Adobe®

PageMaker® 6.5

Illustrated

Kevin G. Proot
Saint Louis University

COURSE
TECHNOLOGY

ONE MAIN STREET, CAMBRIDGE, MA 02142

an International Thomson Publishing company I(T)P®

Cambridge • Albany • Bonn • Boston • Cincinnati • London • Madrid • Melbourne • Mexico City
New York • Paris • San Francisco • Singapore • Tokyo • Toronto • Washington

Adobe® PageMaker® 6.5 — Illustrated is published by Course Technology

Managing Editor:	Nicole Jones Pinard
Product Manager:	Jennifer Thompson
Production Editor:	Roxanne Alexander
Developmental Editor:	Sasha Vodnik
Composition House:	GEX, Inc.
QA Manuscript Reviewer:	John McCarthy, Seth Freeman, Chris Hall
Text Designer:	Joseph Lee
Cover Designer:	Joseph Lee

© 1998 by Course Technology—I⊤P®

For more information contact:

Course Technology
One Main Street
Cambridge, MA 02142

International Thomson Editores
Seneca, 53
Colonia Polanco
11560 Mexico D.F. Mexico

International Thomson Publishing Europe
Berkshire House 168-173
High Holborn
London WC1V 7AA
England

International Thomson Publishing GmbH
Königswinterer Strasse 418
53277 Bonn
Germany

Nelson ITP, Australia
102 Dodds Street
South Melbourne, 3205
Victoria, Australia

International Thomson Publishing Asia
60 Albert Street, #15-01
Albert Complex
Singapore 189969

ITP Nelson Canada
1120 Birchmount Road
Scarborough, Ontario
Canada M1K 5G4

International Thomson Publishing Japan
Hirakawacho Kyowa Building, 3F
2-2-1 Hirakawacho
Chiyoda-ku, Tokyo 102
Japan

Trademarks

Course Technology and the Open Book logo are registered trademarks of Course Technology. Illustrated Projects and the Illustrated Series are trademarks of Course Technology.

I⊤P® The ITP logo is a registered trademark of International Thomson Publishing Inc.

Some of the product names and company names used in this book have been used for identification purposes only and may be trademarks or registered trademarks of their respective manufacturers and sellers.

Disclaimer

Course Technology reserves the right to revise this publication and make changes from time to time in its content without notice.

ISBN 0-7600-5569-6

Printed in the United States of America

10 9 8 7

From the Illustrated Series™ Team

At Course Technology we believe that technology will transform the way that people teach and learn. We are very excited about bringing you, instructors and students, the most practical and affordable technology-related products available.

▶ The Development Process

Our development process is unparalleled in the educational publishing industry. Every product we create goes through an exacting process of design, development, review, and testing.

Reviewers give us direction and insight that shape our manuscripts and bring them up to the latest standards. Every manuscript is quality tested. Students whose backgrounds match the intended audience work through every keystroke, carefully checking for clarity and pointing out errors in logic and sequence. Together with our own technical reviewers, these testers help us ensure that everything that carries our name is as error-free and easy to use as possible.

▶ The Products

We show both how and why technology is critical to solving problems in the classroom and in whatever field you choose to teach or pursue. Our time-tested, step-by-step instructions provide unparalleled clarity. Examples and applications are chosen and crafted to motivate students.

▶ The Illustrated Series™ Team

The Illustrated Series™ Team is committed to providing you with the most visual introduction to microcomputer applications. No other series of books will get you up to speed faster in today's changing software environment. This book will suit your needs because it was delivered quickly, efficiently, and affordably. In every aspect of business, we rely on a commitment to quality and the use of technology. Each member of the Illustrated Series™ Team contributes to this process. The names of all our team members are listed below.

The Team

Cynthia Anderson	Mary-Terese Cozzola	Jeanne Herring	Elizabeth Eisner Reding
Chia-Ling Barker	Carol M. Cram	Meta Chaya Hirschl	Kim Rivers
Donald Barker	Kim T. M. Crowley	Jane Hosie-Bounar	Art Rotberg
Ann Barron	Catherine DiMassa	Steven Johnson	Neil Salkind
David Beskeen	Stan Dobrawa	Mary Kemper	Gregory Schultz
Ann Marie Buconjic	Shelley Dyer	Bill Lisowski	Ann Shaffer
Rachel Bunin	Linda Eriksen	Chet Lyskawa	Dan Swanson
Joan Carey	Jessica Evans	Tara O'Keefe	Marie Swanson
Patrick Carey	Lisa Friedrichsen	Harry Phillips	Jennifer Thompson
Maxine Effenson Chuck	Jeff Goding	Nicole Jones Pinard	Sasha Vodnik
Brad Conlin	Michael Halvorson	Katherine T. Pinard	Jan Weingarten
Pam Conrad	Jamie Harper	Kevin Proot	Christie Williams
			Janet Wilson

Preface

Welcome to *Adobe PageMaker 6.5 – Illustrated*. This highly visual book offers new users a hands-on introduction to Adobe PageMaker and also serves as an excellent reference for future use.

▶ Organization and Coverage

This text contains twelve units that cover basic PageMaker skills. In these units students learn how to design, build, edit, and enhance PageMaker publications. In Unit L, students apply these skills as they work on additional PageMaker projects.

▶ About this Approach

What makes the Illustrated approach so effective at teaching software skills? It's quite simple. Each skill is presented on two facing pages, with the step-by-step instructions on the left page, and large screen illustrations on the right. Students can focus on a single skill without having to turn the page. This unique design makes information extremely accessible and easy to absorb, and provides a great reference for after the course is over. This hands-on approach also makes it ideal for both self-paced or instructor-led classes.

▶ Notes for Macintosh Users

The step-by-step instructions and screen illustrations in this book feature Adobe PageMaker 6.5 for use with Windows 95. However, you can still follow this book if you are using a Macintosh. PageMaker 6.5 for Windows 95 has almost the same visual appearance and functionality as it does for the Macintosh. Where there are differences in the lessons, we have created special instructions called **For Macintosh Users**. These appear in the margin as alternate steps for Macintosh users to follow.

Each lesson, or "information display," contains the following elements:

Tips for Macintosh Users: The steps and figures in this book feature PageMaker 6.5 for Windows. However, the two software releases are *very* similar. Where there are differences, specific steps are given.

Each 2-page spread focuses on a single skill.

Concise text that introduces the basic principles in the lesson and integrates the brief case study.

PageMaker 6.5

Saving a Publication

You must save a file to disk in order to store it permanently. As you work on your publication, it's a good idea to save it every 10 or 15 minutes. Frequent saving prevents losing your work unexpectedly in case of a power or equipment failure. It's also a good practice to save your work before you print it. You will save all the files on your Student Disk. ✎ Joe wants to save his publication with the name Letterhead.

Steps

1. Click File on the menu bar, then click Save As
   See Figure B-13. The Save Publication dialog box opens.

2. Make sure your Student Disk is in the appropriate drive

3. Click the Save in list arrow

4. Click 3½ Floppy (A:)
   If you are storing your practice files on a network, click the appropriate drive.

5. Select the filename in the File name text box if necessary, then type Letterhead
   Filenames can contain up to 250 characters. These characters can be lower- or uppercase letters, numbers, or any symbols.

6. Click Save
   The Save Publication dialog box closes, and the publication is saved as a file named Letterhead.p65 on your Student Disk. PageMaker adds .p65 to the end of the file. This is called a file extension and helps Windows identify the program that created each file. The filename appears in the title bar at the top of the page window. After looking over the letterhead one more time, Joe decides that he wants to change "Blvd." to "Boulevard."

7. Double-click the word Blvd, type Boulevard, then press [Delete] to delete the period
   Now that Joe has changed his publication he needs to save it again.

8. Click File on the menu bar, then click Save
   The Save command saves the changes to a file that has already been named. Table B-4 shows the difference between the Save and Save As commands.

MacintoshUser
This replaces Steps 3 and 4.
3. Click Desktop
4. Click Student Disk, then click Open
Resume at Step 5.

QuickTip
You can use the shortcut key combination [Ctrl] [S] to save a file (Macintosh users: press [S]).

MacintoshUser
This replaces Step 7.
7. Double-click the word Blvd, type Boulevard, then press [del] (not [delete]) to delete the period
Resume at Step 8.

▶ PM B-14   **CREATING A PUBLICATION**

Hints as well as trouble-shooting advice and design tips right where you need it — next to the step itself.

Clear step-by-step directions, with what students are to type in red, explain how to complete the specific task.

Every lesson features large-size, full-color representations of what the students' screen should look like after completing the numbered steps.

Quickly accessible summaries of key terms, toolbar buttons, or keyboard alternatives connected with the lesson material. Students can refer easily to this information when working on their own projects at a later time.

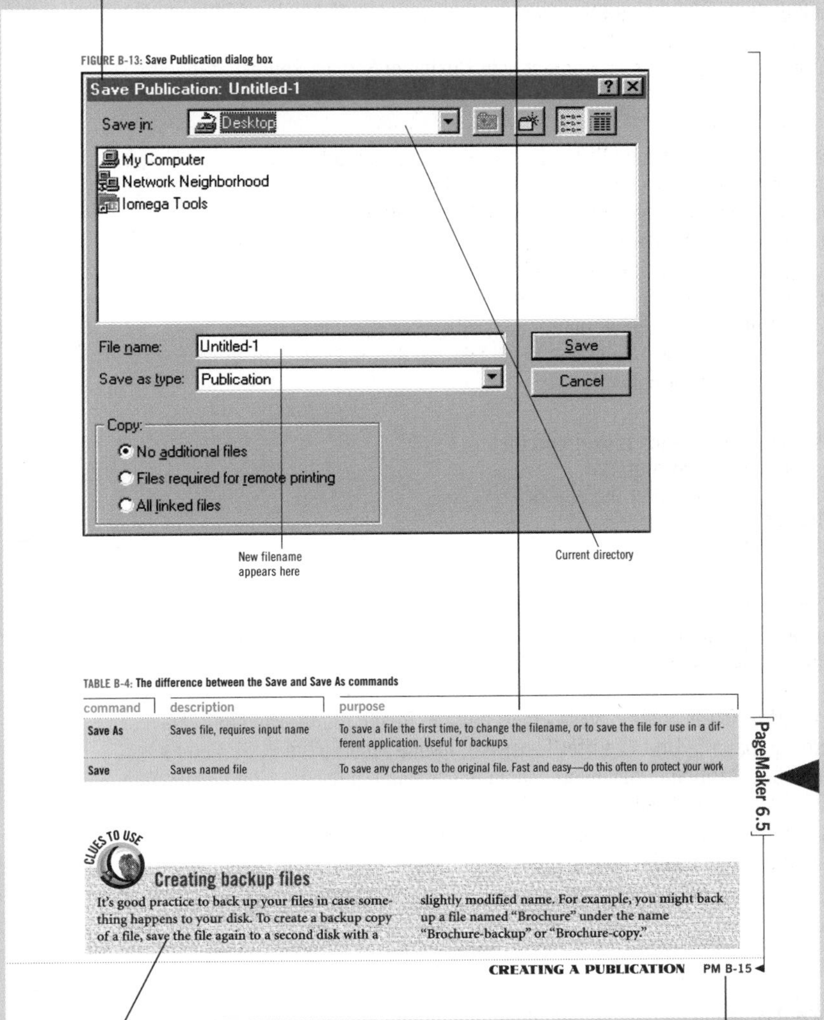

Other Features

The two-page lesson format featured in this book provides the new user with a powerful learning experience. Additionally, this book contains the following features:

▶ **Real-World Skills**
The skills used throughout the textbook are designed to be "real-world" in nature and representative of the kinds of activities that students will encounter when working with PageMaker.

▶ **Design Workshop**
At the end of Units B-K students are asked to critique the design on the PageMaker publication they created in that unit. Students develop critical thinking skills as they evaluate whether their publication is effective as well as visually pleasing.

▶ **End of Unit Material**
Each unit concludes with a Concepts Review that tests students' understanding of what they learned in the unit. The Concepts Review is followed by a Skills Review, which provides students with additional hands-on practice of the skills they learned in the unit. The Skills Review is followed by Independent Challenges, which pose case problems for students to solve. The Independent Challenges allow students to learn by exploring and to develop critical thinking skills. Visual Workshops that follow the Independent Challenges help students to develop critical thinking skills. Students are shown completed documents and are asked to re-create them from scratch. Additional projects are featured in Unit L, where students can apply the PageMaker skills they've learned.

FIGURE B-13: Save Publication dialog box

Save Publication: Untitled-1

Save in: Desktop

My Computer
Network Neighborhood
Iomega Tools

File name: Untitled-1   Save
Save as type: Publication   Cancel

Copy:
● No additional files
○ Files required for remote printing
○ All linked files

New filename appears here

Current directory

TABLE B-4: The difference between the Save and Save As commands

command	description	purpose
Save As	Saves file, requires input name	To save a file the first time, to change the filename, or to save the file for use in a different application. Useful for backups
Save	Saves named file	To save any changes to the original file. Fast and easy—do this often to protect your work

CLUES TO USE

Creating backup files

It's good practice to back up your files in case something happens to your disk. To create a backup copy of a file, save the file again to a second disk with a slightly modified name. For example, you might back up a file named "Brochure" under the name "Brochure-backup" or "Brochure-copy."

PageMaker 6.5

CREATING A PUBLICATION PM B-15

Clues to Use boxes provide concise information that either expands on one component of the major lesson skill or describes an independent task that is in some way related to the major lesson skill.

The page numbers are designed like a road map. PM indicates the PageMaker section, B indicates the second unit, and 15 indicates the page within the unit.

Instructor's Resource Kit

The Instructor's Resource Kit is Course Technology's way of putting the resources and information needed to teach and learn effectively into your hands. With an integrated array of teaching and learning tools that offer you and your students a broad range of technology-based instructional options, we believe this kit represents the highest quality and most cutting edge resources available to instructors today. Many of these resources are available at www.course.com. The resources available with this book are:

Course Test Manager Designed by Course Technology, this cutting edge Windows-based testing software helps instructors design and administer tests and pre-tests. This full-featured program also has an online testing component that allows students to take tests at the computer and have their exams automatically graded.

Course Faculty Online Companion This new World Wide Web site offers Course Technology customers a password-protected Faculty Lounge where you can find everything you need to prepare for class. These periodically updated items include lesson plans, graphic files for the figures in the text, additional problems, updates and revisions to the text, and links to other Web sites. This new site is an ongoing project and will continue to evolve throughout the semester. Contact your Customer Service Representative for the site address and password.

Course Student Online Companion Our second Web site is a place where students can access challenging, engaging, and relevant exercises. They can find a graphical glossary of terms found in the text, an archive of meaningful templates, software, hot tips, and Web links to other sites that contain pertinent information. We offer student sites in the broader application areas as well as sites for specific titles. These new sites are also ongoing projects and will continue to evolve throughout the semester.

Student Files To use this book students must have the Student Files. See the inside front or inside back cover for more information on the Student Files. Adopters of this text are granted the right to post the Student Files on any stand-alone computer or network.

Instructor's Manual This is quality assurance tested and includes:
- Solutions to all lessons and end-of-unit material
- Unit notes which contain teaching tips from the author
- Extra Independent Challenges
- Transparency Masters of key concepts
- Task References

Solutions Files These files have been quality assurance tested and contain solutions to all End-of-Unit material and Extra Independent Challenges.

Photography Credits Unit A: Eiffel Tower photo, Joyelle Proot, page 3; Beach photo, Thomas J. Fischer, page 5; Big Ben photo, John Reiker, page 5; Unit C: Eiffel Tower Far, Joyelle Proot, page 7; St. Peter's Square, Joyelle Proot, page 7; Unit D: Caribbean bay photo, Thomas J. Fischer, page 19; Unit E: New York Skyline, Kevin G. Proot, page 27; Unit F: The Needle, Kevin G. Proot, page 5; Airplane, Kevin G. Proot, page 9; St. Louis, Gateway Arch, Kevin G. Proot, page 7; Unit H: Lighthouse, Kevin G. Proot, page 9; Unit I: Rome Arch, Joyelle Proot, page 5; St. Peter's Cathedral, Joyelle Proot, page 7.

CLUES TO USE

The Illustrated Family of Products

This book that you are holding fits in the Illustrated Series – one series of three in the Illustrated family of products. The other two series are the Illustrated Projects Series and the Illustrated Interactive Series. The Illustrated Projects Series is a supplemental series designed to reinforce the skills learned in any skills-based book through the creation of meaningful and engaging projects. The Illustrated Interactive Series is a line of computer-based training multimedia products that offer the novice user a quick and interactive learning experience. All three series are committed to providing you with the most visual and enriching instructional materials.

Contents

PageMaker 6.5

Contents

Modifying Text   PM D-1

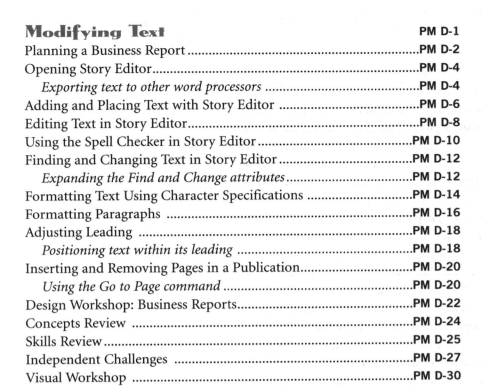

Contents

Working with Graphics

Contents

Using Advanced Graphics

Contents

Working with Long Publications

Contents

PageMaker 6.5

Getting Started

with Adobe PageMaker 6.5

Objectives

► **Define desktop publishing software**
► **Start PageMaker 6.5 and open a publication**
► **View the PageMaker publication window**
► **Set the zero point and use ruler guides**
► **Work with tools in the toolbox**
► **View a publication**
► **Use the Zoom tool**
► **Get Help**
► **Close a publication and exit PageMaker**

Adobe PageMaker 6.5 is a popular desktop publishing application for the Windows and Macintosh platforms. In this unit you will learn how to start PageMaker and how to use the elements of the PageMaker window. You will also view a publication, use online Help, close a publication, and exit the application. ✐ Joe Martin works in the Marketing Department at New World Airlines. Before installing PageMaker, the Marketing Department used third parties to produce all company publications, which was both time-consuming and expensive. Patricia Fernandez, the communications manager, wants Joe to use PageMaker to create many of the publications in-house.

PageMaker 6.5

Defining Desktop Publishing Software

PageMaker is a desktop publishing application. A **desktop publishing application** lets you integrate text, graphics, spreadsheets, and charts created in different applications into one document on a personal computer, condensing into hours what used to take days in traditional publishing. With PageMaker, you can create many types of publications, including brochures, newsletters, and even books. A **publication** is any document produced in PageMaker. Figure A-1 shows one example of a publication. Some types of publications you can create with PageMaker are listed in Table A-1. Joe is excited about using PageMaker. He knows that some of the benefits of using PageMaker include:

Details

 Saving money
By creating publications in-house at New World Airlines, Joe saves the cost of hiring graphic designers to create the company's publications.

 Saving time
In the past, Joe had to consider the time third parties spent completing the publication. Depending on a designer's workload, it took a few days to a week to finish publications. Now Joe can control when publications will be completed and work them into his agenda—not someone else's.

 Controlling the production process
By creating the company's publications at his personal computer, Joe has control of all the steps in the production process—from design to final layouts.

 Providing security
Some publications that Joe needs to create contain special airline fares or confidential company financial data. In the past, New World Airlines managers were apprehensive about sending this information outside the company.

 Offering color
Joe creates many color publications. Some use just one color in a particular area, called a **spot color**. Other publications, such as a color advertisement, use four basic colors (known as the **process colors**) printed over each other to create other colors. The result is a **full-color** publication. PageMaker lets you create spot and full-color publications.

TABLE A-1: **Examples of PageMaker publications**

publication	examples
Periodical	Magazines, newsletters, newspapers
Promotional	Advertisements, flyers, press releases, prospectuses
Informational	Brochures, bulletins, catalogs, data and fact sheets, schedules, programs
Stationery	Business cards, envelopes, fax cover sheets, interoffice memos, letterheads
Instructional	Training manuals, employee handbooks
Presentation	Overheads, posters

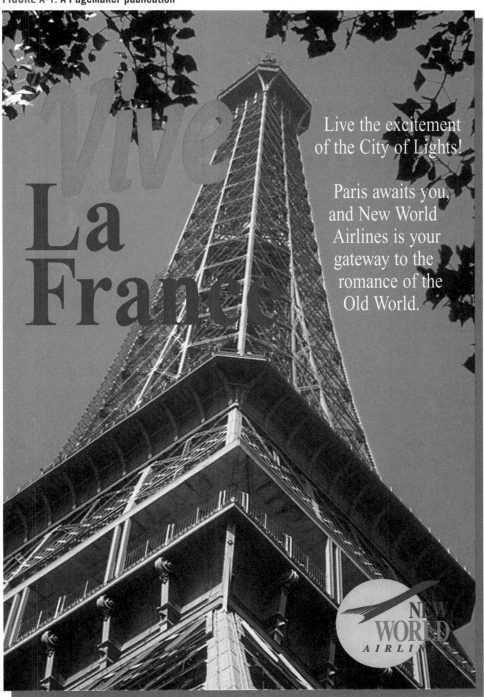

Live the excitement
of the City of Lights!

Paris awaits you,
and New World
Airlines is your
gateway to the
romance of the
Old World.

PageMaker 6.5

Starting PageMaker 6.5 and Opening a Publication

Because every computer can have a different hardware and software configuration, the procedure you use for starting PageMaker might be different from the one described here, especially if your computer is connected to a network. Ask your instructor or technical support person if there are any special procedures for starting PageMaker on your computer. To view the window in which you create PageMaker publications, you need to open an existing publication or create a new one. In this lesson you will open a file from your Student Disk. See your instructor or technical support person for a copy of the Student Disk if you do not already have one. Make sure you have made a working copy of your Student Disk before using any of the files on it. ◄━━━━ Joe wants to start PageMaker and open a newsletter he created earlier to review it.

 Steps

 MacintoshUser

This replaces Steps 1-3.
1. Make sure the hard drive window is open
2. Double-click the Adobe PageMaker 6.5 folder icon
3. Double-click the Adobe PageMaker 6.5 application icon

Resume at Step 4.

1. Make sure the Windows desktop is open, then click the **Start button** on the taskbar
The Start menu opens on the desktop.

2. On the Start menu, point to **Programs**
The Start menu remains open as you point, as shown in Figure A-2. The program listings on your Programs menu will vary from the ones shown in the figure depending on the programs installed on your computer.

3. On the Programs menu, point to **Adobe**, point to **PageMaker 6.5**, then click the **Adobe PageMaker 6.5 icon**
If Adobe is not listed on your Programs menu and Adobe PageMaker 6.5 is listed on the menu, then click Adobe PageMaker 6.5 to start PageMaker. PageMaker opens and displays the PageMaker window. Next, Joe opens his PageMaker publication.

4. Insert your Student Disk in the disk drive, click **File** on the menu bar, then click **Open**
The Open Publication dialog box opens, as shown in Figure A-3. The files, directories, and drive names on your computer might be different from those shown in the figure.

 MacintoshUser

This replaces Steps 5 and 6.
1. Click Desktop
2. Click Student Disk, then click Open
3. In the filename list box, click UNIT_A-1.p65, then click OK

5. Click the **Look in list arrow**, then click **3½ Floppy (A:)**
You might need to scroll up to bring the 3½ Floppy (A:) icon into view. The list of files on the disk in drive A appears in the filename list box.

6. In the filename list box, click **UNIT_A-1**, then click **Open**
Depending on your computer configuration, your screen might show the publication name with the file extension. In that case, click UNIT_A-1.p65 to open the publication. Pages 2 and 3 of the publication, UNIT_A-1.p65, appear, as shown in Figure A-4. UNIT_A-1.p65 contains the New World Airlines company newsletter *Wings*. The newsletter includes a photograph, text, and the company logo at the bottom of the page. If the filename does not appear in the title bar at the top of the screen as shown, then click the publication window Maximize button.

FIGURE A-2: Windows 95 desktop

Click to start
PageMaker
Program

FIGURE A-3: Open Publication dialog box

Look-in list arrow

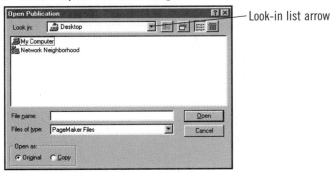

FIGURE A-4: Pages 2 and 3 of UNITA-1.P65

Filename appears
in the title bar

Viewing the PageMaker Publication Window

When you open a publication in PageMaker, it appears in the publication window. The **publication window** is the area that includes the page where you modify an existing publication or create a new one. Joe's newsletter appears in the publication window. Familiarize yourself with the elements of the publication window by comparing the descriptions below with Figure A-5.

QuickTip

To hide the rulers in the publication window, click View on the menu bar, then click Hide Rulers. To show them again click View, then click Show Rulers.

 Rulers are located on the top (horizontal ruler) and left (vertical ruler) of the window. You use the rulers to size and align your text and graphics precisely and accurately.

 The **menu bar** contains menus where you choose PageMaker commands.

 The **zero point marker** is the intersection of the horizontal and vertical rulers. The **zero point** is the point at which the zero marks on the rulers intersect.

 The **publication page** is the solid-lined, boxed area in which you create and modify text and graphics to build a publication. The maximum page size allowed in PageMaker is 42 inches by 42 inches. The publication page can be displayed as a single page or with two facing pages. The publication page is shadowed on the bottom and outer page borders so that you can see if you are working on a right or a left page.

 Master page icons appear to the left of the page icons and access the right and left master pages. **Master pages** are nonprinting pages used for placing text and/or graphics that will appear on all pages of the publication.

 The **margin guides** are magenta-colored boxes inside the page borders. The margin guides show you where the margins are relative to the page borders. The vertical margin guides in this publication are obscured by blue **column guides**, vertical lines that indicate columns.

 Page icons are numbered rectangles that appear in the lower-left corner of the publication window. They represent the pages in a publication. To move to a different page, click the desired page icon.

 The **toolbox** contains 14 tool icons that you use to create and modify text and graphics. The toolbox is a **floating palette**, which is a movable window within the publication window. You can work with it just like any other window—it has a title bar and a Close button.

 The **pasteboard** is the white area surrounding and including the publication page. You can use the pasteboard as a work area to hold text or graphics until you place them in your publication. Any area beyond the pasteboard is represented by yellow or another color other than white.

Scroll bars are located on the right and bottom edges of the window. You use them to display portions of the pasteboard that are not visible in the current view.

FIGURE A-5: PageMaker publication window

Publication Page   Pasteboard   Horizontal ruler   Toolbox

Menu bar

Zero point marker

Vertical ruler

Master page icons

Publication window

Margin guide   Page icon   Column guides   Scroll bars

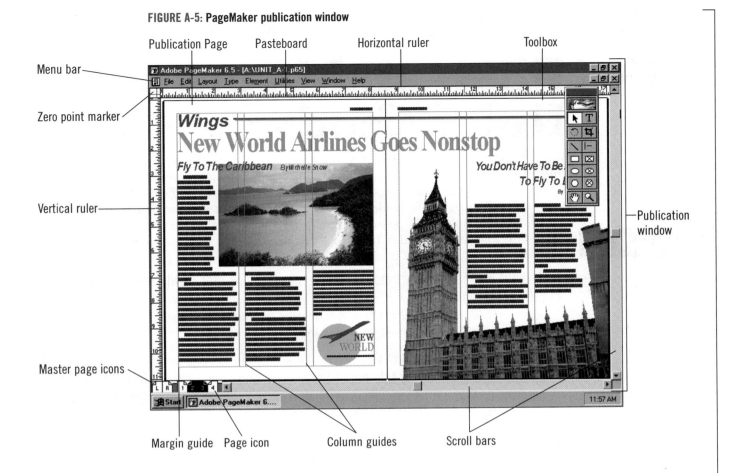

PageMaker 6.5

Setting the Zero Point and Using Ruler Guides

You can easily place and precisely align text and graphics on a page in PageMaker by using its ruler guide system. **Ruler guides** are nonprinting lines that usually appear in blue on the screen. You move a ruler guide onto a page by clicking the area occupied by either the horizontal or vertical ruler and dragging the guide into place. Publication pages accommodate up to 40 ruler guides. The **zero point** is the point at which the zero marks on the rulers meet. The default zero point is the top left page border. Try setting the zero point and using the ruler guides now.

Steps

1. Without pressing the left mouse button, move the pointer slowly around the publication window

   As you move the pointer, watch as the **pointer guides**, dotted lines in the horizontal and vertical rulers, follow the pointer. Try changing the zero point.

2. Make sure your toolbox is in the upper-right corner of the PageMaker window; if it is not, move the pointer into the title bar of the toolbox, press and hold the **left mouse button**, drag the toolbox until its outline is in the upper-right corner of the PageMaker publication window, then release the mouse button

3. Position the pointer on the zero point marker ⊞, press and hold the **left mouse button**, then drag the pointer down and to the right to the point where the top and left margin guides meet

   Notice that as you drag, the zero point icon appears in reverse, and the intersection of two dotted lines that go the length and width of the window follows the movement of the pointer.

4. Release the mouse button

   See Figure A-6. The zero point is now at the intersection of the top and left margin guides. Now try creating a horizontal ruler guide.

5. Position the pointer over the horizontal ruler, then press and hold the **left mouse button**

   The pointer changes to ↖.

6. Drag down until the pointer guide on the vertical ruler is at the 5" mark, then release the mouse button

   A dotted line moves with ↖. See Figure A-7. After you release the mouse button, the ruler guide changes to blue and stays on the page. Don't worry if it is not exactly at the 5" mark. You can reposition the ruler guides anywhere on the publication page.

7. Position the pointer over the horizontal ruler, then drag a second **ruler guide** to the 1" mark on the vertical ruler

   If you didn't move the ruler guide exactly to the 1" mark, position the tip of the pointer on the ruler guide, then drag it again. You can remove a ruler guide anytime by dragging it off the publication page.

8. Drag the **ruler guide** at the 1" mark up or down until it is off the publication page and on the pasteboard or the horizontal ruler, then release the mouse button

   The ruler guide disappears. You create and remove vertical ruler guides in the same manner.

QuickTip

To hide all the ruler guides in the publication window, click View on the menu bar, then click Hide Guides. To show them again click View, then click Show Guides.

FIGURE A-6: The repositioned zero point

Zero point marker ———

New zero point ———

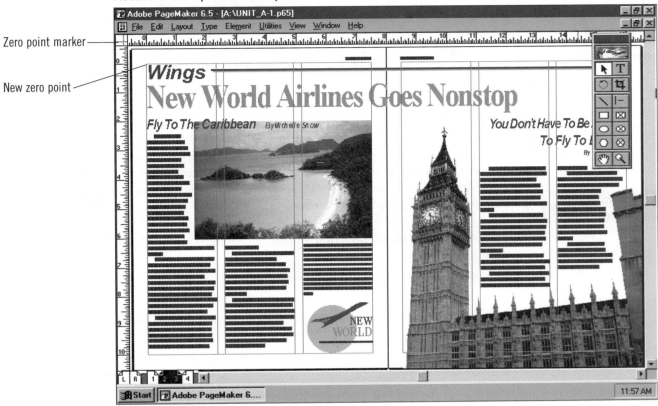

FIGURE A-7: Placing the ruler guides

Ruler guide ———

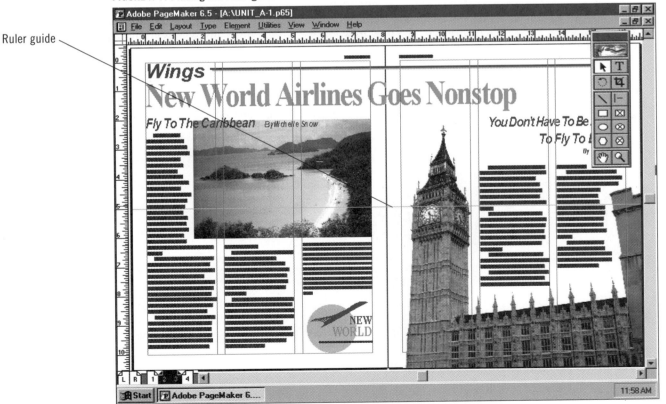

Working with Tools in the Toolbox

Just as conventional designers use their tools (rulers, pens, and knives) to create publications, users of desktop publishing software use electronic tools to perform the same tasks. PageMaker's **toolbox** appears in its own small window on the publication window. The toolbox gives today's designers the same range of tools that conventional designers use, but these electronic tools have even more capabilities. Each of the 14 tools is represented by an icon in the toolbox, and each tool has a different mouse pointer shape when it is selected. See Table A-2 for a list of the tools, their pointer shapes, and brief descriptions of their functions. 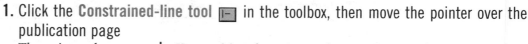 Joe needs to use one of the tools to add a line to his newsletter.

Steps

1. Click the **Constrained-line tool** in the toolbox, then move the pointer over the publication page

   The pointer changes to ✚. You position the pointer where you want to begin drawing the line.

2. Position ✚ above the logo on page 2 directly on top of the third column's left column guide

   See Figure A-8. If it is positioned correctly, you will not be able to see the blue column guide under the vertical line of ✚.

3. Press and hold the **left mouse button**, then drag the pointer across the column until ✚ is on the right margin guide, but do not release the mouse button

   A line appears as you drag the pointer.

4. Move ✚ down the page until the line jumps down by 45 degrees

   See Figure A-9. The line drawn by the Constrained-line tool is always straight at a 45-degree angle.

5. Move ✚ back up the right margin guide until the line is straight across the page, then release the mouse button

   When you release the mouse button, the line stays on the screen as shown in Figure A-10.

FIGURE A-8: Positioning the Constrained-line tool

Ruler guide

Constrained-line pointer

Column guide

Constrained-line tool

FIGURE A-9: Changing the angle of a constrained line

Line moved down 45-degrees

Pointer

FIGURE A-10: The final line

New line

TABLE A-2: Toolbox tools

tool	icon	pointer	description
Pointer			Selects, moves, and resizes objects
Text			Allows you to enter and modify text
Rotating			Rotates any object around an axis to any angle
Cropping			Adjusts the borders of a graphic by eliminating unwanted portions
Line			Draws a straight line at any angle
Constrained-line			Draws a straight line at an angle in increments of 45 degrees
Rectangle			Draws a rectangle or a square
Ellipse			Draws an ellipse or a circle
Polygon			Draws multisided figures
Hand			Moves view within the page or checks hyperlinks
Zoom			Magnifies or reduces the page view
Frame Tools			Use frame tools to create placeholders for text and graphics

Viewing the Publication

In PageMaker, you can change the **page view**, or the magnification of the page. Table A-3 describes the different views available. Higher magnifications allow you to fine-tune documents. Lower magnifications allow you to view an entire page at once. You can also use the scroll bars to see portions of the publication that are not displayed in the window. Try changing the page view and using the scroll bars now.

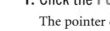 **Steps**

1. **Click the Pointer tool in the toolbox**
   The pointer changes to ▶.

Trouble?

Depending on the size of your monitor, your screen view might look different than the one shown in this and subsequent steps.

2. **Click View on the menu bar, then point to Zoom To**
   The View and Zoom To menus appear, as shown in Figure A-11. The check mark next to the Fit in Window option on the View menu indicates that this is the current view.

3. **On the Zoom To menu, click 200% Size**
   The publication appears at two times its actual size.

4. **Click the down scroll arrow on the vertical scroll bar**
   The page scrolls up a fraction of an inch, revealing a lower section of the page.

5. **Click in the vertical scroll bar anywhere above the scroll box**
   The page moves in a larger increment than when you clicked the down arrow. You use the horizontal scroll bar in the same manner.

6. **Click View on the menu bar, then click Entire Pasteboard**
   A full view of the white pasteboard appears with the pages centered.

QuickTip

To change the view quickly to Actual Size from any other view, press and hold [Shift], then press the right mouse button (Macintosh users: press [⌘][option]). This is called right-clicking. With the keyboard button(s) still pressed, you can press the right mouse button again to change the view to Fit in Window.

7. **Click the Photo of the beach in the upper-right corner on page 2, click View, then click Actual Size**
   The view changes to the actual size of the page with the photo centered in the view. Compare your screen with Figure A-12. Go to the next lesson to learn how to use the Zoom tool.

FIGURE A-11: View menu

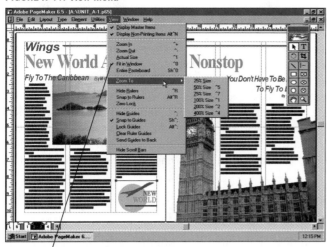

Check mark
indicates this
option is selected

FIGURE A-12: Publication page viewed at its actual size

TABLE A-3: Publication page views

view	keyboard shortcut	description
Fit in Window	[Ctrl][0]	Adjusts page(s) to fill publication window so you see all of the page(s) and some of the surrounding pasteboard
Entire Pasteboard		Displays the entire pasteboard with the page(s) centered on it
25% Size		Displays the page at 25% of the actual size
50% Size	[Ctrl][5]	Displays the page at 50% of the actual size
75% Size		Displays the page at 75% of the actual size
Actual Size	[Ctrl][1]	Displays the publication at the size specified when the publication was created
200% Size	[Ctrl][2]	Displays the page at twice the actual size
400% Size		Displays the page at four times the actual size

CLUES TO USE

Using the grabber hand

Instead of using the scroll bars to move around the pasteboard, you can use the grabber hand. The **grabber hand** acts like a hand on a piece of paper and lets you move the page in any direction in the publication window. To use the grabber hand, press and hold [Alt] (Macintosh users: press and hold [option]), then press and hold the left mouse button. The pointer changes to 🖐, and the page moves in the direction you move the mouse. The grabber hand is active only while you continue to hold the mouse button.

Using the Zoom Tool

Just as you changed the page view using PageMaker's preset magnifications on the View and Zoom To menus, you can also use the Zoom tool to increase the page view at a desired area in the publication window. The Zoom tool is a faster method for changing the page view than using the View menu. Using the Zoom tool from the toolbox, the pointer will change depending on whether you are magnifying or reducing the page view, as shown in Table 1-4. PageMaker makes it easy to switch views anytime during your publication production. Joe wants to use the Zoom tool to magnify his page view so that he can check to make sure the story on page 3 includes New World Airlines' phone number and that the color has been applied to the text in the New World Airlines logo.

Steps

1. Click the **Zoom tool** in the toolbox, then move the pointer onto the publication page
   The pointer changes to 🔍. Joe would like to first reduce the view so he can see the entire page.

MacintoshUser

This replaces Steps 2 and 3.
2. Press and hold [option], then click the mouse button three times, but do not release [option]
3. Release [option], and position 🔍 on the last paragraph of text in the center column on page 3, then click the mouse button once
Resume at Step 4.

2. Press and hold **[Ctrl]**, then click the **left mouse button** three times, but do not release [Ctrl]
   Before clicking, the pointer changes to 🔍. See Figure A-13. The view changes from Actual Size to 25% of the Actual Size view. Notice the pointer has changed to 🔍 meaning you have reached the maximum reduction page view. This page view is also known as Show Pasteboard view. Joe uses the Zoom tool to make sure he included New World Airlines' phone number at the end of the story at the bottom of page 3.

3. Release [Ctrl], and position 🔍 on the last paragraph of text in the center column on page 3, then click the **left mouse button** once
   The page view zooms in to 50% of the actual page size. However, notice 🔍 is no longer on the last paragraph of text. Joe now repositions the pointer on the text he wishes to review.

4. Position 🔍 on the last paragraph of text in the center column on page 3, then click the **left mouse button** twice, making sure the pointer is positioned over the correct paragraph before each click
   See Figure A-14. Joe can now easily read the text in the last paragraph. After viewing the text, Joe decides to use the Zoom tool to reduce the page view so that he can see both pages.

MacintoshUser

This replaces Step 5.
5. Press and hold [option], click the mouse button three times, then release [option]
Resume at Step 6.

5. Press and hold **[Ctrl]**, click the **left mouse button** three times, then release [Ctrl]
   The page view changes so that you can see the entire pasteboard again. If you want to set all pages in a publication to the same view, you could press and hold [Alt], click view on the menu bar and select the desired page view, then release [Alt]. Now Joe decides to look closely at the New World Airlines logo to make sure the word "Airlines" is colored blue.

6. Position 🔍 on the New World Airlines logo at the bottom of the third column of page 2

7. Click the **left mouse button** three times, making sure the pointer is positioned over the logo before each click
   See Figure A-15. The view changes to Actual Size with the New World Airlines logo centered in the view. Now Joe can see that the word "Airlines" is colored blue.

FIGURE A-13: Page view reduced to maximum view

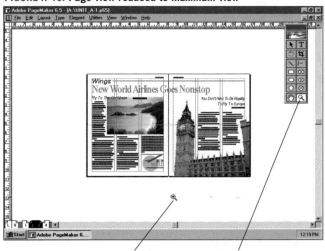

Zoom pointer after releasing [Ctrl]　　Zoom tool selected

FIGURE A-14: Magnified page view

FIGURE A-15: Logo centered in page view

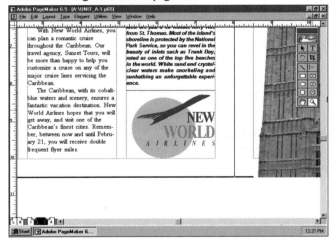

TABLE A-4: Zoom pointers

pointer	description
	Zoom tool for magnifying the page view
	Zoom tool indicating highest page reduction selected
	Zoom tool for reducing the page view

Other methods for changing page view

As you have already learned, PageMaker gives you many different options for changing your page view. You can even change your view while using another tool. Just press [Ctrl][Spacebar]. The pointer automatically changes to ⊕. Then press the mouse button until you reach your desired page view. To reduce the page view while using another tool, press and hold [Ctrl][Spacebar][Alt](in order), then click the mouse button to achieve the desired reduction in the page view. In the previous lesson, the Quick Tip explained how to switch between Fit in Window and Actual Size. You can also toggle between Actual Size and 200% size. Press and hold [Ctrl][Shift] and right-click, and the view will switch to 200%. Right-click again, and you can switch the view to Actual Size.

Getting Help

PageMaker 6.5

PageMaker provides an extensive online Help system that gives you immediate access to definitions, explanations, and useful tips. Help information appears in its own window that you can resize and refer to as you work. ◆ Use PageMaker's online Help to learn how to close a publication and exit PageMaker.

Steps

MacintoshUser

This replaces Step 1.

1. Click [Help Topics] on the menu bar, then click PageMaker Help Topics

Resume at Step 2.

QuickTip

To quickly access Help, press [Shift][F1] (Macintosh users: press [Help Topics], then click the screen element or menu command for which you want more information).

MacintoshUser

This replaces Steps 5-7.

5. In the Index text box, type Quit
(The topic "Quit command" is highlighted in the text box.)

6. Click Display
(The Help window displays an explanation of the Quit command on the File menu.)

7. Click File on the Help Topics window menu bar, then click Quit

---

1. Click **Help** on the menu bar, then click **Help Topics**

The Help window opens listing available Help topics, as shown in Figure A-16.

2. Double-click the topic book **Command Reference** on the Contents tab

A list of PageMaker's menu bar options appears.

3. On the Command Reference list, double-click **File**, then on the File list, double-click **Close**

Help displays an explanation of the Close command on the File menu. This window has its own menu bar and six buttons. See Table A-5 for a description of each button. Read the information on the File Close command.

4. Click the **Help Topics button**, then click the **Index tab**

The Help Topics dialog box opens with the Index tab in front, as shown in Figure A-17. You use this dialog box to locate a specific topic or feature. The insertion point appears in the Index text box.

5. In the Index text box, type **Exit**

As you type each character, the list of available topics scrolls to display topics beginning with those letters. The topic "Exit command" is highlighted in the text box.

6. Click **Display**

The Help window displays an explanation of the Exit command on the File menu. Read the information on the Exit command.

7. Click **File** on the Help window menu bar, then click **Exit**

The Help menu closes and returns you to the publication.

FIGURE A-16: Help window

Help Topics window tabs

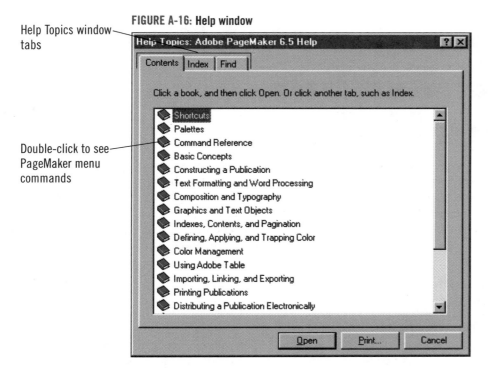

Double-click to see PageMaker menu commands

FIGURE A-17: Help Topics dialog box

Insertion point

List of available topics

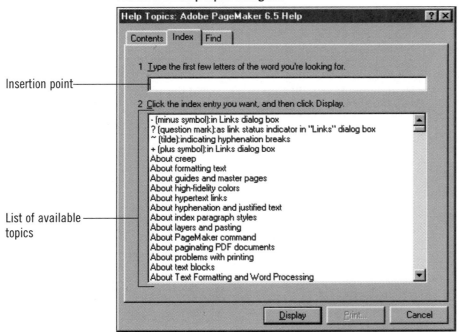

TABLE A-5: Help window buttons

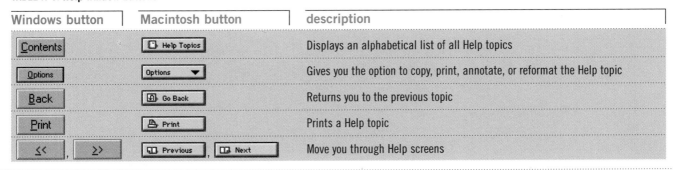

Windows button	Macintosh button	description
Contents	Help Topics	Displays an alphabetical list of all Help topics
Options	Options ▼	Gives you the option to copy, print, annotate, or reformat the Help topic
Back	Go Back	Returns you to the previous topic
Print	Print	Prints a Help topic
<< , >>	Previous , Next	Move you through Help screens

Closing a Publication and Exiting PageMaker

When you are finished working on a publication, you generally save your work, and then close the file. You won't save the changes you made to this publication because you were only practicing. When you close a file, the publication window no longer appears, but PageMaker remains open. When you have completed all your work in PageMaker, you can exit the application. Table A-6 explains the difference between closing a file and exiting PageMaker. Joe is finished reviewing his newsletter, so he closes the publication and exits PageMaker.

Steps

QuickTip

To exit PageMaker and close several files at once, click File on the menu bar, then click Exit (Macintosh users: click File, then select Quit). PageMaker will prompt you to save changes to each publication before exiting.

MacintoshUser

This replaces Step 4.

4. Click File on the menu bar, then select Quit

1. Click **File** on the menu bar
See Figure A-18.

2. Click **Close**
You could also click the Close button in the upper-right corner of the window instead of choosing File Close. A warning box opens, as shown in Figure A-19, asking if you want to save changes to the file before closing. Because this was a practice session, you do not need to save the file.

3. Click **No**
The publication closes, but the menu bar is still visible.

4. Click **File** on the menu bar, then click **Exit**
You could also press and hold [Ctrl], then press [Q] to exit the application *(Macintosh users: [⌘][Q])*. PageMaker closes, and you are returned to the desktop.

FIGURE A-18: Closing a publication using the File menu

Close command ——

Exit command ——

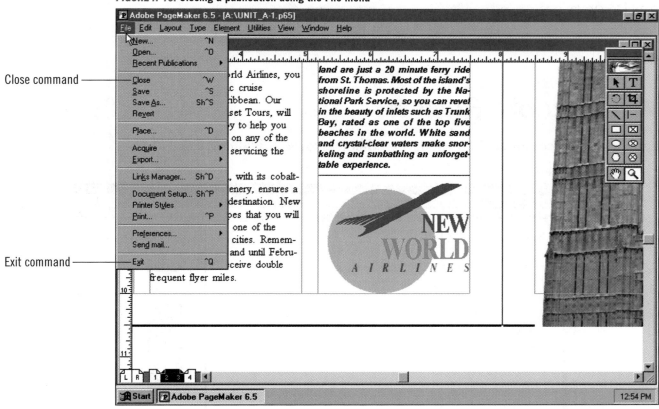

FIGURE A-19: Save changes warning

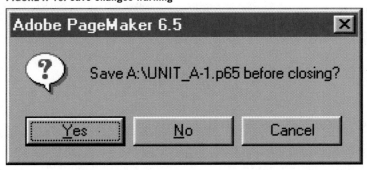

TABLE A-6: PageMaker's Close and Exit commands

closing a file	exiting PageMaker
Puts a file away, closing the active publication window	Puts all files away, closing all open publication windows
Leaves PageMaker loaded in computer memory	Frees computer memory for other uses

PageMaker 6.5

Practice

► Concepts Review

Label each of the publication window elements shown in Figure A-20.

FIGURE A-20

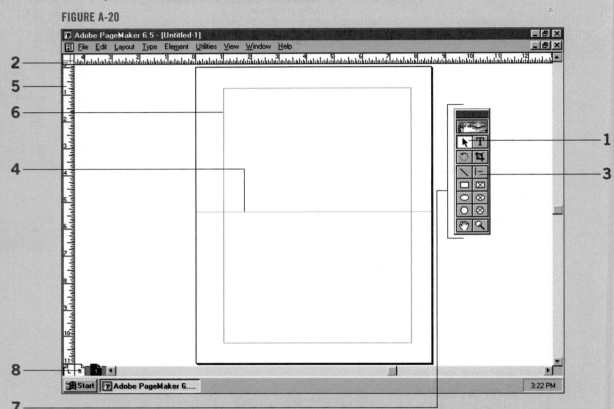

Match each of the terms with the statement that describes its function.

9. Magenta-colored lines that identify the page margins
10. The intersection of the horizontal and vertical rulers
11. Area in which you create and modify text and graphics
12. Work table area that can hold text and graphics
13. Contains tools for creating and modifying text and graphics

a. Zero point marker
b. Pasteboard
c. Margin guides
d. Toolbox
e. Publication page

Select the best answer from the list of choices.

14. **To precisely make small adjustments to a publication, which of the following would you choose from the Zoom To menu?**
    a. Show Pasteboard
    b. 25% Size
    c. Actual Size
    d. 400% Size

15. **Which tool do you use to modify text?**
    a. `T`
    b. `▢`
    c. `╲`
    d. `▸`

16. **Desktop publishing software can create all of the following publications, except:**
    a. Newsletter
    b. Brochure
    c. Advertisement
    d. All of the above can be created in PageMaker

17. **To repeat text and graphics on all pages of a publication, place the text and graphics on the:**
    a. Default pages
    b. Page icons
    c. Master pages
    d. Publication pages

18. **You can get Help in any of the following ways, except:**
    a. Clicking Help Topics on the Help menu
    b. Pressing [F1]
    c. Clicking a topic in the Help window
    d. Minimizing the application window

► Skills Review

1. **Start PageMaker.**
    a. Click the Start button, point to Programs, point to Adobe, click PageMaker 6.5, then click the PageMaker 6.5 icon, or follow the steps you used at the beginning of this unit to open PageMaker.

2. **Open a publication and identify elements in the publication window.**
    a. Click File on the menu bar, then click Open.
    b. Click the Look in list arrow, then click 3½ Floppy (A:) *(Macintosh users: Click Desktop, click Student Disk, then click Open).*
    c. In the filename list box, click UNIT_A-2, then click Open *(Macintosh users: Click UNIT_A-2.p65, then click OK).*
    d. Identify as many elements of the publication window as you can without referring to the unit material.

   e. Click each of the menu options and drag the mouse button through all the commands on each menu. Notice the additional submenus identified by an arrow pointing to the right.

3. **View the publication.**
   a. Click the right scroll arrow on the horizontal scroll bar two times.
   b. Click the down scroll arrow on the vertical scroll bar four times.
   c. Click View on the menu bar, point to Zoom To, then click 25% Size.
   d. Click the New World Airlines logo in the lower-right corner of the publication.
   e. Click View on the menu bar, point to Zoom To, then click 200% Size.
   f. Click View on the menu bar, then click Fit in Window.

4. **Set the zero point and use ruler guides.**
   a. Without pressing the mouse buttons, move the pointer slowly around the publication window. Notice as you move the pointer, the pointer guides follow the pointer on both the horizontal and vertical rulers.
   b. Position the pointer on the zero point marker, press and hold the left mouse button, then drag the pointer to the position where the top and left corners of the publication page meet, then release the mouse button.
   c. Position the pointer over the horizontal ruler, then press and hold the left mouse button.
   d. Drag a ruler guide to the .5" mark (the mark halfway between the 0 and 1 marks) on the vertical ruler, then release the mouse button.
   e. Position the pointer over the horizontal ruler, then drag another ruler guide to the 5" mark on the vertical ruler.
   f. Position the pointer over the vertical ruler, then drag a ruler guide to the 1" mark on the horizontal ruler. (Note that the 1" mark to the left of 0 is actually -1"; be sure to select the 1" mark to the right of 0.)
   g. Drag another ruler guide to the 7" mark on the horizontal ruler.
   h. Position the tip of the pointer on the horizontal ruler guide at the left 5" mark, press and hold the mouse button to select the ruler guide, drag the ruler guide up until it is off the publication page, then release the mouse button.

5. **Explore the toolbox.**
   a. Click the Text tool in the toolbox, then move the pointer across the publication window to the middle of the page. Notice the pointer has changed to $\mathcal{I}$.
   b. Click the Constrained-line tool in the toolbox, then move the pointer across the screen to the middle of the page. Notice the pointer has changed to $+$.
   c. Click the other tools in the toolbox and examine how the mouse pointer changes.
   d. Click the Constrained-line tool in the toolbox.
   e. Position $+$ below the "F" in the word "France."
   f. Press and hold the left mouse button, drag $+$ to draw a line to underline the word, then release the mouse button.

6. **Use the Zoom tool.**
   a. Click the Zoom tool in the toolbox.
   b. Position ⊕ over the text in the first sentence, then click the left mouse button.
   c. Again, position ⊕ over the text in the first sentence, then click the left mouse button two more times.
   d. Press and hold [Ctrl], then click the left mouse button three times.
   e. Position ⊕ on the New World Airlines logo, then click the left mouse button enough times so that the logo is centered in the window. Make sure you place the pointer on top of the logo each time you click the mouse button.

f. Reduce the magnification so you can see the entire publication.

g. Click View on the menu bar, then click Fit in Window.

7. Explore Help.

a. Click Help on the menu bar, then click Help Topics *(Macintosh users: click* Help Topics *on the menu bar, then click PageMaker Help Topics)*.

b. If necessary, click the Contents tab to view the available topics.

c. Double-click Basic Concepts.

d. Double-click Viewing pages.

e. Read the information about Viewing pages, then click the green topic "Magnifying and reducing with the zoom tool" at the bottom of the text.

f. Read about magnifying and reducing with the Zoom tool, then click the Help Topics button.

g. Click the Index tab, type "toolbox palette," then click Display.

h. Move the pointer over the Text tool in the toolbox in the Help Window, then click the left mouse button. Click the other tools to read the purpose of each one.

i. Click the Help Topics button, then select a topic in the list box that you want to know more about, and read the information that appears.

j. When you are finished, click File on the menu bar, then click Exit *(Macintosh users: click Quit)*.

8. Close the publication and exit PageMaker.

a. Click File on the menu bar, then click Close.

b. Click No when you are asked if you want to save UNIT_A-2.p65 before closing.

c. If necessary, use the same technique to close any other documents you might have opened.

e. Click File on the menu bar, then click Exit *(Macintosh users: Click File on the menu bar, then select Quit)*.

► Independent Challenges

1. PageMaker provides an interactive guided tour called "Welcome to PageMaker 6.5" in the CD-ROM version of PageMaker. The interactive program is a brief introduction and demonstration of PageMaker. It includes new feature tutorial movies which demonstrate the new and enhanced features in the current version of PageMaker. In this tour, Adobe PageMaker program developers guide you through the new features and demonstrate how to accomplish various PageMaker commands. You must have Acrobat Reader and QuickTime 2.1.2 to view the tutorial movies.

If you have access to the CD-ROM version of PageMaker 6.5, complete this independent challenge:

1. Double-click the Welcome file in the Tour Adobe PageMaker 6.5 folder to start the tour. If you can't find the file for this program, ask your instructor or technical support person where it is located.

2. Click Tutorials, click Using Layers, then click Movie at the bottom of the screen to view a step-by-step tutorial on layers.

3. When the tutorial movie finishes, click the ? icon on the bottom of the screen to see a Help screen that includes an explanation of the navigation icons.

4. After you are through reading the Help screen, press [Esc], then press [Alt][F4] to quit and exit the Welcome file *(Macintosh users: press [Esc], then press [⌘][Q]*.

2. The tutorial movies located in the "Welcome to PageMaker 6.5" guided tour contain references to printable steps along with sample art and publications which demonstrate new features of PageMaker 6.5. These are located in the Tour Adobe PageMaker 6.5's Tutorials folder.

If you have access to the CD-ROM version of PageMaker 6.5, complete this independent challenge:

1. Double-click the Frames folder located in the Tour Adobe PageMaker 6.5's Tutorials folder. If you can't find the file for this program, ask your instructor or technical support person where it is located.
2. Double-click the Adobe Acrobat Frames file to open it, and view step-by-step instructions on working with frames.
3. When you are finished reading the instructions, click File on the menu bar, then click Exit to close Acrobat Reader *(Macintosh users: click Quit)*.
4. Double-click the PageMaker Frames file in the Tutorials folder to open and view a sample PageMaker document that was created using frames.
5. When you are done viewing the PageMaker document, click File on the menu bar, then click Exit to close PageMaker *(Macintosh users: click Quit)*.

3. Some examples of how PageMaker can be used are mentioned at the beginning of this unit. Search for examples of publications that could be produced using PageMaker and compile them into a sample design packet.

To complete this independent challenge:

1. Gather at least five different publications. Make sure at least one of your samples is in full color and another includes only spot color.
2. Keep this design packet. Refer to it as necessary as you learn about design features in later units.

4. You work in the marketing department of a company that competes with New World Airlines. Your organization has decided to create some of its publications in-house in order to try and save money. They would also like to have an edge over the competition by announcing new flights and discount rates as early as possible.

1. Search the World Wide Web for an international airline's home page.
2. Sketch a document that you could use as a guideline for creating an attractive publication in PageMaker for your airline. The document might announce new flights that an airline has added or discount rates that they are offering.
3. Be sure to include a company logo and all of the relevant information that your customers will need.

PageMaker 6.5

Creating
a Publication

Objectives

▶ **Plan a publication**
▶ **Create a new publication**
▶ **Place a graphic**
▶ **Resize and move a graphic**
▶ **Add text and lines to a publication**
▶ **Format text**
▶ **Save a publication**
▶ **Print a publication**
▶ **Design Workshop: Letterhead**

Now that you know how to start PageMaker, use the online Help system, move around a PageMaker publication window, and use PageMaker tools, you are ready to plan and create your own publication. When working with a publication, you can include text and graphics created in other application programs. You can also use PageMaker's tools to create and modify text and graphics directly in your publication. After you create a publication, you can save and print it. Joe Martin needs to create a new company letterhead for New World Airlines. Creating simple publications is one of the many ways that PageMaker is useful for businesses.

Planning a Publication

Before you create a publication in PageMaker, you need to plan and design it. Planning and designing a publication organizes your thoughts and ideas about what to include and how it should look. At the beginning of each unit, you will learn design tips for creating different types of publications. One of Joe's first assignments is to create a new letterhead for New World Airlines. Letterhead should be eye-catching and memorable. It should contain the company logo and the company name, and can also contain the company address, telephone and fax numbers, and electronic mail address. Joe keeps the following guidelines in mind as he plans and designs the letterhead:

Details

Place the company logo in a logical position on the page

A company's logo is used in almost all forms of visual communication to reinforce the connection between the graphic logo and the company name. Logos on letterhead are often at the top of the page, but they can run down a side or be at the bottom. The logo should be large enough to catch the reader's attention, but not so large that it is overwhelming. Joe decides to place the New World Airlines logo at the top of the page in the center.

Include the company address and any relevant telephone numbers

The placement of the address and telephone numbers is usually based on the placement of the logo. Joe decides to put the company's address and toll free telephone number below the logo.

Consider adding the company motto or slogan

Adding the motto or slogan is not required, but it can help reinforce the company's image. Joe decides to put the New World Airlines slogan, "The Wings of America," above the address line.

Evaluate the final design, and add lines, boxes, or shading, if necessary

Joe wants the logo and the address line to be visually distinct from the rest of the page, so he adds a thin horizontal line below the logo. Figure B-1 shows Joe's sketch of the letterhead.

FIGURE B-1: Joe's sketch of the new letterhead

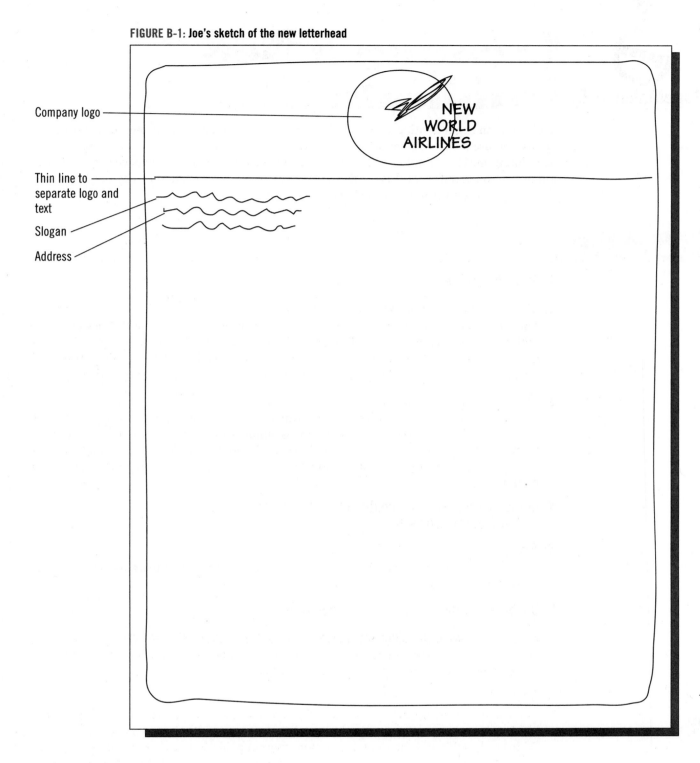

Company logo

Thin line to separate logo and text

Slogan

Address

NEW WORLD AIRLINES

PageMaker 6.5

Creating a New Publication

Before you can begin creating a new publication, you need to select the settings for the pages. To do this, you use the Document Setup dialog box. These settings become the default settings for the publication. The **default settings** determine the general layout of each page in the publication unless you specify otherwise. ✐ Joe begins creating the letterhead by opening a new publication and setting the page defaults.

1. **Start PageMaker**

2. **Click File on the menu bar, then click New**
   The Document Setup dialog box opens, as shown in Figure B-2. Table B-1 describes the options in the Document Setup dialog box. The company letterhead is a one-page publication that will be on standard 8½" × 11" paper, so most of the PageMaker default settings are fine. Because this is only a single-page publication, Joe turns off the Double-sided option.

3. **Click the Double-sided check box**
   Turning this feature off sets each page individually instead of grouping even and odd pages together. Notice that the Facing pages option is dimmed and that the margin options change from "Inside" and "Outside" to "Left" and "Right." Joe looks at his sketch again and sees that he wants to put the logo close to the top edge of the page, so he decides to change the top margin to .5".

4. **In the Margins section, double-click the Top text box**
   The current value, 0.75, is **selected**, or highlighted.

5. **Type .5**
   The top margin is now set at .5". Next, Joe sets the right and bottom margins to be the same as the left margin, 1".

6. **Double-click the Right text box, then type 1**

7. **Press [Tab] twice to select the value in the Bottom text box, then type 1**
   You can place the insertion point in a text box in dialog boxes by clicking in the text box or by pressing [Tab] to move from option to option.

8. **Click OK**
   The Document Setup dialog box closes, and a new Untitled publication window with a blank publication page opens, displaying a letter-size page with the top margin guide set at .5" from the edge and the right and bottom margin guides set at 1" from the edge. Notice that there is only one master page icon because this is a single-sided publication and the number of pages is set at 1.

FIGURE B-2: **Document Setup dialog box**

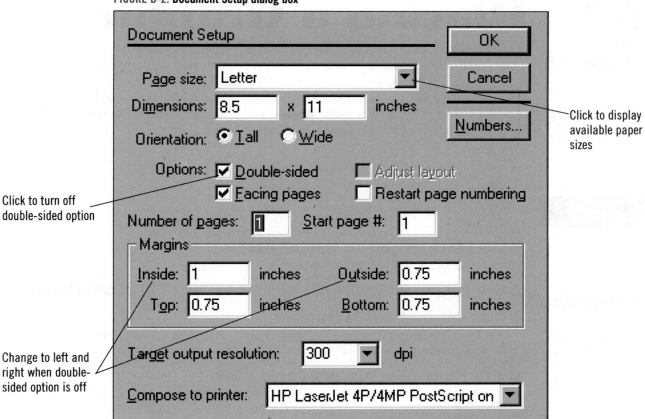

Click to turn off
double-sided option

Click to display
available paper
sizes

Change to left and
right when double-
sided option is off

TABLE B-1: **Document Setup dialog box options**

option	description
Page size	Select a standard paper size or choose Custom to specify your own dimensions
Dimensions	Enter custom page dimensions; if you change the page dimensions to nonstandard measurements, Custom is automatically displayed in the Page size list box
Orientation	Choose Tall (vertical) or Wide (horizontal)
Double-sided	Indicate that a publication has left and right pages
Facing pages	Only available when Double-sided is checked; when selected, displays left and right pages side by side
Restart page numbering	For publication files that are linked, or connected, to another publication file, starts the page numbering at the specified start page number instead of continuing from the end of the publication it is linked to
Number of pages	Specify the total number of pages in the publication
Start page #	Specify the first page number of the publication
Margins	Specify the margins for the publication
Target printer resolution	Choose the **resolution**, or print quality, measured in dots per inch (the higher the number of dots, the better the image quality); you can choose a higher resolution only if you have a higher resolution printer
Compose to printer	Specify the printer on which you plan to print this publication

PageMaker 6.5

Placing a Graphic

With PageMaker, you can easily import, or include, graphics in your publication. **Graphics** are images created in a drawing or painting program or photographs or art scanned into the computer using a scanner. You import graphic files using the Place command on the File menu. Placing graphics allows you to enhance your page layouts with images that cannot be created with PageMaker's basic design tools. ▰▰▰ Joe has already scanned the New World Airlines logo. He now wants to place it at the top of the letterhead.

Steps

1. **Click File on the menu bar, then click Place**
   The Place document dialog box opens.

2. **Make sure your Student Disk is in the disk drive, then click the Look in list arrow**

   MacintoshUser

   This replaces Steps 2 and 3.
   2. Make sure your Student Disk is in the disk drive, then click Desktop
   3. Double-click Student Disk Resume at Step 4.

3. **In the Look in list, click 3½ Floppy (A:)**
   A list of files on your Student Disk appears in the File name list box. Only the files that can be imported into a PageMaker publication are listed.

4. **In the File name list, click Logo, then click Open**
   The Place document dialog box closes, and the pointer changes to ⊠ *(Macintosh users:* ▦ *).* This pointer identifies the format of the graphic file as Tagged Image File format. There are other graphic file formats and each format has a place pointer. Each type of graphic file gives a different resolution and takes up a different amount of disk space. See Table B-2 for a description of graphic file types.

   DesignTip

   Try to position the upper-left corner of the place pointer where you want the upper-left corner of the graphic to be. This saves time moving the graphic to the correct position after it is placed.

5. **Position the top border of ⊠** *(Macintosh users:* ▦ *)* **along the top margin guide with the pointer guide on the horizontal ruler at 3.25", as shown in Figure B-3**
   Notice the top border of the pointer is on top of the top margin border.

6. **Click the left mouse button**
   The graphic appears on the page and the pointer changes back to ▸, as shown in Figure B-4. The **selection handles**, the small black squares at the corners and sides of the graphic, indicate that the graphic is selected.

FIGURE B-3: TIF pointer on the publication page

Pointer guide at 3.25"

TIF place pointer

Left margin is 1"

One page icon indicates that this is a single-page publication

One master page icon indicates Double-sided option is off

Top margin is .5"

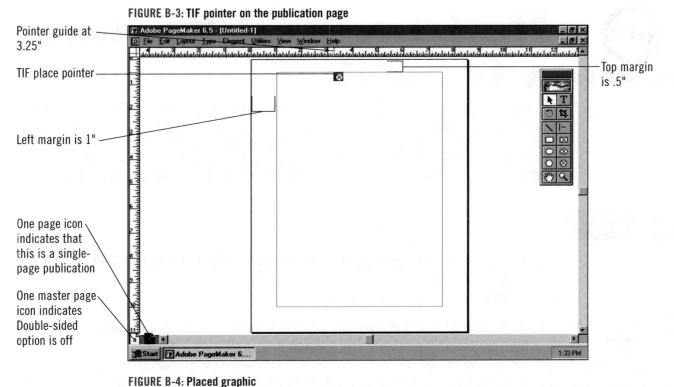

FIGURE B-4: Placed graphic

Pointer changes shape

Selection handles

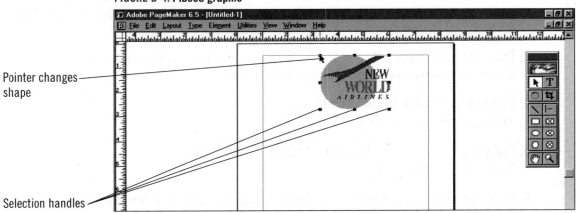

TABLE B-2: Graphic file types

place pointer	Macintosh place pointer	file extension	description
		.BMP	Bitmap file. Image created by dot resolution; used in Windows Paint application
		.EPS	Encapsulated PostScript file. File created using PostScript code to create an image. EPS files are usually large
		.PIC	Picture/Draw file. Generally geometric drawings or charts and graphs
		.TIF	Tagged Image File Format. A standardized file format used by most major software developers for standard drawing, paint, and scanned images

Resizing and Moving a Graphic

PageMaker 6.5

An **object** is an item, such as a graphic logo or a line, that you can select and then size or move. Usually when a graphic is imported, it is not the correct size, so you need to resize it. You can resize graphics by dragging the selection handles to make the graphic larger or smaller. You can also move objects between pages or onto the pasteboard for temporary storage outside the page. Joe needs to resize the New World Airlines logo so that it takes up less space at the top of the page.

Steps

1. **If the graphic is not selected, position the pointer ▶ in the middle of the logo, then click to select it**
   Clicking once on a graphic selects it.

Trouble?

If you forget to press [Shift] when you resize a graphic and the proportions are no longer true, resize it again, this time pressing [Shift].

2. **Move the pointer to the lower-right corner handle of the logo, press and hold [Shift], then press and hold the left mouse button**
   The pointer changes to ↘, and a box appears around the graphic to show you its dimensions. See Figure B-5. Pressing [Shift] while you resize a graphic maintains the proportions of the graphic as you resize it. By dragging a corner handle, you change the length and width of the image simultaneously.

3. **Drag the handle until it is at the 5.25" mark on the horizontal ruler**
   Use the pointer guides to help you size the logo correctly.

4. **Release the mouse button and [Shift]**
   The logo is resized as shown in Figure B-6.

Trouble?

If your toolbox is not visible, click Window on the menu bar, then click Show Tools.

5. **Click the Pointer tool ▶ in the toolbox, if necessary**
   The pointer changes to ▶.

6. **Click anywhere on the New World Airlines logo to select it, if necessary**

DesignTip

The easiest way to determine the measurement of a graphic you are resizing is to move the zero point to the upper-left corner of the image.

7. **Position the pointer anywhere over the logo, but not over any of the handles, then press and hold the left mouse button**
   The pointer changes to ▶ (Macintosh users: ✋). Note that if you hold down the mouse button too long no outline appears. If you clicked one of the handles, you would resize the object instead of moving it.

8. **Drag the logo to the upper-left corner of the page so that the top and left borders of the outline overlap the top and left page margins, then release the mouse button**
   If the border has disappeared, then position the left pointer guide on the horizontal ruler at the 1" mark. When you release the mouse button, the logo appears in its new location. Compare your screen with Figure B-7.

Trouble?

If you accidentally resize a graphic instead of moving it, click Edit, then select Undo stretch to return the graphic to its original size.

9. **Click anywhere on the page, except on the logo, to deselect the graphic**

FIGURE B-5: Preparing to resize the logo

Pointer guide in horizontal ruler

Pointer guide in vertical ruler

Outline shows the dimension of the graphic

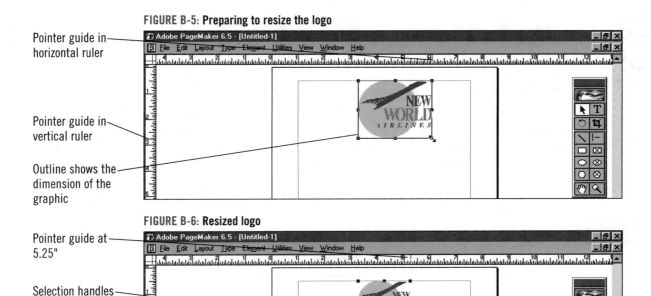

FIGURE B-6: Resized logo

Pointer guide at 5.25"

Selection handles indicate the graphic is still selected

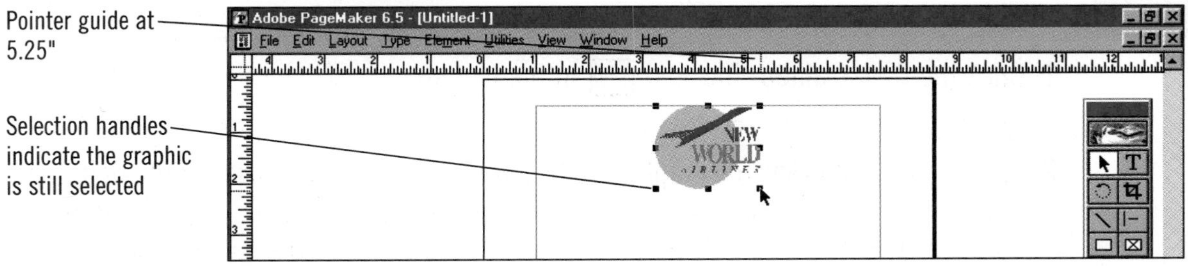

FIGURE B-7: Repositioned logo

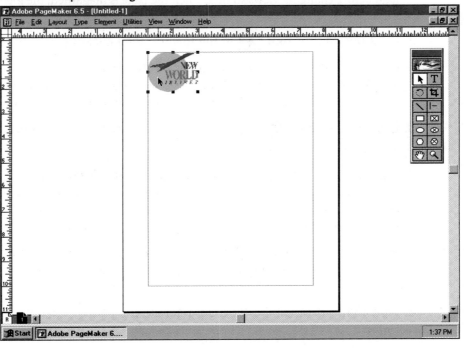

CLUES TO USE

Distorting the image design

Sometimes you will want to resize a graphic without maintaining its proportions. To do this, you drag a selection handle without pressing [Shift]. This distorts the image. When you need to fit an image within a certain area, it can be helpful to distort it. Distortion can also be used as a method of creative design in your publication. It is important to make sure that the distortion does not affect the integrity of the image. If you decide to resize an image to its original proportions after it was distorted, press [Shift], then drag the handle to the desired size, and the graphic will again be proportionally sized.

Adding Text and Lines to a Publication

PageMaker provides tools with which you can add text and lines to a publication easily and quickly. To add text to a publication, you select the Text tool from the toolbox, click the page, and then type. To add a straight line to a publication, you use the Constrained-line tool, which you used earlier. ✒ Joe needs to add the company's address and telephone number to the letterhead. He also wants to draw a line to separate the logo from the rest of the page.

1. Click the **Constrained-line tool** |─| in the toolbox
   The pointer changes to ✛.

2. Position ✛ just below the graphic on the left margin guide, and drag to the right until the ✛ is directly on top of the right margin guide, then release the mouse button
   See Figure B-8. A horizontal line appears just below the logo. Next Joe wants to add the company address. First, he changes the view so that he can see the letters he types. Joe selects the logo before changing views so that, when the page is magnified, the logo will be centered on the screen.

3. Click the **Pointer tool** ▶ in the toolbox, then click the **logo** to select it

4. Click **View** on the menu bar, then click **Actual Size**
   The screen appears at 100% with the selected logo in the center of the screen. Now Joe is ready to enter the airline's address and telephone number with the Text tool.

5. Click the **Text tool** T in the toolbox, then position the pointer over the page
   The pointer changes to I.

6. Click I below the line you drew and next to the left margin guide
   A blinking cursor appears, also called the insertion point. The **cursor** shows where the next character you type will appear. If you click in the wrong place, reposition the cursor by clicking I again in the correct place.

7. Type **"The Wings of America"** (include the quotation marks), then press **[Enter]**
   Notice that characters appear as you type and the cursor moves down one line when you press [Enter]. See Figure B-9.

8. Type **1845 North Lindbergh Blvd.** (include the period), then press **[Spacebar]** three times

9. Type **Charlotte, NC 28204** and press **[Spacebar]** three times, then type **800-HORIZON**

QuickTip

If you make a typing error, press [Backspace] to erase the error, then type the correct text (Macintosh users: press [delete].

FIGURE B-8: **Horizontal line added**

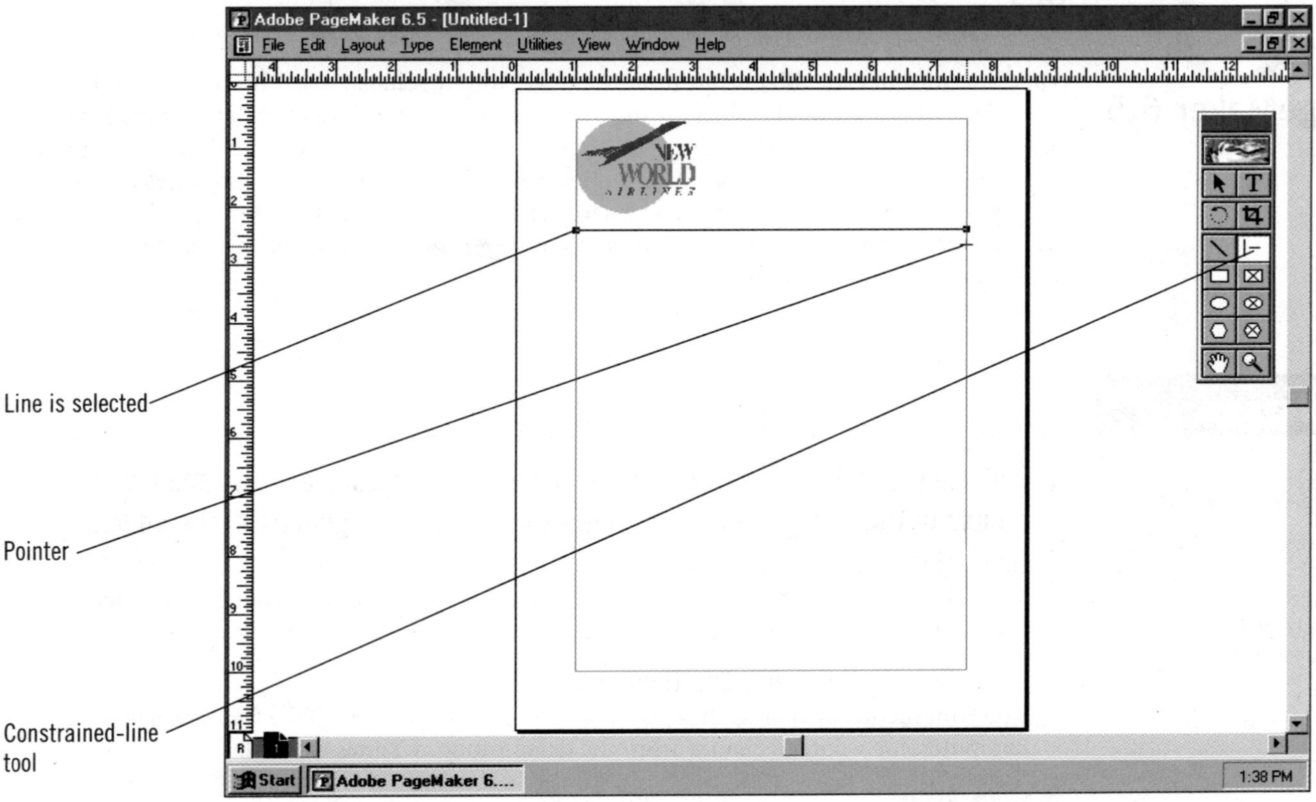

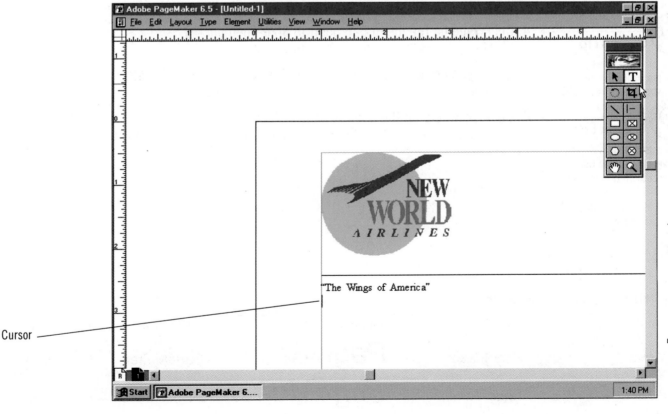

Line is selected

Pointer

Constrained-line
tool

FIGURE B-9: **Text entered on a page**

"The Wings of America"

Cursor

Formatting Text

When you **format** text, you change its appearance. You can change the font, size, and style of the text. The **font** is a set of characters using a specific design. The size of the characters is usually measured in points. A **point** is ½ of an inch. The style of the text is how the design is displayed, for example, in italics or bold. Table B-3 shows examples of fonts, sizes, and styles available in Windows. The easiest way to format text is to select the text you want to format, and then choose the appropriate command from the Type menu. 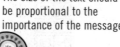 Joe wants to format the company's address and telephone number.

QuickTip

To select a word quickly, double-click it with I.
To select an entire line quickly, triple-click anywhere in it with I.

1. Position the Text tool pointer I at the end of the address line, press and hold the **left mouse button**, drag I to the left until you reach the beginning of the address line, then release the mouse button

   The address line is selected, as shown in Figure B-10. If you accidentally select the line above, click outside the highlighted area to deselect the text and try again.

2. Click **Type** on the menu bar, then point to **Font**

   The Font menu appears, as shown in Figure B-11, with a list of all the fonts available on your computer. Joe wants to change from the default font of Times to Arial.

3. Click **Arial**

   Notice that the font changes. Next, Joe thinks that the address line will look better if the text is smaller.

DesignTip

The size of the text should be proportional to the importance of the message.

4. Click **Type** on the menu bar, point to **Size**, then click **9**

   Joe also wants to italicize the address line.

5. Click **Type** on the menu bar, point to **Type Style**, then click **Italic**

   The selected text now reflects all the changes you made.

QuickTip

To change font, size, and style at the same time, select the text to change, right-click, click Character, then make your changes in the dialog box.

6. Click anywhere on the page to deselect the text

   Joe is pleased with the letterhead. Compare your screen with Figure B-12.

TABLE B-3: Types of fonts and formatting

font	12 point	24 point	12 pt bold	12 pt italic
Arial	PageMaker	PageMaker	**PageMaker**	*PageMaker*
Century Schoolbook	PageMaker	*PageMaker*	**PageMaker**	*PageMaker*
Times New Roman	PageMaker	PageMaker	**PageMaker**	*PageMaker*

FIGURE B-10: Selected text

Selected text ⎯⎯⎯⎯⎯⎯⎯
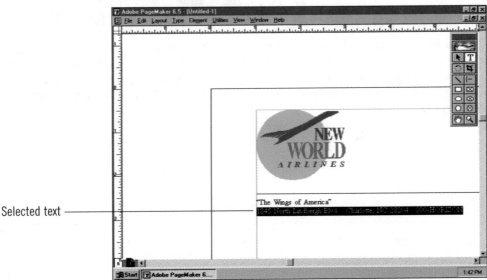

FIGURE B-11: Font menu

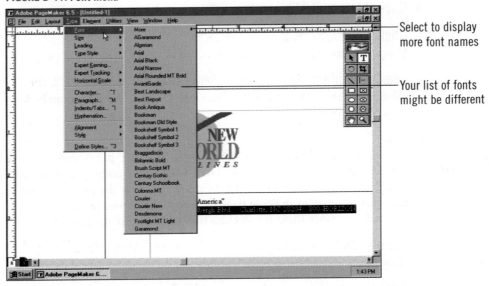

Select to display
more font names

Your list of fonts
might be different

FIGURE B-12: Joe's completed letterhead

9-point italicized
type ⎯⎯⎯⎯⎯⎯
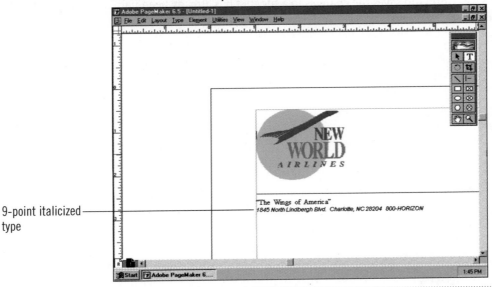

PageMaker 6.5

PageMaker 6.5

Saving a Publication

You must save a file to disk in order to store it permanently. As you work on your publication, it's a good idea to save it every 10 or 15 minutes. Frequent saving prevents losing your work unexpectedly in case of a power or equipment failure. It's also a good practice to save your work before you print it. You will save all the files on your Student Disk. Joe wants to save his publication with the name Letterhead.

1. **Click File on the menu bar, then click Save As**
   See Figure B-13. The Save Publication dialog box opens.

2. **Make sure your Student Disk is in the appropriate drive**

MacintoshUser

This replaces Steps 3 and 4.
3. Click Desktop
4. Click Student Disk, then click Open
Resume at Step 5.

3. **Click the Save in list arrow**

4. **Click 3½ Floppy (A:)**
   If you are storing your practice files on a network, click the appropriate drive.

5. **Select the filename in the File name text box if necessary, then type Letterhead**
   Filenames can contain up to 250 characters. These characters can be lower- or uppercase letters, numbers, or any symbols.

QuickTip

You can use the shortcut key combination [Ctrl] [S] to save a file (Macintosh users: press [S]).

6. **Click Save**
   The Save Publication dialog box closes, and the publication is saved as a file named Letterhead.p65 on your Student Disk. PageMaker adds .p65 to the end of the file. This is called a **file extension** and helps Windows identify the program that created each file. The filename appears in the title bar at the top of the page window. After looking over the letterhead one more time, Joe decides that he wants to change "Blvd." to "Boulevard."

MacintoshUser

This replaces Step 7.
7. Double-click the word Blvd, type Boulevard, then press [del] (not [delete]) to delete the period
Resume at Step 8.

7. **Double-click the word Blvd, type Boulevard, then press [Delete] to delete the period**
   Now that Joe has changed his publication he needs to save it again.

8. **Click File on the menu bar, then click Save**
   The Save command saves the changes to a file that has already been named. Table B-4 shows the difference between the Save and Save As commands.

FIGURE B-13: Save Publication dialog box

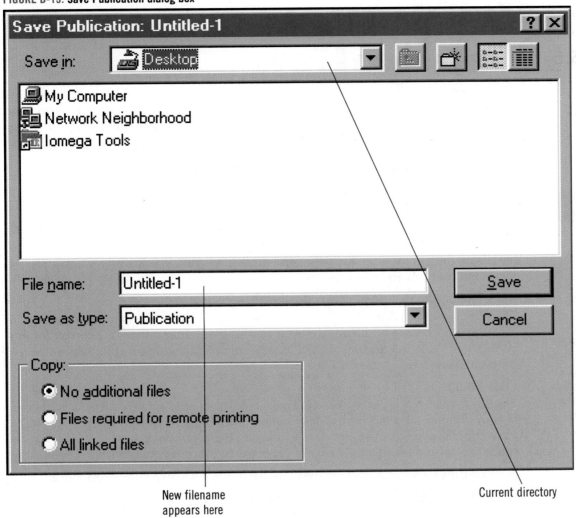

New filename
appears here

Current directory

TABLE B-4: The difference between the Save and Save As commands

command	description	purpose
Save As	Saves file, requires input name	To save a file the first time, to change the filename, or to save the file for use in a different application. Useful for backups
Save	Saves named file	To save any changes to the original file. Fast and easy—do this often to protect your work

CLUES TO USE

Creating backup files

It's good practice to back up your files in case something happens to your disk. To create a backup copy of a file, save the file again to a second disk with a slightly modified name. For example, you might back up a file named "Brochure" under the name "Brochure-backup" or "Brochure-copy."

PageMaker 6.5

Printing a Publication

Printing a publication allows you to edit, or proof, your work. Sometimes it's easier to see how the elements work together on a page in a printed publication than on the screen. You also print your publication when it is completed. When you print your publications on a laser printer, you capitalize on one of desktop publishing's strengths—creating camera-ready copy at your desk. **Camera-ready copy** is paper copy that is ready to be photographed for reproduction without further alteration. With the New World Airlines letterhead saved to disk, Joe prints it to show it to Patricia Fernandez, his manager.

Steps

1. Check the printer
Make sure the printer is on, has paper, and is ready to print. If you send a file to a printer that is not ready, an error message appears.

2. Click File on the menu bar, then click Print
The Print Document dialog box opens, as shown in Figure B-14. The name of the printer in the Printer box might be different on your screen. The default settings are correct for this publication. Table B-5 explains the five middle command buttons, each of which opens a different dialog box.

QuickTip

You should always save a publication prior to printing it, as you did in the previous lesson. If anything happens to the file as it is being sent to the printer, you will have a copy of the final version saved to your disk.

3. Click Setup
The Setup dialog box opens as shown in Figure B-15. If you have a PostScript printer attached to your computer, you will have a Paper button instead of a Setup button. Click Paper. The Print Paper dialog box opens, as shown in Figure B-16. You can choose the paper size on which to print and whether the source of paper will be the trays or a manual feed bypass tray.

4. Make sure the paper selection near the top of the dialog box displays the paper size as Letter

5. Click OK to close the Setup dialog box, then click Print in the Print Document dialog box
If you are using a PostScript printer, you can simply click Print. If any other dialog boxes appear, click OK or Print to close them. A status window appears while the printer receives the publication's information. Note that a Cancel button in the status window allows you to cancel the printing if you want to. Don't worry if you don't have a color printer. Your printer will convert the colors you see on the screen to black, white, and shades of gray. Joe can now exit PageMaker, close the publication, and save his work.

MacintoshUser

6. Click File on the menu bar, click Exit, then click Yes
After Patricia approves the letterhead, Joe will send the file to a professional print shop where the letterhead will be printed in a large quantity with the colors that should appear in the logo.

6. Select File, select Quit, then click Yes.

TABLE B-5: Print Document dialog box buttons

button	description
Document	General settings and options to print the document, including the choice of printer, number of copies, range of pages and orientation
Paper	Settings to change the printing resolution, paper size, and the paper source for PostScript printers
Setup	Settings to change the printing resolution, paper size, and the paper source for non-PostScript printers
Options	Options to choose the scale of the printed publication, from 5% to 1600%, duplex printing (double-sided printing), and options for applying printer marks on the page. Printer marks are used in final output by commercial printers
Color	Settings to determine how color objects in the document will be printed
Features	Printer-specific features for PostScript printers

FIGURE B-14: **Print Document dialog box**

Number of copies

Pages to be printed

Tall orientation
selected

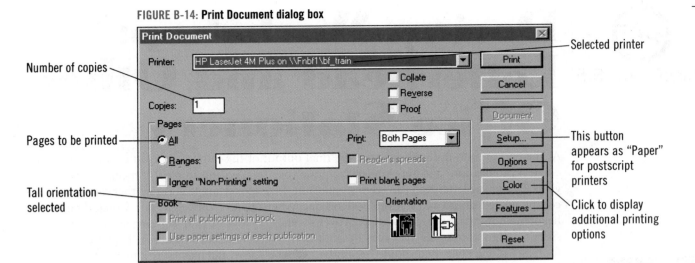

Selected printer

This button
appears as "Paper"
for postscript
printers

Click to display
additional printing
options

FIGURE B-15: **Setup dialog box**

Your printer might
be different

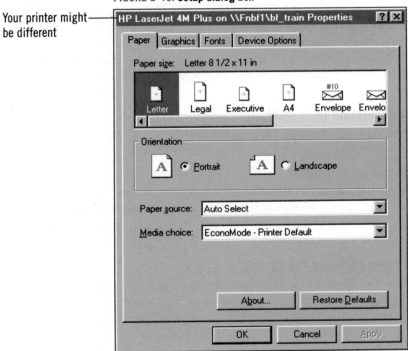

FIGURE B-16: **Print Paper dialog box**

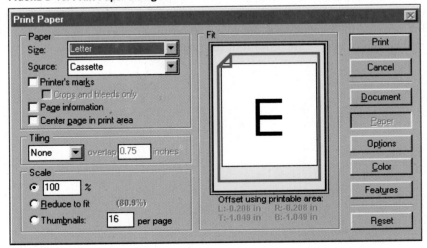

PageMaker 6.5

Design Workshop: Letterhead and Other Office Stationery

At the end of each unit, you will see the final output of the publication you created. After you create a publication, it is important to critique your final output to see if it meets your original goals. Designing letterhead can seem simple, but there are certain techniques that can make your company's letterhead and stationery stand out. When creating office stationery including letterhead, memoranda, business cards, fax cover sheets, and envelopes, it is important to keep a consistent design among all the types of stationery. For example, the placement of the logo and fonts, sizes, and style used should be similar. Joe would like to critique his design of the New World Airlines letterhead shown in Figure B-17 before he gives it to his boss for approval.

Details

Did the logo placement add to the overall design?

Joe added his company logo to the letterhead and moved it from the center to the top left corner of the page. He could have positioned the logo at the top right, in the center, or on the bottom of the page. It seems to be an appropriate size and does not overwhelm the information on the page.

Was all the relevant information included?

Joe did include all the relevant information. He decided not to include the fax number and electronic mail address because these numbers are not appropriate for the general public.

Was the use of the slogan appropriate?

Joe added the New World Airlines slogan to reinforce his company's message. Depending on the audience, slogans or mottoes might not be appropriate or necessary. As with the company information, he could have placed the slogan across the bottom of the page to serve as an anchor, or border, for the overall design of the letterhead.

Did the placement of lines enhance the layout?

Joe separated the logo from the rest of the layout by adding a line below the logo across the page. He could have placed the logo and address vertically down the left side of the page and then added a vertical line from the top to bottom margin to separate this information from the body of the letter.

Are you pleased with the overall appearance of the letterhead?

Joe is pleased because the smaller size and different font of the address distinguish this information from the slogan and from the text of the letters that will be printed on the letterhead. But he could have created a more balanced layout by placing the text above the line in the top-right corner or across the bottom of the page.

"The Wings of America"
1845 North Lindbergh Boulevard, Charlotte, NC 28204   800-HORIZON

Practice

▶ Concepts Review

Label each of the publication window elements shown in Figure B-18.

FIGURE B-18

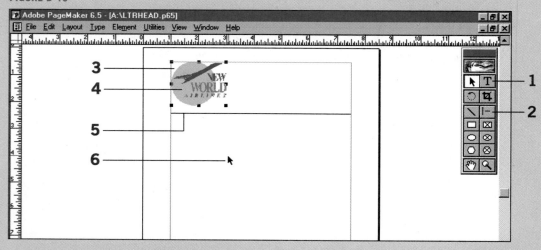

Match each of the terms with the statement that describes its function.

7. **Place**	**a.** Saves the current publication to disk with a new name
8. **Point**	**b.** Command for importing a graphic
9. **Font**	**c.** ½₂ of an inch
10. **Save As**	**d.** Image created in a drawing or painting program
11. **Graphic**	**e.** Specific design of characters

Select the best answer from the list of choices.

12. The term used to describe image quality and clarity of a publication's output is:
    a. Image view   **c.** Laser print
    b. Resolution   **d.** None of the above

13. In the Document Setup dialog box, you can make the following settings, except:
    a. Number of columns   **c.** Number of pages
    b. Size of the page   **d.** Both a and c

14. All of the following are true statements concerning filenames, except:
    a. Filenames are less than eight characters   **c.** Punctuation can be used as the first character
    b. Numbers can be used as the first character   **d.** All of the above are true statements

15. PageMaker allows you to place all of the following, except:
    a. Text files   **c.** Images created with a paint program
    b. Graphic images   **d.** All of the above can be placed

16. While dragging a graphic's corner handle, which key do you press to resize a graphic image proportionally?
    a. [Ctrl]   **c.** [Alt]
    b. [Shift]   **d.** The image automatically resizes proportionally.

► Skills Review

1. Create a new publication.
   a. Start PageMaker, click File on the menu bar, then click New.
   b. In the Document Setup dialog box, make sure Letter appears in the Page size list box.
   c. Make sure the orientation is Tall.
   d. Set all margins to 1" and set the publication as single-sided.
   e. Click OK.
   f. Reposition the zero point to the intersection of the top and left margin guides.
   g. Plan a memo to a coworker asking for approval for new company letterhead design.

2. Place a graphic on a page.
   a. Click File on the menu bar, then click Place.
   b. Insert your Student Disk in the disk drive.
   c. Click the Look in list arrow, then click 3½ Floppy (A:). *(Macintosh users: click Desktop, then double-click Student Disk.)*
   d. Click Logo in the File name list, then click Open.
   e. Position the TIF place pointer ▶ near the top left corner of the publication, then click the left mouse button.
   f. Position ▶ in the middle of the graphic, press and hold the left mouse button, drag the logo to the bottom of the page, then release the mouse button.
   g. Using the rulers as guides, position the top edge of the logo to the .5" mark on the vertical ruler and the right edge of the logo at the 6" mark on the horizontal ruler.
   h. Deselect the graphic by clicking outside of the graphic's boundaries.

3. Resize and move the graphic.
   a. Select the graphic by positioning the pointer in the middle of the logo, and clicking the left mouse button.
   b. Move the pointer to the lower-left corner handle of the logo, press and hold [Shift], then press and hold the left mouse button.
   c. Drag the handle to resize the graphic so the bottom edge is at 2" on the vertical ruler, then release the mouse button and [Shift].
   d. Drag the logo until it is centered between the left and right margins.

4. Add text to the publication.
   a. Click the Text tool in the toolbox.
   b. Position the Text tool pointer Ⅰ at the left margin below the logo, then click the left mouse button.
   c. Click View on the menu bar, then click Actual Size.
   d. Type "MEMO", then press [Enter] twice.
   e. Type the following address information:

TO:	Patricia Fernandez
FROM:	Joe Martin
DATE:	January 12, 1999
RE:	Letterhead & Envelope Design

   f. Press [Enter] twice to leave a blank line after the address information.
   g. Continue typing the following memo:
   Enclosed you will find the final draft for the company letterhead. I believe these designs meet your specifications. If you have any questions, please call me.
   Pending your approval, the printer informed me that the final production of the letterhead could be completed in one week.

5. Format text.
 a. Place the pointer at the beginning of the word "MEMO," then drag the pointer to the end of the word.
 b. Change the size to 14 points.
 c. Change the style to Bold.
 d. Change the style to Underline.
 e. Click anywhere on the page to deselect the text.

6. Add lines to the publication.
 a. Click the Constrained-line tool in the toolbox.
 b. Position the Constrained-line tool pointer ╋ on the left margin guide just below the word "MEMO."
 c. Press and hold the left mouse button, then drag the pointer from the left margin to the right margin. The screen will scroll automatically. Release the mouse button.
 d. Position ╋ below the words "RE: Letterhead."
 e. Press and hold the mouse button, drag the pointer from the left margin to the right margin, then release the mouse button.
 f. Draw a third line below the one you just drew.
 g. Deselect the line by selecting the Pointer tool in the toolbox.
 h. Click the third line to select it.
 i. With the line selected, press [Delete] to remove the unnecessary line.

7. Save the publication.
 a. Make sure your Student Disk is still in the disk drive.
 b. Save the file as "Memo1".

8. Print the publication and exit PageMaker.
 a. Click File on the menu bar, then click Print.
 b. Click the Paper button or Setup button, depending on your printer.
 c. Make sure the paper size selected is Letter.
 d. If you are in the Print Paper dialog box, click Document to return to the Print Document dialog box. If you are in the Print Setup dialog box, then click OK *(Macintosh users: then click Cancel)*.
 e. Make any other adjustments necessary.
 f. Click Print to print the file.
 g. Save and close your document, then exit PageMaker.

► Independent Challenges

1. You are the graphic designer for Johnson Printing Company. Your manager has asked you to create letterhead, memo letterhead, and a business card design. The logo is shown in Figure B-19 and is located on your Student Disk as Jlogo.

FIGURE B-19

To complete this independent challenge:

1. Plan the letterhead, the memo letterhead, and the business card by sketching them on paper.
2. Open a new single-sided one-page publication with one-inch margins on all sides, and save it as Johnson letterhead to your Student Disk.
3. Place the image Jlogo on the page. Resize the logo to a more appropriate size. Move the logo to an appropriate position.

4. Draw a line on the page, if necessary.

5. Use the Text tool to add text for the address and phone number.

6. Save your work. Then print the publication and close the file.

7. Open a new single-sided one-page publication with one-inch margins on all sides, and save it as Johnson memo to your Student Disk.

8. Place the logo Jlogo on the page. Resize the logo to an appropriate size. Move the logo to an appropriate position.

9. Add a single line in a location that you feel enhances the design of the memo.

10. Use the Text tool to add the words "MEMO", "TO:", "FROM:", "DATE:", and "RE:" in the appropriate places.

11. Save your work. Then print the publication and close the file.

12. Open a new single-sided publication. In the Document Setup dialog box, choose Custom in the Page size list box and make the dimensions 2" x 3.5", make all four margins equal to .25", and choose Wide as the orientation.

13. Save the publication as Johnson business card to your Student Disk.

14. Place the logo Jlogo on the page. Resize it so it fits within the page margins, then move it to the position on your business card indicated by your design sketch.

15. Type your name, title, the company's address, and telephone number.

16. Select your name, change the type style to bold, and change the type size until it is the size you want. Change the size and style of the company address and telephone number.

17. Save your work. Then print the publication and close the file.

18. Submit all printouts.

2. You are a free-lance graphic artist hired by your school or company to redesign their stationery. Obtain a sample of the letterhead or memo letterhead currently in use. Compare this example to what you learned in this unit and think about the following:

- Is a logo used in the publication? Is the logo large enough to be seen but not overwhelming?
- Is all the relevant information included? Should you include a fax number or the electronic mail address?
- Is the company's or school's slogan included in the letterhead? Is it appropriate to include it.
- Do you need a graphic to separate the logo and company information from the body text of the letterhead?

To complete this independent challenge:

1. Sketch a new design for the letterhead.

2. What information did you include? Why?

3. Did you include the company's or school's slogan? Why or why not?

4. Did you include any graphics? Explain.

5. Evaluate the overall appearance of the letterhead. Are you pleased with it? Sometimes it helps to not look at a design for a day and then reevaluate it. Now, what do you think?

3. Your school or company liked your new design for their letterhead so much that they would like you to go ahead and create the new letterhead for them using PageMaker 6.5.

To complete this independent challenge:

1. Use the hand sketch of the letterhead you designed in Independent Challenge 2 to create a new letterhead.

2. If you have access to a drawing program, create a logo and place it in your publication.

3. Save the publication as Letterhead 2 to your Student Disk.

4. Print the publication and close the file.

5. Submit your printout.

4. Like Joe Martin, you work in the marketing department of an airline. You have been asked to create a new company letterhead for your organization.

To complete this independent challenge:

1. Search the World Wide Web for information on an airline of your choice or use the same airline as in the first unit.
2. Using the information that you find, sketch a design for the airline's letterhead including a logo and a slogan. Make sure to keep the guidelines in mind that you learned in Unit 2 as you plan and design the letterhead.
3. Use the hand sketch of the letterhead that you designed to create a letterhead in PageMaker 6.5.
4. If you have access to a painting or drawing program, create a logo that can be placed in the publication.
5. Critique your final letterhead to make sure that it meets the goals that you planned.
6. Save the publication as My Letterhead to your Student Disk. Then print and close the file.
7. Submit your sketch, your printout, and the critique of your original goals.

▶ Visual Workshop

You are the marketing manager for a delivery company called Chuck Xpress Delivery & Parcel Service. You have been asked by the owner to create letterhead for the company. Use Figure B-20 as a guide for how the completed letterhead should look. Set the margins to .75" on all sides. Place the graphic located on your Student Disk called Chuck, increase the size of the graphic and move it. Using the Text tool add the company address and slogan. Using the Constrained-line tool, add lines to the letterhead. Save the file as Chuck letterhead to your Student Disk, and print a copy of the new letterhead.

FIGURE B-20

PageMaker 6.5

Working
with Text

Objectives

- ▶ **Plan a fact sheet**
- ▶ **Create columns**
- ▶ **Import and place text**
- ▶ **Control the text flow**
- ▶ **Manipulate text blocks**
- ▶ **Move and resize text blocks**
- ▶ **Drag-place text**
- ▶ **Use reverse text**
- ▶ **Design Workshop: Fact sheets**

Now that you know how to create a publication in PageMaker, you are ready to learn more about working with text. In this unit, you will learn how to create columns, how to import, place, and manipulate text, and how to format headlines.  Joe Martin needs to create a fact sheet describing package tours that New World Airlines has arranged with Sunset Tours, a travel agency.

Planning a Fact Sheet

A **fact sheet** is an informational publication. It can contain one page or a set of pages that describes in detail the company's products or services. Fact sheets usually contain large amounts of text, so it is important to plan the layout carefully and use graphical elements to support the text. As part of the publicity campaign on the New World Airlines package deals with Sunset Tours, Joe wants to create fact sheets that describe available tours to Europe and Asia. Travel agents at Sunset will send the fact sheets to potential customers who request more information about specific vacation packages. Joe plans to describe charters to three different cities. He keeps the following guidelines in mind as he plans his first fact sheet:

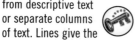

Keep the layout simple
While it is important to catch the reader's attention, fact sheets should provide detailed information about a product or service in a succinct and organized way. If your fact sheet relies too heavily on creative design, some of your message might get lost. Joe has decided to have three columns. Each column will provide information about a specific tour.

Keep the format consistent among fact sheets in a series
Fact sheets in a series should present repetitive types of information consistently. Joe's fact sheets will provide the same information: name of tour, description, and point of response. **Point of response** is the phone number or the address where the reader can respond to information in the fact sheet. Formatting this text in the same manner creates a consistent look.

DesignTip

Use lines to provide structure in your publication. A line can separate headlines from descriptive text or separate columns of text. Lines give the layout some creativity without burdening the reader with too many graphical elements.

Use graphical elements strategically to enhance the overall layout
Graphical elements is an umbrella term that describes anything on a page other than the text. Graphical elements, such as lines or photos, can make your fact sheets more interesting. Because fact sheets should provide information, graphical elements should support the text without overshadowing the message you are trying to convey. Joe decides to include a photograph of a famous site in each city.

Include a headline that instantly conveys the purpose of the fact sheet
Publications with a lot of text can be so intimidating that the reader might simply ignore the fact sheet; therefore, the headline should convey the purpose of the publication immediately and clearly. Joe wants a headline identifying the purpose of his fact sheet across the top of the page. He also decides to set the headline for his fact sheet in **reverse text**, white text on a black background, so the reader will know at the first glance what information the fact sheet contains.

Use high-quality paper stock
People keep fact sheets as reference material, so it's important to print a fact sheet on paper able to withstand repeated handling.

Figure C-1 shows Joe's final sketch of his fact sheet.

FIGURE C-1: Joe's sketch of his fact sheet

Reverse text

PageMaker 6.5

Creating Columns

One way of presenting text is to organize the information into columns. To create a column in PageMaker, you use column guides. **Column guides** define columns on a publication page to control the flow of text or to help you align text and graphics. In the Column Guides dialog box, you specify how many columns you want on the page and the space between columns, called the **gutter**. PageMaker allows up to 20 columns on one page. ✐ Joe begins setting up the fact sheet by creating three columns.

Steps123 4

1. **Start PageMaker, click File on the menu bar, then click New**
   The Document Setup dialog box opens.

2. **Click the Double-sided check box to turn this option off**

3. **Change all margin settings to .5", then click OK**
   The Document Setup dialog box closes, and a new blank publication opens in the publication window.

4. **Click Layout on the menu bar, then click Column Guides**
   The Column Guides dialog box opens, as shown in Figure C-2.

5. **In the Number of columns text box, type 3**
   This tells PageMaker to create three columns on the publication page. The default gutter is .167", which is about 1/6". Although he can change the gutter, Joe accepts the amount of space specified by PageMaker.

6. **Click OK**
   The dialog box closes and blue column guides (if you're using a color monitor) appear on the page dividing the page into three equal columns, as shown in Figure C-3.

DesignTip

Most publications should have no more than four to five columns per page, depending on the page size. This is because the narrower the column, the harder it is to read the text.

FIGURE C-2: Column Guides dialog box

FIGURE C-3: Page with three columns

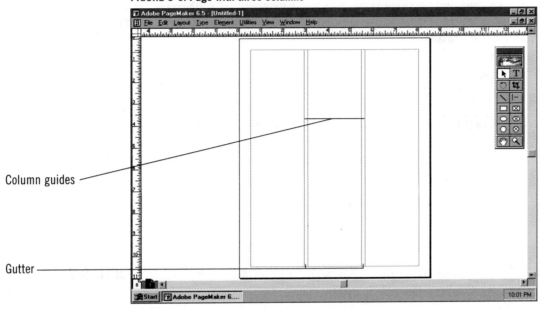

Column guides

Gutter

FIGURE C-4: Adjusting column widths manually

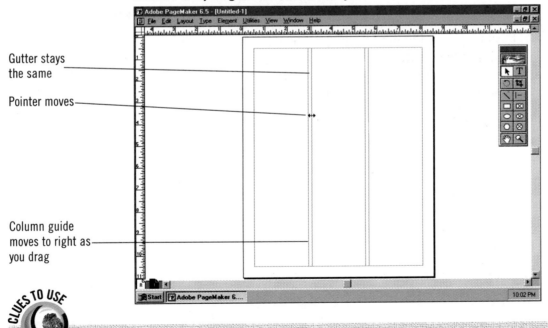

Gutter stays
the same

Pointer moves

Column guide
moves to right as
you drag

CLUES TO USE

Changing column widths

PageMaker automatically creates columns of equal width. You can change these widths by simply moving the column guides. After you create the number of columns you want, position the pointer over one of the two lines that make up the column guide, then press and hold the left mouse button. The pointer changes to ↔. Drag the column guide to widen or narrow the column width. As you move the column guide, the width of the gutter does not change. In Figure C-4, the first column is wider.

PageMaker 6.5

Importing and Placing Text

Just as you imported graphics into your publication, you can import text files from word processing applications, using the Place command on the File menu. Importing text and graphics will save you time; you won't have to re-create anything you've created in another application. See Table C-1 for a partial list of word processing file types that you can place in a PageMaker publication. ◀━━━ Joe has a fact sheet that already contains the photographs he needs. He needs to open that file. Then he wants to place in his publication a point of response that he wrote using a word processing application.

Steps 1 2 3 4

1. Click **File** on the menu bar, click **Close**, then click **No** when asked if you want to save "Untitled-1"

   The untitled publication with the three columns is now closed. Next you will open the file UNIT_C-1.p65, which contains columns and the photos that Joe has already placed.

2. Open the file UNIT_C-1 from your Student Disk

   Now you can place the point of response text.

3. Click **File** on the menu bar, then click **Place**

MacintoshUser

This replaces Step 4.

4. Select the drive containing your Student Disk if necessary, click UNIT_C-2 in the File name list box, then click OK. Click OK in place of Open when opening publications in subsequent lessons.

Resume at Step 5.

4. Select the drive containing your Student Disk if necessary, click **UNIT_C-2** in the File name list box, then click **Open**

   The pointer changes to ▦. Unlike the pointers for placing graphic files, the text placement pointer shape does not change depending on the type of text file being placed. When the manual text flow pointer appears, it is said to contain, or be **loaded**, with text.

5. Position ▦ in the third column at the top margin, as shown in Figure C-5, then click the **left mouse button**

   The text appears on the page bordered on the top and bottom by empty windowshade handles, as shown in Figure C-6. The **windowshade handles** define the **text block**, which is an object that consists of horizontal lines above and below the text. The width of the text block is determined by the width of the page or column.

FIGURE C-5: Manual text flow pointer

Manual text flow pointer

Photos already placed

Logo already placed

FIGURE C-6: Text block on placed page

Text block

Selection handle

Windowshade handle

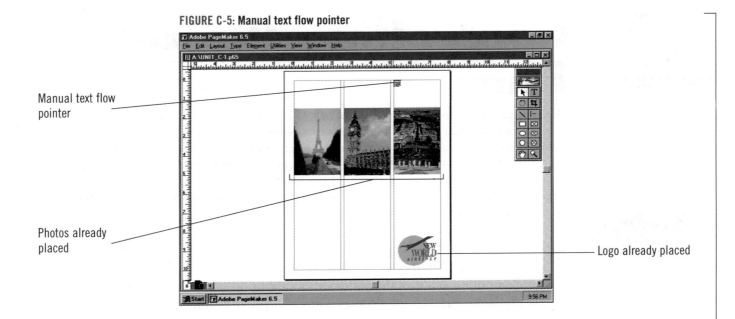

TABLE C-1: Types of word processing files that PageMaker accepts

file extension	word processing application
.WKS	Microsoft Works
.DOC	Microsoft Word Macintosh and Microsoft Word for Windows
.DOC	MultiMate
.WPD	Corel WordPerfect
.RTF	Rich Text Format
.TXT	Text or ASCII file

Controlling the Text Flow

There are three ways you control the flow of text in a publication: automatic (Autoflow), semi-Autoflow, and manual flow. When the **Autoflow** feature is turned on, text you place flows from one column to the next, filling up as many columns and pages as necessary. Table C-2 reviews the three methods of text flow. The Sunset Tours representative, Sheree Jackson, gave Joe a text file containing a description of her company's tours to Europe. Joe is ready to place the text describing the tours in his fact sheet. Because he wants to control where he places text in the columns, he will turn the Autoflow option off.

1. Click Layout on the menu bar, then make sure there is no check mark before the Autoflow option listed at the bottom of the menu
   The default for PageMaker is for the Autoflow feature to be turned off. See Figure C-7.

2. If there is a check mark beside the Autoflow option, click Autoflow to turn it off

3. Click File on the menu bar, then click Place

4. Select the file UNIT_C-3 from your Student Disk, then click Open

5. Position 📄 in the first column at the left margin guide at the 5.25" mark on the vertical ruler, then click the left mouse button
   The text is placed and flows from the pointer down the page to the bottom margin of the first column. A triangle appears in the windowshade handle at the bottom of the column, indicating more text needs to be placed, as shown in Figure C-8.

6. Click the windowshade handle ▽ at the bottom of the first column
   The pointer changes to 📄 .

7. Position 📄 in the second column at the 5.25" mark on the vertical ruler, then click the left mouse button
   Once again, text flows within the column to the bottom of the page. This time an empty windowshade handle ▽ appears at the bottom of the second column, indicating there is no more text to be placed. See Figure C-9. Notice that the windowshade handle at the top of the second column contains a plus sign ⊕ . This indicates that the text is **threaded**, or connected, to another text block, in this case, the text block in the first column.

8. Click File on the menu bar, then click Save to save the changes to the publication

QuickTip

When the text flow pointer is loaded, you can switch between manual flow and semi-Autoflow by pressing and holding [Shift], and you can switch between manual flow and Autoflow by pressing and holding [Ctrl] (Macintosh users: you can switch between manual flow and Autoflow by pressing and holding [⌘]).

FIGURE C-7: Autoflow option turned off

No check mark indicates Autoflow option is turned off

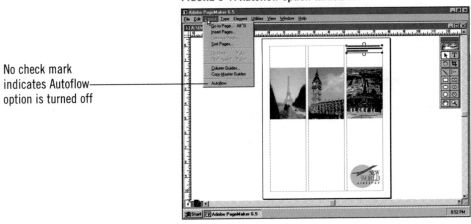

FIGURE C-8: Placed text flowing to the bottom of first column

Pointer guide at 5.25"

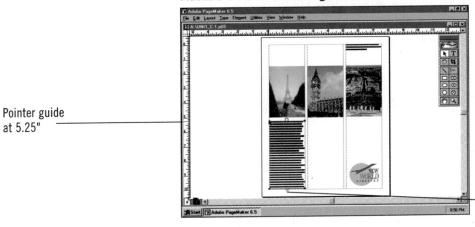

Indicates more text needs to be placed

FIGURE C-9: Threaded text block

Indicates text is threaded from another text block

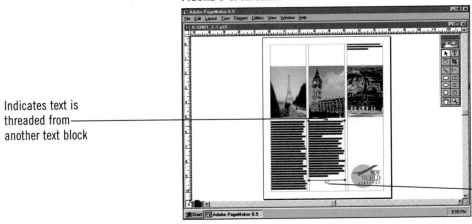

Indicates the end of a text block

TABLE C-2: Text flow methods

method	pointer	description
Manual		Text flows from the insertion point to the bottom of a column or page. You have to specify where to place additional text, if necessary
Autoflow		Text flows from one column to the next, filling up as many columns and pages necessary to place the text
Semi-Autoflow		With Autoflow turned off, press and hold [Shift] while placing text. Text flows to the bottom of the page or column; then the semi-Autoflow text pointer automatically appears ready to place more text

Manipulating Text Blocks

You can change the size and shape of any text block on a page. When you select a text block, the windowshade handles appear across the top and bottom borders of the text block. You change the length of a text block by dragging the windowshade handle up or down. Joe wants to change the length of the text blocks so that the text under each photo corresponds to that photo.

Steps

QuickTip

Use ruler guides to make sure text blocks are aligned across all columns.

1. **Click the text block in the first column**
   This selects the text block in the first column.

2. **Click View on the menu bar, then click Actual Size**
   The text in the first column describes Paris and London. Joe needs to manipulate the text blocks so that the text under each photo corresponds to the photo in the column.

3. **Position the pointer on the bottom windowshade handle, then press and hold the mouse button**
   The pointer ↕ appears, as shown in Figure C-10.

4. **Drag the windowshade handle ↯ up to the end of the paragraph describing Paris, France, under the words "Versailles and the Fontainebleau Forest," then release the mouse button**
   After you release the mouse button, the text from the end of the first column now appears at the beginning of the second column. If you didn't drag the windowshade handle up far enough in the first column, or dragged it too far, click it again, then drag it to the correct position.

5. **Click the text block in the second column**
   The text has flowed past the bottom of the column, as shown in Figure C-11.

6. **Scroll down to see the bottom of the text block in column two**

7. **Drag ↯ up so that only the paragraph describing London, England, appears in the text block**
   Don't worry if it takes a couple of tries to position the paragraph.

Trouble?

If your text block is wider than the one shown in Figure C-12, you can easily resize it by dragging either the top or bottom handle on the right edge until it is even with the right ruler guide for the column.

8. **Click ↯ at the bottom of the second column**
   The pointer changes to 📰.

9. **Position 📰 in the third column at the 5.25" mark on the vertical ruler, then click the left mouse button**
   The text "Rome, Italy" should be at the top of the third column, as shown in Figure C-12. The empty windowshade handle ↯ appears at the bottom of the third column.

FIGURE C-10: Changing the length of the text blocks

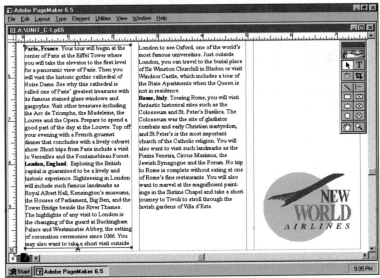

FIGURE C-11: First column after text block is resized

Paragraph describing London moved to top of second column

Ending paragraph describing London

Text flows past bottom of column

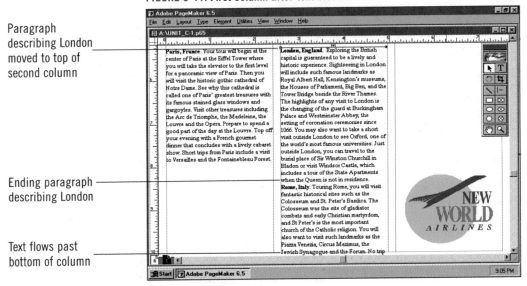

FIGURE C-12: Second column after resizing text block

Text describing Rome

Indicates end of text block

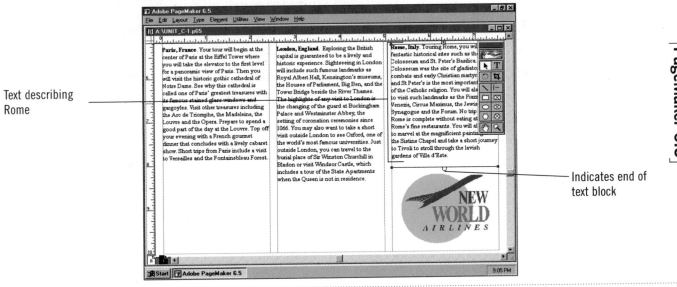

Moving and Resizing Text Blocks

One of PageMaker's most powerful options is its extensive ability to manipulate the dimensions and location of text blocks. The process for sizing and moving text blocks is similar to the method used for graphics. Joe decides to move the text block containing the point of response to the bottom of the page. He will resize it so it stretches across the three columns.

MacintoshUser

This replaces Step 1.
1. Press [⌘][0]
Resume at Step 2.

Trouble?

If the pointer does not change to 🖐 when you try to move a text block, release the mouse button, then select the text block to try again.

1. Press **[Ctrl][0]** (zero) to change to Fit in Window view

2. Click anywhere on the text block containing the point of response located in the upper-right corner of the page

3. Position the pointer in the middle of the text block, then press and hold the **left mouse button**
The pointer changes to 🖐.

4. Drag the **text block** to the lower-left corner of the page inside the left margin guide, then release the mouse button
Now Joe wants to stretch the text across the columns.

5. Position the pointer over the selection handle at the lower-right corner of the text block, then drag the handle to the right margin guide in the third column, but do not release the mouse button
The pointer changes to ↖ as you drag the handle, and a box appears around the text block to show its dimensions, as shown in Figure C-13.

6. When you are satisfied with the new dimensions, release the mouse button
The text is now resized from margin to margin, as shown in Figure C-14. The text block on your screen might be in a different spot depending on how far you dragged the text block. The text block in Joe's fact sheet needs to be moved again because it overlaps the logo.

7. Position the pointer in the middle of the text block, drag the text block down until it is just above the bottom margin guide, then release the mouse button

8. Click **File** on the menu bar, then click **Save** to save the changes to the publication

FIGURE C-13: **Resizing a text block**

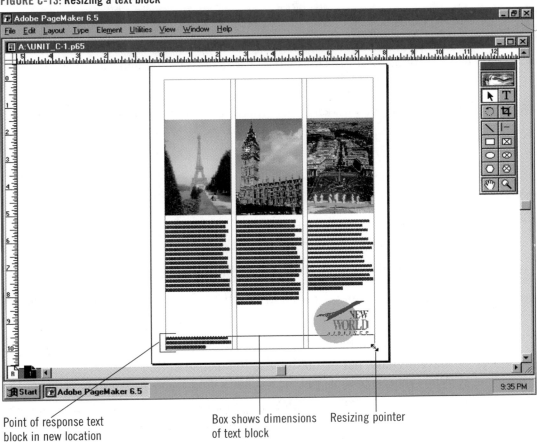

Point of response text
block in new location

Box shows dimensions
of text block

Resizing pointer

FIGURE C-14: **The resized text block**

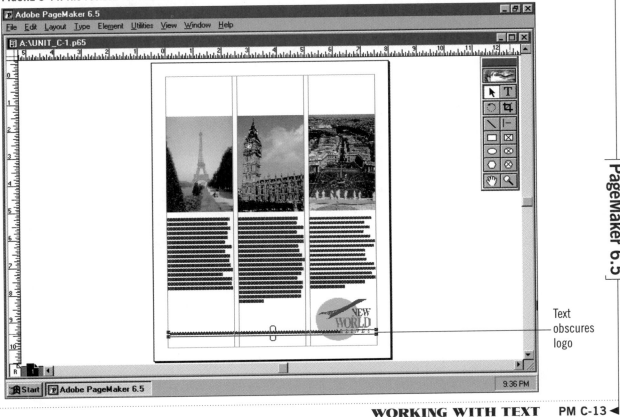

Text
obscures
logo

Drag-Placing Text

In addition to resizing and moving a text block, you can automatically position text across columns or a page using the drag-place method. The **drag-place method** allows you to define the size of a text block at the same time you import text from another location. You can use this method with both manual and automatic text flows. You can also drag-place graphics. Joe wants to place a headline that his co-worker Sheree created across the top of all three columns in his fact sheet.

Steps

1. Click **File** on the menu bar, then click **Place**

2. Select the file **UNIT_C-4** from your Student Disk, then click **Open**

3. Position the manual text flow pointer ▦ at the intersection of the top and left margin guides

4. Drag ▦ down to the 1.25" mark on the vertical ruler and all the way to the right margin guide, but do not release the mouse button
A box appears to show you the text block dimensions, as shown in Figure C-15.

5. When you are satisfied with the text block dimensions, release the mouse button
The headline appears in a text block that stretches from margin to margin, as shown in Figure C-16. The text does not span from margin to margin because the point size isn't big enough. The text, which was formatted as a large point size and bold in the word processed file, retains its format when it is placed in a PageMaker publication. In the next lesson you will learn how to use PageMaker features to make the headline more eye-catching and how to more effectively use the space in the headline text block.

6. Click **File** on the menu bar, then click **Save** to save the changes to the publication

FIGURE C-15: Drag-placing a text block

Box
shows
dimen-
sions of
text block

Manual
text flow
pointer

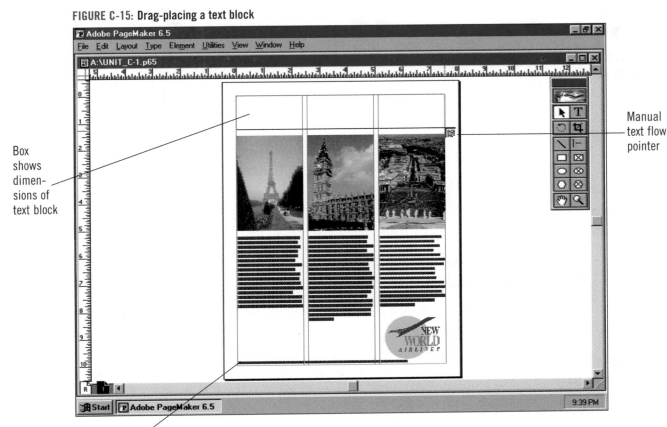

Point of response
text block just above
bottom margin

Text block stretches
across columns

FIGURE C-16: Headline placed across three columns

Headline
already
formatted

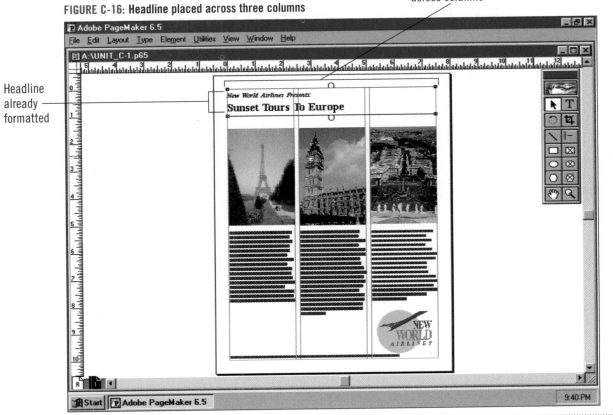

PageMaker 6.5

Using Reverse Text

Headlines in publications need to be eye-catching. One way to do this is to draw a box around the headline and use reverse text. **Reverse text** is white or lightly shaded letters and lines against a dark background. The contrast makes the text more noticeable. Joe formats the headline on the fact sheet with reverse text. He also wants to draw a box around the headline.

Steps

1. Click the **Text tool** [T] in the toolbox, then drag I over the two lines of text containing the headline to select them

2. Click **Type** on the menu bar, point to **Alignment**, then click **Align Center**
   The headline is centered in the text block.

Trouble?

If you have trouble finding text that is reversed, click Edit on the menu bar, then click Select All to display the windowshade handles of all the text blocks.

3. Click **Type** on the menu bar, point to **Type Style**, then click **Reverse**
   The text changes to white, and because it's on a white background, it seems to disappear. (Selecting text reverses both text and background colors, so currently both the text and background are black.)

4. Click the **Rectangle tool** [□] in the toolbox
   The pointer changes to ┼.

5. Position ┼ at the top left intersection of the margin guides, drag the pointer to the 1" mark on the vertical ruler and the right edge of the third column, then release the mouse button
   A box appears with selection handles around it, as shown in Figure C-17. Next, Joe needs to make this box black.

6. Click **Element** on the menu bar, point to **Fill**, then click **Solid**
   The box fills with black. The box is an object that is on top of the text block. To see the text in the text block, Joe needs to move the box behind, or in back of, the text block.

DesignTip

Reverse text is an effective method to draw the reader's attention to headlines or subheadlines if the type is large enough.

7. Click **Element** on the menu bar, point to **Arrange**, then click **Send to Back**
   The selected object, in this case the box, is sent behind the white text, so you can read the white text on the black box. See Figure C-18. This technique is called **layering**. Satisfied with his fact sheet, Joe saves and prints it. Note that depending on your printer this might take moments or minutes. Also, if you do not have a color printer, your printout will look different.

8. Save, print, and close your document

FIGURE C-17: A box drawn across three columns

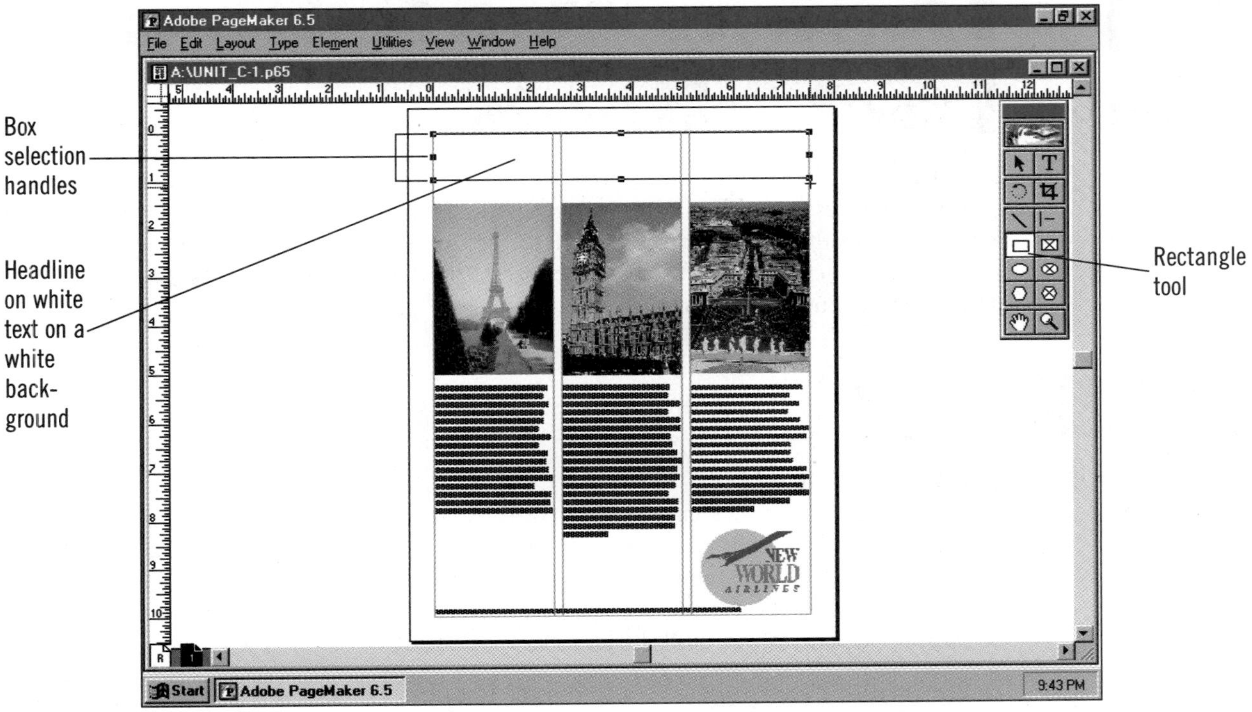

Box selection handles

Headline on white text on a white background

Rectangle tool

FIGURE C-18: White text on black background

White text shows up on black background

Box still selected

Box filled with black behind the text block

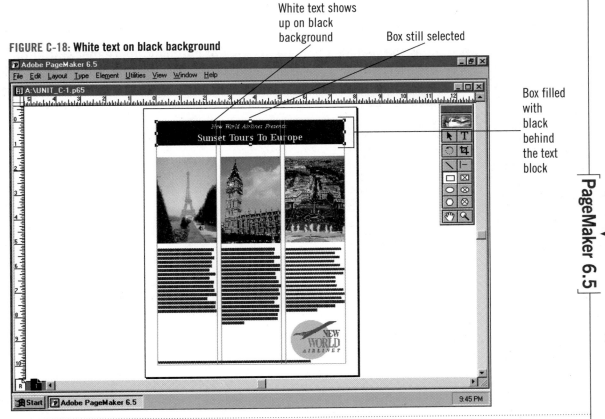

PageMaker 6.5

Design Workshop: Fact Sheets

Fact sheets are important publications for many companies. These documents describe products and services available, and are often the first contact with potential customers. It is therefore important that fact sheets convey all the information in an organized fashion. Consistency is essential in fact sheets that describe multiple products or services. Joe critiques his design for the European tours fact sheet shown in Figure C-19.

Details

Is the layout simple?

You should try to balance large amounts of text with graphical elements. Graphical elements help to break up the text. When you add graphical elements, be careful not to add too many, or the publication will look cluttered. Joe's layout is simple and well-balanced. Each of the three columns contains a photo and an equal amount of text. The headline at the top and the point of response at the bottom pull the fact sheet together.

Is the format consistent with other fact sheets?

It is important to portray your company's products and services in an organized fashion to the reader. Joe will create additional fact sheets for the other Sunset Tours in Europe and Asia. He will use the same layout that includes a headline, small photos, an equal amount of text describing the specific tour destination, and the point of response.

Do the graphical elements on the page enhance the overall layout?

Graphical elements can help the reader gain an immediate understanding of the purpose of the publication. Joe has included photos of some of the most famous landmarks of Europe to help stimulate the reader's desire for travel. He also used the New World Airlines logo to help identify which airline flies to Europe. Both of these graphical elements enhance the fact sheet message.

Does the headline achieve its goal of catching the reader's attention?

Using reverse text immediately draws the attention of the reader to the fact sheet. Joe could have used a bolder font like Arial and a larger point size to make his headline more striking. Before he completes the other fact sheets in the series, he will make these changes to the headlines.

FIGURE C-19: Completed European Vacation fact sheet

New World Airlines Presents:
Sunset Tours To Europe

Paris, France. Your tour will begin at the center of Paris at the Eiffel Tower where you will take the elevator to the first level to get a panoramic view of all of Paris. Then you will visit the historic gothic cathedral of Notre Dame. See why this cathedral is called one of Paris' greatest treasures with its famous stained glass windows and gargoyles. Visit other treasures including the Arc de Triomphe, the Madeleine, the Louvre and the Opera. Prepare to spend a good part of the day with the Louvre. Top off your evening with a French gourmet dinner that concludes with a lively cabaret show. Short trips from Paris include a visit to Versailles and the Fontainebleau Forest.

London, England. Exploring the British capital is guaranteed to be a lively and historic experience. Sightseeing in London will include such famous landmarks as Royal Albert Hall, Kensington's museums, the Houses of Parliament, Big Ben, and the Tower Bridge beside the River Thames. The highlight of any visit to London is the changing of the guard at Buckingham Palace and Westminster Abbey, the setting of coronation ceremonies since 1066. You may also want to take a short visit outside of London to see Oxford, one of the world's most famous universities. Just outside of London you can travel to the burial place of Sir Winston Churchill in Bladon or visit Windsor Castle, which includes a tour of the State Apartments when the Queen is not in residence.

Rome, Italy. Touring Rome, you will visit fantastic historical sites such as the Colosseum and St. Peter's Basilica. The Colosseum was the site of gladiator combats and early Christian martyrdom, and St Peter's is the most important church of the Catholic world. You will also want to visit such landmarks as the Piazza Venezia, Circus Maximus, the Jewish Synagogue, and the Forum. No trip to Rome is complete without eating at one of Rome's fine restaurants. You will also want to marvel at the magnificient paintings in the Sistine Chapel or take a short journey to Tivoli to stroll through the lavish gardens of Villa d'Este.

NEW
WORLD
A I R L I N E S

For more information about New World Airlines/Sunset Tours to Europe, call your travel agent or call us at 1-800-HORIZON.

Practice

► Concepts Review

Label each of the numbered publication window elements shown in Figure C-20.

FIGURE C-20

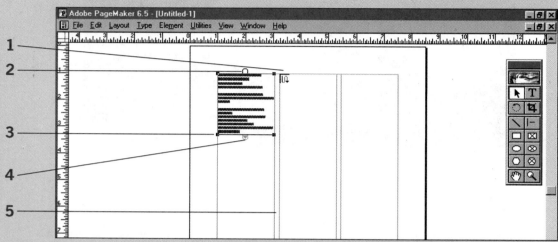

Match each term with the statement that describes its function.

6. Gutter   a. Defines the area of a text block
7. Autoflow   b. Automatically places all text from one column to another until all text is placed
8. Column guide   c. Helps control the flow of text and alignment of graphics
9. Windowshade handle   d. The ability to define the size of the text block
10. Drag-placing   e. Space between columns

Select the best answer from the list of choices.

11. When creating fact sheets you should include the following:
    a. Detailed information about a product or service
    b. Graphic elements that instantly convey a message
    c. Small headlines that don't overshadow the graphic elements
    d. All of the above

12. Fact sheets are used for:
    a. Conveying a message instantly
    b. Product descriptions
    c. A call for action
    d. Both a and b
    e. All of the above

13. A gutter is:
    a. The space between margins and the end of the page
    b. The space between columns
    c. The margin of a column
    d. None of the above

14. You can automatically place all text from one column to the next, filling up as many pages as necessary, using:
    a. Drag-placing
    b. Autoflow
    c. Semi-Autoflow
    d. Balance columns

▶ Skills Review

1. **Create a publication with three columns.**
   a. Start PageMaker and make sure your Student Disk is in the disk drive.
   b. Open the file UNIT_C-5 from your Student Disk.
   c. Click Layout on the menu bar, then select Column Guides.
   d. In the Number of columns text box, type "3," then click OK.
   e. Click the Pointer tool in the toolbox, if it is not already selected.
   f. Position the pointer on the right column guide for the first column guide, press and hold the mouse button, then drag the column guide 1" to the right to create a customized column size.
   g. Click Layout on the menu bar, click Column Guides, type "3" in the Number of columns text box to reset the column guides, then click OK.

2. **Place text on the page using Autoflow.**
   a. Click File on the menu bar, then click Place.
   b. Select the drive containing your Student Disk, click the file UNIT_C-3, then click Open.
   c. Click Layout on the menu bar, then make sure a check mark appears before the Autoflow option indicating the option is turned on. If it is not turned on, click it; otherwise, click Layout again to close the menu *(Macintosh users: release the mouse button to close the menu)*.
   d. Move the Autoflow text pointer ⏫ to the top of the first column, then click the left mouse button.
   e. Make sure the text flows on the page inside the first two columns.

3. **Manipulate text blocks.**
   a. Click View on the menu bar, then select Actual Size.
   b. Scroll to the bottom of the first column.
   c. Use the Pointer tool in the toolbox to select the first text block.
   d. Position the pointer on the bottom windowshade handle.
   e. Press and hold the mouse button, then drag the windowshade handle ⊞ up to move the bottom of the text block to the 5.5" mark on the vertical ruler.

4. **Move and resize the text block.**
   a. Click the Zoom tool in the toolbox, move ⊕ onto the page, press [Ctrl] *(Macintosh users: press [option])*, then click the left mouse button two times.
   b. Move ⊕ to the middle of the publication, then click the left mouse button.
   c. Click the Pointer tool in the toolbox.
   d. If necessary, scroll so that the whole page is visible in the publication window.
   e. Move ▶ in the middle of the text block in the first column, then press and hold the left mouse button.
   f. Drag the text block so the bottom of the text block touches the bottom margin guide on the page.
   g. Drag the text block in the second column so the top of the text is aligned with the top line of text in the first column. Use a ruler guide to assist you in aligning the text.
   h. Click File on the menu bar, then click Document Setup. In the Document Setup dialog box, change the left and right margins to .5", then click OK.
   i. Click Layout on the menu bar, select Column Guides, type "3" in the Number of columns text box to reset the column guides, then click OK.
   j. Drag the text block back to the left margins of their columns, then use the text block selection handles to resize both text blocks to fit within their respective column guides.
   k. Make sure the top lines of text are still aligned.

5. Drag-place text.

  a. Click Layout on the menu bar and click AutoFlow to deselect it.

  b. Click File on the menu bar, then select Place.

  c. Select the drive containing your Student Disk, click the file UNIT_C-2, then click Open *(Macintosh users: click OK)*.

  d. Position the manual text flow pointer 🔲 at the left margin guide just above the text.

  e. Drag-place the text so that it is positioned across the first two columns above the body text.

6. Create a headline in reverse text.

  a. Click View on the menu bar, then click Actual Size.

  b. Use the Text tool in the toolbox to type the following two lines at the top of the page:
    Paris, London and Rome
    Escorted Tour from $2,500

  c. Use the Text tool to highlight the text you just typed, click Type on the menu bar, point to Font, then select Arial *(Macintosh users: select Helvetica)*.

  d. Click outside of the highlighted text to deselect it.

  e. Select the first line of text you typed, click Type on the menu bar, point to Size, then click 30.

  f. Select the second line of text you typed, click Type on the menu bar, point to Size, then click 24.

  g. Select both lines of text you typed, click Type on the menu bar, point to Type Style, then click Reverse.

  h. With both lines of text still selected, click Type, point to Alignment, then click Align Center.

  i. Click the Pointer tool in the toolbox, select the text box containing the text you typed, then resize it so the right edge is at the right border of the second column.

  j. Use the Rectangle tool in the toolbox to draw a box from the intersection of the top and left margin guides to the right edge of the second column at the 2" mark on the vertical ruler.

  k. Click Element on the menu bar, point to Fill, then click Solid.

  l. Click Element on the menu bar, point to Arrange, then click Send to Back.

  m. Save your publication as My Fact Sheet to your Student Disk.

  n. Print your publication, then exit PageMaker.

▶ Independent Challenges

1. You work in the Admissions Office at Medfield College. One of your tasks is to standardize the descriptions for all degree programs in the various schools. You decide to keep a consistent format and give each major its own fact sheet. Your next fact sheet is for the bachelor of science degree in management information systems (MIS). The staff of that department provides you with the program description. You need to modify it so it conforms to your standards.

To complete this independent challenge:

1. Open a new one-page, letter-sized publication with three columns using portrait orientation and default margins.
2. Drag-place the file UNIT_C-6 from your Student Disk across the top of the page.
3. Change the font, size, and style of the headline "Medfield College, Management Information Systems" so it is eye-catching and appealing. Use reverse text for the headline.
4. Place the graphic file UNIT_C-7 on the publication page. This file contains a drawing of the building that houses the MIS offices. Resize and move the graphic as necessary.
5. Place the file UNIT_C-8 from your Student Disk on the publication page. The text in this file should flow from one column to another.
6. Manipulate the text blocks and the graphic to make the layout appealing.
7. Use your own judgment to add lines or boxes to enhance the layout of the fact sheet.
8. Save your work as Mis to your Student Disk, print the fact sheet and close the publication.

2. Visit a computer store or an automotive dealer and get the informational fact sheets used to describe the products offered. Review the examples, then redesign one of them to improve its performance. Answer the following questions as you plan your design:

1. Is the layout simple? Or are there too many graphics? Is there a way to cut some of the text and add graphical elements without sacrificing the overall purpose of the publication?
2. Does the headline stand out and immediately catch your attention?
3. Can your overall design be consistently applied to other product description/fact sheets?

To complete this independent challenge:

1. Open a new single-sided, one-page publication and save it as New Fact Sheet on your Student Disk.
2. Create columns in your publication if necessary.
3. Place the file Placehld on your Student Disk in your fact sheet for each graphic you want to include. Use the drag-place method to place the graphics, and resize and move them as necessary.
4. Place the file Texthld on your Student Disk in the publication.
5. Adjust the text flow of the story in the fact sheet as necessary so that the fact sheet is visually balanced. (*Hint*: If there is too much text in the file for your fact sheet, use the Text tool in the toolbox to select some of the text, then press [Delete] to delete it.)
6. Add a headline by typing directly on the page. Format the headline to be eye-catching. Resize and move the text block, and change the alignment of the headline so that it appears where you want it to. (*Hint*: If you are having trouble finding the text block, click the Pointer tool in the toolbox, then click anywhere on the text.)
7. Add a point of response if necessary by typing directly on the page.
8. Add lines as necessary.
9. Save, print, and close the publication.

3. You received a freelance design project from Brian Scleter, owner of Scleter's Used Import Cars and Auto Parts. He wants a simple fact sheet about the mufflers, shocks, and tires in stock at his store. Before Scleter gives you the information needed for the fact sheet, he wants to see a dummy of the sheet. You need to place fake text and a box to simulate where photos will be situated.

To complete this independent challenge:

1. Create a new single-sided document with a Wide orientation. Make the margins .75" on all sides.
2. Create three columns and set .5" between each column.
3. Type the headline, "Scleter's Used Import Cars and Auto Parts" to fit across the top of the page.
4. Format the headline in reverse type with a black background.
5. Place the file PLACEHLD from your Student Disk into the publication three times, and move a copy of each graphic to each column. Use your judgment on how best to balance the page using the graphics.
6. Type a separate subheadline for each of the three columns: "Mufflers...", "Shocks...", and "Tires...". Arrange them in each column so they complement the way you arranged the photos from the previous step.
7. Place the file TEXTHLD from your Student Disk into the publication. This dummy text will simulate the real text you'll create from the information Scleter gives you later. Make the text flow through each of the three columns so the layout appears balanced.
8. Save the file as Factsheet 2 on your Student Disk, then close the publication.

4. You work in the marketing department for a major airline. You have been given the job of creating a fact sheet that describes package tours that your airline has arranged with a travel agency.

To complete this independent challenge:

1. Search the World Wide Web to find information on an airline that is offering package tours in conjunction with a travel agency. You might try searching for tours offered by a travel agency first rather than searching for information on an airline.

WEB WORK

PageMaker 6.5

2. Using the information that you find, sketch a fact sheet for the airline keeping in mind the guidelines that you learned in this unit. Don't forget to include a point of response, graphical elements, and a headline.
3. Create a fact sheet in PageMaker 6.5 using your sketch as a guide.
4. Use the file PLACEHLD on your Student Disk as a dummy graphic file.
5. Use the file TEXTHLD on your Student Disk as a dummy text file, but be sure to replace the text with the information that you find about your particular tour(s) on the World Wide Web.
6. Save the publication as Factsheet 3 on your Student Disk, then print it.
7. Critique your fact sheet design to make sure that it meets your guidelines.
8. Close the publication and submit your printout and your critique.

▶ Visual Workshop

Using Figure C-21 create a new design for Joe's fact sheets. Open the file UNIT_C-9 from your Student Disk. Add two columns to your publication. Place the body text (UNIT_C-3), and resize to match Figure C-21. Drag-place the file UNIT_C-2 across two columns below the photo. Add the reverse text on the top of the publication, and format the headline to be Helvetica, 48 point bold and centered. Finally, type the headline at the bottom of the fact sheet. Format the text to be Helvetica, 48 point bold. Save the publication as Factsheet 4 to your Student Disk.

FIGURE C-21

See Europe Today!

Paris, France. Your tour will begin at the center of Paris at the Eiffel Tower. Take the elevator to the first level to get a panoramic view of all of Paris. Then you will visit the historic gothic cathedral of Notre Dame. See why this cathedral is called one of Paris' greatest treasures with its famous stained glass windows and gargoyles. Visit other treasures including the Arc de Triomphe, the Madeleine, the Louvre and the Opera. Prepare to spend a good part of the day at the Louvre. Top off your evening at a French gourmet dinner concluding with a lively cabaret show. Short trips from Paris include a visit to Versailles and the Fontainebleau Forest.

NEW WORLD AIRLINES

London, England. Exploring the British capital is guaranteed to be a lively and historic experience. Sightseeing in London will include such famous landmarks as: Royal Albert Hall, Kensington's museums, the Houses of Parliament, Big Ben, and the Tower Bridge beside the River Thames. The highlight of any visit to London is the changing of the guard at Buckingham Palace and a visit to the Westminster Abbey, the setting of coronation ceremonies since 1066. You may also want to take a short visit outside of London to see Oxford, one of the world's most famous universities. Also outside of London is the burial place of Sir Winston Churchill in Bladon and the Windsor Castle, which includes a tour of the State Apartments when the Queen is not in residence. **Rome, Italy**. Touring Rome, you will visit fantastic historical sites such as the Colosseum and St. Peter's Basilica. The Colosseum is the site of gladiator combats and early Christian martyrdom, and St Peter's is the most important church of the Catholic world. You will also want to visit such landmarks as the Piazza Venezia, Circus Maximus, the Jewish Synagogue, and the Forum. No trip to Rome is complete without eating at one of Rome's fine restaurants. You will also want to marvel at the magnificient paintings in the Sistine Chapel or take a short journey to Tivoli to stroll through the lavish gardens of Villa d'Este.

For more information about New World Airlines/Sunset Tours to Europe, call your travel agent or call us at:

1-800-HORIZON

Modifying

Text

Objectives

- ▶ **Plan a business report**
- ▶ **Open story editor**
- ▶ **Add and place text with story editor**
- ▶ **Edit text in story editor**
- ▶ **Use the spell checker in story editor**
- ▶ **Find and change text in story editor**
- ▶ **Format text using character specifications**
- ▶ **Format paragraphs**
- ▶ **Adjust leading**
- ▶ **Insert and remove pages in a publication**
- ▶ **Design Workshop: Business reports**

PageMaker has many features to help you create professional-looking publications. A built-in word processor called story editor allows you to edit, format, and then check the spelling of text. You can also format paragraphs, change the space between lines of text, and add or delete pages. Joe Martin will use these features as he completes his first big project, a five-page business report that proposes expanding New World Airlines' flights into the Caribbean.

Planning a Business Report

When developing a business report, consider that most business people have limited time to read your document. Your goal should be to create high-impact reports and proposals that take advantage of innovative design and concise writing. It's important that the report be organized in a logical, consistent, and sequential fashion. A report that quickly and clearly conveys a message using a creative design captures the attention of busy people. New World Airlines' marketing director, Sarah Pohl, wants to add flights to the Caribbean. Working with Sarah, Joe plans a concise report proposing these additional flights. This proposal will be read by the president and vice presidents of the company. Joe created the thumbnail sketches shown in Figure D-1 as he planned the proposal. A **thumbnail** is a small sketch that shows only the large elements of the page. He uses the following guidelines to create a high-impact proposal:

Details

 Use a coherent writing style

Keep report language simple, clear, and concise. Use headlines and subheads to organize the report in a logical, consistent, and sequential fashion. Joe makes sure that his proposal has logical headlines, and he writes concisely and clearly.

 Include an abstract

An **abstract** is a summary at the beginning of the report. The abstract highlights the main points of the report. Joe's proposal will include a short, one-paragraph abstract. Joe decides to place the abstract on the proposal's cover.

 Add a businesslike cover

The cover sets the tone for the report. It should not entertain the reader, rather it should emphasize the importance of the report and introduce the visual style used in the report. The cover for Joe's proposal will include a title, the logo for New World Airlines, and the names of the people who prepared the proposal.

 Include graphics to enhance text pages

By using graphics, you can balance the excessive text used in reports. Graphics include charts, tables, photographs, or illustrations. The graphics should reinforce the information in the report. Joe plans to include photos of the Caribbean and charts to show how New World Airlines' revenue will increase with the new flights.

 Maintain a consistent design

Using a consistent design provides continuity through all sections of the report.

 Consider using a three-column page layout

A columnar layout allows you to include more text on a page. A page with three columns gives you more flexibility in placing graphics. Layouts with only one or two columns limit the size of graphics, and letter-size pages look cramped with more than three columns. Joe decides to use three columns for the body of the proposal so he needs to use graphics that are one, two, or three columns wide.

Opening Story Editor

You can edit text in the PageMaker publication window, but this can be slow. If you have to insert a large amount of text in PageMaker, use PageMaker's story editor. **Story editor** is a word processing program within PageMaker. In addition to inserting text, you can edit text, check the spelling of all the words in a publication, and find text and change it to other text. Joe already wrote the proposal and placed it in his publication. Now he is ready to create the abstract for the business proposal using story editor and place it on the cover.

Steps

1. **Start PageMaker, then open the file UNIT_D-1 from your Student Disk**
   This file contains Joe's proposal. The cover page of the proposal, page 1 of the publication, appears in the publication window. Joe wants to place the abstract in the middle of the page, but he wants it to be wider than the middle column. He decides to add ruler guides ½" from either side of the middle column guides to help him place the abstract text block.

2. **Drag a ruler guide to the 6" mark on the horizontal ruler**

3. **Drag another ruler guide to the 2½" mark on the horizontal ruler**
   See Figure D-2. Joe is ready to type the abstract.

4. **Click Edit on the menu bar, then click Edit Story**
   The story editor window appears as shown in Figure D-3. The Story option replaces the Layout option in the menu bar, and the Element option no longer appears. The publication window is visible behind the story editor window. The left side of the story editor window is where style names appear. The filename of the current publication and the story name appear in the title bar.

5. **Move the pointer anywhere over the right side of the story editor window**
   Notice that the pointer changes to $\mathcal{I}$.

6. **Move $\mathcal{I}$ anywhere over the left side of the story editor window**
   Notice that the pointer changes to $\mathcal{k}$.

CLUES TO USE

Exporting text to other word processors

You might need to export text created in PageMaker to a word processing program such as Corel WordPerfect or Microsoft Word. You do this by selecting Text from the Export submenu on the File menu. If you do this in layout view, you first need to use the Text tool in the toolbox to select the text you want to export. The Export Document dialog box opens as shown in Figure D-4. You can choose to save text in a specific word processing program's format or in a **text-only format**, which saves the text without the formatting originally applied in PageMaker. A text-only file can be imported into most word processors. After you click Save (*Macintosh users: OK*), a new text file, separate from the original PageMaker file, is created. You can export only text, not graphics or page layouts.

FIGURE D-2: Page 1 of the proposal with ruler guides

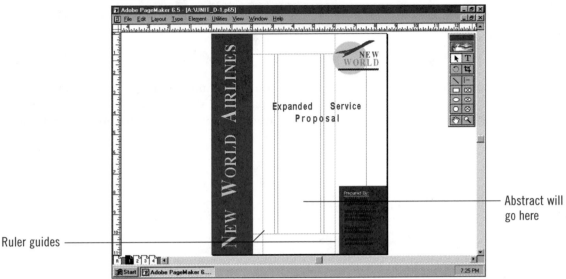

Ruler guides

Abstract will
go here

FIGURE D-3: The empty story editor window

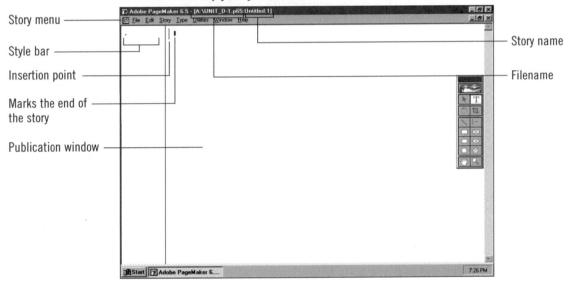

Story menu

Style bar

Insertion point

Marks the end of
the story

Publication window

Story name

Filename

FIGURE D-4: Export Document dialog box

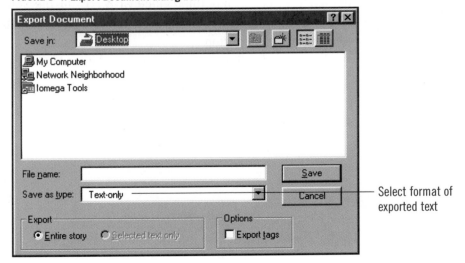

Select format of
exported text

PageMaker 6.5

Adding and Placing Text with Story Editor

Story editor is especially helpful when you make multiple changes to a story that spans several text blocks on multiple pages, because the entire story displays in the story editor window. With story editor open, Joe is ready to type the text of the abstract and place it in the publication.

Steps

1. Type **ABSTRACT** then press [Enter]

2. Click Story on the menu bar, then click Display ¶
If the command Display ¶ already has a check mark next to it, then this option is already turned on, so skip this step. The Display ¶ command displays nonprinting characters such as paragraph markers, spaces, and tab markers. ¶ is the symbol for a new paragraph. Displaying the nonprinting symbols makes it easier to precisely place the cursor within the story.

QuickTip

Remember that if the toolbox is covering your view, you can move it by clicking the toolbox's title bar, then dragging it to a new position.

3. Type **New World Airlines has mapped success in the past 10 years by offering competitive pricing, quality,** but do not press [Enter]
Don't worry if you make typing errors. You will find out how to correct them in a later lesson. Depending on the size of your screen, a word or words may have moved down to the next line while you typed. This feature is called **word wrap**. The only time you press [Enter] is to start a new paragraph. Notice that spaces are represented by dots between words.

4. Type the rest of the abstract shown in Figure D-5
Now Joe needs to place the abstract in the publication.

5. Click Story on the menu bar, then click Close Story
You could also click the close button on the story editor window. A small dialog box opens giving you three options: Place, Discard, or Cancel. See Table D-1 for a description of each of these commands. Joe wants to place the story.

6. Click Place
Story editor closes, and page 1 appears in layout view. The pointer changes to ▦.

Trouble?

If you see ▽ at the bottom of the text block, drag it down below the bottom margin guide to finish placing the text, then drag the text block up until all the text is above the bottom margin.

7. Position ▦ on the left ruler guide at 8.25" on the vertical ruler, drag-place the pointer to the intersection of the right ruler guide and the bottom margin guide, then release the mouse button
The abstract is placed on page 1, as shown in Figure D-6.

8. Click File on the menu bar, then click Save to save your changes

FIGURE D-5: The abstract in the story editor window

Non-printing
paragragh marker

Word wraps
automatically to
the next line

Non-printing space
markers

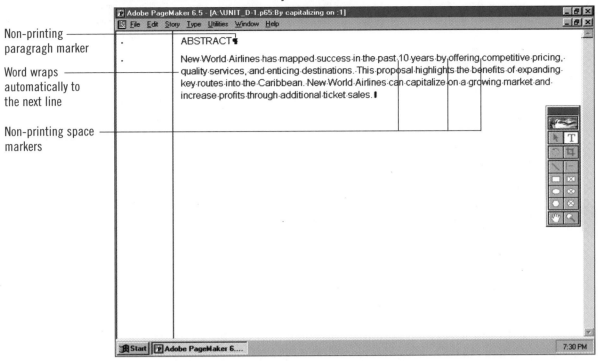

FIGURE D-6: Abstract on page 1

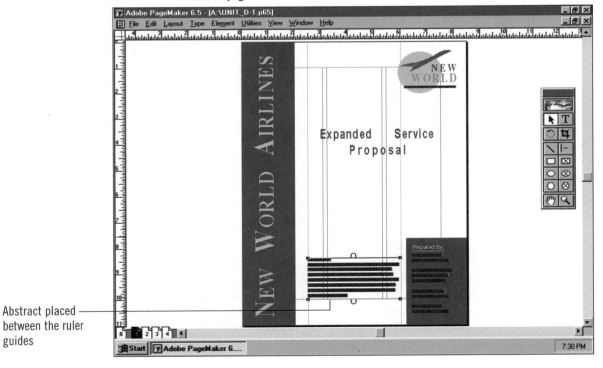

Abstract placed
between the ruler
guides

TABLE D-1: Dialog box commands to place story editor text

command	description
Place	Closes story editor and opens the layout view
Discard	Deletes the text you just typed and returns to the layout view
Cancel	Stops the action and keeps story editor open

Editing Text in Story Editor

You can use story editor to edit any story in a publication, even if the story was placed from another word processor. When you use story editor to edit your stories rather than making changes directly in the publication, you can see all parts of a story at one time, even if the story is threaded over multiple pages. You edit text by deleting and retyping characters or by using the Cut, Copy, and Paste commands on the Edit menu. When you cut or copy selected text, you place the selected text on the Clipboard. The **Clipboard** is a temporary storage area for cut or copied text or graphics. See Table D-2 for brief descriptions of the Cut, Copy, and Paste commands and their corresponding keyboard shortcuts. 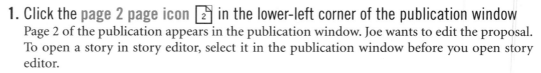 After looking over the proposal, Joe wants to move one of the paragraphs in the publication.

Steps 1 2 3 4

1. **Click the page 2 page icon 2 in the lower-left corner of the publication window**
   Page 2 of the publication appears in the publication window. Joe wants to edit the proposal. To open a story in story editor, select it in the publication window before you open story editor.

QuickTip

You can access story editor quickly by triple-clicking a text block with the Pointer tool pointer ▶.

2. **Click the text block in the first column, click Edit on the menu bar, click Edit Story, then click Story on the menu bar, and click Display ¶**
   Story editor opens with the text of the proposal in the story editor window. The word "Normal" appears several times in the style area. Normal is the name of the style that was imported with the text. Notice that the filename of the story is the first few words of the story. Don't worry about any spelling errors you may notice; you will correct them later.

3. **Click I at the beginning of the second paragraph, then triple-click the left mouse button to highlight the entire paragraph**
   Make sure the entire paragraph including the ¶ symbol is selected, as shown in Figure D-7.

4. **Click Edit on the menu bar, then click Cut**
   PageMaker removes the selection from the story editor and places it on the Clipboard.

Trouble?

If you use [Delete] *(Macintosh users: [del])* by mistake instead of the Cut command to delete something, click Edit on the menu bar, then click Undo Delete *(Macintosh users: Undo Edit).*

5. **If necessary, scroll using the vertical scroll bar so that the paragraph beginning with "Existing aircraft" is visible**

6. **Click I at the beginning of the paragraph that begins "Existing aircraft"**
   The insertion point appears at this point.

7. **Click Edit on the menu bar, then click Paste**
   PageMaker pastes the contents of the Clipboard at the insertion point, as shown in Figure D-8. The paragraphs will run together if you didn't highlight the paragraph marker at the end of the paragraph you moved. If the paragraphs run together here, press [Enter] to insert a new paragraph marker. Joe notices that the second sentence in the paragraph he just moved begins with "Bye," and it should begin with "By."

8. **Drag I over the "e" in "Bye" to select it**

MacintoshUser

This replaces Step 9.
9. Press [del]

9. **Press [Delete]**
   The "e" is deleted from the story. When you use this method of deleting text, the deleted text is not placed on the Clipboard, and you cannot use the Paste command to paste it back into the publication.

FIGURE D-7: **Highlighted selection in story editor**

Story name is first
few words of story

Text paragraph
marker highlighted

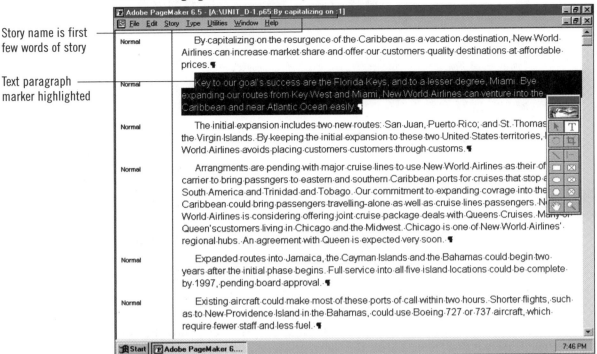

FIGURE D-8: **Paragraph pasted in new location**

Wrong word

Paragraph moved

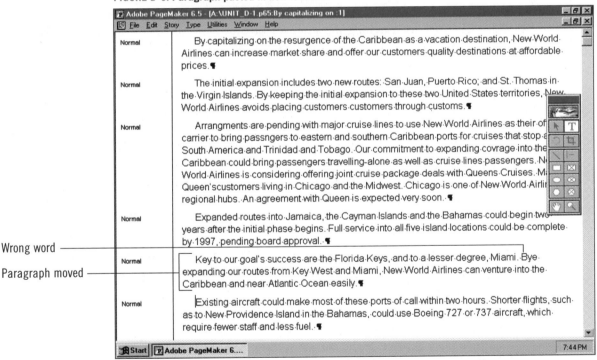

TABLE D-2: **Editing commands**

command	keyboard shortcut	description
Cut	[Ctrl][X]	Removes the selection to the Clipboard
Copy	[Ctrl][C]	Copies the selection to the Clipboard, but leaves the selection in place
Paste	[Ctrl][V]	Moves the Clipboard contents to a new location

PageMaker 6.5

Using the Spell Checker in Story Editor

It's a good idea to check the spelling before you print the publication. You can do this using the spell checker in story editor. You can check the spelling in the current story, a highlighted portion of the story, all stories in the current publication, or all stories in open PageMaker publications. Spell checking is only available in story editor. Joe wants to check the spelling in the current story.

Steps

1. **Scroll to the top of the story editor window so that the beginning of the story is visible, then click I before the "B" in "By capitalizing"**
   PageMaker starts checking spelling from the insertion point, so placing the insertion point here insures PageMaker will check the whole story.

2. **Click Utilities on the menu bar, then click Spelling**
   The Spelling dialog box opens. See Table D-3 for descriptions of the options in the Spelling dialog box. Notice that the Current story radio button is selected. This means that PageMaker will check the spelling in only the current story—that is, the story that is currently displayed in the story editor window.

3. **Click Start**
   PageMaker begins searching the story for unknown words. "Juan" is flagged by the spell checker as a possible misspelled word, as shown in Figure D-9. Juan is not misspelled, but PageMaker does not have Juan in its dictionary. Joe decides to add it to the dictionary because he knows he will use this word in the future.
   NOTE: If you are working in a lab, you might not be allowed to add words to the dictionary; check with your instructor or technical support person before completing the next step. If the first word flagged is "Puerto," then someone else might have already added "Juan" to the dictionary. Read Steps 4, 5, and 6, but do not perform any mouse actions; then continue with Step 7.

4. **Click Add**
   The Add Word to User Dictionary dialog box opens, as shown in Figure D-10. If the word were more than one syllable, PageMaker would insert a tilde (~) to indicate the word would hyphenate if it appeared at the end of a line. Three tildes after a syllable indicate the least desirable place to hyphenate the word.

5. **Click OK to accept PageMaker's changes to the word and to close the dialog box**

6. **Continue making spelling changes to the story, choosing the appropriate action for each potential error**
   When PageMaker identifies a repeated word, click Replace to delete the duplicate. When PageMaker presents a list of words in the Change to list, click the correct spelling to select it, and then click Replace. If the correct spelling is not listed (for example, when PageMaker highlights two words with no space between them), you can edit the word in the Change to text box, and then click Replace. When PageMaker is finished checking the story, the message "Spelling check complete" appears at the top of the Spelling dialog box.

7. **Click the Close button in the upper-right corner of the Spelling dialog box to close it**

Trouble?

If you accidentally clicked Ignore for a word that is spelled incorrectly, you must save the file and exit PageMaker, then reopen the file before the spell check will recognize the misspelled word again.

MacintoshUser

This replaces Step 7.
7. Click the close box in the upper-left corner of the Spelling dialog box

FIGURE D-9: Spelling dialog box with unknown word

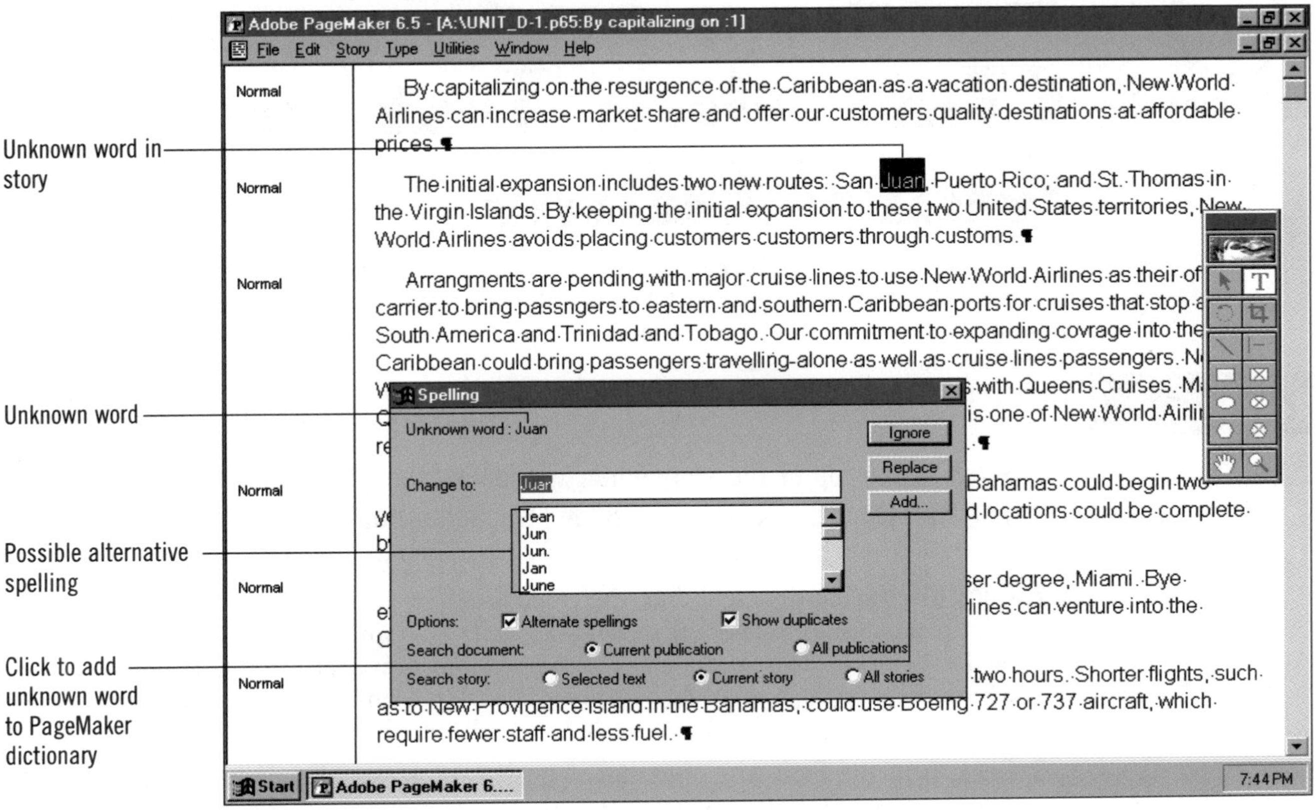

Unknown word in story ──

Unknown word ──

Possible alternative spelling ──

Click to add unknown word to PageMaker dictionary ──

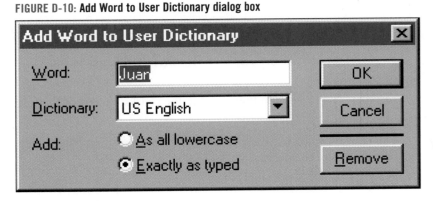

FIGURE D-10: Add Word to User Dictionary dialog box

TABLE D-3: Spelling dialog box options

option	description
Alternate spellings	When turned on, lists alternate spellings for each word the PageMaker dictionary does not recognize; turn this feature off to speed up the spell check
Show duplicates	When turned on, flags duplicate words such as "the the"; turn this feature off to speed up the spell check
Current publication	Checks spelling in the current publication only
All publications	Checks spelling in all open publications
Selected text	Checks spelling in the selected text only
Current story	Checks spelling in the current story only
All stories	Checks spelling in all stories in the current publication

Finding and Changing Text in Story Editor

When you are in story editor, you can use the Change command to search for specific text in a story and change it to different text. You can also search for and change format attributes such as fonts, type styles, or font size.  Joe used the phrase "ports of call" in the proposal. He wants to change it to "destinations."

1. **Scroll to the top of the story editor window so that the beginning of the story is visible, then click ⌶ before the "B" in "By capitalizing"**
   PageMaker searches for the text from the insertion point.

2. **Click Utilities on the menu bar, then click Change**
   The Change dialog box opens, as shown in Figure D-11. If you had selected the Find command on the Utilities menu instead, a similar dialog box would have opened, but the three command buttons for changing text would not appear. You use the Find command to search for specific text only. Joe wants to find the phrase "ports of call" and change it to "destinations."

3. **Click ⌶ in the Find what text box if necessary, type ports of call, click ⌶ in the Change to text box, then type destinations**

4. **Click Find**
   PageMaker searches the story. When it finds the text you typed in the Find what text box, it stops and waits for your approval of the highlighted change. See Figure D-12. PageMaker gives you three choices. Table D-4 describes the Change options.

5. **Click Change**
   The text is replaced with the new text. Joe checks the rest of the story for the phrase.

6. **Click Find next**
   The Search complete dialog box opens. This means that PageMaker did not find any more occurrences of the phrase.

7. **Click OK to close the dialog box**

8. **Click the Close button in the upper-right corner of the Change dialog box to close it**
   The Change dialog box closes. Joe is finished editing the proposal. He wants to return to page view now.

9. **Click Story on the menu bar, then click Close Story**
   Story editor closes and the page view appears.

QuickTip

You cannot find or change text that is a part of a graphical element.

MacintoshUser

This replaces Step 8.
8. Click the close box to close the dialog box

TABLE D-4: Change options

change option	description
Change	Replaces the selected text with the text in the Change to text box
Change & find	Replaces the selected text with the text in the Change to text box, and finds the next occurence of the text in the Find what text box
Change all	Finds all occurences of the text in the Find what text box and changes each of them to the text in the Change to text box

FIGURE D-11: **Change dialog box**

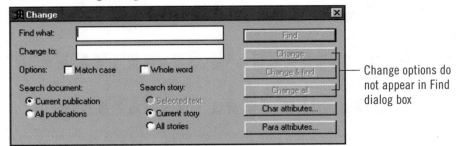

Change options do not appear in Find dialog box

FIGURE D-12: **Change dialog box and found text**

Found text

Click to change found text

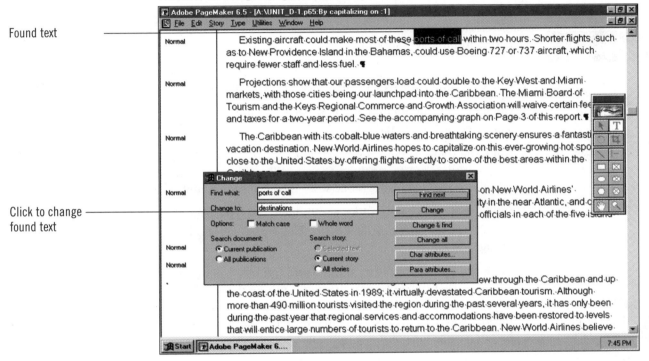

FIGURE D-13: **Change Paragraph Attributes dialog box**

Attributes to search for

New attributes to apply

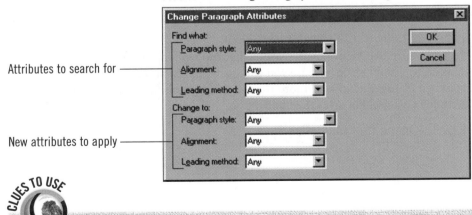

CLUES TO USE

Expanding the Find and Change attributes

You might need to find or change text that is formatted in a particular way. Both the Find and Change dialog boxes contain buttons for Para Attributes (paragraph) and Char Attributes (character). The Change Paragraph Attributes dialog box is shown in Figure D-13. Using this dialog box, you can find and change specific format attributes for paragraph styles, alignment, and leading method. All the attribute dialog boxes contain boxes for setting the attributes you want to find.

Formatting Text Using Character Specifications

You already know how to change text formats using the submenus on the Type menu. If you choose the Character command on the Type menu, you open the Character Specifications dialog box in which you can set multiple formats at once. You can use the Character Specifications dialog box in either layout view or story editor. The current font in the proposal is Arial, a sans serif font that can be difficult to read when it's small. Joe decides to change the font for the entire proposal to a serif font.

Steps

1. Click the **Text tool** [T] in the toolbox, then click ⌶ anywhere in the text

2. Click **Edit** on the menu bar, then click **Select All**
   The Select All command selects all the text in a story.

3. Click the **page 4 page icon** [4], click **View** on the menu bar, then click **Actual Size**
   This will allow you to see the changes you'll make to the text. Notice the text on this page is selected as well because it is one story threaded throughout the publication.

4. Click **Type** on the menu bar, scroll down the list, then click **Character**
   The Character Specifications dialog box opens, as shown in Figure D-14. Joe wants to change the font.

5. Click the **Font list arrow**, scroll down the list, then click **Times New Roman**
   You may need to scroll down the font list using the scroll bar, depending on the number of fonts you have installed. The current font size is 11.5 points. Joe chose this point size when the font was Arial because he didn't think 12 point would fit. Now that he's changed the font he can change the point size to the more common 12 point.

6. Click the **Size list arrow**, then click **12**

7. Click **OK**

8. Click anywhere outside of the selected text block
   This deselects the text. See Figure D-15. Notice that the type in the third column does not flow down as far as it did before because you changed the font and the point size. Letters in the new typeface fit together closer, more than compensating for the increased type size. Satisfied with his changes, Joe saves the publication.

9. Click **File** on the menu bar, then click **Save**

MacintoshUser

This replaces Step 5.
5. Click the Font drop-down box, then click Times

DesignTip

Depending on the font, a range of 10 to 12 points is a good size for a large body of text.

FIGURE D-14: **Character Specifications dialog box**

Click to display list of fonts

Click to display list of sizes

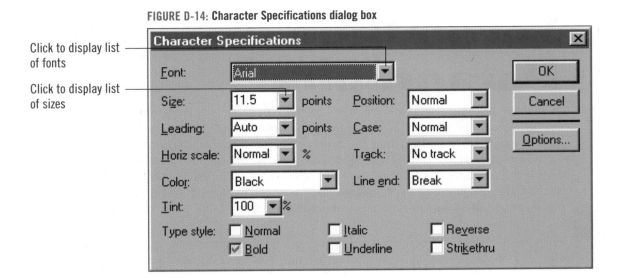

FIGURE D-15: **Character changes applied**

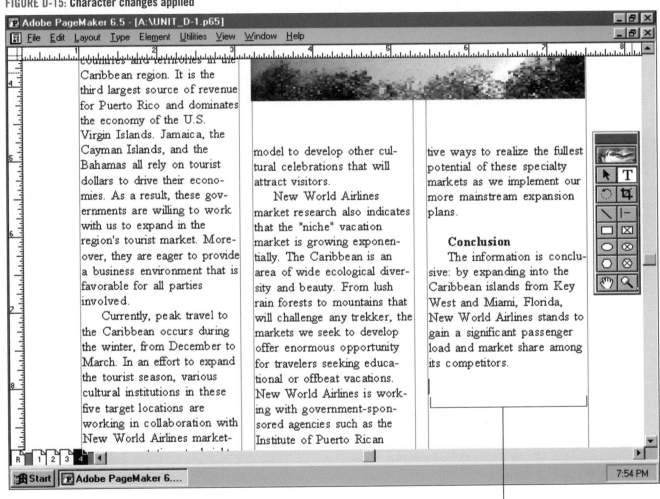

Text reflowed after font and font size changed

Formatting Paragraphs

When you select the Paragraph command on the Type menu, the Paragraph Specifications dialog box opens. You can use this dialog box for a variety of formatting needs. For example, you can set paragraph indents, change the space between paragraphs, adjust the alignment, or turn on widow and orphan control. In PageMaker, a **widow** is a line that begins a paragraph at the bottom of a column or page. In PageMaker, an **orphan** is a line that ends a paragraph but falls at the top of a column or page. Joe thinks the paragraph indent on the paragraphs is too large. He also wants to eliminate widows and orphans.

Steps

1. Click Ⅰ anywhere in the last paragraph, click **Edit** on the menu bar, then click **Select All**

2. Scroll the page until you can see the bottom page margin
   See Figure D-16. Your text might break at slightly different places depending on exactly where you placed the loaded pointer on page 1. Notice any widows and orphans.

3. Click **Type** on the menu bar, then click **Paragraph**
   The Paragraph Specifications dialog box opens. First, Joe wants to decrease the paragraph indents on all the paragraphs in the proposal.

4. Double-click the **First text box** in the Indents section, then type **0.15**
   This sets an indent of .15" on the first line of every paragraph. Next, Joe turns the widow and orphan control on.

5. Click the **Widow control check box**
   A check mark appears in the check box, and widow control is turned on. Now Joe needs to tell PageMaker how many lines of text make up a widow. Joe decides that two lines constitute a widow.

6. Type **2** in the Widow control text box
   See Figure D-17.

7. Click the **Orphan control check box**, then type **2** in the Orphan control text box

8. Click **OK**
   PageMaker moves lines of text up to the next column or page or down to the previous column or page to eliminate widows and orphans.

DesignTip

The absence of widows and orphans in a layout shows quality design.

FIGURE D-16: **Widowed text at the bottom of column two**

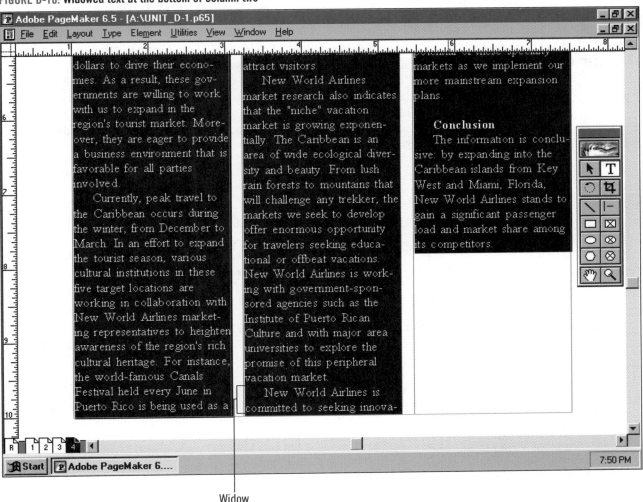

Widow

FIGURE D-17: **Paragraph Specifications dialog box**

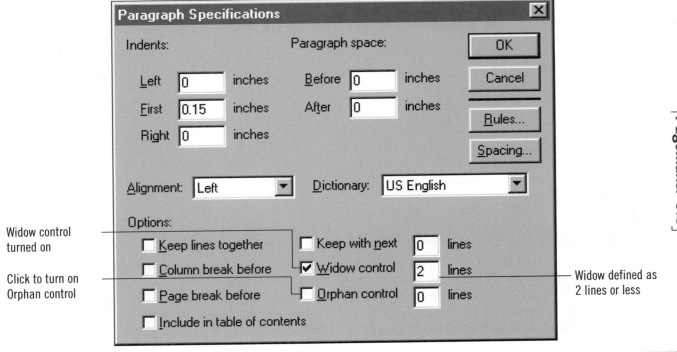

Widow control
turned on

Click to turn on
Orphan control

Widow defined as
2 lines or less

PageMaker 6.5

Adjusting Leading

Leading is the vertical space between lines of text. Specifically, leading is the total height of a line from the top of the tallest characters in the line to the top of the tallest characters in the line below. Like font size, leading is measured in points. PageMaker's default for leading is 20% greater than the font size. This means that if the text is 10 points, the leading would be 12 points. This is referred to as 10 (font size) over 12 (leading), or 10/12. Joe wants to make the lines of text a space and a half apart; in other words, he wants to increase the leading to 50% more than the font size.

Steps

1. Click **View** on the menu bar, then click **Fit in Window**
2. Click the **Text tool pointer** anywhere in the text if necessary
3. Click **Edit** on the menu bar, then click **Select All** if necessary
4. Click **Type** on the menu bar, then click **Character**
   The Character Specifications dialog box opens. Joe wants to increase the space between each line of text.
5. Double-click the **Leading list box** to select the current value, type **18**, then click **OK**
   You could also point to Leading on the Type menu, then select a leading from the submenu. The story flows below the bottom margin of the third column, as shown in Figure D-18. Note that if you try to set different leading in the same line, PageMaker uses the largest leading for the entire line.
6. Click the **Pointer tool** in the toolbox, click the **text block** in the third column, then drag the **windowshade handle** up to the bottom margin even with the second column
   The windowshade handle appears at the bottom of the third column, indicating that there is still text to be placed, as shown in Figure D-19. Joe will need to add additional pages to the proposal.

Trouble?

Depending on the exact placement of text in your publication, the handle may move up higher than the bottom of the second column, due to the widow and orphan control you set earlier.

CLUES TO USE

Positioning text within its leading

PageMaker gives you three choices for adjusting the text once the leading is chosen. **Proportional leading** is the default setting that allows for proportional amounts of space above the tallest character and the lowest character in a line. **Top of caps leading** measures the leading from the highest point on any character in a line. **Baseline leading** measures the leading from the baseline of the line of text. To change the way leading is measured, click Type on the menu bar, click Paragraph, then click Spacing.

FIGURE D-18: **Text after leading is increased**

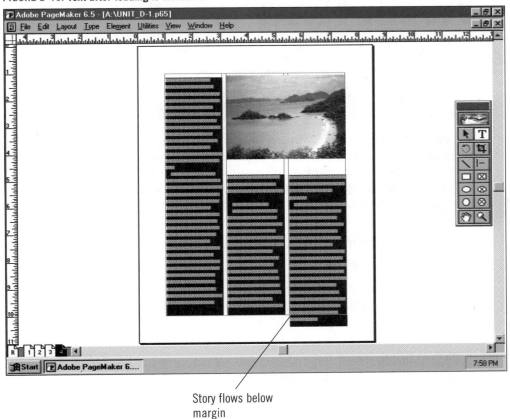

Story flows below
margin

FIGURE D-19: **Text block shortened in the third column**

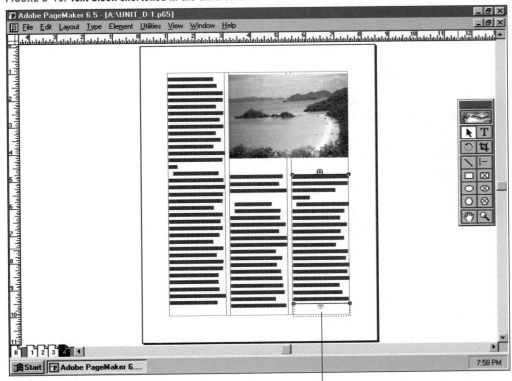

Indicates more text
needs to be placed

PageMaker 6.5

Inserting and Removing Pages in a Publication

You can insert pages before, after, or between the current pages in the publication window. PageMaker allows a maximum of 999 pages in a publication. You can also remove pages from a publication. PageMaker automatically rethreads text blocks and updates page icons when you add or delete pages. Because Joe increased the leading, the text no longer fits on four pages, so he needs to add pages to the publication.

Steps

1. **If the text block in the third column is not selected, click it, then click the window-shade handle** ☟

   This loads the place pointer ⊞ with the text that doesn't fit on page 4.

2. **Click Layout on the menu bar, then click Insert Pages**

   The Insert Pages dialog box opens, in which you specify how many pages you want to insert and where you want to insert them, as shown in Figure D-20.

3. **Type 2 in the Insert Page(s) text box, make sure the box before "the current page" reads after, then click Insert**

   The dialog box closes, and a new page 5 appears in the window. Notice two additional page icons for pages 5 and 6 appear in the lower-left corner of the window. Joe uses the semi-Autoflow method to place the rest of the text.

4. **Press [Shift], then click the semi-Autoflow text pointer** ⫯ **at the top of the first column, but do not release [Shift]**

5. **Click** ⫯ **at the top of the second column, then release [Shift]**

   The windowshade handle ⊔ appears at the end of the text in the second column indicating that there is no more text to place. See Figure D-21. Joe realizes he added one page too many, so he needs to remove page 6.

6. **Click Layout on the menu bar, click Remove Pages, type 6 in the Remove page(s) text box, double-click the through text box, type 6, then click OK**

   An alert message appears, asking if you want to delete the specified pages.

7. **Click OK**

   PageMaker removes page 6. Notice that the page 6 page icon no longer appears in the lower-left corner of the window. Satisfied with the proposal, Joe decides to save and print it.

Time To

✔ Save
✔ Exit

8. **Click File on the menu bar, then click Save; when PageMaker is done saving the file, click File on the menu bar, click Print, click All, then click Print All in the Print document dialog box**

   The publication prints.

Using the Go to Page command

In addition to clicking page icons to move to a specific page in a publication, you can use the Go to Page command on the Layout menu. This command is helpful if you are working on a large multiple-page document (usually more than 20 pages) and all the page icons do not appear at the bottom of the publication window. Click Layout on menu bar, then click Go to Page to open the Go to Page dialog box. Click the Page number radio button, type the page number you want to go to in the text box, then click OK. See Figure D-22.

FIGURE D-20: **Insert Pages dialog box**

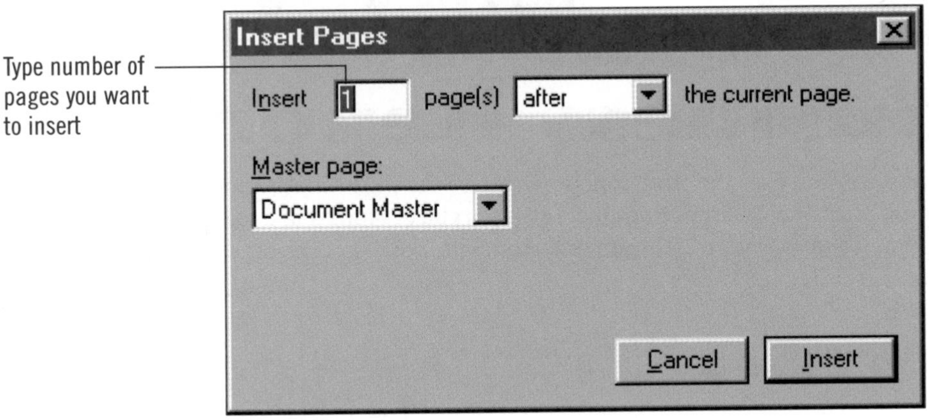

Type number of
pages you want
to insert

Insert Pages ☒

I̲nsert [1] page(s) [after ▼] the current page.

M̲aster page:

[Document Master ▼]

[C̲ancel] [I̲nsert]

No more text
to place

FIGURE D-21: **Text placed on the new page**

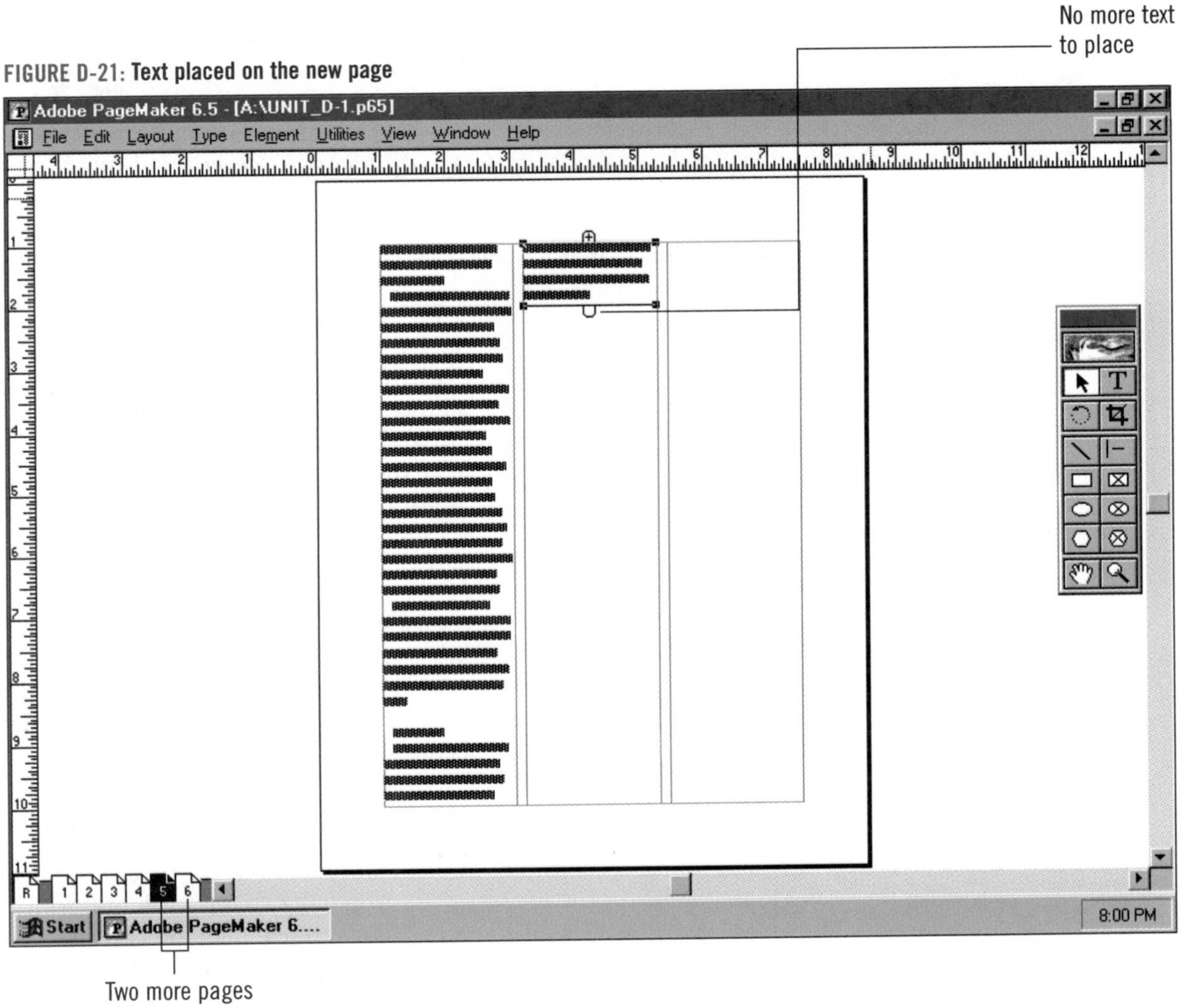

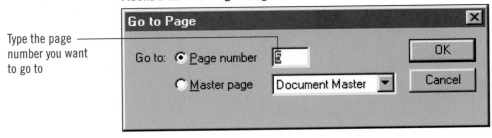

Adobe PageMaker 6.5 - [A:\UNIT_D-1.p65]

F̲ile E̲dit L̲ayout T̲ype E̲lement U̲tilities V̲iew W̲indow H̲elp

R 1 2 3 4 5 6 ◄

Start Adobe PageMaker 6....   8:00 PM

Two more pages

FIGURE D-22: **Go to Page dialog box**

Type the page
number you want
to go to

Go to Page ☒

Go to: ⊙ P̲age number [5]   [OK]

○ M̲aster page [Document Master ▼] [Cancel]

Design Workshop: Business Reports

Using innovative design and concise writing when creating business reports will capture your reader's attention. It's important that the report be organized in a logical, consistent, and sequential fashion. Figure D-23 shows the final proposal. Let's critique the final publication.

Details

Does the cover invite the reader to read the report?

The cover sets the tone for the report. It should emphasize the importance of the report and introduce the visual style used in the report. You should not spend so much time creating the cover page that you sacrifice the quality of the text in the report; however, there are several small additions that can enhance your cover and invite the reader to continue to read the report. The large headline and the abstract on the cover of Joe's proposal immediately let the reader know what the report contains. The New World Airlines logo on the cover adds a nice touch without crowding any important information.

Is the text organized in a logical fashion?

It is critical that the text in a business report be coherent. PageMaker's story editor gives you some of the tools commonly available in word processing applications to edit your stories, including a spell checker and commands for finding and changing text. Joe checked the spelling in his report before he printed it. He also replaced an overused phrase with a better word. Note also that Joe included headlines and subheads within the body of the report to help organize the information.

Are the pages too heavy with text?

If possible, you should balance the excessive text used in reports with graphics. As with a fact sheet, you should add graphics to reinforce the information in the report, not just decorate it. Joe included a chart on page 3 to reinforce text explanations, and photos of the Caribbean on pages 2 and 4 to add interest to the text. Joe also adjusted the leading to space out the text in the proposal, giving the pages more white space. This forced him to add a new page, page 5, to his proposal.

Does each page of the report have a consistent design?

Using a consistent design provides continuity through all sections of the report and makes it easier for the reader to find information. Joe set up the proposal with three columns which gave him more flexibility for placing the text and graphics. His placement of graphics helps the pages look consistent. Looking back, Joe should have included a graphic on page 5 to tie the entire publication together.

NEW WORLD AIRLINES

Expanded Service Proposal

ABSTRACT

New World Airlines has mapped success in the past 10 years by offering competitive pricing, quality services and enticing destinations. This proposal highlights the benefits of expanding key routes into the Caribbean. New World Airlines can capitalize on a growing market and increase profits through additional ticket sales.

Prepared By:

Michelle Snow
New World Airlines

Jennifer Ellen
Greater Caribbean
Board Of Tourism

Timothy Francie
New World Airlines

Joseph Martin
New World Airlines

Expanded Service Proposal

By capitalizing on the resurgence of the Caribbean as a vacation destination, New World Airlines can increase market share and offer our customers quality destinations at affordable prices.

The initial expansion includes two new routes: San Juan, Puerto Rico; and St. Thomas in the Virgin Islands. By keeping the initial expansion to these two United States territories, New World Airlines avoids placing customers through customs.

Arrangements are pending with major cruise lines to use New World Airlines as their official carrier to bring passengers to eastern and southern Caribbean ports for cruises that stop along South America and Trinidad and Tobago. Our commitment to expanding coverage into the Caribbean could bring passengers travel-ling-alone as well as cruise lines passengers. New World Airlines is considering offering joint cruise package deals with Queens Cruises. Many of Queenís customers living in Chicago and the Midwest. Chicago is one of New World Airlineí regional hubs. An agreement with Queen is expected very soon.

Expanded routes into Jamaica, the Cayman Islands and the Bahamas could begin

---

two years after the initial phase begins. Full service into all five island locations could be complete by 1999, pending board approval.

Key to our goal's success are the Florida Keys, and to a lesser degree, Miami. By expanding our routes from Key West and Miami, New World Airlines can venture into the Caribbean and near Atlantic Ocean easily.

Existing aircraft could make most of these destinations within two hours. Shorter flights, such as to New Providence Island in the Bahamas, could use Boeing 727 or 737 aircraft, which require fewer staff and less fuel.

Projections show that our passengers load could double to the Key West and Miami markets, with those cities being our launchpad into the Caribbean. The Miami Board of Tourism and the Keys Regional Commerce and Growth Association will waive certain fees and taxes for a two-year period. See the accompanying graph on Page 3 of this report.

The Caribbean with its cobalt-blue waters and breath-taking scenery ensures a fantastic vacation destination. New World Airlines hopes to capitalize on this ever-growing hot spot so close to the United States by offering

flights directly to some of the best areas within the Caribbean.

Our commitment to this expanding vacation area is based on New World Airlines' well-researched projections of travel trends and airline capacity in the near Atlantic, and our close collaboration with the various governments and tourism officials in each of the five island locations.

New Horizons

Hurricane Hugo did more than damage property when it blew through the Caribbean and up the coast of the United States in 1989; it virtually devastated Caribbean tourism.

Projected Increases In Passengers And Revenues

Passengers In Thousands

Revenues In Thousands

Although more than 490 million tourists visited the region during the past several years, it has only been during the past year that regional services and accommodations have been restored to levels that will entice large numbers of tourists to return to the Caribbean. New World Airlines believe that we are uniquely positioned to capitalize on this expanding service area.

Our market research has shown that vacationers prefer to visit places they perceive as exotic while at the same time they choose destinations that ensure a certain cultural "comfort zone." What makes these five locations particularly attractive for our potential customers, who will be predominantly from the United States, is that English is the official language of most and is widely spoken in all. In addition, the historical European influence on the cultures of these particular Caribbean locations makes them a comfortable choice for travelers, while the island

location satisfies their desire for a "foreign" experience, romance, excitement, and sun.

Strategic Alliances

Tourism is the largest source of revenue for most countries and territories in the Caribbean region. It is the third largest source of revenue for Puerto Rico and dominates the economy of the U.S. Virgin Islands. Jamaica, the Cayman Islands, and the Bahamas all rely on tourist dollars to drive their economies. As a result, these governments are willing to work with us to expand in the region's tourist market. More-

over, they are eager to provide a business environment that is favorable for all parties involved.

Currently, peak travel to the Caribbean occurs during the winter, from December to March. In an effort to expand the tourist season, various cultural institutions in these five target locations are working in collaboration with New World Airlines marketing representatives to heighten awareness of the region's rich cultural heritage. For instance, the world-famous Canals Festival held every June in Puerto Rico is being used as a

---

model to develop other cultural celebrations that will attract visitors.

New World Airlines market research also indicates that the "niche" vacation market is growing exponentially. The Caribbean is an area of wide ecological diversity and beauty. From lush rain forests to mountains that will challenge any trekker, the markets we seek to develop offer enormous opportunity for travelers seeking educational or offbeat vacations. New World Airlines is working with government-sponsored agencies such as the Institute of Puerto Rican Culture and with major area universities to explore the promise of this peripheral vacation market.

New World Airlines is committed to seeking innovative ways to realize the fullest potential of these specialty markets as we implement our more mainstream expansion plans.

Conclusion

The information is conclusive: by expanding into the Caribbean islands from Key

West and Miami, Florida, New World Airlines stands to gain a significant passenger load and market share among its competitors.

Practice

► Concepts Review

Label each of the publication window elements as shown in Figure D-24.

FIGURE D-24

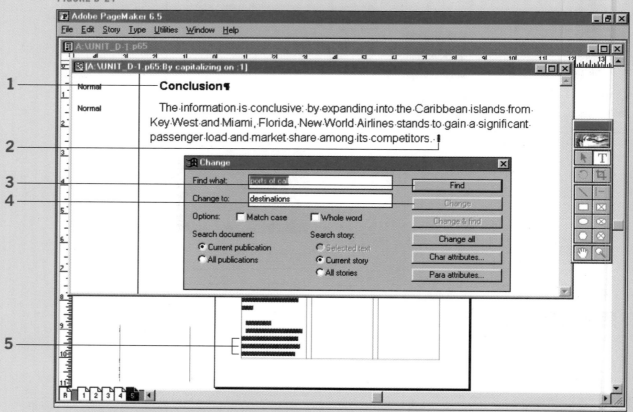

Match each of the terms with the statement that describes its function.

6. Story editor
7. Clipboard
8. Leading
9. Word wrap

a. Temporary storage area for cut or copied text or graphics
b. PageMaker's word processor
c. The automatic movement of the insertion point and text to the next line
d. The space between the lines

Select the best answer from the list of choices.

10. All of the following are advantages of using story editor, except:
   a. You can insert large amounts of text easily
   b. You can make multiple changes to a story that spans several text blocks
   c. You can use powerful utilities such as the spell checker and the Find and Change commands
   d. You can see how the story fits on the page

11. **When you use the spell checker, you can check only:**
    a. The current story
    b. All stories in the current publication
    c. All stories in open PageMaker publications
    d. All of the above

12. **An advantage of using the Character Specifications dialog box is you can:**
    a. Spell Check your entire document
    b. Set multiple formats at one time
    c. Set paragraph specifications
    d. Both b and c

13. **All of the following are true statements about leading, except:**
    a. You change the height of the characters when you set leading
    b. Leading is measured in points, the same as text
    c. PageMaker's default for leading is 20% greater than font size
    d. Leading is automatically set when you choose a different font size

14. **PageMaker's spell checker allows you to:**
    a. Add new words to the dictionary
    b. Check for spelling in all stories in the publication
    c. Find a word accidentally typed consecutively
    d. All of the above

15. **Typing "2" in the Widow control lines text box means PageMaker will:**
    a. Allow two lines together at the end of a page or column
    b. Allow three lines together at the end of a page or column
    c. Allow two lines together at the top of a page or column
    d. Not allow three lines together at the end of a page or column

▶ Skills Review

1. **Place text using story editor.**
   a. Open the file UNIT_D-2 from your Student Disk.
   b. Click Edit on the menu bar, then click Edit Story.
   c. Type the following text:
      Story by Janice Owens
      Janice is a business editor for the New Orleans Star. She has closely monitored the large food warehouse chains nationwide because many of these companies are headquartered in New Orleans and the surrounding areas in Louisiana. She can be reached at her office at (504) 564-5433 or through e-mail at Owens@NOSTAR.VCA.
   d. Click Story on the menu bar, then click Display ¶.
   e. Make sure there are no extra spaces between any two words.
   f. Click Story on the menu bar, then click Close Story.
   g. Click Place.
   h. Drag-place the story below the headline across all three columns, and drag the window shade handle down to fit text if necessary.

2. Insert pages.

    a. Click Layout on the menu bar, then select Insert Pages.

    b. Make sure that "after" is selected for the position of the new pages.

    c. Type "4" in the Insert page(s) text box, then click Insert.

    d. Move to page 1 by clicking the page 1 page icon in the lower-left corner of the publication window.

    e. Click the Pointer tool ▣ in the toolbox, move the pointer ▶ to the middle of the text block in column 3, click to select the column, then click the bottom windowshade ▽ once to load the place text pointer.

    f. Click the page 2 and 3 page icon ▣▣.

    g. Click Layout on the menu bar, then click Autoflow.

    h. Move the place text pointer to the top of page 2 in the first column, then place the text.

3. Edit text in story editor.

    a. Return to page 1, position the pointer over the main story, then triple-click to open the story editor.

    b. Make sure the Display ¶ option is selected.

    c. Using the text cursor, highlight the entire second paragraph including the paragraph symbol.

    d. Click Edit on the main menu, then click Cut.

    e. Position the insertion point at the beginning of the paragraph that begins "Kemper cited..."

    f. Click Edit, then click Paste to place the text that you just cut.

    g. Highlight the last sentence in the second new paragraph of the story, then press [Delete] *(Macintosh users: press [del])*.

4. Use the spell checker in story editor.

    a. Move the insertion point to the beginning of the story.

    b. Click Utilities on the menu bar, then click Spelling.

    c. Click Start.

    d. Click "food" in the list of alternative spellings for "fod," then click Replace.

    e. Click Ignore when "Kemper" is highlighted.

    f. Click Ignore when "Isis" is highlighted.

    g. Click Ignore when "Lombardo" is highlighted.

    h. Click the correct spelling for "success," then click Replace.

    i. Continue spell checking the text.

    j. When you are finished, close the Spelling dialog box.

5. Find and change text in story editor.

    a. Move the insertion point to the beginning of the story.

    b. Click Utilities on the menu bar, then select Change.

    c. Type the text "Kemper Foods" in the Find what text box.

    d. Type "Kemper Distributors Inc." in the Change to text box.

    e. Click Find to select the first occurrence of the text you are searching for.

    f. Click Change to change the text to the replacement text.

    g. Find all occurrences of the text you are searching for and change them to the new text.

    h. When you are finished, close the Change dialog box.

    i. Click Story on the menu bar, then click Close Story.

6. Format text using character specifications.

    a. Click the Text tool in the toolbox, then click anywhere in the main story on page 1.

    b. Click Edit on the menu bar, click Select All to highlight all the text in the main story in the publication.

   c. Click Type on the menu bar, then select Character.

   d. Click the Font list arrow, then click Arial *(Macintosh users: click Helvetica)*.

   e. Double-click the Size text box, then type "10".

   f. Click OK to close the Character Specifications dialog box.

7. Adjust the leading.

   a. Make sure all the text in the main story is still selected.

   b. Click Type on the menu bar, point to Leading, then click 20.

   c. Click the pages 2 and 3 page icon 2 3 .

   d. Click the Pointer tool in the toolbox, then click the last text block and determine if there is more text to be placed by looking at the windowshade.

   e. If necessary, move the bottom windowshade up to fit the text in the last column.

   f. Click the windowshade at the end of the last text block and continue to flow the text to the next page.

8. Format paragraphs.

   a. Make sure all the text in the main story is still selected.

   b. Click Type on the menu bar, then click Paragraph.

   c. Change all of the paragraph indents to .15".

   d. Turn on widow control and define a widow as one line.

   e. Click OK to close the Paragraph Specifications dialog box.

   f. If necessary, adjust the text in the last text block to flow to the last column.

9 Remove pages.

   a. Click Layout on the menu bar, then click Remove Pages.

   b. Remove pages 4 and 5.

   c. Save your work and print the publication.

   d. Close the publication, then exit PageMaker.

▶ Independent Challenges

1. As the on-site desktop publisher for Johnson Printing, you need to petition your manager for an upgrade of your computer equipment. You must justify the expense in a report that proves the upgrade will ensure an increase in productivity. The increase in productivity will translate into more time to do more projects, which equals more revenue. You decide to make the report simple and straightforward.

To complete this independent challenge:

1. Create a new four-page single-sided publication with three columns using the default margin. Save the publication as Johnson proposal to your Student Disk.
2. Place the file JLOGO, the Johnson Printing logo, on page 1, which is the cover page. Open a new story in story editor, and then type a headline and your name to go on the cover page. Place these elements anywhere on the page. Format this text. Add other design elements to the cover page to make it more eye-catching.
3. The graphic file CHART on your Student Disk contains a chart showing how much your productivity will be increased if you get the upgraded equipment. Place this chart on page 3. Drag-place it across the two left columns starting in the upper-left corner of the publication. The bottom of the graphic should be at the 4" mark on the vertical ruler.
4. Type a headline on page 2 that corresponds to the computer request for Johnson Printing. Stretch the headline's text block across all three columns. Format the headline.
5. Place the file PROPOSAL on pages 2 through 4. This text is the same as the text you placed earlier in the unit for New World Airlines. Here, you're using it as dummy text, which is sample text placed in a document strictly for the purposes of design approval. Place each block manually, and ignore any leftover text that might have flowed to page 4.
6. Open the dummy text in story editor, and write a custom introduction for Johnson Printing. Make the introduction two paragraphs long with at least three sentences per paragraph describing your goals for upgrading the computers at Johnson Printing.
7. Select the introduction you just typed, and then open the spell checker and check the spelling in your introduction.
8. Deselect the introduction, move the insertion point to the beginning of the story, and then use the Change command to find the phrase "New World Airlines" and change it to "Johnson Printing Company."
9. Close story editor and evaluate the final design. Is the proposal too text heavy? Do you need to increase the leading? Would a different font be easier to read? Do you need to add more graphics? Make any changes necessary.
10. Save and print your work, and close your publication.

2. Find a copy of at least two different companies' versions of reports. They can be annual reports, although the design in a project as large as an annual report may differ from the previous discussions of reports.
   To complete this independent challenge:

1. Analyze the writing style of the report. Can you tell who the intended audience is?
2. Critique the reports using the guidelines discussed in this unit along with other criteria that you establish. How effective is the design to the readability of the publication? Do elements of design withdraw or enhance the complete report?
3. How would you improve the look, the writing tone, or the writing quality of the report?

3. Choose an issue or problem at your school or place of employment that you would like to address. Use PageMaker to create either a proposal for the school's board of trustees, your department, your boss, or the president of your company. Define the issue, and then discuss your proposed solution.

To complete this independent challenge:

1. Open a new single-sided publication with at least four pages. Save it as My proposal to your Student Disk.
2. Create a cover page that includes a short two- to three-paragraph abstract describing the contents of your report. Make sure the cover page is eye-catching.
3. Place the file JLOGO as a dummy graphic file, or if you have another graphic file you would like to use, use that instead. Consider placing a second graphic in the publication. On your final printout, label these graphics to identify what they would be if you were not using dummy files.
4. Type the text of your proposal in story editor. Use the spell checker to check the spelling. Place the text in the publication. Add the necessary pages to place the entire text or remove empty pages.
5. Format the text of the proposal. Change the font, size, and leading as necessary. Consider double-spacing the text.
6. Add headlines and subheadlines to enhance the overall appearance of your report.
7. Evaluate the final design. Do you need to add any lines to visually separate graphics and text? Do the pages have a consistent design? Is your cover page eye-catching without looking cluttered? Make any necessary changes.
8. Save and print the publication.

4. As the president of your senior class, you have been chosen to put together a proposal for your senior class trip. You have decided to use PageMaker, which you are learning in one of your computer classes, to create the proposal to present to the school board. Your peers want you to design an attractive, high-impact proposal that will justify the expense to the school board and convince them that your senior trip will be very educational.

To complete this independent challenge:

1. Search the World Wide Web for information on traveling to the destination of your choice.
2. Create a thumbnail sketch of a four-page proposal, keeping in mind the guidelines that you learned in this unit.
3. Using the sketch as a guide, create your proposal in PageMaker. You may use the file JLOGO on your Student Disk as a dummy graphic file, but be sure to label these graphics on your final printout.
4. Create your proposal's text in story editor, and don't forget to use the spell checker.
5. When you are done formatting the proposal and enhancing its appearance, critique the final design to make sure that you have followed the guidelines you learned in this unit, and that the proposal is going to capture the school board's attention.
6. Save your proposal as Class trip to your Student Disk, print the publication, and exit PageMaker.
7. Be sure to hand in all printouts along with the critique of your design.

▶ Visual Workshop

You are an investment manager for Omaha Investor Group Inc. You have been asked to create a report as shown in Figure D-25. Open the file on your Student Disk called UNIT_D-3. Create an abstract on the front cover of your report. Use story editor with the Display ¶ option on to type the following:

INTRODUCTION
This report is a supplement to the information found in the annual Omaha Investors Group Plan Summary booklet and is provided to help you understand the characteristics of your investment options. Please note that the historical data in this report is provided for information purposes only and should not be used to predict the future performance of group funds.

Place the text as shown in Figure D-25. Then go to page 2 in the publication and open the text inside the story editor. Using the Cut and Paste options, highlight and cut point #3 and move it above point #2. Renumber the points. Then spell check all stories in the publication, and then use the change command to find the text "Windlow Stock Fund" and replace it with "Altoffz Growth Stock Fund." Close the story editor. Then highlight the entire text and change the font to Times New Roman, 12 point *(Macintosh users: change the font to Times, 12 point)*. With the text still highlighted, change the leading to 24 point. Insert two pages and continue to flow the text. Turn on the Widow control and Orphan control and set to 2 lines. Remove any unnecessary blank pages. Finally, add bold formatting and change the font to Arial *(Macintosh users: Helvetica)* for the section headings and fund names in the fund description section. Save and print the document.

FIGURE D-25

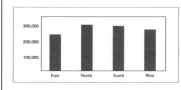

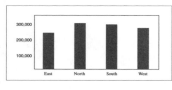

PageMaker 6.5

Working
with Multiple Pages

Objectives

► **Plan a newsletter**
► **Use master pages**
► **Create multiple master pages**
► **Edit master pages layout**
► **Apply master pages**
► **Use styles**
► **Define styles**
► **Apply styles**
► **Edit styles**
► **Balance columns**
► **Rearrange pages**
► **Mask objects**
► **Design Workshop: Newsletters**

Making multiple-page publications cohesive and consistent is one of PageMaker's strengths. In this unit, you will learn about master pages and styles and how they help control repetitive elements and type usage in multiple-page publications. Text and graphics placed on the master pages appear on all pages of your publication. Styles enhance productivity by quickly applying set attributes to paragraphs and by modifying a style to change its appearance throughout the publication. Also, you will learn about features designed to improve the layout of your publication.

In this unit, Joe Martin uses PageMaker to enhance the final appearance of the New World Airlines quarterly frequent flyer newsletter.

Planning a Newsletter

Newsletters are one of the most common types of publications produced using PageMaker. The challenge is to create a newsletter that will capture the reader's attention. Before creating your newsletter in PageMaker, take time to determine the overall layout of your newsletter. Joe needs to design *Wings*, the New World Airlines frequent flyer newsletter, which he has sketched in Figure E-1. The newsletter is on letter-size paper and is eight pages long. Joe takes the following points into consideration as he plans the layout:

Details

Include a flag at the top of the newsletter

The **masthead**, **nameplate**, or **flag**, is the graphical element that serves as your identification and gives a purpose to your newsletter. The flag includes the name of the newsletter and the date of the publication. It might also include the volume number, the company name or the source of the newsletter, and other identifications. Be careful not to crowd the area with too much information. Joe creates a flag using a drawing application, and he places it at the top of page 1.

Focus the attention of the reader on the main story on each page

The reader should immediately know which story is the most important story on each page. Creating a main focus gives readers a place to begin reading the pages of the newsletter. The headline for the main story can be larger than other headlines on the page. Generally, the importance of stories ranks from the top left to the bottom right because of the natural way we read. The story about bonuses on special trips is the most important story on page 8, so Joe places it on the page's upper-left corner.

Use graphics to show the information's importance

Graphics capture the reader's attention and motivate him or her to read the story. Generally, graphics associated with the main story are larger. Smaller stories might not even contain graphics. Joe designs the first three pages of the newsletter to contain many graphics, especially pages 2 and 3, which represent a **spread**, or two facing pages that can work together in one design package.

Use shading, lines, or white space to break up text

You don't want to congest your newsletter by having stories run into each other. Try to include only one or two stories on a page for a newsletter of this size. However, there might be times when you have many short stories on a page; in these cases, use shading or lines to separate the stories. Joe uses page 8 of the newsletter as a "catch-all" for the shorter stories and plans to use shading on one of the stories to help it stand out from the other three stories on the page.

DesignTip

Too many fonts distract the reader. A small newsletter should contain only two fonts, one for headlines and one for body text. Use type styles (bold, italic, etc.) to create contrast without changing the font.

Select appropriate fonts for headlines and body text

Like photos and graphics, the headline must invite your audience to read the story. In general, you should design headlines in a bold font no smaller than 18 points. Headlines compete for attention on the page, so you need to visually separate them from the page's other design elements. Body text is usually a serif font 10 to 12 points in size. Joe plans to use a mix of styles for headlines and use 12-point Times New Roman for body text.

FIGURE E-1: Joe's sketch of his newsletter

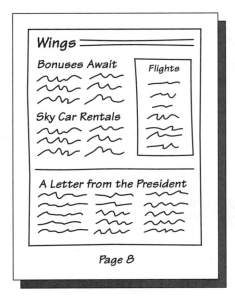

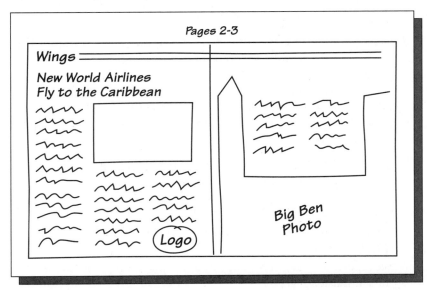

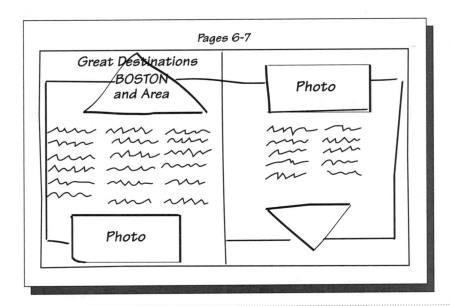

Using Master Pages

Master pages are nonprinting pages that serve as templates for the entire publication. All items, including text, graphics, and guides, that you place on the master pages appear on every page of the publication. Master pages are helpful when you are working on a multiple-page publication. If a publication contains double-sided pages, you can choose whether to place elements on either the left or right master page. Joe wants to add the page number to the upper-right corner of all even-numbered pages. He wants to add the date to the upper-left corner of each odd-numbered page.

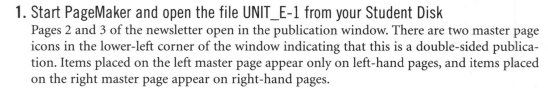

1. **Start PageMaker and open the file UNIT_E-1 from your Student Disk**
   Pages 2 and 3 of the newsletter open in the publication window. There are two master page icons in the lower-left corner of the window indicating that this is a double-sided publication. Items placed on the left master page appear only on left-hand pages, and items placed on the right master page appear on right-hand pages.

2. **Click the master page icon** [L R] **in the lower-left corner of the publication window**
   [L R] becomes highlighted, and the left and right master pages appear on the screen. The pages are blank, except for column guides that separate each page into three columns. Joe added the column guides when he first started designing the newsletter. This way, the column guides appear on every page, and Joe had to set the guides only once. He also had placed the Wings logo and a line for the tops of the pages to help create a consistent design for each page.

3. **Click View on the menu bar, click Actual Size, then scroll the page to view the upper-right corner of the left master page**

4. **Click the Text tool** [T] **in the toolbox, then drag-place a text block just above the third column about one column-width wide, type Page, press [spacebar], then press [Ctrl][Shift][3]**
   See Figure E-2. "Page LM" appears at the insertion point. LM is the page number symbol for the left master page.

5. **Click Type on the menu bar, point to Alignment, then click Align Right**
   The text becomes right-aligned in the text block.

6. **Click the pages 2 and 3 page icon** [2 3]

7. **Position the pointer near the top of the publication page where pages 2 and 3 intersect, then press [Ctrl] and right-click**
   See Figure E-3. The information you typed on the master pages appears on these pages. The number 2 replaces the LM page number symbol.

Trouble?

Master pages cannot be deleted but you can delete any element placed on the master pages as you would on a normal page.

MacintoshUser

This replaces Step 4.

4. Click the Text tool, drag-place a text block above the third column one column-width wide, type Page, press [spacebar], then press [⌘] [option] [P].

MacintoshUser

This replaces Step 7.

7. Position the pointer near the top of the publication page where pages 2 and 3 intersect, then press [⌘] [option] and click.

FIGURE E-2: Page number symbol on left master page

Page number
symbol

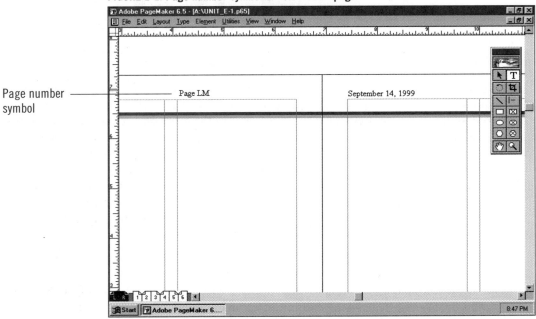

FIGURE E-3: Page 2 page number and date

Page number
replaces symbol

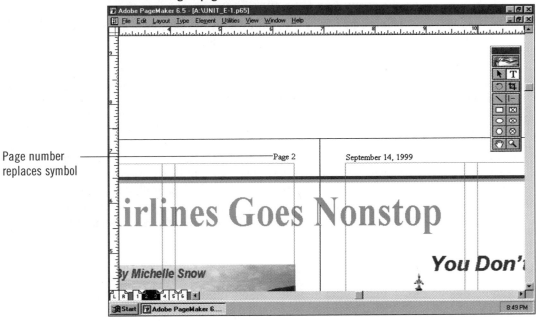

CLUES TO USE

Hiding and partially displaying master page items

The Display Master command allows you to hide all the elements you add to the master pages. When Display Master Items is checked (the default), all items on the master page appear on all the pages in the publication window. When Display Master Items is unchecked, the master page items disappear from view. Sometimes you might want to hide only certain elements from a master page. For example, you might want to display a graphic but not a page number. To hide the unwanted elements, draw a box around the element, click Element on the menu bar, click Fill, then click Paper. You might have to remove the line as well, depending on your default line weight.

Creating Multiple Master Pages

Using master pages you can add page numbers, repetitive graphic elements, and headers and/or footers to all the spreads in your publication at once. However, these master page objects can limit your ability to create unique page layouts because the elements are included on all pages of the publication. To remove some or all of the master page elements from a page can be very time-consuming, especially in multiple-page publications. PageMaker allows you to create multiple master pages. You have the option to create a master page based on an existing publication page or to create a master page from scratch. ◣━━ Joe wants to create a new master page from an existing page spread that he has already begun to design. This spread will highlight facts and photos about one New World Airlines destination. The new master page spread will be named "Great Destinations" and can be used for other spreads in the newsletter.

Steps

1. Click the **pages 4 and 5 page icon** 〔4|5〕
The "Great Destinations" two-page spread opens. Joe has created a new spread, but he doesn't want to include the Wings logo and lines that are automatically placed on his page layout by the master pages. In order to create the new master pages, Joe must first open the Master Pages palette.

QuickTip
To quickly display the Master Pages palette, press [Ctrl][H] (Macintosh users: no keyboard shortcut exists for this action).

2. Click **Window** on the menu bar, then click **Show Master Pages**
The Master Pages palette appears on the publication window. See Figure E-4. Joe clicks the right arrow on the palette to examine the Master Pages menu.

3. Click the **right arrow** ▶ on the Master Pages palette
The Master Pages menu appears. See Figure E-5. The Master Pages palette contains a menu that allows you to create new master pages from scratch or from existing publication pages. The palette menu contains other commands related to working with master pages. Joe needs to give his new master pages a name.

Trouble?
If the Master Pages palette covers a screen element you're working with, click on its title bar and drag it out of the way. If you can't see the full names of the master pages listed on the palette, click and drag the borders of the palette to resize it.

4. Click **Save Page as** on the Master Pages menu, type **Great Destinations**, then click **Save**
The highlight in the lower-left corner of the publication window moves from 〔4|5〕 to 〔L|R〕. All the elements and the page layout from pages 4 and 5 are automatically copied to the new master page spread called Great Destinations. The new name appears on the Master Pages palette. Now Joe can remove the Wings logo and other items not needed in the new master page layout.

FIGURE E-4: Master Pages palette

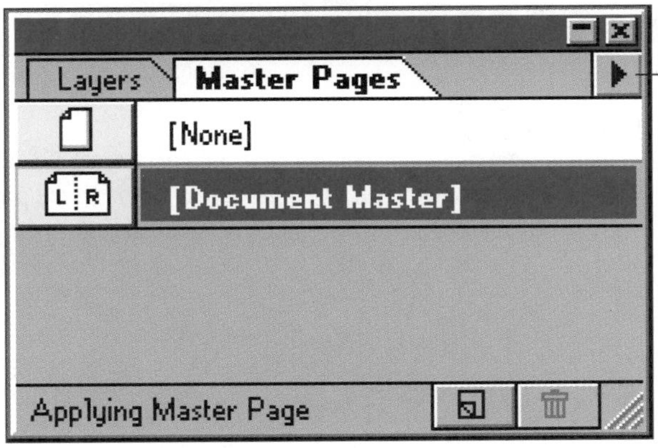

Layers | **Master Pages** | ▶ —— Click to display
Master Pages menu

[None]

[Document Master]

Applying Master Page

FIGURE E-5: Master Pages menu

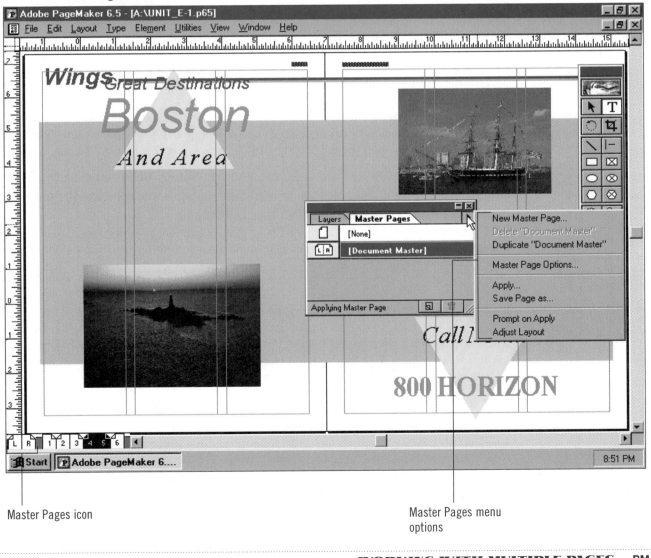

Master Pages icon

Master Pages menu
options

Editing Master Pages Layout

Joe needs to remove the information about Boston from these pages to make them applicable to any destination. Joe now removes the word Wings and the lines on the master pages.

MacintoshUser

This replaces Steps 2 and 3.

2. Move the pointer to the top of the window at the intersection of the left and right master pages, then press [⌘] [1], click the horizontal heavy blue line on the left master page, press and hold [Shift] while you click the gray line on the left master page, release [Shift], then press [Delete]

3. Click the blue line on the right master page, press and hold [Shift] and click the gray line on the right master page, release [Shift] press [Delete], then press [⌘] [0] (zero)

Resume at Step 4.

1. Click the Pointer tool ▶ in the toolbar, click the word Wings to select its text box, then press [Delete]

   This removes the logo from the Great Destinations master pages but not from the original Document Master pages used in the rest of the newsletter.

2. Move the pointer to the top of the window at the intersection of the left and right master pages, then press [Ctrl] and right-click, click the horizontal heavy blue line on the left master page, press and hold [Shift] while you click the gray line on the left master page, release [Shift], then press [Delete]

3. Click the blue line on the right master page, press and hold [Shift] and click the gray line on the right master page, release [Shift], press [Delete], then press [Ctrl] and right-click

   The page view returns to Fit to Window. You can see that the blue and gray lines are gone across the spread. Joe now needs to delete all text and graphic objects that refer to Boston so that all that will remain in the master pages is the basic Great Destinations layout.

4. Click inside the Boston text block, press and hold [Shift] while you click the photo on the bottom of the page, press and hold [Shift] again while you click the photo on the top of the right master page, then press [Delete]

   See Figure E-6. Now all that remains on the Great Destinations master pages is the colored box across both pages, Great Destinations triangle objects, and the page number and date.

5. Click the pages 4 and 5 page icon ▢▢ in the lower-left corner of the publication window

   Joe notices his original page layout remains the same including the placement of the Wings logo. The Master Pages palette shows that the current pages are still using the original Document Master master pages. You need to apply the new Great Destinations master pages to this spread. However, before you do this, you should delete elements on these pages that are already part of the Great Destinations master pages.

6. Click the colored box in the background of page 4, press and hold [Shift] while you click the colored box in the background of page 5, click the words Great Destinations, and click the words 800 HORIZON, release [Shift], then press [Delete]

   Now your spread includes only the custom objects for the layout on Boston. In the next lesson you will apply the Great Destinations master page layout design.

FIGURE E-6: The completed Great Destinations master pages

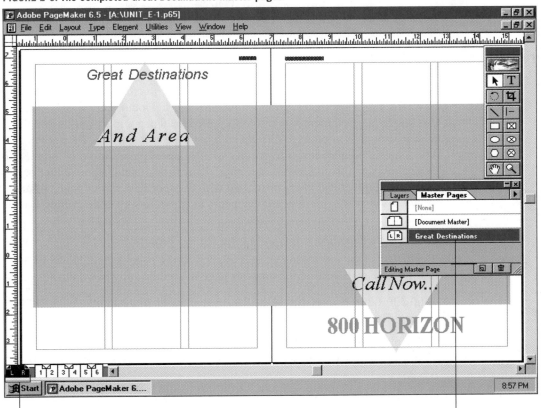

Master pages icons highlighted

New master page spread created

FIGURE E-7: New Master Page dialog box

Enter name here

Adjust settings to new spread

Creating a new master page from scratch

To create a new master page from scratch, click New Master Page on the Master Pages menu. The New Master Page dialog box opens. See Figure E-7. Type the name of the new master page in the Name text box. For a two-page layout, set the margins, number of columns, and the space between the columns, for both the left and right pages. After you complete the new settings, click OK (Macintosh users: click Create). The new master page appears in the publication window. You can now continue by adding the text and graphics you want for the new master page.

PageMaker 6.5

Applying Master Pages

Even though you have created a new master page, it has no effect until you apply it to pages in your document. All PageMaker publications include a Document Master page layout. The Document Master page elements are initially applied to all pages in a publication. You can change a page or page spread by applying a different master page to it from the Master Pages palette. The Insert Pages command allows you to specify which master page should be applied to all newly created pages. You can also edit any master page at any time during page production. The changes will be applied instantly to all pages formatted with the specified master page.  Joe would like to apply the Great Destinations master pages to the page spread describing Boston.

1. Click **Great Destinations** on the Master Pages palette
   See Figure E-8. The new master page is applied to the page spread. However, Joe would like to modify the Great Destinations master page to contain only two columns on each page.

2. Position the pointer over the left and right master page icons ⌐L R⌐, then right-click
   The Master Pages pop-up list appears. See Figure E-9.

3. Click **Great Destinations** on the pop-up list
   The publication window displays the Great Destinations master pages that Joe created.

4. Click **Layout** on the menu bar, click **Column Guides**, type **2** in the Number of columns text box, then click **OK**
   The Great Destinations master pages now have only two columns. Now return to pages 4 and 5 to see the change.

5. Click the **pages 4 and 5 page icon** ⌐4 5⌐
   The page layout is automatically changed to two columns.

6. Click the **pages 2 and 3 page icon** ⌐2 3⌐
   Notice that [Document Master] is now highlighted on the Master Pages palette, reflecting the master pages choice for these pages.

7. Click **Layout** on the menu bar, then click **Insert Pages**
   The Insert Pages dialog box opens. Joe will add 2 new pages based on his new Great Destinations master pages.

8. Make sure **2** is entered in the Insert Page(s) text box, click the **Master page list arrow**, click **Great Destinations** in the list box, then click **Insert**
   Two new pages based on the Great Destinations master pages are added to the publication after the current page.

MacintoshUser

This replaces Step 2.
2. Position the pointer over the left and right master page icons ⌐L R⌐, then click and hold the mouse button
3. Drag down to select Great Destinations on the pop-up list, then release the mouse button
Resume at Step 4.

QuickTip

To quickly insert pages at the end of a publication using specific master pages, select the name on the Master Pages pop-up list, then press [Ctrl][Alt][Shift] [G] (Macintosh users: [⌘] [option] [shift] [G]).

Quickly applying master pages to multiple pages

To quickly apply the same master page to multiple pages in a publication, click the Apply command on the Master Pages menu. The Apply Master dialog box opens. See Figure E-10. Click the Page range radio button, then specify the page numbers in the Page range text box. You can type in a range of pages that are not consecutive using commas to separate the page numbers. Use a hyphen to separate the first page and the last page in a series. You can also check the Set left and right pages separately option to apply different master pages to the left and right pages. When you have completed your selections, click Apply.

FIGURE E-8: **New master page applied**

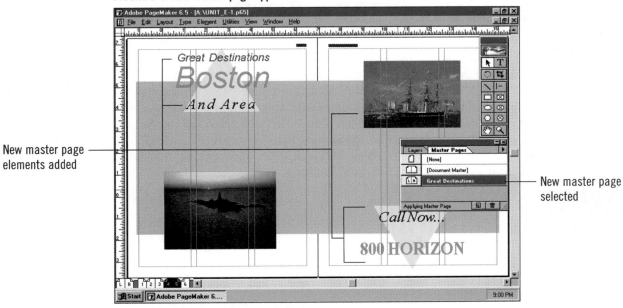

New master page
elements added

New master page
selected

FIGURE E-9: **Master Pages pop-up list**

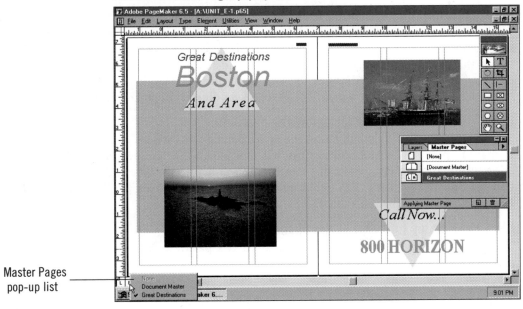

Master Pages
pop-up list

FIGURE E-10: **Apply Master dialog box**

Enter page
numbers to apply
selected master
pages here

Using Styles

You define styles using the Define Styles command on the Type menu. **Styles** are sets of formatting instructions that you name, save, and apply to paragraphs. Styles let you quickly apply formatting instructions to text with a simple click on the Styles palette. Using styles saves time and formats text consistently throughout a multiple-page publication. After you define styles, the style names appear on the Styles palette. You can also edit styles at any time. Once you edit a style, all occurrences of the style on the open publication are automatically updated with the new formatting instructions.   Joe has already created styles for the headlines and the body text of the newsletter. Now he needs to create a style for the cutlines. Cutlines are text describing photos or graphics in a newsletter.

Steps

1. Click the **page 8 page icon**

2. Click **Window** on the menu bar, then click **Show Styles**
   The Styles palette appears with the styles that Joe already created listed. Like the toolbox, the Styles palette is a floating palette. You can move it anywhere around the screen and resize it.

3. If necessary click the **Text tool** in the toolbox, then click the **Text tool pointer** anywhere within the headline about SkyCar Rentals on page 8
   The style Reg. Headline is highlighted in the Styles palette, as shown in Figure E-11. This style defines the text as Arial, 24 points, bold, left-justified, with autoleading. **Justified** means that the space between characters will be adjusted so that the text is aligned to a particular margin. Left-justified aligns the text along the left margin. **Leading** is the space between lines. **Autoleading** means that PageMaker adjusts the spacing automatically.

4. Click the anywhere in the story below the headline
   The style Body text is highlighted on the Styles palette. This style is defined as Times New Roman, 11 points, 12-point leading, justified, first indent at 0.167 inches, and autohyphenation. **Autohyphenation** means that PageMaker will hyphenate words automatically. Note that the Body text style for this publication has been changed from the PageMaker default Body text style described in Table E-1.

5. Click the **Pointer tool** in the toolbox
   The [No style] option is highlighted on the Styles palette because no text is presently selected.

PageMaker's default styles

When you open a new publication, a set of default styles already exists. See Table E-1 for a description of the default styles. The style description includes the style that it is based on, which style will be applied to the next paragraph, and all of the formatting instructions to be applied by the style. The "+" (plus sign) signifies each formatting instruction that you add to the style. You can modify these styles and their names to suit your publication or remove them from the styles list and start a new list.

FIGURE E-11: Styles palette

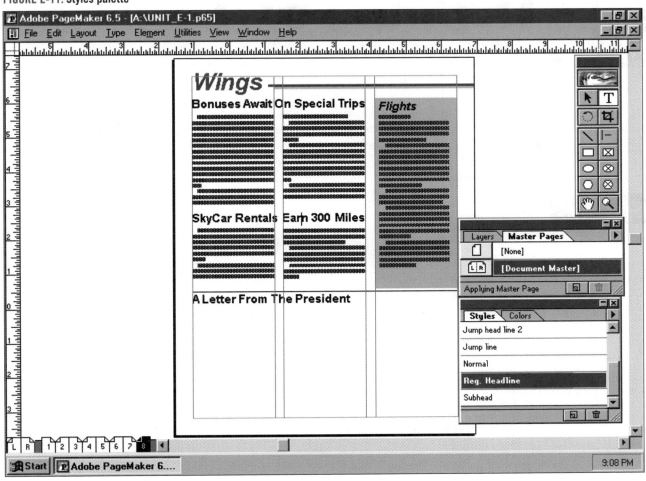

TABLE E-1: PageMaker's default styles

style name	description
[Selection]	No style + face: Times New Roman + size: 12 + leading: auto + flush left + hyphenation
Body text	next: Same style + face: Times New Roman + size: 12 + leading: auto + flush left + first indent: 0.333 + hyphenation
Caption	next: Same style + face: Times New Roman + italic + size: 10 + leading: auto + flush left
Hanging indent	next: Same Style + face: Times New Roman + size: 12 + leading: auto + flush left + left indent: 0.167 + first indent: -0.167+ hyphenation
Headline	next: Same Style + face: Times New Roman + bold + size: 30 + leading: auto + flush left + incl TOC
Subhead 1	Headline + next: Same style + size: 18
Subhead 2	Subhead 1 + next: Same style + size: 12

Defining Styles

The Based on list box lets you select a style to base your new style upon. For example, the Reg. Headline used for headlines on page 4 is based on the 60 point Headline style. When you select a style from the Based on list box, PageMaker copies the formatting attributes for the new style. You then can modify these attributes. The Next style list box lets you select the style that applies to the next paragraph in a story if that paragraph does not already have a style. The Cutline style is based on the "No style" selection from the Styles palette. PageMaker assigns the formatting characteristics from the Selection default. PageMaker also provides predesigned templates which already have the style defined for you. ✍ Joe continues defining the Cutline style by selecting character and paragraph formats.

Steps

1. **Click Type on the menu bar, then click Define Styles**
   The Define Styles dialog box opens. See Figure E-12. Because the insertion point was in the body text when you opened the Define Styles dialog box, [Selection] appears at the top of the Style list. Joe continues defining the Cutline style by selecting character and paragraph formats.

2. **Click New**
   The Style Options dialog box opens with the insertion point in the Name text box. Each of the four buttons on the bottom right side of the dialog box opens a corresponding dialog box. You set specifications in each of these dialog boxes for the style you are creating. Joe decides to name the new style "Cutline".

3. **Type Cutline in the Name text box**
   See Figure E-13.

4. **Click Char**
   The Character Specifications dialog box opens.

MacintoshUser

This replaces Step 5.
5. Click the Font list box, click Helvetica, then type 10 in the Size list box

5. **Click the Font list box, click Arial, then click the Size list box and type 10**

6. **Click the Italic check box in the Type style section, click OK, then click Para in the Style Options dialog box**
   The Paragraph Specifications dialog box opens. Because some of the cutlines are more than one line long, Joe wants the Cutline style to be justified.

7. **Click the Alignment list arrow, click Justify, then click OK**
   The Paragraph Specifications dialog box closes. The description of the style at the bottom of the dialog box reflects the changes you made. The Justify command forces text to align between both the right and left margins. See Figure E-14.

8. **Click OK**
   The Style Options dialog box closes. The new Cutline style name is highlighted in the Style list box in the Define Styles dialog box.

9. **Click OK to close the Define Styles dialog box**
   You return to the publication window. Cutline is now listed on the Styles palette.

FIGURE E-12: Define Styles dialog box

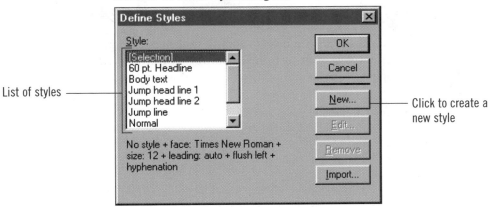

List of styles

Click to create a
new style

FIGURE E-13: Style Options dialog box

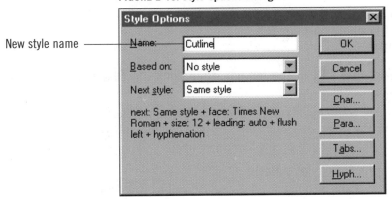

New style name

FIGURE E-14: Style Options dialog box after Cutline style is defined

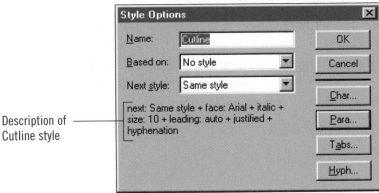

Description of
Cutline style

Using PageMaker's predesigned templates

To save you time and energy, you can choose one of PageMaker's predesigned templates as a starting point for creating your own publications. You can choose from three different newsletter templates. These newsletter templates have dummy text and graphics laid out on the page which you replace with your own text and graphic objects. The templates also include styles for headlines, body text, titles, and cutline captions. Other publications that you can create from predesigned templates include: mailing labels, brochures, calendars, labels or linings for cassettes, compact discs, or video tapes, envelopes, fax cover sheets, invoices, manuals, or purchase orders. To open a predesigned template, click Window on the menu bar, point to Plug-in Palettes, then click Show Scripts. Double-click the Template folder and choose a template by double-clicking. After you choose your desired template, rename the new untitled file to leave the original template unchanged. You could also create your own template by clicking the Template radio button in the Save publication as dialog box.

PageMaker 6.5

PageMaker 6.5

Applying Styles

Once you've defined a style, you need to apply it to the text. To apply a style, you select the characters or paragraph you want to format, and then click the style name in the Styles palette. Joe applies his new Cutline style to the cutlines in the newsletter.

Steps 1 2 3 4

1. Click the **pages 2 and 3 page icon** [2|3], then scroll down until you can see the cutline below the photo on page 2
   See Figure E-15.

2. Click the **Text tool** **T** in the toolbox, then click the **Text tool pointer** ⌶ anywhere within the cutline text block
   The style won't be applied if you use the Pointer tool to select the text block; the text must be selected or the insertion point must be in the paragraph you are applying the style to. Notice [No style] is selected on the Styles palette.

3. Click **Cutline** on the Styles palette
   The cutline text changes to match all the specifications you defined earlier. See Figure E-16. If text format does not change, click Undo on the Edit menu, make sure the insertion point is in the correct paragraph and repeat this step.

4. Click the **page 1 page icon** [1]
   Page 1 appears in the publication window.

5. Click ⌶ anywhere within the cutline under the photo, press **[Ctrl]** and right-click to change the view to Actual Size, then click **Cutline** on the Styles palette
   The text changes to conform to the Cutline style.

6. Click the **pages 2 and 3 page icon** [2|3]

MacintoshUser

This replaces Step 5.
5. Click ⌶ anywhere within the cutline under the photo, press [⌘] [1] to change the view to Actual Size, then click Cutline on the Styles palette

FIGURE E-15: Text before Cutline style is applied

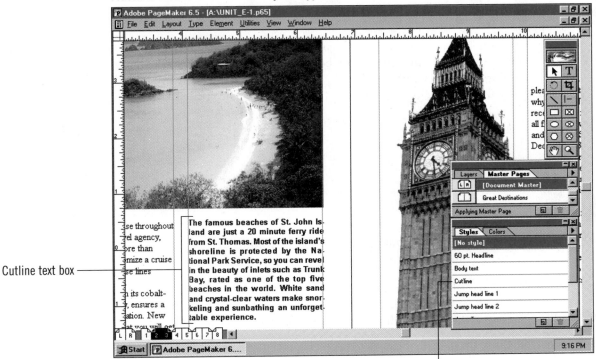

Cutline text box

New style on styles palette

FIGURE E-16: Text after Cutline style is applied

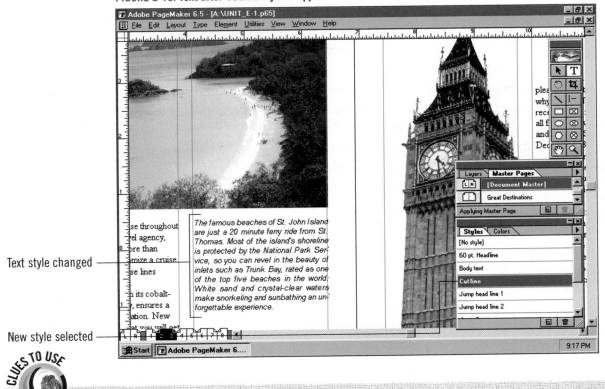

Text style changed

New style selected

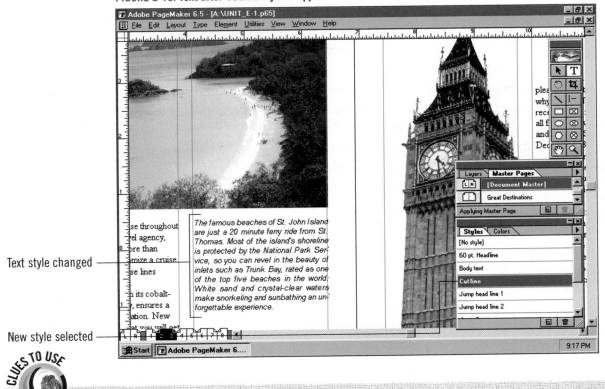

CLUES TO USE

Formatting text after applying a style

You can edit text after applying a style using commands available on the Type menu. Any changes you make to a selected range of text affect only that text. When you further format text with an applied style, a plus sign (+) appears behind the name of the style on the Styles palette. This tells you that additional formatting changes have been made to the style after it was originally applied to that text.

Editing Styles

PageMaker 6.5

After you define a style, you can change it at any time. When you edit a style definition in the Define Styles and Edit Style dialog boxes, PageMaker automatically updates all occurrences of the style in the open publication. You don't have to select every paragraph that is formatted with that style. ◢ Joe wants to edit the Cutline style he created.

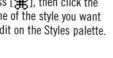

Steps

QuickTip

To open the Style Options dialog box quickly, press and hold [Ctrl] (Macintosh users: press [⌘]), then click the name of the style you want to edit on the Styles palette.

MacintoshUser

This replaces Steps 5 and 6.
5. Make sure the mouse pointer is on the page spread, then press [⌘] [0] (zero) and click the mouse button
6. Press [⌘], then click 60 pt. Headline on the Styles palette

Resume at Step 7.

1. Click **Type** on the menu bar, then click **Define Styles**
   The Define Styles dialog box opens.

2. Click **Cutline** in the Style list, then click **Edit**
   The Style Options dialog box opens. Joe wants to increase the font size of the cutline and change the color to blue to make the text stand out more.

3. Click **Char**
   The Character Specifications dialog box opens.

4. Click the **Size list box**, type **11**, click the **Color list arrow** and click **Blue**, then click **OK** three times
   The Define Styles dialog boxes close, and Cutline is highlighted on the Styles palette. See Figure E-17. The description of the style has automatically changed throughout the publication. The text style in the caption on page 2 now reflects the changes you made.

5. Make sure the mouse pointer is on the page spread, then press [Ctrl] and right-click
   The view changes to Fit in Window. Joe wants to adjust the 60 pt. Headline style so that the text flows across all columns to the far right margin on page 3.

6. Press [Ctrl], then click **60 pt. Headline** on the Styles palette
   The Style Options dialog box opens.

7. Click **Char**

8. Click the **Horiz scale list arrow**, click **130**, then click **OK** twice
   See Figure E-18. Notice that the headline now flows across the entire page spread.

9. Save the publication

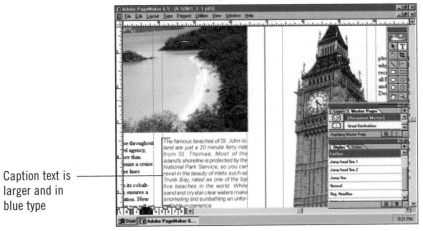

Caption text is larger and in blue type

FIGURE E-18: Headline style modified

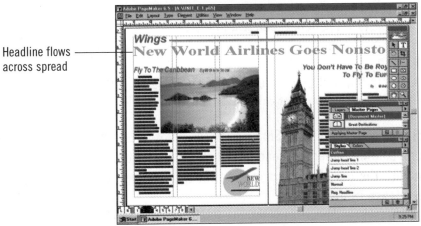

Headline flows across spread

FIGURE E-19: Import styles dialog box

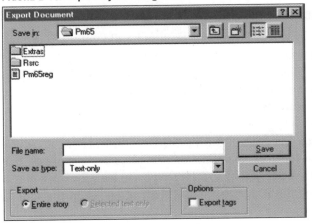

Importing styles from another PageMaker publication

Each publication has its own set of styles. You can add styles from another PageMaker publication to the publication you are working on. Open the Define Styles dialog box, then click Import. The Import styles dialog box opens, as shown in Figure E-19. Select the filename of the publication you want to copy the style from, then click OK twice to close the Import styles and Define Styles dialog boxes. PageMaker imports the styles. If the message "Import over existing files?" appears, note that PageMaker will write over styles with the same name when you copy styles from another publication.

Balancing Columns

PageMaker 6.5

Newsletter or magazine designs appear more organized when all columns are **balanced**, or the same length. PageMaker contains a feature called **Balance Columns** that lets you easily align the tops or bottoms of text blocks threaded in a story on a single page or facing pages. Balance Columns is a PageMaker Plug-in. When you use Balance Columns, PageMaker calculates the average length of each text block and resizes them to equal lengths across the number of columns they span. Balancing columns manually usually requires a few minutes worth of moving windowshade handles and text blocks. Using the Balance Columns feature, PageMaker performs the calculations within seconds. ✏️ Joe improves the layout of his newsletter by balancing the text blocks of a story he places on page 8.

Steps

Trouble?

If you receive messages about missing fonts and text specifications, click OK for each message; PageMaker will place the text without the formatting included in the file.

Trouble?

The plug-ins must be installed in order to use them. They install automatically with a standard installation of PageMaker. If you don't have this plug-in, ask your instructor or technical support person.

1. Click the **page 8 page icon** ⬚, click **View** on the menu bar, click **Actual Size**, then use the scroll bars to center the lower third of page 8 in the publication window
   Page 8 appears in the publication window.
2. Click **File** on the menu bar, click **Place**, click **UNIT_E-2** from your Student Disk, then click **Open**
3. Click 📋 in the first column under the headline "A Letter From The President"
   The letter flows into the first column. The windowshade ▽ indicates more text needs to be placed.
4. Click ▽, press and hold **[Shift]**, click the **semi-automatic text-flow icon** in the second column under the headline, click in the third column at a point even with the top of the text in the first two columns to place the rest of the story, then release **[Shift]**
   See Figure E-20. The story contains three text blocks of uneven lengths across three columns. Joe wants to balance these columns to make the president's letter appear as one "unit" on the page.
5. Click the **Pointer tool** 🖈 in the toolbox, click the **text block** in column 1, press and hold **[Shift]**, click the **text blocks** in columns 2 and 3, then release **[Shift]**
6. Click **Utilities** on the menu bar, point to **Plug-ins**, then click **Balance Columns**
   The Balance columns dialog box opens, as shown in Figure E-20. Joe wants to align the columns at the top and balance all three columns. This means PageMaker aligns the tops of the windowshade handles of the selected text blocks and balances the text blocks so their bottom lines are even across all three columns.
7. Click the **Balance Column Top icon** ⊞ in the Alignment section of the dialog box
   Now Joe needs to decide where to place the lines of text that cannot be divided equally among the selected text blocks. He decides to have the extra lines, if any, added to the left column.
8. Click the **Balance Column Left icon** ⊞ in the Add leftover lines section of the dialog box
9. Click **OK** to close the dialog box, then click anywhere outside the page to deselect the text blocks if necessary
   See Figure E-22. The columns are now balanced.

FIGURE E-20: Columns before balancing

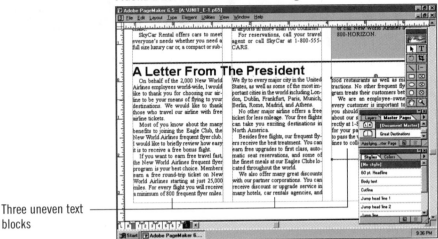

Three uneven text blocks

FIGURE E-21: Balance columns dialog box

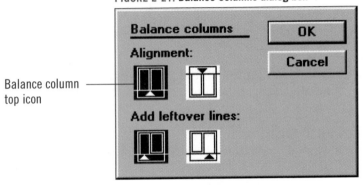

Balance column top icon

FIGURE E-22: Columns after balancing

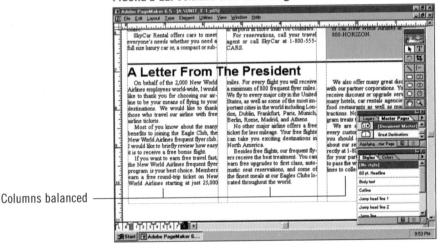

Columns balanced

PageMaker plug-ins

PageMaker plug-ins provide customized features to automate repetitive or complex publishing tasks. PageMaker 6.5 is shipped with 16 plug-ins for Windows and 18 plug-ins for the Macintosh. Third-party vendors also supply plug-ins to enhance PageMaker. All of the plug-ins are listed in the Plug-ins submenu on the Utilities menu. PageMaker separates plug-ins into three categories: text plug-ins, page layout plug-ins, and color and printing plug-ins. The text plug-ins can create drop caps and add bullets and numbering for lists. The plug-ins for page layout can balance columns and sort pages. The plug-ins for color and printing allow you to define printer styles, build booklets, and create keylines. You will learn about several of the plug-ins provided by PageMaker in this book.

Rearranging Pages

PageMaker 6.5

You can rearrange the order of pages easily by using the Sort Pages command. Each page is represented by a small **thumbnail**—which is a miniature rendering of the page—that you can drag to a new location using the mouse. Rearranging pages does not alter the text in a story.  Joe would like to reposition pages 2 and 3 after the Great Destinations page spread that is now on pages 4 and 5.

Steps

Trouble?

Depending on the resolution of your screen, you might not see icons as detailed as those shown in Figure E-23.

Trouble?

Screen redraw time after changes can be slow when the Show detailed thumbnails option is selected.

1. Click Layout on the menu bar, then click Sort Pages

The Sort Pages dialog box opens. See Figure E-23. You may have to wait a minute or two while PageMaker creates the thumbnail for each page. If necessary, click and drag the bottom right corner of the dialog box so all pages are visible. Joe selects pages 2 and 3 to be moved after the present pages 4 and 5.

2. Click and hold the left mouse button on the page 2 thumbnail

Clicking the page 2 thumbnail selects both pages 2 and 3. Now Joe drags the pages to the new location.

3. Drag the selection after page 5

A black bar appears after page 5 indicating where the selection will be inserted. See Figure E-24.

4. Release the mouse button

The pages automatically are rearranged. Notice that two page number icons appear beneath each thumbnail affected by the move. The original page number icon is dimmed and the new page number appears to its left. Joe is satisfied with the new arrangement and closes the Sort Pages dialog box.

5. Click OK

PageMaker performs the sort and the dialog box closes. This process may take several minutes, depending on the speed of your computer.

6. Save the publication

CLUES TO USE

Resizing the Sort Pages thumbnails

After you select the Sort Pages command, you can reduce or enlarge the sizes of the thumbnails for the current publication. You can enlarge, reduce, or display a more detailed view of selected thumbnails or of all of them at once. In the Sort Pages dialog box, click the Magnifying tool [🔍] or the Reduction tool [🔍] to increase or decrease, respectively, the size of all thumbnails. To see detailed icons for all thumbnails instead of generic placeholders, click Options. The Options dialog box opens, as shown in Figure E-25. Click the Show detailed thumbnails check box, then click OK. To view only selected thumbnails in more detail, select the thumbnails you want to view in the Sort Pages dialog box, then click Detail.

▶ PM E-22 **WORKING WITH MULTIPLE PAGES**

FIGURE E-23: Sort Pages dialog box

Pages of current
document appear
as thumbnails

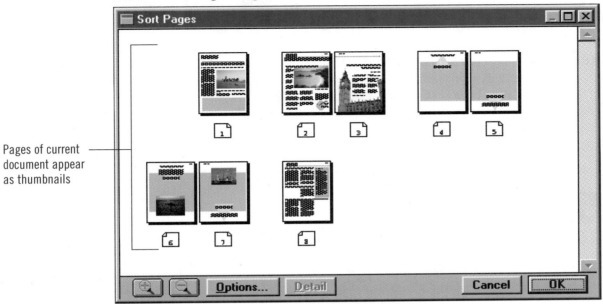

FIGURE E-24: Insertion point for rearranged pages

Pages selected
to move

Bar indicates
where pages will
be inserted

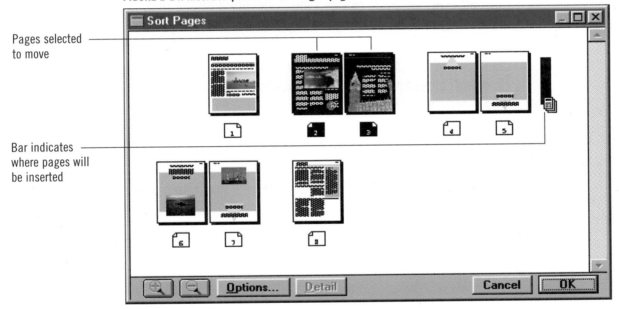

FIGURE E-25: Sort Pages Options dialog box

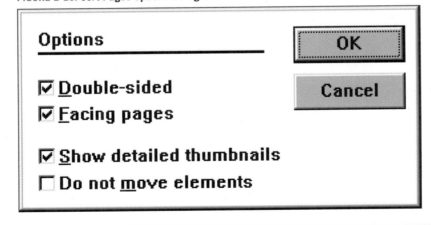

Masking Objects

The Mask command in PageMaker allows you to display a portion of an object through a drawn figure created using one of PageMaker's tools. To create the mask, simply place the drawn object, such as a circle, ellipse, box, or rectangle, on top of the object you wish to mask, click Element on the menu bar, and then click Mask. Joe would like to complete the Boston Great Destinations spread by placing a mask on top of the photo on page 6.

1. Click the **pages 6 and 7 page icon**

2. Click the **Ellipse tool** in the toolbox, move the **Ellipse tool pointer** + to the 6" mark on the horizontal ruler and the 6.25" mark on the vertical ruler

3. Press and hold **[Shift]**, click and hold the **left mouse button**, drag the **circle** till the right edge of the circle reaches the 2.75" mark on the horizontal ruler, release the mouse button, then release [Shift]
   See Figure E-26. Now Joe needs to select both the mask and the object to be masked.

4. Click the **Pointer tool** in the toolbox, click anywhere on the outside line of the circle object, press and hold **[Shift]**, then click the **photo** beneath the circle
   Both objects are now selected.

5. Click **Element** on the menu bar, then click **Mask**
   The photo is masked by the circle object. See Figure E-27. You can now move or resize the masked object.

6. Move the pointer in the middle of the masked object, then click once to select it

7. Drag the masked object down .25"
   The masked item moves down in page layout, giving you more room to place text.

8. Save and print the publication, then exit PageMaker

QuickTip

To undo masking, select the masking object or the masked object, click Element on the menu bar, then click Unmask.

FIGURE E-26: Drawn object over object to be masked

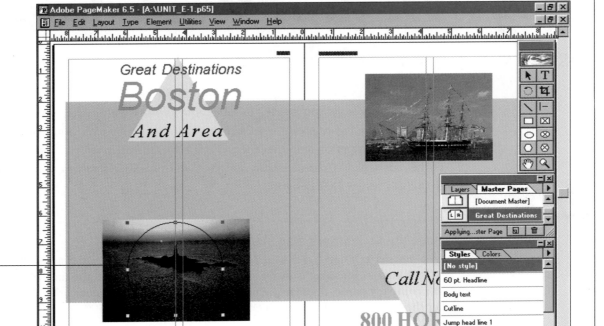

Circle object
created over
the photo

FIGURE E-27: Masked photo

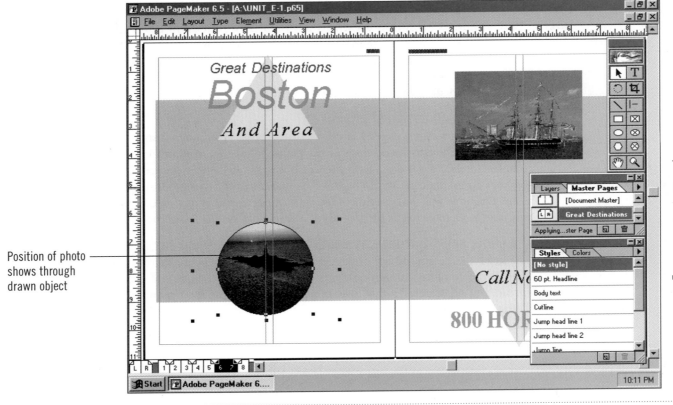

Position of photo
shows through
drawn object

Design Workshop: Newsletters

Although most of this newsletter was completed when you opened the publication, this unit provided the lessons you needed to learn how to work with master pages and defining styles. Before creating your newsletter, you must carefully plan your overall layout to capture your reader's attention and draw the reader's eye to the main story. Pages 1, 4, 5, and 8 of the redesigned Wings newsletter for New World Airlines' frequent flyers are shown in Figure E-28. Let's review Joe's design.

Details

Does the newsletter's flag stand out?
The newsletter's flag serves as a graphic that quickly identifies the newsletter for readers. The Wings logo in Joe's flag is easily identifiable. Joe also includes the date of the publication and the company name. Because the newsletter is published only quarterly, Joe decides not to clutter the flag with a volume number.

Does the newsletter's first page invite the reader to continue to read the newsletter?
The first page is design-intensive. A large photo and creative headline make the first glance at the newsletter a noticeable one. Readers are instantly drawn to the story after seeing the photo and reading the headline. They want to discover why they should "start spreadin' the news."

Are the pages too congested or too crowded?
Joe wanted to make page 1 visually appealing. To accomplish this, he sacrificed the space needed to place other stories or photos on this page. The result is a strong first page. Page 8 acts as a "catch-all" page for Joe, where he placed the continuation of the page 1 story, which is called a **jump**, and other smaller, less important stories. He separates the information presented on page 8 with lines and a box shaded gray.

Is the reader's attention drawn to the main story on each page?
Only page 8 contains more than one story, so the stories on the other pages compete only with graphics for attention. On page 8, the story about special trips is understood to be the most important because it is at the top of the page. Joe placed the jump from page 1 next to the top story and shaded it gray to separate it.

Was the spread designed effectively?
Joe used the spread on pages 4 and 5 to write a large headline that spans both pages. Although there are separate stories on each of the pages, Joe's large headline acts as a main title relating to both stories. Page 4 deals with the Caribbean while page 5 concerns Europe, but both pages together stress the New World Airlines' commitment for flying nonstop to most of its destinations. The large pop-out graphic of Big Ben on page 5 shows quality design. A photo reproduced this large on a page needs the benefit of a spread to "give it room" on the page.

If a photo splits the page, is it still considered a spread design?
The key to successful design of page spreads is the theme being shared among all items on the page. If the contents contain no overriding theme, then the pages should not be designed as a spread, but separately. In this case, nonstop service is the theme, and all materials relate to it. The space between the towers helps to provide a bold graphic on one of the pages and acts as a border for the Europe story.

FIGURE E-28: Pages 1, 4, 5, and 8 of the newsletter

Practice

► Concepts Review

Label each of the publication window elements shown in Figure E-29.

FIGURE E-29

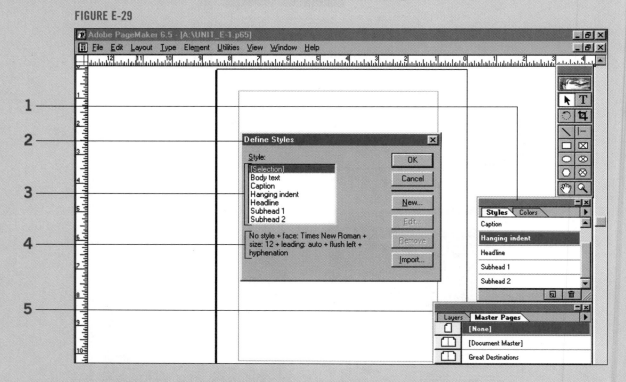

Match each of the terms with the statement that describes its function.

6. Flag
7. Cutline
8. Master page
9. Style
10. Plug-ins

a. Text attributes
b. Elements placed here appear on all pages
c. Place where the title, date, and other identification information appears in a newsletter
d. The description of photos or graphics
e. Customized features to automate repetitive or complex publishing tasks

11. Which of the following is not a guideline for creating a design?
    a. The overall layout should focus the reader's attention.
    b. Use many fonts for variety.
    c. Use space, shading, or lines to break up sections of text.
    d. Design headlines to draw the reader's attention.
12. Which of the following is true about master pages?
    a. They are a template for the entire publication.
    b. They allow you to add page numbers.
    c. They are the best page to place graphics.
    d. Both a and b

13. **Ruler and column guides set on master pages:**
    a. Appear on all pages
    b. Appear only on pages you define
    c. Appear only on the master pages
    d. Cannot be set on the master pages

14. **Cutlines are:**
    a. Preview areas in a newsletter
    b. Text describing photos or graphics
    c. Subheadlines
    d. Both a and b

▶ Skills Review

1. **Use the master pages to add page numbers.**
    a. Start PageMaker and open the file UNIT_E-3 from your Student Disk.
    b. Click the master page icon in the lower-left corner of the publication window.
    c. Press [Shift] while right-clicking within the publication page, then scroll to see the lower-left corner of the right master page *(Macintosh users: Press [⌘] [option] while clicking within the publication page, then scroll to see the lower-left corner of the right master page).*
    d. Click the Text tool **T** in the tool box, position the pointer ▶ below the bottom margin guide, then drag-place a text block across the bottom of the three columns of the right master page.
    e. Type "Holistic Health News" followed by three spaces, then type a hyphen (-) followed by one space.
    f. Press [Ctrl][Shift][3] to insert the page number symbol *(Macintosh users: Press [⌘] [option][P]).*
    g. Click Type on the menu bar, point to Alignment, then click Align Center.
    h. Click the Constrained-line tool |– in the toolbox, position the pointer ┼ at the intersection of the bottom margin and the left margin guide, and drag across the bottom margin guide to the right margin guide, then release the mouse button.
    i. With the line still selected, click Element on the menu bar, point to Stroke, then click 4 pt.
    j. Click the Pointer tool ▶ in the toolbox, click the line you just drew, press and hold [Shift], then click the text block for the line of text you typed.
    k. Click Edit on the menu bar, then click Copy.
    l. Click Edit, click Paste, then position the pointer on the line you just pasted, and drag it to the corresponding position on the left master page.
    m. Click the page 1 page icon. Notice that the page number appears at the bottom of the page.
    n. Click View on the menu bar, then click Display Master Items to turn off the display of the master page items on page 1.

2. **Create multiple master pages.**
    a. Click the pages 4 and 5 page icon.
    b. Click Window on the menu bar, then click Show Master Pages.
    c. Click the right arrow on the Master Pages palette, then click Save Page as.
    d. Type "Exercise" in the text box, then click Save.
    e. Click the Jogging text box, then press [Delete].
    f. Position the pointer below the bottom margin guide on the left master page, then click the page number text box, press and hold [Shift], click the line object, then press [Delete].
    g. Repeat Step f to delete the page number text and line object on the right master page.

   h. Click pages 4 and 5 page icon.

   i. Click Edit and click Select All, press and hold [Shift] and click Jogging to deselect it, then press [Delete]. All that remains on the layout is the Jogging text box, the page number text boxes, and the line objects.

3. Apply and edit master pages.

   a. Click Exercise in the Master Pages palette.

   b. Right-click the master page icon.

   c. Click Exercise on the Master Pages pop-up list.

   d. Click Layout on the menu bar, then click Column Guides.

   e. Type "2" in the Number of columns text box, then click OK.

   f. Click the pages 2 and 3 page icon.

   g. Click Layout, then click Insert Pages.

   h. Make sure 2 is selected in the Insert Page(s) text box and "after" is selected in the Current Page list box.

   i. Click the Master page list arrow, click Exercise, then click Insert.

   j. Click the pages 6 and 7 page icon, then click the Jogging text box.

   k. Click Edit on the menu bar, then click Copy.

   l. Click the pages 4 and 5 page icon, then press [Ctrl][V].

   m. Click the Text tool **T** in the toolbox, highlight the word "Jogging", then type "Cycling".

4. Define styles.

   a. Click the Pointer tool **▶** in the toolbox, click Type on the menu bar, then click Define Styles.

   b. In the Define Styles dialog box, click New.

   c. In the Name text box, type "Headline".

   d. If necessary, click the Based on list box, then click No style.

   e. If necessary, click the Next style list box, click Same style then click Char.

   f. Click the Font list arrow, then click Arial. Click the Size list box, then type "24".

   g. Click the Bold check box in the Type style section.

   h. Click OK three times to close the dialog boxes.

5. Apply the Headline style to the newsletter headlines.

   a. Click Window on the menu bar, then click Show Styles to display the Styles palette.

   b. Click the pages 2 and 3 page icon.

   c. Click the Text tool **T** in the toolbox, then click the pointer in the headline that reads "Plants Process..." at the top of page 2.

   d. Click Headline in the Styles palette.

   e. Click the pointer in the headline that reads "Organically Grown..." at the bottom of page 2.

   f. Click Headline in the Styles palette.

   g. If necessary, scroll to make all of page 3 visible in the publication page.

   h. Repeat Steps e and f to apply the Headline style to the headline that reads "Going Mainstream..." at the bottom of page 3.

6. Edit a style.

   a. Click Type on the menu bar, then click Define Styles.

   b. Click Body text in the Style list, click Edit then click Para.

   c. Click the Alignment list arrow, then click Justify.

   d. Click OK twice to return to the Define Styles dialog box.

   e. Click Headline in the Style list, click Edit, then click Char.

   f. Click the Size list box, then type "26". Click OK three times to close the dialog boxes.

7. Balance columns.

   a. If necessary, scroll to make all of page 2 visible in the publication page.

b. Click the Pointer tool ▶ in the toolbox, then select the text blocks under the headline "Organically Grown Controversy" by pressing and holding [Shift] while clicking the text blocks.

c. Click Utilities on the menu bar, point to Plug-ins, then click Balance Columns.

d. If necessary, click the Balance Column Top icon in the Alignment section.

e. If necessary, click the Balance Column Left icon in the Add leftover lines section.

f. Click OK to close the dialog box.

g. Click File on the menu bar, click Place, click the file CHALL1 on your Student Disk, then click Open.

h. Click the text placement icon in the first column of page 3, below the headline "Going Mainstream..." then place the remaining text for this story in the second and third columns.

i. Repeat Steps b through f to balance the placed text, then apply body text style and rebalance the columns.

8. Rearrange pages.

a. Click Layout on the menu bar, then click Sort Pages.

b. If the pages appear as gray boxes, click Options, click the Show detailed thumbnails check box, then click OK.

c. Click the pages 2 and 3 thumbnails, drag the selection after pages 4 and 5, release the mouse button.

d. Click OK then click the pages 4 and 5 page icon to confirm the changes have taken place.

9. Mask an object.

a. Click the pages 8 and 9 page icon.

b. Click the Ellipse tool ⬭ in the toolbox.

c. Press and hold [Shift] while you draw a circle inside the color photo of New York on page 9.

d. Click the Pointer tool ▶ in the toolbox.

e. Click the photo to select it, then press and hold [Shift] while you click the circle you drew.

f. Click Element on the menu bar, then click Mask. Save and print your publication.

▶ Independent Challenges

1. As the marketing agent for BioLabs, Inc, you create a newsletter for the health research company. Your budget is small, but the expectation is great. You decide the newsletter will be the front and back of a letter-size page.

1. Create a new double-sided publication with two letter-size pages called Biolabs newsletter.

2. Add column guides to the master pages that divide each page into three columns.

3. Type the name of the newsletter on page 1. Use the Line and Shape tools to add interest to the flag. Use shading and text formatting to make the flag interesting. Add a line for the date and company name.

4. Place four stories into the newsletter: CHALL1, CHALL2, CHALL3, and CHALL4 (all located on your Student Disk).

5. Add lines, boxes, and shading as necessary to separate stories in the page layout.

6. Create styles for the newsletter. Create a style for headlines, body text, cutlines, and subheadlines.

7. Make sure the columns are evenly balanced to give the newsletter a professional appearance.

8. Evaluate the final design. Does the use of graphics enhance the overall layout of the newsletter? Save and print the publication.

2. You have been hired by the program manager at local radio station to create a newsletter to be sent to all WKMRN Club Members.

1. Create a double-sided publication with two letter-size pages, and save it as WKMRN newsletter.

2. Create a master page for the cover page and a different master page layout for rest of the pages of the newsletter. Add page numbers and columns to the master pages.

3. Create an interesting flag on page one. Hide all master page items on this page.

4. Create styles for headlines and body text. Then add headlines and place stories from your Student Disk.

5. Make sure all columns are evenly balanced using the balance columns addition, then save and print your publication.

3. You work in the marketing department of a large travel agency. Your boss has asked you to come up with a creative publication that will attract your customers' attention and keep them up to date on the agency's most recent developments.

1. Use the World Wide Web to search for information on a travel agency.
2. Create a sketch of your four-page newsletter, using the guidelines that you learned in this unit.

3. Create your newsletter in PageMaker using your sketch. Create and apply master pages. Because you do not want all pages of the publication to be the same, you will need to create more than one master page. You can use the dummy text file TEXTHLD and the dummy graphic file PLACEHLD from your Student Disk.

4. Be sure to include a flag, headlines, subheadlines and cutlines in your newsletter. Define and apply styles to the different elements in your publication. Edit the styles as you wish.

5. Balance all of the columns, add or delete pages, and rearrange pages to make your newsletter more attractive.

6. Apply a mask to at least one of the objects in your newsletter.

7. Critique your final newsletter to make sure that it follows the design guidelines you learned in this unit.

8. Save your newsletter as My newsletter. Print the newsletter.

► Visual Workshop

Joe Monikamp, director of Public Relations at Medical Technology Institute, has hired you to create the body of the quarterly newsletter called *Health Link,* as shown in Figure E-30. Open the file UNIT_E-4 from your Student Disk. On the master pages, place the page number and the name of the newsletter on the left master page. On the right master page include the page number with the words "Spring Issue" and the year.

FIGURE E-30

PageMaker 6.5

Working
with Graphics

Objectives

► **Plan an advertisement**
► **Change line weights and styles**
► **Crop a graphic**
► **Rotate an object**
► **Stack objects**
► **Create a shadow box**
► **Wrap text around a graphic**
► **Add a custom text wrap**
► **Create a polygon**
► **Use frames**
► **Design Workshop: Advertisements**

Working with graphics in PageMaker is much like working with text. You can resize, manipulate, and rotate graphics in ways similar to text blocks. In this unit you will learn to crop and rotate graphics, manipulate the stacking order of objects, add text that wraps around graphics, and draw rectangles. Joe Martin needs to create a quarter-page advertisement for the local newspaper. He began placing graphics on the page, but he needs to finish the design.

Planning an Advertisement

Most advertisements try to initiate an immediate response from the reader. Some ads help build awareness of a specific product or company. It is important that you consider the ultimate purpose or goal of your advertisement when planning and creating it. New World Airlines' advertising director, Carlos Bruno, wants to create an ad promoting nonstop flights from St. Louis to Toronto to be placed in the business section of a local St. Louis newspaper. Working with Carlos, Joe starts to plan the quarter-page ad, as shown in Figure F-1. Joe decides to use photos from a stock photography catalog as the ad's foundation and to write the small amount of text in the ad himself. The advertisement will be black and white because the business section requires that all ads be black and white. The following guidelines will help Joe produce an effective ad:

Build the ad around strong visual elements

Large headlines or graphics should attract the readers' attention. Once caught, their attention focuses to other aspects of the ad, such as the text or a way to respond. Joe sets the page size according to the newspaper's specifications for a quarter-page ad. The ad is 6.25" wide and 10.5" tall. Joe uses photos of monuments in St. Louis and Toronto rather than text in his ad. He thinks the design will have more impact by using photos. The headline type is also large and bold.

Organize the ad's layout

Because print advertising is expensive, there is a tendency to put as much information as possible into an advertisement to justify the cost. However, too much information or a poor design confuses the reader. A good ad is designed to be read top to bottom with a simple message at the top and specific details at the bottom. Joe's design literally moves the reader down the ad with his use of arrows and a continuing headline.

Visually separate the ad from other items on the page where it will appear

With all the information included in newspapers and magazines, it is important to make your ad stand out on the page. Increasing the thickness of the border is one solution. Another solution is to use white space around the ad to separate it from the other page items. Joe uses white space to set off his ad.

Encourage a quick response

Similar to a flyer, an ad's main goal is to elicit a response from the reader. The reader should be given a clear course of action, such as an address or phone number for more information. For some advertisements, this would include the price of the product or service. Because the ad is for the airline and not a specific travel agency, Joe's design calls for placing the New World Airlines logo and 800 number in the ad.

PageMaker 6.5

Changing Line Weights and Styles

When you draw lines and shapes, you can change the line weight and the line style. **Line weight** is the thickness of the line, and **line style** is the line's design, such as single, double, dashed, or reverse line. Lines are measured in **points**; 72 points equal one inch, so a 72-point line would be 1" thick. The default line style is a 1-point single line. Joe has worked on his ad. He has already placed the graphics and the text. Now he wants to add a double-line box around his ad for a border and a thick line under one of the words.

Steps

1. **Start PageMaker and open the file UNIT_F-1 from your Student Disk**
   The ad Joe started working on appears in the publication window. First, Joe draws a box around the entire ad.

2. **Click the Rectangle tool** 🔲 **in the toolbox, position + over the intersection of the top and left page margins, then drag to the lower-right corner of the ad**
   The rectangle appears with handles indicating it is selected.

3. **Click Element on the menu bar, point to Stroke, then click the 4pt single line in the list**

MacintoshUser

This replaces Steps 4.

4. Position + near the left center handle of the box, then press [⌘][1] to change the view

4. **Position + near the left center handle of the box, then press [Ctrl] and right-click to change the view**
   See Figure F-2. The line has changed from a 1-point line to a 4-point line.
   Next, Joe wants to add a line under the word "here" in the headline "Is here."

5. **Use the scroll bars to position the headline Is here in the publication window**

6. **Click the Constrained-line tool** |‑ **in the toolbox, then position + under the word here aligning the vertical bar on the pointer with the bottom left serif in the letter "h"**
   Make sure you leave a small amount of white space between the word and the pointer.

QuickTip

To create a white line on a dark background shade or color, select the line, click Element on the menu bar, point to Stroke, then click Reverse.

7. **Drag + from the "h" to the right side of the period**
   A 1-point line appears under the word. Joe wants to make this line thicker because the type is so big.

8. **With the line still selected, click Element on the menu bar, then point to Stroke**
   Notice the check mark next to 1pt. If a different line weight is selected on your screen, someone changed the default line weight; just continue with the next step.

9. **Click the 4pt single line**
   See Figure F-3. The line changes to a 4-point line.

DesignTip

Extra white space will help an ad stand out more than overuse of shading or lines.

10. **Click File on the menu bar, then click Save**

FIGURE F-2: 4-point single line box

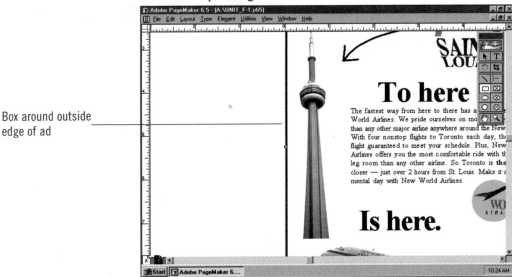

Box around outside edge of ad

FIGURE F-3: 4-point single line added

Thicker line added to balance heavy text

Creating custom line weights

PageMaker lets you create custom line weights from 0 to 800 points. To create a custom line weight, select Custom on the Stroke submenu to open the Custom Stroke dialog box shown in Figure F-4. You can choose a style from the Stroke style list box, then enter a point size in the Stroke weight text box. Make sure the Transparent background check box is checked if you want to see through a pattern-style line with blank spaces, such as the space between the two lines on a double line.

FIGURE F-4: Custom Stroke dialog box

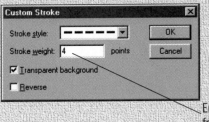

Enter point size from 0 to 800

Cropping a Graphic

PageMaker's Cropping tool lets you remove a portion of a graphic you don't want. Cropping changes how the graphic looks, but it does not permanently delete any portion of the graphic. The only photo of St. Louis in the stock photography catalog included the words "Saint Louis" beneath the photo. Using PageMaker's cropping tool, Joe crops the photo so the words are no longer visible.

1. Scroll the publication window so that the arch graphic is centered in it

2. Click the **Cropping tool** ▣ in the toolbox
   The pointer changes to ↯ .

3. Click the **arch graphic** to select it
   The graphic's selection handles appear.

4. Position ↯ over the bottom middle handle, then press and hold the **left mouse button**
   The pointer changes to ↕ See Figure F-5.

DesignTip

If you resize a graphic after cropping it, it will remain cropped.

5. Drag ↕ up to the white space just above the words "Saint Louis," then release the mouse button
   Portions of the graphic disappear as you move the pointer up. Once a graphic is cropped, you can move it around inside its boundaries.

6. Position ↯ on top of the arch graphic, then press and hold the **left mouse button**
   A box appears around the graphic and the pointer changes to ✋.

7. Move ✋ up, but do not release the mouse button
   The words you cropped reappear at the bottom of the graphic, but now the top of the arch is cropped off. See Figure F-6. The extent to which the graphic scrolls around inside the boundaries is limited to how much you cropped the graphic.

DesignTip

Cropped graphics take longer to print than graphics that aren't cropped.

8. Move ✋ down until the graphic has scrolled down as far as it will go, then release the mouse button
   The graphic should now look like Figure F-7.

9. Click **File** on the menu bar, then click **Save**

FIGURE F-5: Cropping a graphic

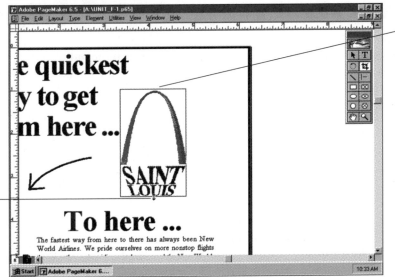

Graphic boundaries

Use this pointer to crop text

FIGURE F-6: Moving a graphic inside its boundaries

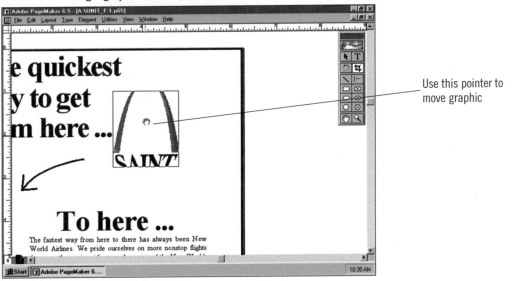

Use this pointer to move graphic

FIGURE F-7: Graphic after cropping

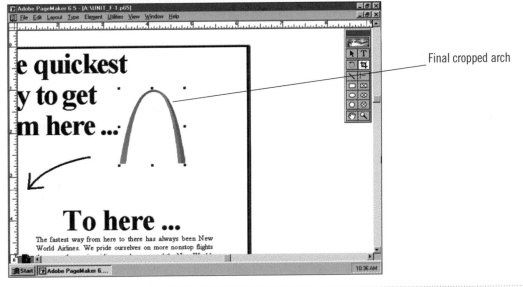

Final cropped arch

Rotating an Object

The Rotating tool in the toolbox lets you rotate graphics by 360 degrees at increments of .01 degree. Joe created the arrow in a drawing application and placed it in the ad. Now he wants to add another arrow to the ad but one that points in the opposite direction. The arrow will extend from the "Is here" headline to the logo on the tail of the plane. He decides to copy the existing arrow and rotate it.

Steps

1. **Click the Pointer tool in the toolbox**
   First Joe will copy the graphic. You copy graphics the same way you copy text.

2. **Click the arrow graphic to select it, click Edit on the menu bar, then click Copy**
   PageMaker copies the graphic to the Clipboard.

3. **Click Edit, then click Paste**
   PageMaker pastes the arrow on top of the original arrow, offset to the bottom right. The pasted arrow is selected. This graphic is considered line art. **Line art** consists of graphics drawn as outlines of objects. Black and white cartoons are examples of line art.

4. **Drag the selected arrow to the right of the "Is here" text block**
   PageMaker scrolls the page view as you drag the element down the page. See Figure F-8. The precise location of the graphic isn't crucial because you can move it into position later.

5. **Position ▸ over the top right corner handle, press and hold [Shift], drag the pointer to the left to reduce the graphic to about 50% of the original size, then release [Shift]**
   See Figure F-9. The space you need to fill with this arrow is much smaller than the corresponding space at the top of the ad.

6. **Click the Rotating tool in the toolbox**
   The pointer changes to ✳.

DesignTip

To rotate an object in exact 45-degree increments, press [Shift] while you are rotating the object.

7. **Position ✳ at the center of the selected arrow graphic, then click and drag the pointer outward from the center at approximately the 4 o'clock position and drag around the center point counter-clockwise to the 10 o'clock position, then release the mouse button**
   See Figure F-10. As you dragged, a rotation lever followed the pointer from the starting point to the ending position. You rotate lines, text blocks, and other objects the same way you rotated the graphic.

Trouble?

Rotated objects, especially TIFF images, can slow the overall printing time for a publication.

8. **Click the Pointer tool in the toolbox, then, if necessary, move the rotated graphic so the arrow points from the "Is here" text block to the New World Airlines logo on the airplane's tail**
   You might need to reduce the graphic further so the tips of the arrow don't cover parts of the text block or the airplane's tail. Joe uses this arrow to create a visual link between the words of the headline and the logo.

9. **Save the publication**

FIGURE F-8: Moving a duplicated graphic into position

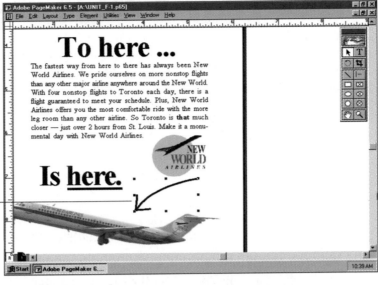

Duplicated arrow

FIGURE F-9: Resized graphic

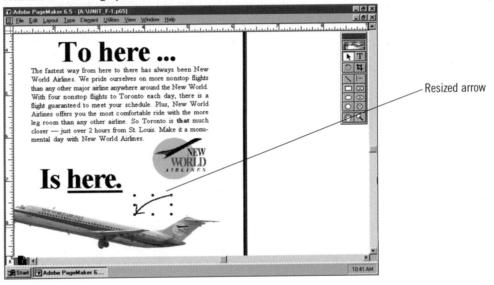

Resized arrow

FIGURE F-10: Rotated graphic

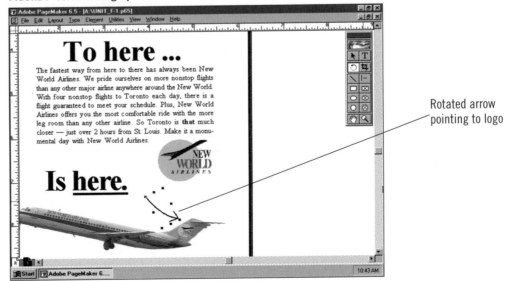

Rotated arrow
pointing to logo

Stacking Objects

PageMaker 6.5

Graphics in a publication are not always imported from one file. They can consist of several objects imported from other applications or created in PageMaker and stacked on top of each other. When objects are **stacked**, they overlap each other as shown in Figure F-11. ◢▬▬ Joe wants to increase the size of the arch. He will resize it, then check to make sure that the larger object does not cover anything else in the ad.

Steps 1234

1. Scroll to the top of the page until the arch is centered in the window

2. Click the **arch graphic** to select it, move the pointer over the top right handle, press and hold **[Shift]**, then click and drag the resizing pointer ↗ toward the upper-right corner of the ad's border without touching the border itself

   See Figure F-12. The top left portion of the arch graphic now covers the end of the text block to the left, so the "t" in the word "quickest" seems to have disappeared. PageMaker imports photos with a solid white background. Joe needs to fix this by sending the arch to the back of the layout.

3. Click **Element** on the menu bar, point to **Arrange**, then click **Send to Back**

   All of the text block's characters appear because the arch block now lies behind the text block.

4. Use the scroll bars to center the bottom third of the ad in the publication window

5. Save the publication

FIGURE F-11: **Two objects stacked to create a shadow box**

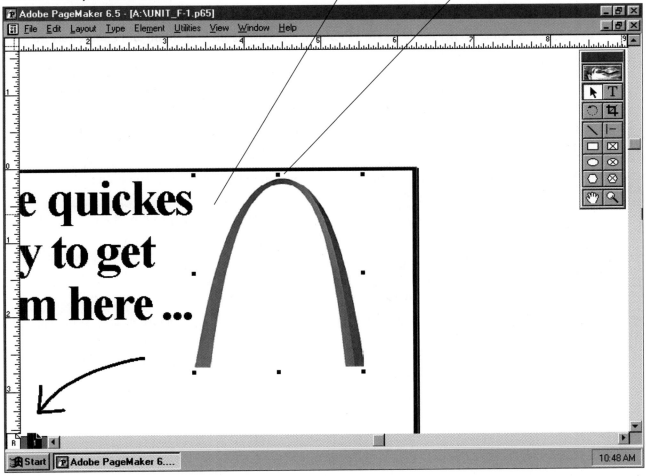

box 1

box 2

Box 1 (top stack)

Box 2 (bottom stack)

The "t" is stacked
under graphic

Top of arch does
not touch the page
border

FIGURE F-12: **Graphic covers text**

Adobe PageMaker 6.5 - [A:\UNIT_F-1.p65]

File   Edit   Layout   Type   Element   Utilities   View   Window   Help

e quickes
y to get
m here ...

Start   Adobe PageMaker 6....   10:48 AM

Graphic backgrounds

The area surrounding an imported graphic is either transparent or filled with solid white. PageMaker imports line art images with transparent backgrounds; it imports **grayscale images**, like the arch, needle, or the jet in this publication, with shades of gray and a white background. In grayscale TIFF images, any space not occupied by shades of gray contains white.

PageMaker 6.5

Creating a Shadow Box

You can use PageMaker's stacking capabilities to create shadow boxes. A **shadow box** is a box with a drop shadow on two sides. To create a shadow box, draw a box, copy the box, fill the copied box with black, and finally send it to the back of the stacking order. ✐━━ Joe wants to create a shadow box to make the point of response stand out on the bottom of the advertisement.

Steps

QuickTip

Whenever you move an object, PageMaker retains the stacking order of the moved object.

1. Click the **box** that surrounds the phone number to select it, click **Edit** on the menu bar, then click **Copy**

2. Click **Edit**, click **Paste**, then click **Element** on the menu bar, point to **Fill**, then click **Solid**
   PageMaker pastes a copy of the box on top of the phone number and box and offsets it to the lower right. Changing the Fill to Solid shades the box black. Next, Joe needs to change the stacking order to make this look like a shadow box.

3. Click **Element** on the menu bar, point to **Arrange**, then click **Send to Back**
   See Figure F-13. PageMaker sends the black box behind the phone number text block and the original box. Now you can't see the phone number because the original box is transparent so the black box shows through between the text characters. You need to fill the original box with solid white, or what PageMaker calls "Paper."

4. Click the **box** you originally copied, click **Element**, point to **Fill**, then click **Paper**
   PageMaker fills the box with white, and the box now covers the phone number.

5. Click **Element**, point to **Arrange**, then click **Send to Back**
   PageMaker sends the white box to the back of the stacking order. Joe needs to use the Send to Back command again on the black box to set the stacking order correctly.

6. Click the **box** filled with solid black, click **Element**, point to **Arrange**, then click **Send to Back**
   See Figure F-14. The black box is now behind both the white box and the phone number. The white box sits between the phone number and the gray box.

7. Save the publication

FIGURE F-13: Black box sent to back

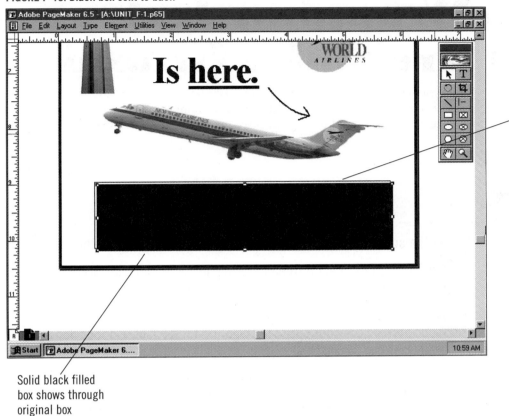

Original box is
transparent

Solid black filled
box shows through
original box

FIGURE F-14: Shadow box with proper stacking order

Solid black box
sent to back

Original box now
filled with solid white

Wrapping Text Around a Graphic

When you wrap text around a graphic, you make text flow around the graphic object at a specific distance. Wrapping text offers a unique way of blending text and graphics in a layout. Joe wants text to wrap around the logo he places on top of the descriptive text.

Steps

1. Use the scroll bars to center the New World Airlines logo in the publication window

2. Click the **logo** to select it, then drag the logo and place it toward the right side of the ad on top of the body text

3. Click **Element** on the menu bar, then click **Text Wrap**
   The Text Wrap dialog box opens. See Figure F-15. See Table F-1 for a description of the icons in the Text Wrap dialog box.

4. Click the **Rectangular Wrap option icon** to turn on text wrapping
   The Wrap-all-sides Text flow icon is automatically selected. This means that PageMaker will flow the text around all four sides of the graphic. PageMaker sets the **standoff**, or the amount of space between the graphic being wrapped and the text, to .167".

5. Click **OK**
   Your screen should look similar to Figure F-16. You might need to move the logo slightly to better match the figure. The standoff is indicated by the nonprinting dotted-line barrier around the logo. You can move any of the standoff lines by dragging them when the graphic is selected.

6. Save the publication

Trouble?

You cannot wrap text around a text block, only around graphic objects.

FIGURE F-15: Text Wrap dialog box

Click to wrap text around default borders

Click to wrap text on all four sides of graphic

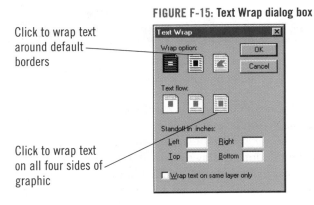

FIGURE F-16: Wrapped graphic

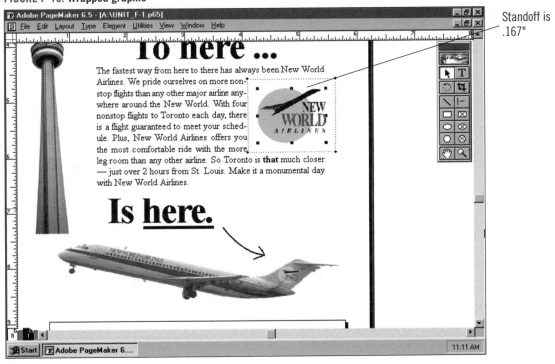

Standoff is .167"

TABLE F-1: Text Wrap dialog box icons

button	name	description
	No Boundary Wrap option	Text flows on top of the graphic object
	Rectangular Wrap option	Text flows around a graphic object in a rectangular fashion, and you can control the amount of white space between the graphic and the text
	Custom Wrap option	Text flows around an irregularly shaped graphic; you will learn about this option in the next lesson
	Column-break Text flow	Text wraps around to the top of the graphic, then continues to flow in the next column or page
	Jump-over Text flow	Text wraps to the top of the graphic, then continues below the graphic's bottom boundary
	Wrap-all-sides Text flow	Text wraps the graphic on all four sides

PageMaker 6.5

Adding a Custom Text Wrap

When you place a graphic in a publication, the graphic has an invisible rectangular border. If you want to custom-wrap text around the shape of a graphic, you can change the standoff to match the shape of the graphic. To custom-wrap the graphic, you first need to apply the Rectangular Wrap option and then change the standoff by dragging the standoff lines using definition points. **Definition points** define the shape of the standoff. You add definition points to the standoff line by clicking the standoff. By default, four definition points are placed at the corners of a rectangular text wrap. Joe wants to customize the text wrap so it follows the curve of the New World Airlines logo. By curving the text wrap, Joe fits the ad copy as tightly around the logo as possible, making the text and the logo act as one graphic unit.

Steps

1. With the logo still selected, click on the **left side standoff line** near the upper-left corner, as shown in Figure F-17
   This adds a definition point to the standoff line.

2. Position the pointer over the point you just added, then press and hold the **left mouse button**
   The pointer changes to $+$.

3. Drag the pointer to a location closer to the curved surface of the logo, as shown in Figure F-18
   Keep some white space between the logo and the text so they don't run together.

DesignTip

To prevent text from being redrawn each time you adjust a text wrap boundary, press and hold [spacebar] as you create and move definition points.

4. Add about eight more definition points to the standoff line around the left, bottom, and top curved portions of the graphic, and then drag each point to the logo after you add it
   You should not allow more than ¼" of space between the text and logo. Your screen should look similar to Figure F-19—it's okay to have more definition points. With each point you add and move into position, PageMaker rewraps the text block around the graphic.

5. Click **View** on the menu bar, then click **Fit in Window**

6. Click anywhere on the pasteboard to deselect the graphic, then evaluate the text wrap
   Make any adjustments necessary to the size of the logo or the position of the text block to achieve the proper amount of space between the logo and the text.

Trouble?

A custom text wrap's definition points will be deleted if you later convert the text wrap to its default rectangular standoff.

7. Save your publication

FIGURE F-17: Adding a definition point to a standoff line

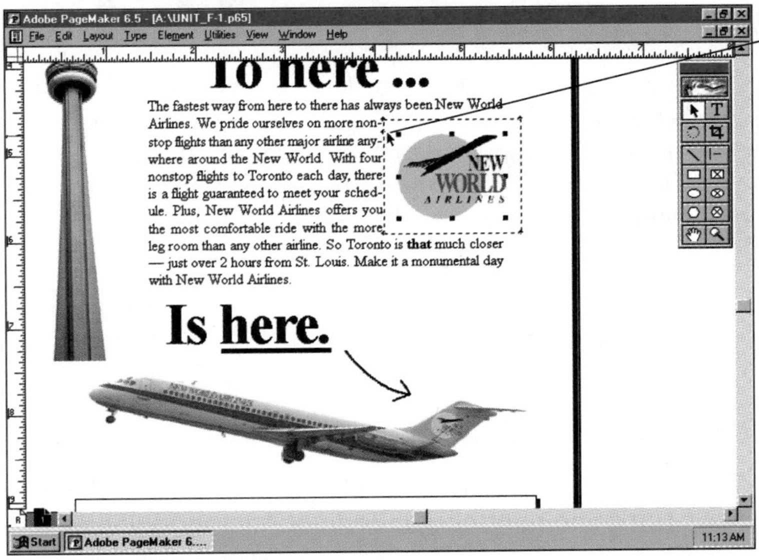

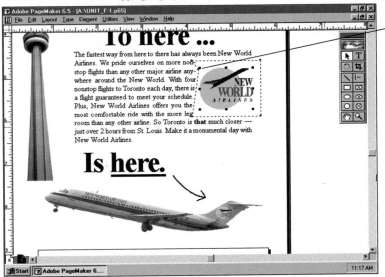

Added definition point

FIGURE F-18: Custom-wrapping a graphic

Dragged definition point

FIGURE F-19: Custom text wrap applied

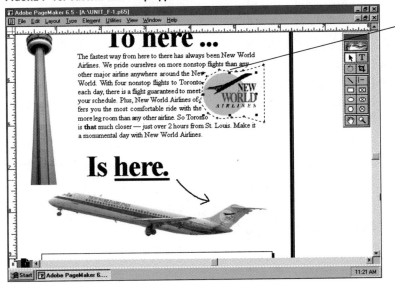

Standoff is curved around circle

Creating a Polygon

PageMaker allows you to create multisided objects or stars using the Polygon tool. You specify the number of sides of the polygon, from 3 to 100 sides. Joe wants to create a star-shaped polygon with reverse text that will resemble a stamp. He wants to place it next to the 800 number. The stamp will remind potential customers to ask about New World Airlines' frequent flyer program, called the Eagle Club.

Steps

MacintoshUser

This replaces Step 1.

1. Move ▶ over the left edge of the shadow box containing the phone number, then press [⌘][1] to change the view to Actual Size

1. Move ▶ over the left edge of the shadow box containing the phone number, then press [Ctrl] and right-click to change the view to Actual Size

2. Click the **Polygon tool** in the toolbox, move + to 8½" on the vertical ruler and slightly to the right of zero on the horizontal ruler, press and hold [Shift], then drag down and to the right until the side of the polygon almost touches the letter "C" in Call, then release the mouse button and [Shift]
   See Figure F-20. A five-sided polygon appears on the page. Your polygon might have more than five sides based on the default polygon setting for number of sides. Joe now needs to modify the shape of the polygon to resemble a star.

3. Click **Element** on the menu bar, then click **Polygon Settings**
   See Figure F-21. The Polygon Settings dialog box opens. First Joe needs to set the number of sides.

4. Type **25** in the Number of sides text box, then press [Tab] twice
   After you press [Tab], PageMaker displays the effect of your choice of sides in the Preview box. Next Joe needs to determine the Star inset value to create the stamp effect.

MacintoshUser

This replaces Step 4.

4. Type 25 in the Number of Sides text box, then press [Tab] once

5. Type **20** in the Star inset text box, press [Tab], then click **OK**
   Twenty percent (20%) represents a small star inset. Now Joe is satisfied with the star; however, he wants to change the fill setting of the polygon to Solid and create reverse text inside the polygon.

6. Click the **Pointer tool** in the toolbox, click the polygon that you just created, click **Element**, point to **Fill**, then click **Solid**
   Now Joe needs to add the reverse text. He uses the Text tool to define the size of his text block.

7. Click the **Text tool** T in the tool box, click inside the polygon at the upper-left corner of the polygon and drag to the lower-right corner of the polygon, as shown in Figure F-22, then release the mouse button
   PageMaker creates a text block. Now Joe needs to set the type specifications for the block before he begins to type the text.

MacintoshUser

This replaces Step 8.

8. Substitute Helvetica for Arial

8. Click **Type** on the menu bar, click **Character**, in the Character Specifications dialog box click **Arial** in the Font list box, type **10** in the Size text box, click the **Bold check box**, click the **Reverse check box**, then click **OK**

9. Click **Type** on the menu bar, point to **Alignment**, click **Align Center**, then type **Ask About the Eagle Club**
   See Figure F-23. You may need to resize or move your text block to fit your text inside of the polygon.

Time To
- ✔ Save
- ✔ Print
- ✔ Close

FIGURE F-20: **Five-sided polygon created**

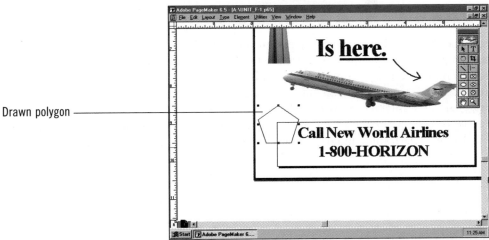

Drawn polygon

FIGURE F-21: **Polygon Settings dialog box**

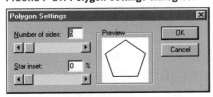

FIGURE F-22: **Defining the text box**

Creating custom size text box for the reverse text

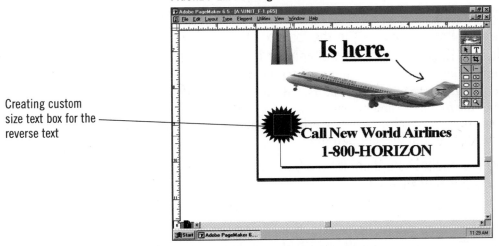

FIGURE F-23: **The reverse text block**

Reverse text displayed inside black star

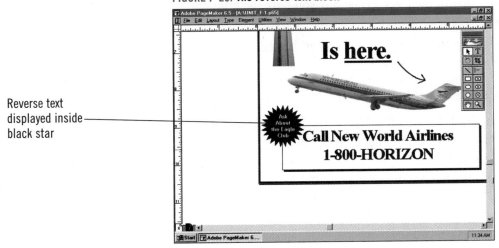

PageMaker 6.5

Using Frames

Frames are placeholders that allow you to design your page layout before placing final versions of text and graphics. Your layout can contain either graphic frames, text frames, or both text and graphic frames. Frames are objects that can be manipulated to have stroke and fill attributes. Text placed in frames can be threaded to other text frames so that text can flow between frames. Joe wants to modify the ad he has created to serve as a standard advertisement that can easily be changed by local New World Airlines advertising coordinators. These coordinators will place into the frames photos of cities they will use to advertise New World airline flights.

Steps

1. Open the file UNIT_F-2 from your Student Disk
   The ad Joe completed now appears in the publication window. Joe has already created a frame at the top of his page for the picture of the arch. He would like to create an additional frame that he will use to place a picture of Toronto's Needle in this advertisement.
2. Click the **Rectangle Frame tool** in the tool box, position + at the 0.25" marker on the horizontal ruler and the 2.5" marker on the vertical ruler, then drag down to the 1" marker on the horizontal ruler and the 7.5" marker on the vertical ruler
   See Figure F-24. Joe is satisfied with the basic design of his advertisement. However, PageMaker automatically places a 1-point rule line on the frame's border. Joe will remove the stroke border.
3. Click the **Pointer tool** in the toolbox, click the **frame** you just drew, press and hold **[Shift]**, click the **frame placeholder** in the top right corner of the page, release [Shift], click **Element** on the menu bar, point to **Stroke**, then click **None**
   The 1-point stroke border disappears, but a nonprinting gray border still appears to remind you of the frame size and placement. Joe will save the publication and use a copy of the file for creating his ad. This allows the original publication to be used to create different advertisements based on the same layout.
4. Save the publication, then use the Save as command to save a copy of the publication as **Advertisement 1**
   Joe is now ready to place a graphic photo inside the frame he just created.
5. Click the **frame** you just created, click **File** on the menu bar, click **Place**, then click **UNIT_F-3** located on your Student Disk, but do not click Open
   Notice that in the Place dialog box you have the option to place the image as an independent graphic or within the selected frame. Joe wants to place the graphic within the frame
6. Make sure the **Within frame option button** is selected, then click **Open**
   The graphic is now inside the frame, as shown in Figure F-25. You can also attach graphics already place in your publication to frames. However, once a graphic is placed inside of a frame, text cannot be added to the same frame.
7. Click the **frame** in the top corner of the publication, press **[Shift]**, click the **arch graphic** on the pasteboard, release [Shift], click **Element**, point to **Frame**, then click **Attach Content**
   The graphic is placed inside of the frame. Joe is satisfied with his final layout. To detach a graphic from a frame, select the graphic frame, click Element, click Frame, then click Delete Content.
8. Save the publication, then exit PageMaker

MacintoshUser

This replaces Steps 5 and 6.

5. Click the frame you just created, click File on the menu bar, select Place, then select UNIT_F-3 from your Student Disk, but do not click OK
6. Make sure the Within frame option button is selected, then click OK

Resume at Step 7.

FIGURE F-24: Text frame drawn on the publication page

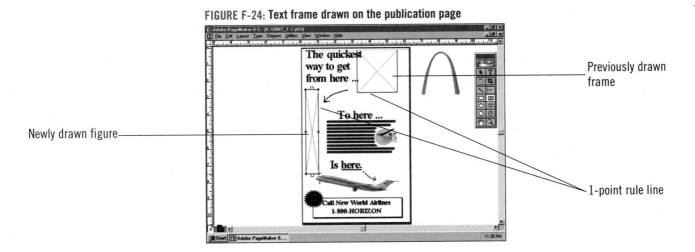

Newly drawn figure

Previously drawn frame

1-point rule line

FIGURE F-25: Frame with a graphic attached

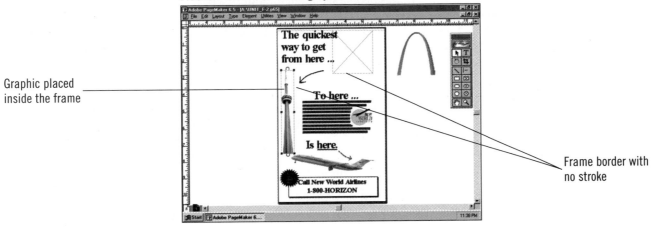

Graphic placed inside the frame

Frame border with no stroke

CLUES TO USE

Using text frames

Text can be placed into frames and be threaded between multiple frames. To place text into multiple frames, press [Shift], select all the frames to be used, click File, then click Place. The text frames will have handles similar to normal text blocks, indicating threaded frames. Text can also be placed in circle or polygon drawn objects. See Figure F-26. Different stroke fills can be added by simply selecting the text frame, clicking Element, clicking Fill, then clicking Stroke.

FIGURE F-26: Circle text frame

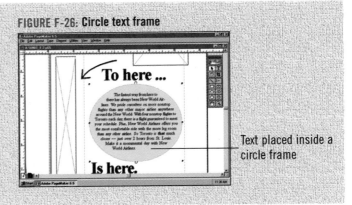

Text placed inside a circle frame

PageMaker 6.5

Design Workshop: Advertisements

A successful advertisement should provide a clear course of action or form a positive image of a company or product. Let's evaluate Joe's design, shown in Figure F-27.

Details

Does the ad achieve its goal?

Graphics are the first things people see when looking at a page, followed by the text. Joe's design of blending text and graphics makes the ad's goal clear: New World Airlines offers service from St. Louis to Toronto. Joe used well-known symbols of each city to inform people about the service. The monuments in each of these cities form a better visual picture for the reader than simply typing the names of the cities in the ad.

Is the ad well organized?

The three photos in Joe's ad break up separate blocks of text in the ad. The short headlines in a large, bold typeface and the arrow graphics help smooth the transition between the photos. Although Joe made the graphics the central focus of the ad, he still needed text to elaborate on the services being offered. He placed the first and largest headline on the top left so it would be read first. The rest of the information flows from left to right and top to bottom.

Will the ad stand out on the newspaper page?

Unless it is a full-page ad, a newspaper ad can get lost in the crowd of other ads and news stories. Joe realized his ad would lose impact in the crowded travel section of the local newspaper, so he used simple graphics and plenty of white space to help set off his ad from other ads. He achieved a crisp-looking ad that is free from crowded text blocks and discount prices common to the rest of the business section.

How will the color of the ad affect the impact?

Although studies show a reader is more apt to view color areas on a page before black and white ones, this doesn't detract from the successful design of this ad. In the end, an ad's success is determined by its response, not by the amount of color used. Sometimes using a single color ink, in this case black, can be a greater challenge to designers because creativity is seemingly limited. Together, black and white form the best contrast to one another. More often than not, you will be forced to work using black as your only color, so it's important to have a good design. Joe used black and white to his advantage by using quality photographs and large, bold graphics. He blended those with a generous use of white space to help each graphic element stand on its own.

Practice

► Concepts Review

Label each of the publication window elements as shown in Figure F-28.

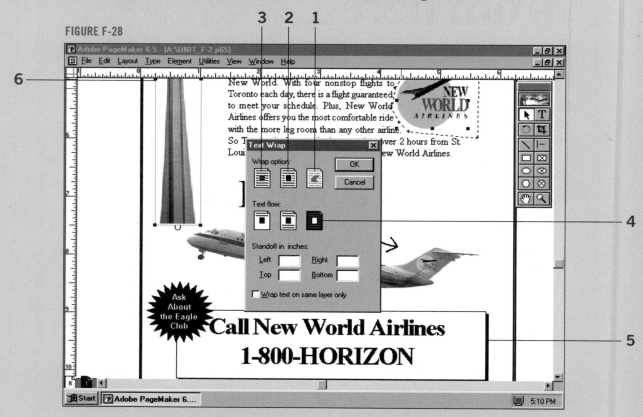

FIGURE F-28

Match each of the terms with the statement that describes its function.

8. Standoff
9. Line weight
10. Text wrap
11. Line art

a. Graphics drawn as outlines of objects
b. Text around a graphic
c. Amount of space between a graphic and wrapped text
d. Thickness, measured in points

12. **How many points equal an inch?**
    a. 24
    b. 36
    c. 60
    d. 72

13. **All of the following statements about cropping are true, except:**
    a. Cropping permanently deletes a portion of the graphic.
    b. Cropping changes only the view of the graphic.
    c. You can crop a graphic as many times as you wish.
    d. All of the above are true.

14. **You can rotate a graphic:**
    a. At 45-degree increments
    b. At increments of .01 degree
    c. Only at 90-degree increments
    d. Both a and b

15. **When you move a layered object, it:**
    a. Can never be sent to its original layer
    b. Moves all of the layered objects
    c. Always moves to the top layer
    d. None of the above

16. **Rectangular wrap option allows you to wrap text:**
    a. Only around boxes
    b. Around graphic objects in rectangular fashion
    c. Only on top of the graphic
    d. All of the above

17. **When using text wraps, you can control the space between the graphic and the text by:**
    a. Adjusting the standoff measurement
    b. Creating a custom wrap
    c. Both a and b
    d. None of the above

18. **You can only change the line style on:**
    a. Rectangles
    b. Lines
    c. Circles
    d. All of the above

PageMaker 6.5

▶ Skills Review

1. Draw a border around an advertisement

a. Start PageMaker and open the file UNIT_F-4 from your Student Disk.

b. Click the Rectangle tool in the toolbox, position ╋ over the upper-left corner of the advertisement just outside the page margin border.

c. Drag the pointer to the lower-right corner of the advertisement just outside the margin border.

d. Click the Pointer tool in the toolbox.

e. Click the box you just drew to reselect the box.

f. Click Element on the menu bar, point to Stroke, then click the 4pt single line.

g. Click the Rectangle tool in the toolbox.

h. Draw a second box around the headline and body text describing Sunset Travel Tours.

i. Click Element, point to Stroke, then click the 2pt single line.

2. Crop a graphic.

a. Place the graphic file UNIT_F-5, located on your Student Disk, in the advertisement.

b. Click the Cropping tool in the toolbox, then select the graphic you just placed.

c. Position 🔲 on the bottom left handle, press and hold the left mouse button.

d. Crop the graphic until you can no longer see the plane on the left.

e. Position 🔲 on top of the graphic, then press and hold the left mouse button.

f. Move the graphic within its border until you see the plane that you cropped from the image, then release the mouse button.

g. Click Edit on the menu, then click Undo Crop.

h. Click the Pointer tool in the toolbox.

i. Click the graphic to select it, then drag the graphic to the white area to the left of the text.

3. Rotate an object.

a. Make sure the Pointer tool is selected from the toolbox, then click the plane to select it.

b. Click the Rotating tool in the toolbox.

c Position ✛ in the center of the selected graphic, then rotate the graphic so the front of the plane angles toward the sky, similar to the rotation of the plane in the New World Airlines logo in Figure F-27.

d. Click the Pointer tool in the toolbox, then click the plane graphic.

e. Position ▸ over the bottom left handle, press and hold [Shift].

f. Click and drag the handle to the left and enlarge the plane graphic to about 25% more than its original size.

g. Drag the graphic so it is entirely within the border you just drew around the entire advertisement and overlaps the body text but not the headline.

h. Click outside the plane graphic to deselect the graphic.

4. Create a shadow box and stack objects.
   a. Click the Rectangle tool in the toolbox.
   b. Create a third border box that is wider than the original border box horizontally, but shorter vertically. Placement should be similar to that of the black box in Figure F-29.
   c. Make sure the box you just drew is selected.
   d. Click Element on the menu bar, point to Fill, then click Solid.
   e. Click Element, point to Arrange, then click Send to Back.
   f. Make sure your layered boxes are well-aligned. If you have to move the solid box more to the center, use the Pointer tool to select it, then drag it to center it better.
   g. Click the Pointer tool in the toolbox, then select the first box you drew (the box outside the page's margins).
   h. Click Element, point to Fill, then click Paper.
   i. Click Element, point to Arrange, then click Send to Back.
   j. Click the black box again, then click Element, point to Arrange, then click Send to Back.

FIGURE F-29

5. Wrap text around a graphic.
   a. Select the plane graphic.
   b. Click Element on the menu bar, then click Text Wrap.
   c. Select the Rectangular Wrap option icon. Use the default standoff settings.
   d. Click OK to close the Text Wrap dialog box.
   e. Select the text to the right of the graphic.
   f. Position the pointer ⤡ on the top left handle of the text block, then drag it toward the left margin, but do not go as far as the left margin.

6. Add a custom text wrap.
   a. Select the plane graphic.
   b. Select the plane's right standoff line, then add eight definition points.
   c. Position the pointer ▶ on top of one of the definition points, then drag each point to reshape the text wrap around the plane outline.
   d. Continue to reshape the definition points to reshape the plane's standoff to create a custom wrap around the plane.
   e. Click outside the plane to deselect the graphic. Arrange elements to fit if necessary.

7. Create a star-shaped polygon.

   a. Click the Polygon tool in the toolbox.

   b. Move + to an area of the screen containing empty white space.

   c. Drag to create a polygon to fit in the white space area.

   d. Click Element on the menu bar, then click Polygon Settings.

   e. Type "15" in the Number of sides text box.

   f. Press [Tab] twice to preview the multisided object. *(Macintosh users: Press [tab] once.)*

   g. Type "25" in the Star inset text box.

   h. Press [Tab] to preview the star inset.

   i. Click OK.

   j. Click the Pointer tool in the toolbox, click the star to select it, then click Element, point to Fill, then click Solid.

   k. Click the Text tool in the toolbox, then click the pointer inside the star to create a new text block.

   l. Click Type on the menu bar, click Character, select Arial *(Macintosh users: Select Helvetica)*, 11 points, bold, and reverse text, then click OK.

   m. Click Type, click Alignment, then click Align Center.

   n. Type "Travel with the World's leading tour company" and adjust the text block or reduce the size of the text to fit inside the star.

8. Add a frame for a graphic.

   a. Click the Rectangle Frame tool in the toolbox, position + at the 3" marker on the vertical ruler and the 1" marker on the horizontal ruler, then drag down to the 5" marker on the vertical ruler and the 5" marker on the horizontal ruler.

   b. Make sure the frame is still selected, click Element on the menu bar, point to Stroke, then click None.

   c. Click the Pointer tool in the toolbox, click the frame, press [Shift], click the airplane graphic, click Element, point to Frame, then click Attach Content.

   d. Drag the frame as necessary to reposition the airplane graphic.

   e. Save the publication, then print it.

▶ Independent Challenges

1. Create a black and white advertisement for the Board of Tourism for Paris, France. Make the advertisement 7" tall by 5" wide.

   To complete this independent challenge:

1. Open the file UNIT_F-6 from your Student Disk.
2. Place the text file UNIT_F-7, located on your Student Disk.
3. Place the graphic file PARIS, located on your Student Disk over the text you placed.
4. Crop the graphic so that only the tower is visible.
5. Double the size of Paris graphic.
6. Create a custom text wrap so that the text almost touches the right border of the tower.
7. Include a headline.
8. Add a circle behind the partial New World Airlines logo. The circle should be lightly shaded. Then send the circle to the back.
9. Create a shadow box around the entire advertisement.
10. Add a star, place text inside the polygon reminding readers to "Ask about special weekend flights."
11. Create a text frame for the text in the bottom right corner of the ad containing the phone number. Be sure to remove the stroke border. Attach the text to the frame. Reposition the frame, as necessary, to move the text back to the bottom right corner of the ad.
12. Save your work as Paris ad on your Student Disk.
13. Print the publication, then submit the printout.

2. Pick three black and white advertisements from a newspaper. Try to find advertisements that include the following features: varied borders, rotated graphics, layered objects, and text wraps. Evaluate the advertisements, and then be prepared to share your findings with others.

To complete this independent challenge:

1. Critique the advertisements using the guidelines from the first lesson in this unit. Do the graphical features, such as a rotated graphic, enhance the overall design of the advertisement? Or do they detract? Why?
2. Take the best aspects from each advertisement, and then sketch a new advertisement design.
3. Try to include rotated graphics and text wraps. Think of a creative headline, and use a unique border around your advertisement.
4. Add a star or another polygon object to your page layout.
5. Assess whether the designer(s) used black and white creatively. Would these ads look better if multiple colors were used?
6. Submit your evaluation and sketches.

PageMaker 6.5

3. Create an advertisement for a product of your choice. You can choose an existing product or create one yourself. Sketch the layout of your ad on a piece of paper first to determine how you want to relate the text and graphics. You have free reign with the design.

To complete this independent challenge:

1. Create an ad that is 6" tall by 9" wide.
2. Use graphic files on your Student Disk as dummy graphics. Earn extra credit by using graphics from another source, such as a clip art disk, CD-ROM, or scanned images.
3. Use a font you haven't yet used for your headline, and make it at least 100 points in size.
4. Use text to describe the product, but keep the message short. Wrap the text around one of the graphics in your ad. If it adds to the design, use a custom text wrap around the graphic.
5. Take advantage of rotating graphics and stacking objects to create unusual effects.
6. Add a text or graphic frame, and attach the text or graphic to the frame.
7. Save the advertisement as Advertisement 3 on your Student Disk. Print your publication, then submit the printout.

4. You work in the marketing department of a major airline or travel agency. You have been asked by your boss to design a quarter-page, black and white advertisement for a newspaper.

To complete this independent challenge:

1. Search the World Wide Web for information on airline specials or a travel agency's package tours.
2. Make a sketch of your advertisement for the airline or travel agency, using the guidelines that you learned in this unit.
3. Create your ad in PageMaker using the sketch as a guide.
4. Use lines and shapes in your ad, and change the line and border weights and styles to enhance your design.
5. Add graphics to your publication, and crop at least one graphic to remove a portion of it that you don't want to appear in your ad. You can use graphic files from your Student Disk. Rotate one of your graphics.
6. Stack two of the objects in your ad, and create a shadow box to make something stand out.
7. Choose a unique way to wrap the text in the ad around a graphic.
8. Add a frame and attach one of the graphics in your advertisement to the frame. Resize and move the frame as necessary.
9. Critique your final design to make sure it matched your original goals.
10. Save the publication as Advertisement 4 on your Student Disk, and then print the publication. Submit your sketch, all printouts, and your critique.

▶ Visual Workshop

New World Airlines needs an advertisement describing the sights to see in London. Using Figure F-29 as an example, create an advertisement that is 7 by 10 inches. Place the graphic file BIGBEN and resize it as necessary to fit. Create a customized text wrap and place the text file UNIT_F-7 so that it flows inside the graphic. Next place the file UNIT_F-4; crop the graphic and rotate the plane as shown. Create a white box and type "LONDON" inside the box. Create a three-sided object, then rotate it so that one of the points of the triangle points towards the body text describing London. Make sure that you select the three-sided object and send it behind the white box. Add a shadow box around the entire advertisement. Make the line weight of the white box 2 pt. Finally, add a text or graphic frame to your ad, and attach the text or graphic to the frame. Save your file as London ad on your Student Disk.

FIGURE F-29

Formatting

Text

Objectives

- ► **Plan a menu**
- ► **Set publication preferences**
- ► **Define the Control palette in character view**
- ► **Define the Control palette in paragraph view**
- ► **Apply small capitals**
- ► **Adjust the baseline**
- ► **Adjust text spacing**
- ► **Set character widths**
- ► **Set tabs**
- ► **Set indents**
- ► **Use the Bullets and Numbering Plug-in**
- ► **Design Workshop: Menus**

This unit introduces you to more complex text manipulation features in PageMaker which can enhance the appearance of text in your publication. You will learn how to use the Control palette, which contains buttons and options to format character and paragraph attributes quickly. Using the Control palette, you will adjust character and paragraph specifications options that will give the text and overall layout of your publication a professional and distinctive look. You will once again work with styles to modify the width of characters in headings and modify tab and indent settings. ◢▬▬ Joe Martin needs to finish a menu he created for the Eagle Club, a comfortable restaurant and lounge reserved for Gold Club Members of the Eagle Flight Program for frequent flyer passengers.

Planning a Menu

Creating a menu means more than copying a chef's recipes onto a piece of paper. No matter how simple or complex a menu's design, the menu is responsible for being the final point of sale for a restaurant. Menus offer a "smorgasbord" of design opportunities. Menus usually include a lot of text, so you will need to use PageMaker's character and paragraph manipulation features to enhance the overall appearance of the menu. A poorly planned and designed menu actually detracts from the profitability of a food service facility by confusing the customer. ✐ Joe received a handwritten list and description of items for the new Eagle Club menu from Executive Chef Tamara Roche. Tamara carefully selected items for the menu and told Joe that the Surf & Turf special was an item that could bring the most profit because its perceived value is much greater than what it costs to make. This fact helps Joe determine where he places items as he designs the menu.

Details

Determine the menu items of importance
Where you place items on the page directly affects how customers order from the menu. Certain areas of a page or spread of pages are read before others. Areas read first are called **power points** because of their potential impact on the reader. Because the Surf & Turf is the most profitable item for the Eagle Club, Joe makes sure to place the menu item on the top in the center column. He will also place the Chocolate Cake Special as the top entry in the third column.

Create an organized and easy-to-read layout design
Menus tend to include a large amount of information. By adjusting the character spacing, you can "loosen" the text and make it easier to read. You can use PageMaker's text manipulation features such as indents and tabs to help organize overall layout design. Joe will use three columns and will use PageMaker's kerning, character width, and type options commands to enhance the appearance of the text. See Figure G-1 for Joe and Tamara's rough sketch of the menu.

Organize menu items into categories
The Eagle Club's menu items allow Joe to create logical categories, such as appetizers and entrées. The menu items will be organized according to category and flow from first course to beverages.

Produce menus on durable paper
Because menus are constantly in use, it is important to print them on durable card stock paper. **Lamination**, which is a permanent plastic coating, will also preserve the menu. The Eagle Club menus will remain at the tables, but they will receive a lot of use from the sheer volume of passengers stopping at the restaurant to eat each day. Joe will use an 80-pound, light tan card stock paper. He will also have his commercial printer laminate the menus.

Menu banner ——————

Eagle Club

Appetizers

Salads

Entrées

Desserts

Beverages

Setting Publication Preferences

PageMaker lets you customize certain aspects of the application through the Preferences dialog box. In the Preferences dialog box, you can set a measurement system for the horizontal and vertical rulers, change the way text displays in the layout and story editor views, and improve the appearance of quotation marks and apostrophes, among other options. The changes you make in the Preferences dialog box apply only to the open publication. You can set a publication's preferences when you begin a new publication or at any point during the creation of the publication. The printer has asked Joe to submit his publication in **picas**, a measurement system used by many commercial printers. Joe has already begun his Eagle Club menu and needs to change the publication's rulers from inches to picas.

1. Start PageMaker and open the file UNIT_G-1 from your Student Disk

The menu Joe started working on appears in the publication window. Joe uses the Preferences dialog box to change the publication's measurement system.

2. Click File on the menu bar, then point to Preferences, then click General

The Preferences dialog box opens, as shown in Figure G-2.

3. Click the Measurements in list arrow, then click Picas

This changes the unit of measure PageMaker uses in the horizontal ruler in layout view. Six picas equal 1", and 12 points equal one pica. In PageMaker, pica measurement is denoted as 0p1, where the zero is picas and the one is points.

PageMaker allows you to set the unit of measure for the vertical ruler different from the overall measuring system. Joe wants to set his vertical ruler to picas also.

QuickTip

It is best to use only one unit of measurement throughout a publication.

4. Click the Vertical ruler list arrow, then click Picas

Joe has noticed that his PageMaker publications have been taking large amounts of disk space. Joe wants to use the Save Smaller option in the Preferences dialog box to help decrease publication file sizes.

5. Click the Smaller option button in the Save option section

This forces PageMaker to save the publication file as small as possible when you use the Save command. The Save Faster option saves the document more quickly, but gradually increases the file's size on disk.

QuickTip

You can set default settings for all new publications by changing preferences settings when there are no documents open.

6. Click OK to return to the publication window

7. Save the publication

FIGURE G-2: **Preferences dialog box**

Click to display measurement system choices

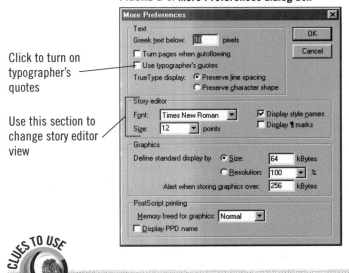

Click to display the More Preference dialog box

Click to save the publication in the smallest file size possible

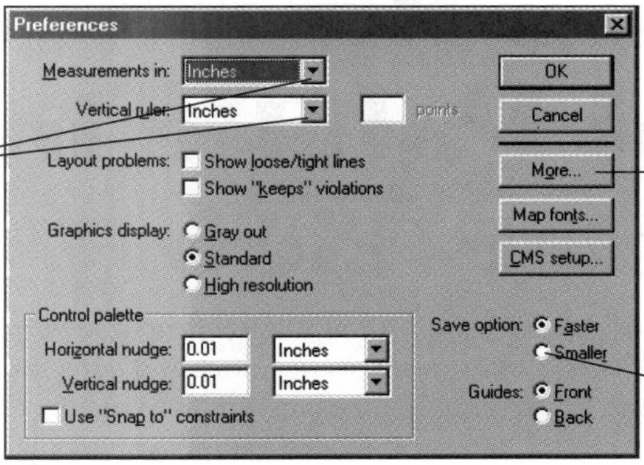

FIGURE G-3: **More Preferences dialog box**

Click to turn on typographer's quotes

Use this section to change story editor view

More Preferences Options

Using story editor can improve your ability to create text or edit long bodies of text in a multiple-page publication. Story editor displays all text using the same font and point size. If you use story editor for any period of time, you might want to change the font and size of the text display in story editor view. The story editor view display font is set inside the More Preferences dialog box. See Figure G-3. Certain fonts are used for screen display, such as Geneva, New York, or even Arial, because they are easier to read. You might have noticed PageMaker uses tick marks

(" and ') for quotation marks and apostrophes. PageMaker gives you the option to convert the appearance of these tick marks to curly marks, or typographer's quotes. **Typographer** refers to someone who designs or sets type in the commercial printing industry. You can use PageMaker's keystroke combinations each time you wish to use a typographer's quote (as described in Table G-1), or you can activate the Use typographer's quotes option in the More Preferences dialog box to use the curly marks automatically when you type quotation marks or apostrophes.

TABLE G-1: **PageMaker's keystroke combinations for typographer's quotes**

character	Windows keyboard shortcut	Macintosh keyboard shortcut
'	[Ctrl][[]	[option][]]
"	[Ctrl][Shift][[]	[option][[ ]
'	[Ctrl][]]	[option][shift][]]
"	[Ctrl][Shift][]]	[option][shift][[ ]

PageMaker 6.5

Defining the Control Palette in Character View

As you already know, PageMaker gives you several different methods to accomplish the same task. To format text, you can use the Character Specifications and Paragraph Specifications dialog boxes, or commands on the Type menu. Another method is to use the Control palette, which lets you quickly apply text formats. The Control palette allows you to change text by switching between two views. You use **character view** for setting type formats and **paragraph view** for setting paragraph formats. You apply format settings by selecting the desired text and clicking one of the format buttons or by changing the text box options on the Control palette.

Below are some of the benefits of using the Control palette and its character features:

 Format character text quickly and easily

Clicking a Control palette button is faster than using the menus. See Table G-2 for a description of the Control palette's character view formatting buttons. Compare the Character Specifications dialog box in Figure G-4 with the Control palette's character view in Figure G-5. Notice the character view allows you to format text by changing type styles, font attributes, and word and character spacing.

 Flexibility to move the Control palette anywhere in the layout or story editor view windows

You show or hide the Control palette by selecting it from the Window menu. You can move the Control palette anywhere in the publication window by clicking its left border below its close box and dragging the palette to the desired location.

QuickTip

A power nudge allows you to increase a nudge setting by a factor of 10 by pressing [Shift] as you click a nudge button.

Change options by precise measurements

Next to most Control palette options are little arrows called **nudge buttons** that allow you to make changes by a preset measurement. When you click a nudge button, PageMaker immediately makes the change. The amount by which the setting changes depends on the default units of measurement setting. The default nudge amount for inches is 0.01". This default nudge can be changed using the Preferences dialog box. You can also make changes by a mathematical factor.

FIGURE G-4: **Character Specifications dialog box**

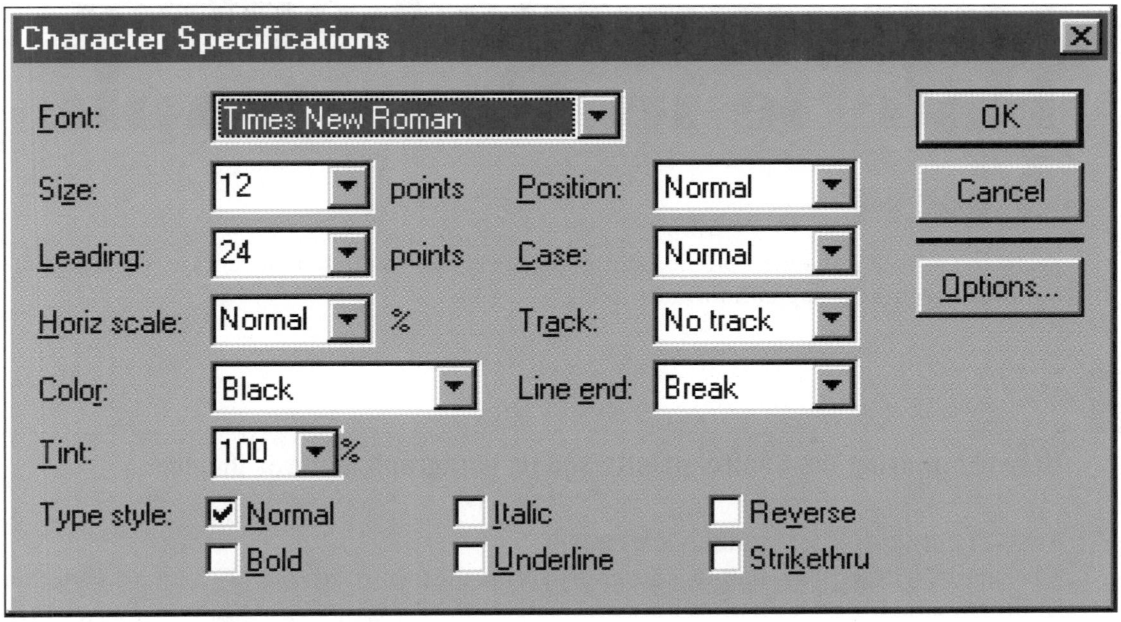

Character Specifications ☒

F̲ont:	Times New Roman ▾		OK
Si̲ze:	12 ▾ points	Position: Normal ▾	Cancel
Leading:	24 ▾ points	Case: Normal ▾	
Horiz scale:	Normal ▾ %	Track: No track ▾	Options...
Color:	Black ▾	Line end: Break ▾	
Tint:	100 ▾ %		

Type style: ☑ N̲ormal ☐ I̲talic ☐ R̲everse
 ☐ B̲old ☐ U̲nderline ☐ Stri̲kethru

FIGURE G-5: **Control palette in character view**

☒ Times New Roman ▾ ◀▾ ↕T 12 ▾ ♠♠♠ No Track ▾ ◀▶ ᴬᵥ
¶ N B I U ⊟ ⊖ C C ⅀ ⅀ ◀▾ ↕ᴬ 14.4 ▾ ◀▶ ⊥ 100% ▾ ◀▾ ᴬᴿ 0 in

TABLE G-2: **Control palette's character view buttons and options**

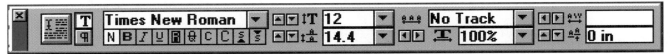

button/box	option	description
🖳	**Apply button**	Applies changes made on the Control palette
¶	**Paragraph view button**	Changes Control palette to paragraph view
Times New Roman ▾	**Font option**	Applies typeface from list of available system fonts to selected text
N B I U ⊟ ⊖	**Type style buttons**	Applies special type styles to selected text: Normal, Bold, Italic, Underline, Reverse, Strikethru
C C	**Case buttons**	Changes the case of text; the left button sets lowercase text in small capital letters, and the right button sets the text in all capitals
⅀ ⅀	**Superscript/subscript buttons**	Changes the size and position of text
◀▾ ↕T 12 ▾	**Type size option**	Sets the point size; type a value in the text box, use the nudge button, or use the list arrow to display available sizes
◀▾ ↕ᴬ 14.4 ▾	**Leading option**	Sets the leading—type a value in the text box, use the nudge button, or use the list arrow to display available sizes of leading; the list includes an auto setting that sets the type to the default leading
♠♠♠ No Track ▾	**Track option**	Sets the tracking or the spacing between characters
◀▶ ⊥ 100% ▾	**Set width option**	Sets the width of characters—100% is the default; you increase the width of the letters by choosing a value greater than 100% and decrease the width with a value less than 100%
◀▶ ᴬᵥ	**Kerning option**	Sets the width between characters
◀▾ ᴬᴿ 0 in	**Baseline shift option**	Raises or lowers the baseline for the selected text

Defining the Control Palette in Paragraph View

Switching to paragraph view on the Control palette allows you to take advantage of the palette's options for setting paragraph formats.

Benefits of using the Control palette and its paragraph features include:

Format paragraph text quickly and easily

Clicking a Control palette button is faster than using the menus. See Table G-3 for a description of the paragraph view formatting buttons. Compare the Paragraph Specifications dialog box in Figure G-6 with the Control palette's paragraph view in Figure G-7. The paragraph view allows you to set alignments, indents, styles, and other settings for one or more paragraphs.

Easily switch between character and paragraph view

You can quickly change the view of your Control palette by clicking the Character view button or the Paragraph view button 9.

MacintoshUser

Note that the Character view displays as T.

TABLE G-3: Control palette's paragraph view buttons and options

button/box	option	description
	Apply button	Applies changes made on the Control palette
T	Character view button	Changes Control palette to character view
[No style] ▼	Paragraph style option	Applies preset styles to selected text
	Alignment buttons	Aligns text to the left or right, centers it, or justifies it on the publication page
0 in	Left indent options	Sets the indent from the left margin
0 in	Right indent options	Sets the indent from the right margin
0 in	First-line indent options	Sets the indent for the first line of the paragraph
0 in	Space before option	Sets the space above the beginning of a paragraph
0 in	Space after option	Sets the space below the last line of a paragraph
0	Grid-size option	Sets the size of the text grid you want to use when the Align-to-grid option is on
	Align-to-grid buttons	Automatically aligns vertically the baselines of adjacent columns (the right button turns the option on and the left button turns if off)
0 in	Cursor position indicator	Tracks the position of cursor on publication page

FIGURE G-6: Paragraph Specifications dialog box

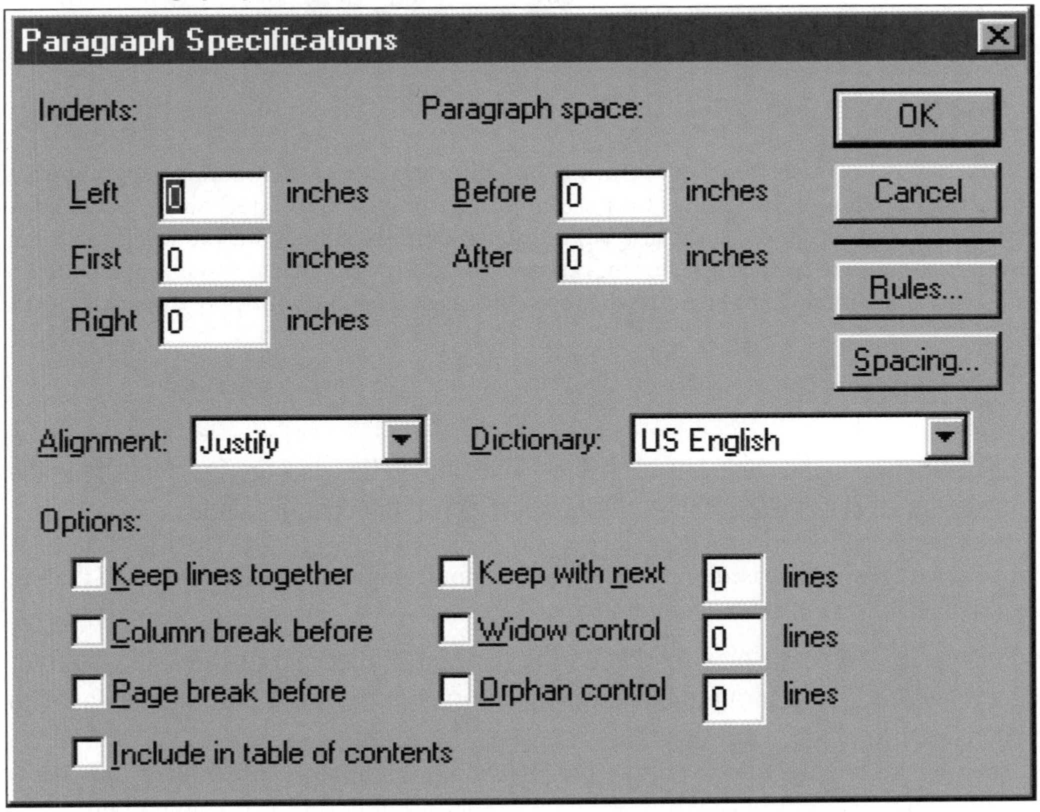
Paragraph Specifications
Indents:
Paragraph space:
OK
Left
0
inches
Before
0
inches
Cancel
First
0
inches
After
0
inches
Rules...
Right
0
inches
Spacing...
Alignment:
Justify
Dictionary:
US English
Options:
Keep lines together
Keep with next
0
lines
Column break before
Widow control
0
lines
Page break before
Orphan control
0
lines
Include in table of contents

FIGURE G-7: Control palette in paragraph view

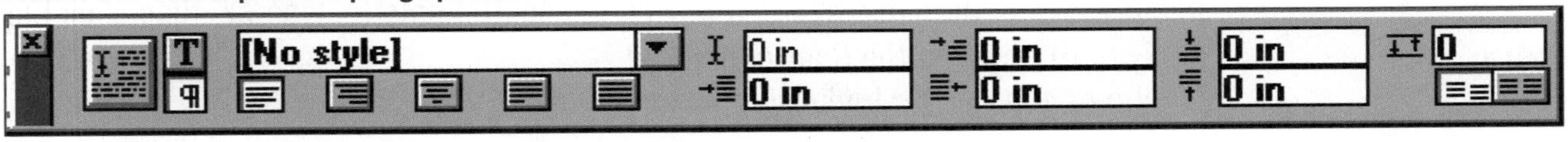
[No style]
0 in
0 in
0 in
0 in
0 in
0 in
0

Performing Arithmetic Adjustments

CLUES TO USE

You can use the Control palette to perform simple arithmetic in any active numeric option by typing the numeric expression into the option's text box. For example, to scale a text headline to three times its size, you would first select the text. Then, using the Control palette character view, in the Type size text box, type "x3" and then click the Apply button. The text headline automatically scales to three times its original size.

PageMaker 6.5

Applying Small Capitals

PageMaker lets you create special effects using the Control palette or the Character Options dialog box. You can choose the settings for position (Superscript or Subscript) and size (All caps, Small caps, or Normal), and you can also adjust the size of the baseline shift. You will learn about adjusting the baseline in the next lesson. Joe wants to add the restaurant's name in reverse type to the menu banner across the top of the page. Then he will apply the small capital feature for an innovative look.

 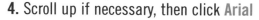

QuickTip

Press [Ctrl]['] (Macintosh users: [⌘][']) to quickly show the Control palette in the publication window.

1. Click **Window** on the menu bar, click **Show Control Palette**, click the **Text tool**  in the toolbox, then click the **Character view button** on the Control palette
   The Control palette appears in character view, as shown in Figure G-8. The size of the control palette may vary based on the resolution of your monitor. Joe wants to define the size of the text block for the restaurant's name.

2. Position Ⅰ at the 30-pica marker on the horizontal ruler and at the 4-pica marker on the vertical ruler, drag to the lower-right corner of the black box, then release the mouse button
   After you release the mouse button, the insertion point appears in the black box. Joe is ready to use the Control palette to set the type specifications for the restaurant's name.

3. Click the **Reverse button** on the Control palette, then click the **Font list arrow** on the Control palette
   The font list appears in the Control palette, as shown in Figure G-9. Joe decides to use the sans serif font Arial for the menu banner.

MacintoshUser

This replaces Step 4.
4. Select **Helvetica**

4. Scroll up if necessary, then click **Arial**

5. Double-click in the **Type size text box** on the control palette, type **72**, then click the **Apply button** on the Control palette
   Joe also needs to set the leading for the text block.

Trouble?

If your screen display is not refreshed after formatting text, simply zoom out and zoom back in.

6. Click the **Leading list arrow** on the Control palette, click **Auto**, then type **Eagle Club**

7. Select the name **Eagle Club**, then click the **Small caps button** on the Control palette
   See Figure G-10. This changes the lowercase text to capital letters that are smaller than regular capital letters. Joe wants to decrease the size of the small caps in relation to the first letter of each word. This option is not available on the Control palette, so Joe opens the Character Options dialog box.

8. Click **Type** on the menu bar, click **Character**, then click **Options**
   The Character Options dialog box opens, as shown in Figure G-11.

DesignTip

To use it effectively, apply the Small caps option only to text that is 14 points or larger.

9. Type **50** in the Small caps size text box, then click **OK** twice
   This changes the lowercase letters to capital letters that are 50% smaller than the size of the corresponding full-sized capital letters.

10. Deselect the text by clicking anywhere outside the text area, then save the publication

FIGURE G-8: Control palette in character view

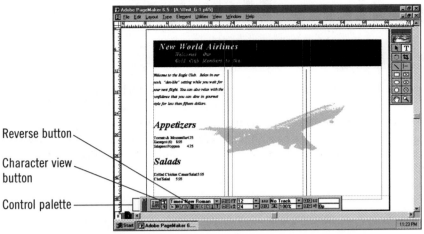

Reverse button

Character view button

Control palette

FIGURE G-9: Font list

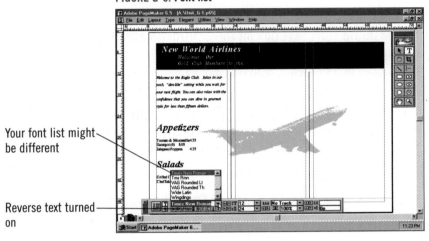

Your font list might be different

Reverse text turned on

FIGURE G-10: Small caps applied to name

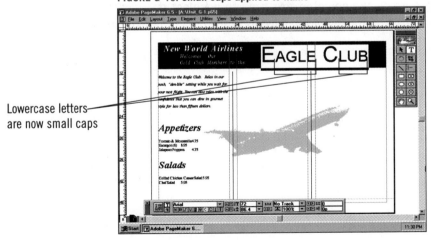

Lowercase letters are now small caps

FIGURE G-11: Character Options dialog box

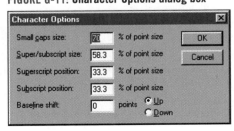

Adjusting the Baseline

You can also create special effects with text by adjusting its position on the baseline. The **baseline** is an imaginary line that text rests on, as shown in Figure G-12. Text can be moved above or below a baseline. You can use the Control palette in character view or the Character Options dialog box to shift the text above or below the baseline in increments as little as a tenth of a point. Joe decides to use the Control palette to shift the baseline of the small capital letters in the restaurant name.

Steps

MacintoshUser

This replaces Step 1.
1. Select "agle" of the word "Eagle," then press and hold [⌘][option] and click the **left mouse button** to change view to Actual Size

1. Select "agle" of the word "Eagle," then press [Ctrl] and right-click to change view to Actual Size

2. Double-click in the **Baseline shift text box** on the Control palette and type **0p6**, then click the **Apply button** 🔳 on the Control palette
   See Figure G-13. Joe decides that a baseline shift of a half a pica is not enough. He is not sure how much more to increase the baseline shift so he decides to use the nudge button.

3. Click the **Baseline shift nudge up button** on the Control palette six times
   Notice that the setting in the Baseline shift text box changes each time you click. Joe decides that a baseline shift of 1p looks the best so he decides to do the same with the word "club."

4. Deselect the text, then select "**lub**" of the word "Club"

5. Double-click in the **Baseline shift text box** on the Control palette and type **1p**, then click 🔳
   See Figure G-14.

6. Click anywhere outside the selected text area to deselect it
   Notice that the baseline of the small capital letters in the restaurant name has been moved up.

7. Save the publication

FIGURE G-12: The baseline

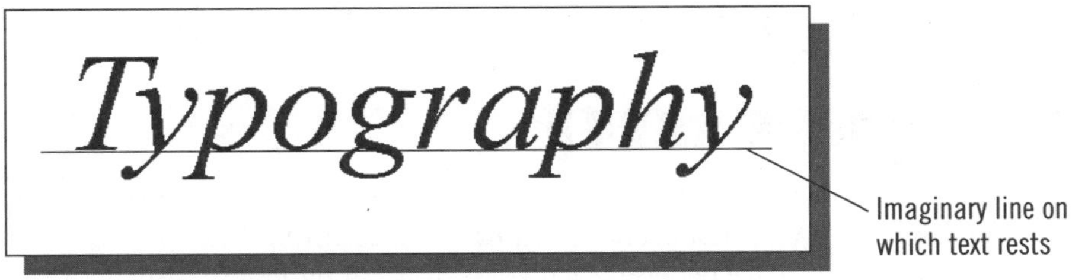

Typography

Imaginary line on which text rests

FIGURE G-13: "AGLE" with a 6-point baseline shift applied

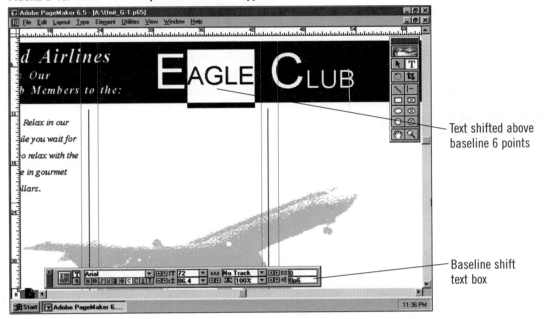

Text shifted above baseline 6 points

Baseline shift text box

FIGURE G-14: Eagle Club with baseline shift applied

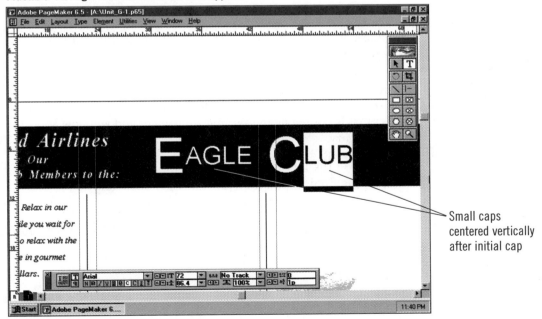

Small caps centered vertically after initial cap

Adjusting Text Spacing

Adjusting word and letter spacing is a powerful PageMaker feature for improving the overall appearance of your publication. You have full control of the space between each character and the amount of space between each word. You can tighten spacing between characters to fit text in a defined area or make headlines and small text easier to read by increasing the spacing.  You can modify word or character spacing using one of three methods. First, you can adjust spacing of both words and letters in a paragraph or selected paragraphs by percentages using the Spacing option in the Paragraph specifications dialog box. Secondly, you can use the Kerning option on the Control palette to specify the exact measurement of space between characters in the selected text. **Kerning** is adjusting space between a pair or range of characters. Finally, you can adjust spacing quickly by choosing one of six predefined spacing defaults using the Track option on the Control palette or in the Character Specifications dialog box. Joe wants to "loosen" the text in the first column to make it easier to read. He also wants to adjust the kerning of the category headings in the menu to make the categories more eye-catching.

Steps

1. Use the scroll bars to position the first paragraph in the first column in the center of the publication window

2. Select the entire paragraph, then click the **Track list arrow** on the Control palette
See Figure G-15. The Track pop-up list appears. See Table G-4 for examples of all six tracking options.

3. Click **Very Loose**
Spacing increases between the characters in the paragraph text. Joe now wants to increase the space between characters for the category headings. He will use the Kerning option because it gives him more control over spacing than tracking does.

4. Use the scroll bars to position the word "Appetizers" in the publication window, then select the word **Appetizers**

5. Double-click in the **Kerning text box** on the control palette, type **.25**, then click the **Apply button** 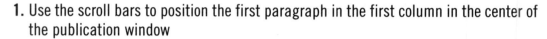 on the Control palette
See Figure G-16. The space between characters is measured in ems. One **em** is equal to the width of a lowercase *m* of the same size and font. Values greater than 0 increase the space between characters, and values under 0 decrease the space. Joe is satisfied with the special effect that is created by the kerning adjustment and will now apply the same setting to the next category.

6. Scroll down the publication, select the word **Salads**, double-click in the **Kerning text box** on the Control palette, type **.25**, then click
You will open a more complete menu in the next lesson, so you can save and close this file.

7. Click **File** on the menu bar, select **Close**, then click **Yes** when you are asked if you want to save your publication

FIGURE G-15: Track pop-up list

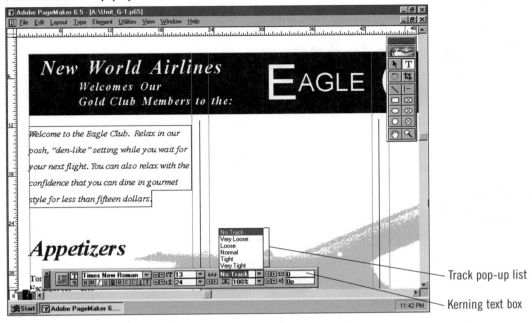

Track pop-up list

Kerning text box

FIGURE G-16: Increased kerning applied to category divider

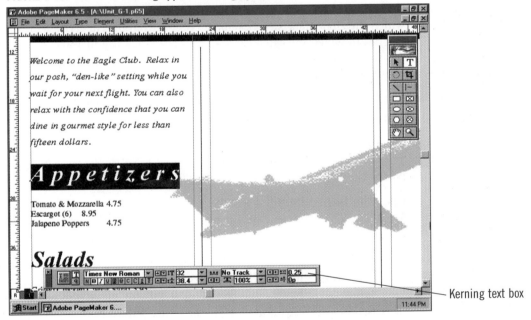

Kerning text box

TABLE G-4: Examples of tracking

example	setting
This is an example of Tracking	No Track
This is an example of Tracking	Loose
This is an example of Tracking	Very Loose
This is an example of Tracking	Normal
This is an example of Tracking	Tight
This is an example of Tracking	Very Tight

PageMaker 6.5

Setting Character Widths

PageMaker gives you the option to change the width of an individual character using the Horizontal scale option. You can set the character width by using either the Control palette or the Character Specifications dialog box. You can scale character width by any percentage from 5% to 250%. The default percentage is 100%. ▰▰▰ Joe would like to widen each character in the category headings. Joe could use the Control palette to adjust the width of the categories, but he decides to adjust all of the category headings at once using the Categories style.

1. **Open the file UNIT_G-2 from your Student Disk**
   This menu is nearly complete.

2. **Click Window on the menu bar, then click Show Styles**
   Joe has set up separate styles for the category headings, item names, and the descriptions.

3. **Click the Text tool [T] in the toolbox, click the heading Appetizers, then press [Ctrl] and right-click to change the view to Actual Size**
   The Categories style is selected in the Styles palette. Joe wants to create a special effect and widen the characters' size. See Table G-5 for examples of styles with applied set widths. Joe decides to widen the category heading's character size to 130% of its actual width. He will modify the widths of all the category headings at once by changing the Categories style. You could use the Control palette to change the width one heading at a time.

MacintoshUser

This replaces Step 3.
3. Click the Text tool [T] in the toolbox, click the heading Appetizers, then press and hold [⌘] [option] and click the left mouse button to change the view to Actual Size

4. **Click Type on the menu bar, then click Define Styles**
   The Define Styles dialog box opens.

5. **Click Categories in the Style list box, click Edit, then click Char**
   The Character Specifications dialog box opens. Notice the current width of the characters is Normal.

6. **Click the Horiz scale list arrow**
   See Figure G-17. You can choose one of the predefined widths or type the desired percentage that you wish to scale the text. Joe wants to draw attention to the category names, so he chooses the largest predefined width setting.

QuickTip

Print your publication to make sure the printed character widths match your screen's character widths.

7. **Click 130, then click OK three times**
   See Figure G-18. Notice the character width for all of the text in Categories style has increased in size. Joe, upon viewing the entire publication, is satisfied with the effect of the widened category headings so he saves his publication.

8. **Save the publication**

FIGURE G-17: Horizontal scale options

Predefined widths

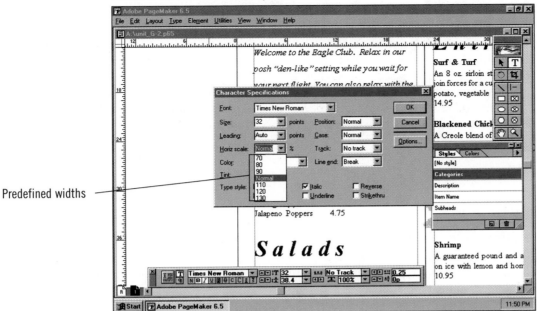

FIGURE G-18: New horizontal width applied to the Categories style

Width of characters increased to fill entire column

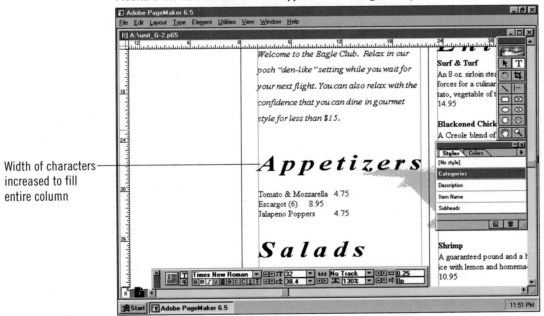

TABLE G-5: Examples of horizontal character widths

width setting	example
80	New World Airlines
Normal	New World Airlines
130	New World Airlines

PageMaker 6.5

Setting Tabs

Tabs, which are nonprinting characters, allow you to position text at specific locations within a text block. Tabs can help you create columns of text within a text block. You can set left, center, right, and decimal tabs. See Table G-6 for a description of the tab icons in the Indents/Tabs dialog box. Tab settings can also include a leader. **Leaders** are repeat patterns between tabbed items. Examples of leaders include repeated dots or dashes. ▰▰▰ Joe wants to add dot leaders to create a visual link between the item description and the price.

Steps

1. **Use the horizontal scroll bar to center column 2 in the publication window**
   Joe could change the tabs for each description individually using the Indents/Tabs option on the Type menu. However, by editing the Description style, Joe changes all of the tabs and leaders in the style at once.

2. **Click Type on the menu bar, then click Define Styles**
   The Define Styles dialog box opens.

3. **Click Description in the Style list box, click Edit, then click Tabs**
   The Indents/Tabs dialog box opens. A small section of the ruler shows the default tabs, and the indent markers reflect the width of the text block. Joe wants to use a right-aligned tab to align the prices near the right margin.

4. **Click the right tab icon** ⬇
   Now, if you click in the tab area located above the ruler, you will set a right-aligned tab.

5. **Click in the tab area around 18 picas**
   See Figure G-19. The exact position of the tab you placed appears in the Position text box. Joe decides to drag the tab closer to the right margin.

6. **Drag the right tab marker to the 19-pica mark**
   The Position text box verifies the location of the tab.

MacintoshUser

This replaces Step 7.
7. Click the **Leader** list
   arrow

7. **Click Leader**
   A list of options for tab leaders appears, as shown in Figure G-20. You choose one of the options from this list, or you can type any character in the Leader text box. The character in the text box then repeats between tabs as a leader.

8. **Click the dotted line option, then click OK three times**
   Dotted lines now fill the space between the last word in the menu item description and the price, as shown in Figure G-21. If any of the menu items do not display leaders, click to the left of the price, then press [Tab] until the leaders appear.

TABLE G-6: Tab icons in the Indents/Tabs dialog box

tab icons	name	description
⬇	Right tab	Sets a right-aligned tab
⬇	Left tab	Sets a left-aligned tab
⬇	Center tab	Sets a tab that centers text under it
⬇	Decimal tab	Sets a tab aligned to a decimal point

FIGURE G-19: **Right tab at the 18-pica mark**

Tab area for setting tabs

Right-aligned tab set at 18-pica mark

18-pica mark

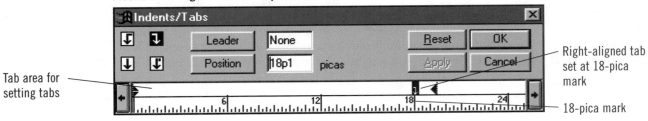

FIGURE G-20: **Leader options**

Click to choose this leader

19-pica mark

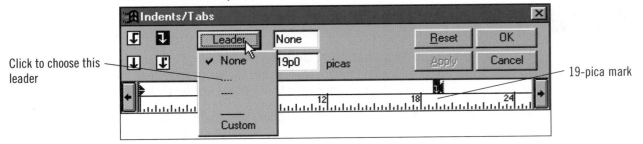

FIGURE G-21: **Tabs and leaders applied to text block**

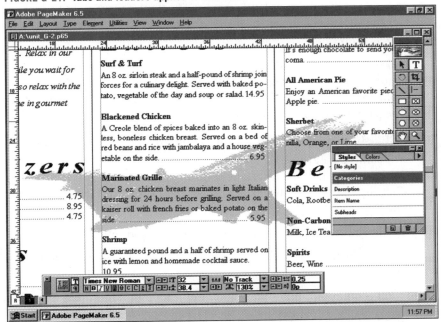

Using the Indents/Tabs Position option

When you work with small monitors, it can be difficult to drag a tab to a specific position on the ruler. The Position option in the Indents/Tabs dialog box allows you to set tabs at smaller increments than your ruler displays. To set a tab using the Position option, type the position of the tab in the text box, click the Position list arrow, then click Add tab. You can also set tabs in increments by clicking Position, then clicking Repeat tab.

PageMaker 6.5

Setting Indents

PageMaker lets you set both indents and tabs within a text block. **Indents** allow you to move text inward from either the right or left margin without changing the original margin settings. You can change indents many different ways. You can use the Control palette, the Paragraph Specifications dialog box, or the Indents/Tabs dialog box. See Table G-7 for a description of the indent icons in the Indents/Tabs dialog box. ➤ Joe wants to indent each of the menu description paragraphs to create a layered effect that will make the menu items stand out from their descriptions.

MacintoshUser

This replaces Step 3.
3. Drag the **left indent marker** ▶ until **4** appears in the Position text box

1. Click **Type** on the menu bar, then click **Define Styles**
The Define Styles dialog box opens. Once again Joe wants to change the indents for all the descriptions at once so he will edit the indent settings for the Description style.

2. Click **Description** in the Style list box, click **Edit**, then click **Tabs**
The Indents/Tabs dialog box opens. Joe decides to indent the descriptions 4 picas from the left column guide.

3. Drag the **left indent marker** ▶ until **4p0** appears in the Position text box
See Figure G-22. Make sure you position the pointer on the lower triangle of ▶. The top triangle moves independently from the bottom, so you need to drag the bottom triangle to set the left indent.

4. Click **OK** three times
All the menu item descriptions now contain a left indent of 4 picas along with their dotted leaders, as shown in Figure G-23. Joe would now like to set a first line indent for the welcome paragraph in the first column. He didn't set a style for this body of text so he will use the paragraph view of the Control palette to set the indent independently.

5. Scroll to display the paragraph of text in the first column, then click ⌶ inside the welcome paragraph
You need to place the insertion point inside the paragraph to which you want to apply the first-line indent. Joe needs to display the Control palette before he can use it to set the indent.

6. If the Control palette is not already displayed, click **Window** on the menu bar, click **Show Control Palette**, then click the **Paragraph view button** 📭 on the Control palette

7. Double-click the **First-line indent text box** on the control palette, type **4p**, then click the **Apply button** 📧 on the Control palette
See Figure G-24. Joe decides 4 picas is too much space for a first-line indent, so he changes the indent to 2 picas.

8. Double-click the **First-line indent text box** again, type **2**, then click 📧
Joe is satisfied with the indents and saves his publication.

9. Save the publication

FIGURE G-22: Indents/Tabs dialog box

Left indent icon at 4 picas

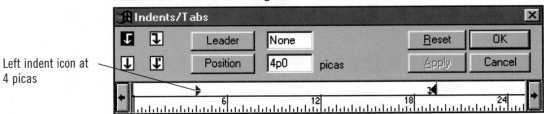

FIGURE G-23: Indents applied to text

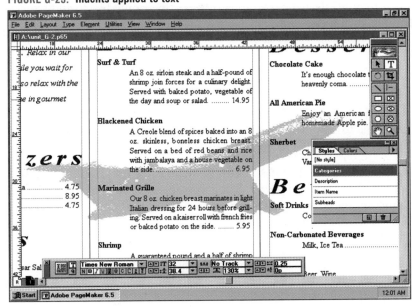

FIGURE G-24: First line indented 4 picas

Welcome paragraph indented

Insertion point

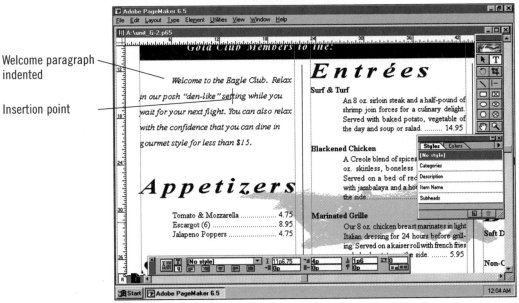

TABLE G-7: Indent icons in the Indents/Tabs dialog box

indent icons	description
	First-line indent
	Left indent
	Right indent

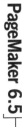

PageMaker 6.5

Using the Bullets and Numbering Plug-in

The Bullets and Numbering Plug-in allows you to use bullets, numbers, or special characters with a tab in front of each selected paragraph. You can use this feature to add bullets or numbers to consecutive paragraphs, to all paragraphs with a specific style, to every paragraph in a story, or to only selected paragraphs. Joe would like to add a special airplane character in front of each menu item.

Steps

1. **Click Ӿ inside the menu item name Surf & Turf in the second column**
   In order to use the Bullets and Numbering Plug-in, the insertion point must be placed inside the text block where the feature will be applied.

Trouble?

If you make a mistake while using the Bullets and Numbering Plug-in, you can use the Revert command on the File menu to reopen the last saved version of the current file.

MacintoshUser

This replaces Steps 4 and 5.
4. Click the Font list arrow, then click Zapf Dingbats
5. Click the airplane character in the first row, ninth column
Resume at Step 6.

2. **Click Utilities on the menu bar, point to Plug-ins, then click Bullets and Numbering**
   The Bullets and numbering dialog box opens, as shown in Figure G-25. You can pick any bullet in the Bullet style section or click Edit to see a list of all the optional characters that can be used instead of a bullet.

3. **Click Edit**
   The Edit bullet dialog box opens, as shown in Figure G-26. All of the characters for the selected font appear in the dialog box. Joe needs to choose the Wingdings font, which contains a special airplane character.

4. **Click the Font list arrow, then click Wingdings**
   Notice that all of the characters from the previous font change to the characters for the Wingdings font. Joe now looks for the airplane character.

5. **Click the airplane character in the second row near the center column**
   The Example box previews the airplane character.

6. **Click OK**
   The Edit bullet dialog box closes and you return to the Bullets and numbering dialog box.

7. **In the Range section, click the All those with style option button**
   This will apply the airplane character to the beginning of each paragraph in the selected style. Notice that Description appears in the list box. Joe needs to change the style to Item Name.

8. **Click the style list arrow, click Item Name, then click OK**
   The airplane character is automatically applied to the front of each paragraph in the Item Name style, as shown in Figure G-27.

9. **Close the Control palette, save the publication, then exit PageMaker**

FIGURE G-25: Bullets and numbering dialog box

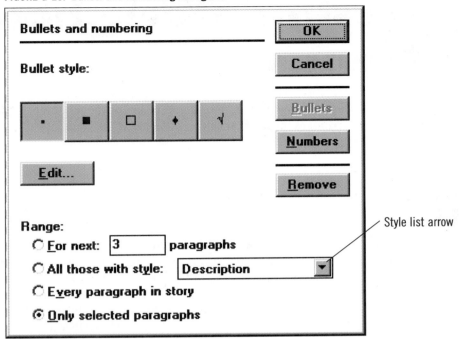

Style list arrow

FIGURE G-26: Edit bullet dialog box

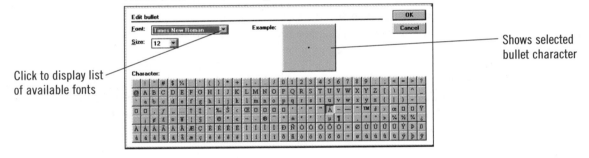

Shows selected
bullet character

Click to display list
of available fonts

FIGURE G-27: Airplane character applied to Item Name style

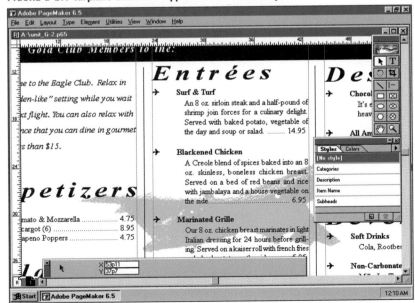

Design Workshop: Menus

A menu needs to provide a creative, concise listing of a restaurant's fare. The menu needs to feature certain selections and give an overall impression of the restaurant. ✎━━ After creating the menu, Joe critiques his work, as shown in Figure G-28.

Details

Does the menu highlight the items it should?

According to Joe's information, the Surf & Turf needed to be featured prominently to help sell it. He placed the menu item at the top of the center column of the menu. Other ways to highlight the menu item could be to reverse the text, place a bullet or other icon next to the menu item to give it special treatment, or change the font to something much bolder. No one way is correct. Usually, a few different techniques can work well together to produce the desired result.

Is the menu well organized?

Joe separated the menu into main sections to help customers select items quickly. He also placed all of the entrées in one column so customers wouldn't have to search the menu for more selections.

What other improvements can Joe make?

By making the menu one color (black), Joe keeps costs down. He plans to take the menu to a local copy center and copy the entire menu on a cream-colored paper stock. The color scheme matches that of the Eagle Club. Joe can easily change menu items to meet the needs of the chef or change the menu seasonally. For example, during Thanksgiving, a turkey dinner could replace the Surf & Turf. To add variety or to add more menu items, Joe could change the size of the menu or possibly rotate the orientation so the menu is tall instead of wide.

New World Airlines
Welcomes Our
Gold Club Members to the:

EAGLE CLUB

Welcome to the Eagle Club. Relax in our posh "den-like" setting while you wait for your next flight. You can also relax with the confidence that you can dine in gourmet style for less than $15.

Appetizers

Tomato & Mozzarella..................4.758.95
Escargot (6).................................
Jalapeno Poppers.........................4.75

Salads

Grilled Chicken Caesar Salad 5.95
Chef Salad 5.95
Spinach & Tomato Salad 4.75
House Salad 2.50
Manager's Special 2.75
Salad and Soup of the Day 3.75

Entrées

Q **Surf & Turf**
An 8 oz. sirloin steak and a half-pound of shrimp join forces for a culinary delight. Served with baked potato, vegetable of the day and soup or salad. 14.95

Q **Blackened Chicken**
A Creole blend of spices baked into an 8 oz. skinless, boneless chicken breast. Served on a bed of red beans and rice with jambalaya and a house vegetable on the side. 6.95

Q **Marinated Grille**
Our 8 oz. chicken breast marinates in light Italian dressing for 24 hours before grilling. Served on a kaiser roll with french fries or baked potato on the side. 5.95

Q **Shrimp**
A guaranteed pound and a half of shrimp served on ice with lemon and homemade cocktail sauce. 10.95

Q **Swordfish**
Meaty, grilled swordfish served with new potatoes and house vegetable. 12.95

Desserts

Q **Chocolate Cake**
It's enough chocolate to send you into a heavenly coma. 3.50

Q **All American Pie**
Enjoy an American favorite piece of homemade Apple pie. 3.50

Q **Sherbet**
Choose from one of your favorite flavors: Vanilla, Orange, or Lime. 1.75

Beverages

Q **Soft Drinks**
Cola, Rootbeer, Lemon-lime........1.25

Q **Non-Carbonated Beverages**
Milk, Ice Tea................................1.25

Q **Spirits**
Beer, Wine..................................2.50

Thank You for your patronage!

Practice

▶ Concepts Review

Label each of the publication window elements shown in Figure G-29

FIGURE G-29

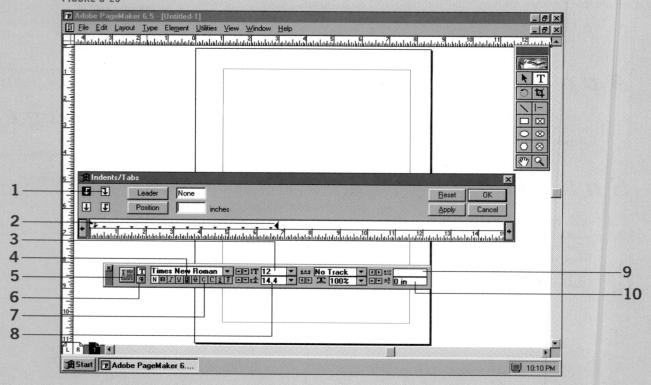

Match each of the statements with the term it describes.

11. **Picas**
12. **Preferences**
13. **Nudge button**
14. **Tracking**
15. **Control palette**

a. Make changes by a preset measurement
b. Space between characters
c. Type of measurement
d. Easily changes character and paragraph settings
e. PageMaker custom settings

Select the best answer from the list of choices.

16. **When you create your page layout, what are the power points?**
    a. The four corners where the margins intersect
    b. The sections of the publication that are read first
    c. The graphics in the lower-left corner
    d. None of the above

17. **Using the Preferences dialog box, you can customize which of the following:**
    a. Measurement system
    b. Quotation marks

    c. Save file size options

    d. All of the above

18. The imaginary line on which characters of type reside is the:

    a. Margin line

    b. Bar

    c. Baseline

    d. Either b or c

19. The Track option in the Character Specifications dialog box allows you to:

    a. Choose one of six predefined spacing defaults

    b. Manually set the space between characters

    c. Track the amount of space taken up on a page

    d. Track the letter size of a paragraph

20. The Kerning option on the Control palette allows you to

    a. Set the tracking for paragraphs

    b. Choose a predefined spacing default

    c. Change the text size

    d. Manually set the space between characters

21. PageMaker's default setting for tabs is:

    a. Every .25"

    b. Every .5"

    c. Every 1"

    d. There is no default setting

22. Leaders refer to:

    a. Repeated patterns between tabs

    b. Default tab settings

    c. Decimal tab settings

    d. Both b and c

23. Indents allow you to:

    a. Set tabs within text

    b. Move text up or down within a column

    c. Move text inward from either the right or left margin

    d. Both a and b

24. Using the Control palette in character view, you can modify the following, except:

    a. Font size

    b. Type style

    c. Rotate text

    d. None of the above

25. Using the Control palette in paragraph view, you can modify the following, except:

    a. Indents

    b. Space between paragraphs

    c. Widows and orphans

    d. None of the above

26. Character width can be set using the:

    a. Font menu

    b. Control palette

    c. Character Specifications dialog box

    d. Both b and c

► Skills Review

1. Set preferences.

a. Start PageMaker and open the file UNIT_G-3 from your Student Disk.

b. Click File on the menu bar, point to Preferences, then click General.

c. Select Picas from the Measurements in list box.

d. Select Picas from the Vertical ruler list box.

e. In the Guides section, click the Back radio button.

f. Select the Smaller option in the Save section to decrease the size of the saved publication file.

g. Open the More Preferences dialog box.

h. In the Text section, select the Use typographer's quotes option.

i. Click OK twice to close the dialog boxes.

2. Apply small capitals.

a. Click the Text tool in the toolbox.

b. Move the pointer to the beginning of the headline and select the headline.

c. Press [Ctrl] and right-click to change the view to Actual Size *(Macintosh users: Press [⌘][option] and click the mouse button).*

d. Click Type on the menu bar, then click Character.

e. Select the Small caps option from the Case list box.

f. Click Options.

g. Type "50" in the Small caps size text box.

h. Click OK twice.

3. Adjust the baseline.

a. Deselect the text by clicking outside the highlighted area.

b. Highlight the "he" in "The."

c. Click Window on the menu bar, then click Show Control Palette.

d. Apply a baseline shift to the headline by clicking the Baseline shift nudge down button twice.

e. Readjust the baseline shift by clicking the Baseline shift nudge up button six times.

f. Adjust the baseline shift to your preference.

g. Deselect the text, then highlight the "iberty" in "Liberty" and apply the same baseline shift as you chose for "The."

h. Apply the same baseline shift to the "lub" in "Club."

i. Press [Shift] and right-click to change the view to Fit in Window *(Macintosh users: Press [⌘][0] and click the mouse button).*

4. Adjust text spacing.

a. Select the entire menu text. (*Hint*: Do not include headline.)

b. Select the Very Loose track option on the Control palette.

c. Deselect the text by clicking outside the highlighted area.

d. Select the headline.

e. Press [Ctrl] and right-click to change the view to Actual Size *(Macintosh users: Press [⌘][option] and click the mouse button).*

f. Click the Kerning nudge up button on the Control palette to add space between the characters until the headline touches both the left and right margins.

g. Deselect the text by clicking outside the highlighted area.

h. Press [Ctrl] and right-click to return the view to Fit in Window *(Macintosh users: Press [⌘][0] and click the mouse button).*

5. Set character widths.

   a. Click Type on the menu bar, then click Define Styles.

   b. Remove all styles by clicking each style individually and then clicking Remove.

   c. Click New.

   d. Type "Category" in the Name text box.

   e. Click Char.

   f. Select Arial *(Macintosh users: Helvetica)*, 14 points, bold, and small caps (be sure to deselect Italic).

   g. Click the Horiz scale list arrow, then click 130.

   h. Set the baseline shift to Zero.

   i. Click OK three times.

   j. If necessary, click Window on the menu bar, then click Show Styles.

   k. Press [Ctrl] and right-click to change the view to Actual Size *(Macintosh users: Press [⌘][option] and click the mouse button)*.

   l. Select the menu category heading "Appetizers" and apply the Category style.

   m. Apply the same style to all of the menu category headings.

6. Set indents.

   a. Make sure the insertion point is in a text block with no style applied, click Type on the menu bar, then click Define Styles.

   b. Click New.

   c. Type "Description" in the Name text box.

   d. Click Char.

   e. Select the Times New Roman font and a point size of 11, then click OK *(Macintosh users: Select Times, 10 points, then click OK)*.

   f. Click Tabs.

   g. Drag the first-line indent icon to the 1p mark.

   h. Click OK three times.

   i. Click inside the first description paragraph.

   j. Apply the Description style.

   k. Apply the Description style to the rest of the menu descriptions, including those that list only a price.

7. Set tabs.

   a. Click Type on the menu bar, then click Define Styles.

   b. Click Description in the Style list box, then click Edit.

   c. Click Tabs.

   d. Click the right tab icon.

   e. Click the ruler at the 18-pica mark.

   f. Select the dotted line leader option.

   g. Click OK three times.

8. Use the Bullets and Numbering Plug-in.

   a. Click the pointer in the category heading "Appetizers".

   b. Click Utilities on the menu bar, point to Plug-ins, then click Bullets and Numbering.

   c. Select the diamond or a character of your choice.

   d. In the Range section, click the All those with style **option** button.

   e. Click in the All those with style list box, then click Category.

   f. Click OK.

   g. Save your publication, then exit PageMaker.

▶ Independent Challenges

1. You are a cook at a New York pizza shop called Tainted's Basement Pizza Parlor. The owner, Avis Figlioni, asks you to create a new menu. Avis wants the menu to be one page with two columns in a page size smaller than 8½" × 11". He wants to list his appetizers and salads in the left column and the pizzas and different toppings in the upper-right corner of the menu. Below the pizzas, Avis wants to list the beverages and the Friday night happy hour pizza and drink specials. The clientele at the pizza parlor is mostly college students and young adults, so the design needs to be creative but legible.

To complete this independent challenge:

1. Create a rough sketch of the menu indicating the different categories of foods and the different graphics you want to use.
2. Create a new document 5" wide by 9" tall, then save it as Pizza menu on your Student Disk. Use the Document Setup dialog box for the margins and the size of the menu. Use the Preferences dialog box to set typographer's quotes and greeked text. Use pica measurement and choose the Save Faster option.
3. Place the graphic file UNIT_G-4 in your publication, then place the menu text from the file UNIT_G-5. These files are located on your Student Disk.
4. Use small caps for the headlines and subheadlines.
5. Adjust the tracking for the fonts you choose to enhance their appearance.
6. Set tab leaders between the menu items and their prices.
7. Save your publication, then print it and submit the printout and your sketch.

2. Collect three menus from local restaurants. Critique the menus using the design guidelines from this unit by answering the following questions:

- Does the menu adequately use the power points? What is the first thing you see when you open the menu?
- Does the overall design organize the categories of food in a simple, easily understood format?
- Does the menu contain too much text? Is there too much text because of the number of items in the menu or is it because of extensive explanations of the menu items.
- Does the menu offer too many choices? Studies show restaurant guests look at a menu for 1.5 minutes. Can you make your choices easily in this time frame?

Now try to re-create one of the menus using the techniques learned in this unit. Use the Control palette as much as possible for both character and paragraph formatting modifications. Before creating the new menu in PageMaker, draw a rough sketch of the menu.

To complete this independent challenge:

1. Open a new document and modify the following preferences: use the metric measuring system (millimeters), choose the Save Smaller option, set greeked text at 8 points, and set typographer's quotes.
2. Adjust tracking and letter spacing to give the type the correct look.
3. Use tab leaders between menu items and prices.
4. Save your publication as Sample menu to your Student Disk.
5. Print the new menu, then submit the printout and your sketch.

3. You have been asked to create a menu for Carlos and Gellis' Country Style Restaurant. The menu should be one-sided, with a Wide orientation so that Carlos and Gellis can also use the menu as a placemat.

To complete this independent challenge:

1. Create a sketch of your menu first, and then create a new document in PageMaker using your sketch as a guide.
2. Modify the Preferences dialog box to include the pica measurement system, the Save Smaller option, and the typographer's quotes.
3. Place the menu text from the file UNIT_G-5 in your publication.
4. Use small caps for the headlines and subheadings.
5. Adjust the font size and the tracking.
6. Set tab leaders between menu items and their prices.
7. Use the Bullets and Numbering Plug-in to place a special character in front of each category on the menu.
8. Save your publication as Placemat menu on your Student Disk, then print your menu.

4. You work for a prestigious design firm in New York City. Your boss has asked you to create a new menu for a well-known restaurant in the city. This could be your big break. If the client likes your design, you will get that promotion you have been waiting for. You decide to use PageMaker to design the most attractive and eye-catching menu possible. The restaurant manager has requested that the design be in black-and-white, as their menus get so much use that they must be reprinted often. She also told your boss that their printer requires that the publication be submitted in picas.

To complete this independent challenge:

1. Use the World Wide Web to search for information on a famous restaurant located in New York City.
2. From the information that you find, create a thumbnail sketch of your menu keeping in mind the guidelines that you learned in this unit.
3. Set your menu's preferences before you add the menu text. You should be able to find a restaurant that offers some or all of their menu items on the World Wide Web. If not, make up some of your own dishes and be sure to include the prices.
4. Use reverse type for the restaurant's name and apply the Small caps option. Also, make the name more attractive by adjusting its position on the baseline.
5. Adjust the character width of any menu categories that you use to make the design more eye-catching. Also, increase the kerning in your menu descriptions using the Control palette.
6. Add dot leaders to separate your descriptions from the prices, and indent each of the menu description paragraphs.
7. Add a special character before the restaurant's most desirable menu item.
8. Save your menu as NYC menu on your Student disk, and then print it. Critique your menu and turn in your sketch, all printouts, and your critique.

► **Visual Workshop**

Mike and Celeste McInscent, owners of the new uptown bar and grill called Blue Moon, have contracted your graphic design agency to create their menu. Open the file UNIT_G-6 from your Student Disk. Enhance the overall appearance of text in the draft to make a menu similar to the one shown in Figure G-30.

FIGURE G-30

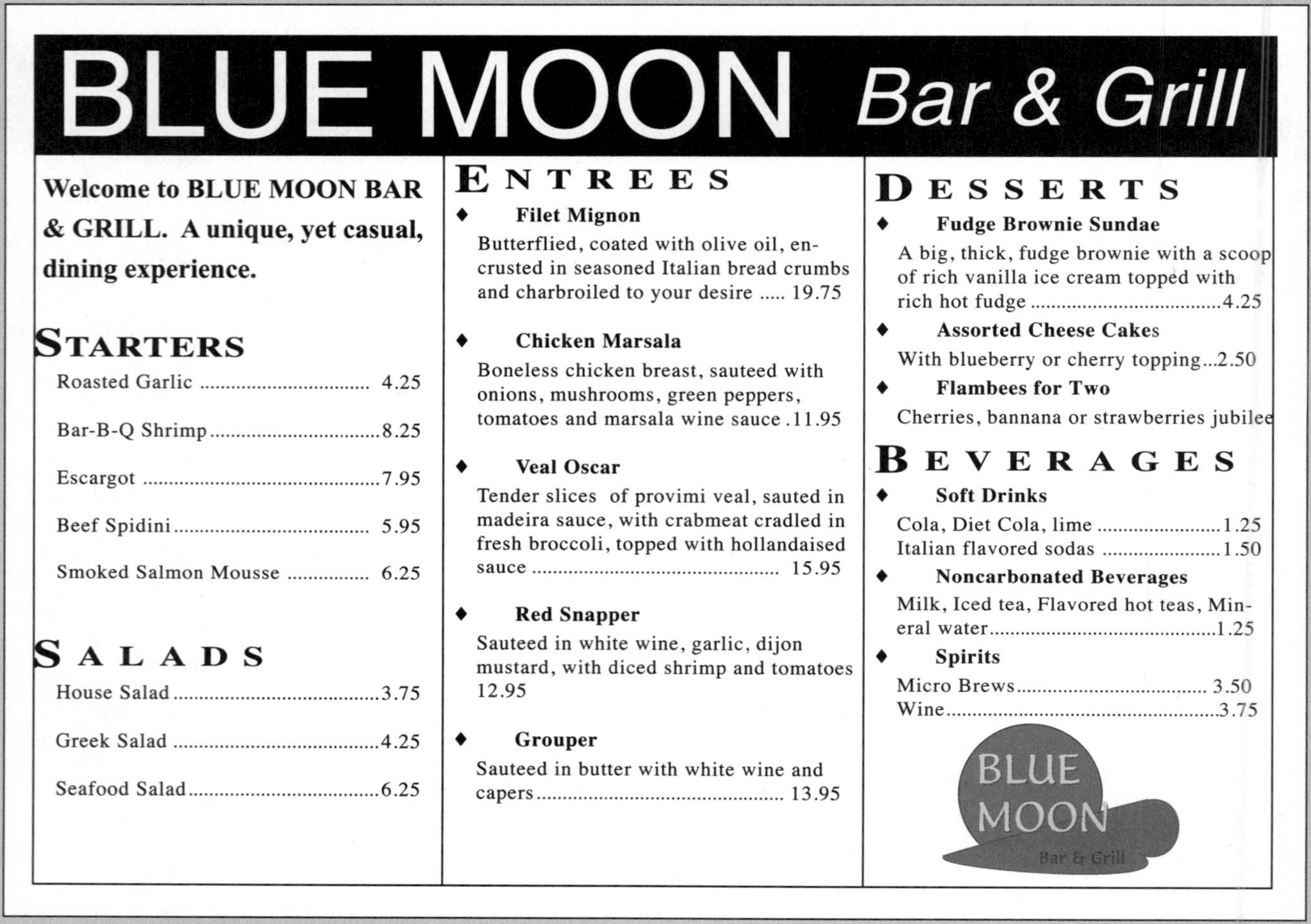

BLUE MOON *Bar & Grill*

Welcome to BLUE MOON BAR & GRILL. A unique, yet casual, dining experience.

STARTERS

Roasted Garlic	4.25
Bar-B-Q Shrimp	8.25
Escargot	7.95
Beef Spidini	5.95
Smoked Salmon Mousse	6.25

SALADS

House Salad	3.75
Greek Salad	4.25
Seafood Salad	6.25

ENTREES

♦ **Filet Mignon**
Butterflied, coated with olive oil, en-crusted in seasoned Italian bread crumbs and charbroiled to your desire 19.75

♦ **Chicken Marsala**
Boneless chicken breast, sauteed with onions, mushrooms, green peppers, tomatoes and marsala wine sauce .11.95

♦ **Veal Oscar**
Tender slices of provimi veal, sauted in madeira sauce, with crabmeat cradled in fresh broccoli, topped with hollandaised sauce 15.95

♦ **Red Snapper**
Sauteed in white wine, garlic, dijon mustard, with diced shrimp and tomatoes 12.95

♦ **Grouper**
Sauteed in butter with white wine and capers.. 13.95

DESSERTS

♦ **Fudge Brownie Sundae**
A big, thick, fudge brownie with a scoop of rich vanilla ice cream topped with rich hot fudge 4.25

♦ **Assorted Cheese Cakes**
With blueberry or cherry topping...2.50

♦ **Flambees for Two**
Cherries, bannana or strawberries jubilee

BEVERAGES

♦ **Soft Drinks**
Cola, Diet Cola, lime 1.25
Italian flavored sodas 1.50

♦ **Noncarbonated Beverages**
Milk, Iced tea, Flavored hot teas, Mineral water..1.25

♦ **Spirits**
Micro Brews.................................... 3.50
Wine..3.75

PageMaker 6.5

Using
Advanced Graphics

Objectives

► **Plan a poster**
► **Use the Control palette in object view**
► **Minimize PageMaker file sizes**
► **Scale a graphic**
► **Place an inline graphic**
► **Modify an inline graphic**
► **Skew an object**
► **Reflect an object**
► **Change an object's links**
► **Use layers**
► **Use image control**
► **Design Workshop: Posters**

You can use PageMaker's advanced graphics capabilities to improve the overall appearance of your publication. In this unit you will use the object view of the Control palette to modify text blocks and graphics quickly and precisely. To manage your files better, you will also learn how to minimize a PageMaker publication file size and place a graphic in a line of text. Using the Control palette in object view and the Image Control dialog box, you will learn to manipulate graphics to create special effects, such as skewing and reflecting. ✎ Joe Martin needs to develop several advertising posters for New World Airlines flights to the New England area.

Planning a Poster

Posters follow many of the same rules as other advertising publications but on a larger scale. Posters usually contain large, color graphics and bold type. Although full-color posters can be expensive, they are often worth the expense because they can create an instant and lasting impact on viewers. ▰▰▰▰ Joe's next task is to plan a series of posters advertising New World Airlines destinations. His first poster will advertise new flights to the New England area and will target people who are going to New England for a vacation.

Details

Create a proof version of poster

A **proof version** is a smaller scaled, less costly version of the final poster. You can use a proof version for editing purposes and for previewing the final output. Because posters are costly to produce, Joe wants to be sure of a successful design in a less costly form before he proceeds. The proof version will be an 8" × 14" page size. After Joe is satisfied with his proof version of the poster, he will send his PageMaker publication file to the commercial printer. The printer will create another proof to make sure the printing equipment can produce the correct color output. Once Joe approves this version, the commercial printer will then print the poster scaled to the final dimensions at 24" × 42" poster size.

Use colorful, striking graphics

Posters are meant to be on display. Whether tacked up on a wall or placed in a frame, posters have a longer life span than most other forms of advertising. For a successful design, you need to use graphics or photography that is pleasing and memorable. Joe uses a photo of a lighthouse from a stock photography catalog. This photo dominates Joe's sketch of the poster. See Figure H-1.

Use bold text in a unique way

If you plan to use text on your poster, it should be large and bold so it jumps out at the viewer. Joe will use the words "New England" in bold blue type; then he will add a clip art graphic of a lobster to help make the words "New England" stand out.

Use paper stock that is durable

Picking out the type of paper your poster will be printed on depends on the amount of money you have budgeted for your project. Poster paper can be expensive, especially when a thicker card stock paper is chosen. The thicker the paper, the longer the poster will last. Joe decides to use a 60-pound glossy paper so the poster can be rolled into a mailing tube and sent to travel agencies across the country.

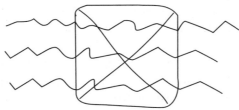

PHOTO

NEW ☒ ENGLAND

1-800-HORIZON

PageMaker 6.5

Using the Control Palette in Object View

The Control palette can appear in character view, paragraph view, and object view. **Object view** gives you the ability to create unique effects with graphic images and to modify or transform them easily and uniformly. To **transform** an object means to change its appearance by sizing, rotating, skewing, reflecting, or cropping. You have complete control of graphic objects in the publication window. See Table H-1 for a description of the object view options. Joe uses the Control palette in object view as he develops the poster. He understands, and hopes to take advantage of, all of the following features and benefits that it offers:

Details

 ## Additional graphics capabilities

The Control palette in object view gives you the ability to reflect and skew graphic objects. **Reflecting** means flipping an object either from top to bottom or from right to left. **Skewing** allows you to stretch the object at an angle, giving it a distorted appearance. Joe wants to use both of these features to create a box positioned behind both the top and bottom headlines on his poster. These two new features are available only on the Control palette. See Figure H-2.

 ## Precise measurement transformations

You can rely on the rulers and your own judgment to size, rotate, or move graphics using the mouse. However, using the object view of the Control palette, you can enter exact measurement values for sizing, rotating, and moving graphic objects. Joe will use the Control palette to determine the exact dimensions of the New England photo.

 ## Transform objects from a specific reference point proxy

The **proxy** on the Control palette is a graphical representation of a selected object. You must choose one **reference point** which is an edge, corner, or center of the graphic, to serve as the base that remains stationary as you transform your graphic, as shown in Figure H-3. Joe will select the proxy reference point before he sizes, skews, and reflects the graphic objects in his poster.

 ## Transform multiple objects at once

You can rotate, reflect, or move multiple objects at one time using the Control palette. This method allows for a quick and easy way to transform graphics. However, you cannot scale or skew multiple objects at one time. Remember that to select multiple objects you can use the selection marquee or the shift-click method. Joe will not be using this feature in this lesson but will remember to use it if he formats multiple objects in his other posters.

FIGURE H-2: **Control palette in object view**

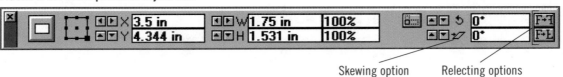

Skewing option   Relecting options

FIGURE H-3: **The proxy reference point**

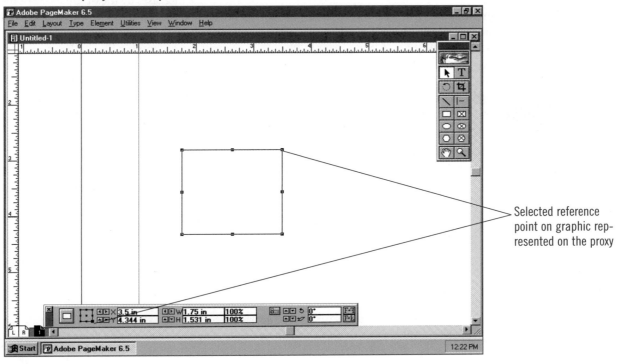

Selected reference point on graphic represented on the proxy

TABLE H-1: **Control palette's object view buttons and options**

button/box	option	description
◀▶ X 0 in	**Position X option**	Coordinate for the reference point on the horizontal ruler
▲▼ Y 0 in	**Position Y option**	Coordinate for the reference point on the vertical ruler
◀▶ W 0 in 100%	**Width sizing option**	Sets the horizontal measurement value of the selected object
▲▼ H 0 in 100%	**Height sizing option**	Sets the vertical measurement value of the selected object
	Scaling button	Sizes a graphic proportionally or nonproportionally
	Cropping button	Conceals part of the graphic
	Proportional scaling on indicator	Sizes an image to any percentage of its original dimensions
	Proportional scaling off indicator	Sizes height and width dimensions independently
	Printer resolution scaling button	Scales a placed graphic image to match the resolution of the target printer
▲▼ ↺ 0°	**Rotating option**	Changes the rotation position of an object; you can adjust the rotation by .1° increments using the proxy reference point
▲▼ ✐ 0°	**Skewing option**	Changes the skew position of an object; you can adjust the skew by .1° increments from the proxy reference point
F→]	**Horizontal reflecting button**	Flips a selected object horizontally
F→↓	**Vertical reflecting button**	Flips a selected object vertically

PageMaker 6.5

Minimizing PageMaker File Sizes

Each time you place a graphic, your publication's file size increases by the original size of the placed graphic. You can minimize the size of your PageMaker publication by turning off the option for storing a copy of a graphic in the publication. When you no longer store a copy of the placed image in the publication, it is important to keep the original source graphic file on the same disk as your PageMaker publication file. PageMaker needs to link the publication file to the source file to display the placed graphic at the highest resolution on your screen and in the final printed output. Joe has a limited amount of space on his disk; therefore, he decides to minimize the size of his PageMaker publication file by turning off the Store copy publication option.

1. **Start PageMaker and open the file UNIT_H-1 from your Student Disk**

   The poster Joe started working on earlier appears in the publication window. Joe needs to place the lighthouse photo in the poster. Before he does this, he first wants to change the link option defaults for graphic objects that will minimize his publication's file size.

QuickTip

To change the linking default settings for all new publications, open the Link Options: Defaults dialog box when no publications are open.

2. **Click Element on the menu bar, then click Link Options**

   The Link Options: Defaults dialog box opens. See Figure H-4. In the Graphics section, the Store copy in publication check box is selected; the Update automatically check box is not.

3. **Click the Store copy in publication check box in the Graphics section to deselect this option**

   Turning off this option turns on the Update automatically option. This ensures that the placed graphics will be linked to their original source files, so that PageMaker will have the necessary information to display the graphics at the highest quality on the screen and in printed output. Note that turning off the Store copy in publication option only affects all future placed objects; it does not affect graphic objects previously placed in a publication.

4. **Click OK**

   The Link Options: Defaults dialog box closes. Now that Joe has turned off the Store copy in publication option, he can place the photo in the poster.

5. **If necessary, click Window on the menu bar, then click Show Control Palette**

   The Control palette appears in object view. Notice that as you drag the pointer across the pasteboard, the values in both the Position X and Y text boxes change to reflect the exact position of the pointer. Instead of using the publication window's rulers, Joe will use the Control palette to determine the precise position where he would like to place the photo.

MacintoshUser

This replaces Steps 6 and 7.
6. Click File on the menu bar, click Place, select the graphic file UNIT_H-2 from your Student Disk, then click OK; the pointer changes to 🔳
7. Move 🔳 to display "1 in" in the Position X text box and "1 in" in the Position Y text box on the Control palette, as shown in Figure H-5
Resume at Step 8.

6. **Click File on the menu bar, click Place, select the graphic file UNIT_H-2 from your Student Disk, then click Open**

   The pointer changes to ⊠. Joe uses the Control palette to specify the reference point for the exact placement.

7. **Move ⊠ to display "1 in" in the Position X text box and "1 in" in the Position Y text box on the Control palette, as shown in Figure H-5**

8. **Click the left mouse button**

   The graphic appears in the layout at the position specified in Step 7. In the next lesson Joe will enlarge the photo.

9. **Click File on the menu bar, then click Save**

   If you had not turned off the Store copy in publication option, your PageMaker publication file would have been around 475 kilobytes in size as compared to its present size of about 100 kilobytes.

FIGURE H-4: Link Options: Defaults dialog box

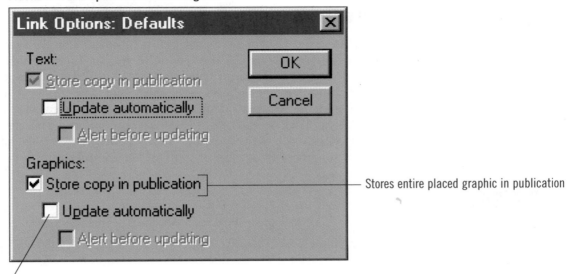

Stores entire placed graphic in publication

Select to ensure that
the placed graphic
will be linked to its
original source file

FIGURE H-5: Using the Control palette to place a graphic precisely

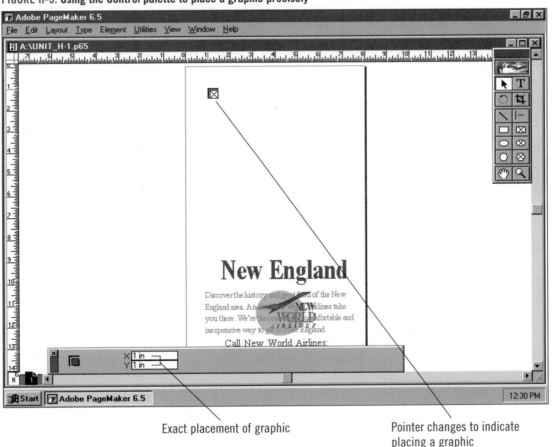

Exact placement of graphic

Pointer changes to indicate
placing a graphic

PageMaker 6.5

Scaling a Graphic

When a graphic is selected, the Control palette displays its coordinates on the page, its dimensions, and the percentage its size has been increased or decreased. The Control palette allows you to **scale** an object by decreasing or increasing the dimensions of its size either proportionally or nonproportionally. The advantage of manipulating an object with the Control palette is the precision of entering figures for the exact measurements for the object. You can use a proxy reference point on the Control palette as a base from which PageMaker transforms the selected object. You can also crop objects. Joe wants to proportionally resize the New England lighthouse photo to make it more prominent on the page. He will use the Control palette to do this.

1. If the lighthouse photo is not selected, click the Pointer tool ▶ in the toolbox, then click the graphic to select it

   Eight handles appear to indicate the graphic is selected, as shown in Figure H-6. Notice on the Control palette that the top left proxy reference point is also selected. The dimensions displayed in the Position X and Y text boxes apply only to the upper-left corner of the selected graphic, which is represented by the top left reference point on the proxy.

   Joe is satisfied with the placement of the upper-left corner of the graphic, but he would like to resize his photo proportionally to give a 1" margin to each side of the photo. With the top left proxy reference point selected, he will change the width of the photo to be 6" wide, and let PageMaker automatically determine the final proportional length.

2. Make sure the top left proxy reference point on the Control palette is selected; if it isn't, click to select it

   This reference point will be the base point that will remain constant as Joe resizes the photo.

3. Make sure the Control palette displays the Proportional–scaling on indicator 🔲, if not, click the Proportional–scaling on indicator 🔲 to change it to 🔲

   This is a **toggle button**, which changes between the two options when you click it.

Trouble?

Any sizing changes you make to a graphic can be undone by typing "100" in the size percentage boxes on the Control palette.

4. Double-click the value in the Width sizing (W) text box on the Control palette, type 6, then click the Apply button 🔲

   See Figure H-7. With Proportional scaling selected, Joe was able to enter 6" for the width size. PageMaker automatically scaled the height size dimension to approximately 7.9 inches, maintaining the size of the graphic proportionally.

5. Click in the pasteboard to deselect the graphic

6. Save the publication

CLUES TO USE

Using the Control palette to crop a graphic

You can use the Control palette in object view to crop a graphic precisely. With the graphic selected, click the Cropping button 🔲 on the Control palette. Select your base reference point on the proxy, then enter values in the Position X and Position Y text boxes or in the Height and Width text boxes. Then click the Apply button to accept your modifications.

FIGURE H-6: Graphic coordinates on the Control palette

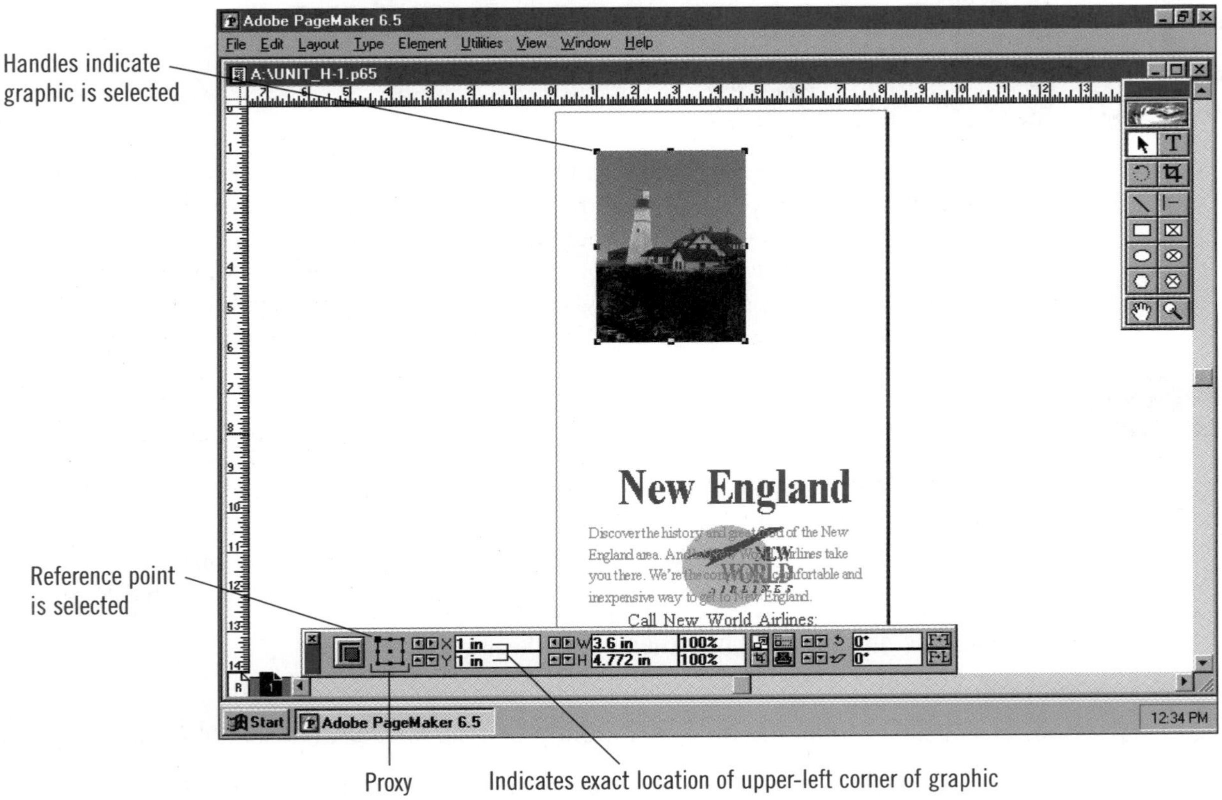

Handles indicate
graphic is selected

Reference point
is selected

Proxy

Indicates exact location of upper-left corner of graphic

FIGURE H-7: PageMaker proportionally sized photo

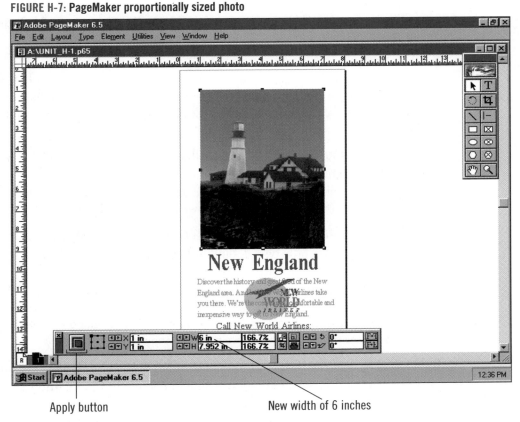

Apply button

New width of 6 inches

PageMaker 6.5

Placing an Inline Graphic

PageMaker allows you to place graphics within text blocks. This feature is commonly referred to as **inline graphics.** In the previous unit, the graphics you placed were "independent," meaning that you move them freely within the layout view. Inline graphics remain within the text block. The inline graphic moves when the text block or the text in the text block moves. 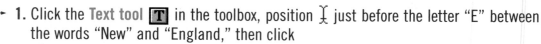 Joe wants to personalize the headline "New England" by adding an inline graphic of a lobster. Joe feels that the inline graphic will give the name "New England" a strong identity and enhance his poster.

Steps

QuickTip

You can import graphics as inline graphics using story editor.

MacintoshUser

This replaces Step 3.
3. Select the graphic file UNIT_H-3 from your Student Disk, but do not click OK

MacintoshUser

This replaces Step 5.
5. Click OK

MacintoshUser

The Macintosh Apply button is **T**.

1. Click the Text tool **T** in the toolbox, position **I** just before the letter "E" between the words "New" and "England," then click
   The Control palette changes to character view because you chose the Text tool. The inline graphic will be placed at the exact position of the insertion point in the text block.

2. Click **File** on the menu bar, then click **Place**
   The Place dialog box opens.

3. Select the graphic file UNIT_H-3 from your Student Disk, but do not click Open

4. Make sure the **As inline graphic option button** in the Place section at the bottom of the dialog box is selected
   Because you selected the Text tool before you opened the Place document dialog box, PageMaker automatically assumed that you wanted to place a graphic in text. If this were not the case, you could select the As independent graphic option button.

5. Click **Open**
   The lobster graphic appears between "New" and "England," as shown in Figure H-8. If you were to select the Pointer tool to move or resize the text block, PageMaker would adjust the graphic as if it were a word in the text block. Joe decides the headline would look better at the top of the poster.

6. Click the **Pointer tool** in the toolbox, position **k** on top of the word New, then click the **left mouse button**
   The text block with the inline graphic is selected. The Control palette switches to object view. Joe enters the exact coordinates of where he wants the text block positioned.

7. Make sure the **top left proxy reference point** is selected, double-click the value in the **Position X text box**, type **0**, double-click the value in the **Position Y text box**, type **0**, then click the **Apply button**
   See Figure H-9. The text block moves to the zero point on the page. The text block with the inline graphic appears below the top page border, but the photo covers the text block slightly. Joe decides to move the photo below the New England text block by changing the coordinate for the photo's reference point on the vertical ruler to 2".

8. Position **k** over the New England photo, click to select it, make sure the top left proxy reference point is selected, double-click the value in the **Position Y text box**, type **2**, then click the **Apply button**
   The photo moves below the text block; the heading is brought to the front.

9. Save the publication

FIGURE H-8: **Lobster graphic placed in text**

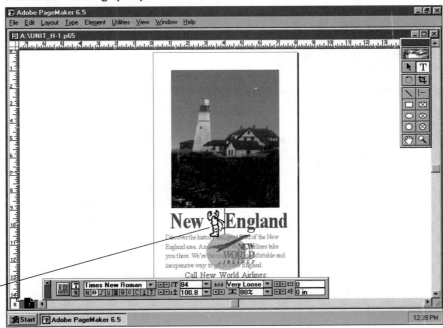

Inline graphic

FIGURE H-9: **Text block moved to the top of the page**

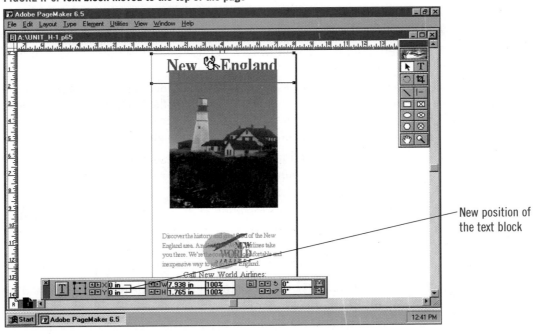

New position of
the text block

Advantages and disadvantages of using inline graphics

One advantage of using an inline graphic is the ability to keep related text and graphics together. When you move the text block, the graphic moves with text. This is particularly useful for figures with captions. You can align an inline graphic using the same commands you use to align text. One disadvantage of using inline graphics is that when you enter or delete text, the graphic moves; therefore the graphic continuously moves during editing. Another disadvantage is the inability to move the graphic independently of the text. You can move the graphic only when you move the entire block of text. Finally, you cannot use the text wrap option on a selected inline graphic. To wrap text around an inline graphic, you need to use tabs, spacing, indents, or line spacing.

Modifying an Inline Graphic

As you learned in the last lesson, when you move a text block, the inline graphic moves with it. If you had rotated the text block, the inline graphic would have rotated the same degree as the text block. In this lesson you will learn how to transform an inline graphic independently from its text block. You can size and rotate an inline graphic within its position in the line of text. You can also adjust the inline graphic's baseline position. When you place an inline graphic, PageMaker automatically places the graphic two-thirds above the baseline, independent of the paragraph's leading. Depending on your desired layout, you can edit the vertical baseline position of an inline graphic manually or adjust the space before and after the inline graphic. Joe decides to resize the lobster graphic to make it smaller. After reducing the size, Joe wants to adjust the graphic's baseline position to center it vertically in the text block.

MacintoshUser

This replaces Step 1.
1. Position the Pointer ⬈ over the lobster inline graphic, click to select it, then press [⌘][1] to change the view

QuickTip

Try to size or adjust inline graphics to fit within the paragraph's leading value.

1. **Position the Pointer ⬈ over the lobster inline graphic, click to select it, then press [Ctrl] and right-click to change the view**
   See Figure H-10. Notice on the Control palette the Baseline shift option has replaced the proxy and Position X and Y options. The Control palette includes only the features that can be used to transform inline graphics such as skewing and rotating. Joe first needs to decrease the width size of the inline graphic to exactly 80% of the original size.

2. **Make sure the Proportional scaling on indicator ⬚ on the Control palette is selected, double-click the Width sizing percentage text box, type 80, then click the Apply button ⬚**
   The inline graphic is resized to 80% of its original size, as shown in Figure H-11. If you get an error message, check that you typed 80 in the percentage box and not in the text box (containing the measurement "in"). Joe then decides to adjust the graphic's baseline shift so the bottom of the inline graphic lies on the imaginary baseline.

3. **Position ⬈ over the inline graphic, then press and hold the left mouse button**
   See Figure H-12. The pointer changes to ⬍ allowing you to move the graphic either up or down in relationship to the baseline.

4. **Drag ⬍ until the graphic's baseline shift displays 0 in in the Baseline shift text box on the Control palette, then release the mouse button**
   Joe is satisfied with the baseline position of the graphic; however, he thinks the graphic is too close to the letter "E" in England. He wants to insert a space before the letter "E."

5. **Click the Text tool T in the toolbox, click I between the graphic and the letter "E" in England, then press [Spacebar]**
   The inline graphic is now centered between the words in the headline text. Joe is pleased with the effect of placing the lobster graphic with the words "New England."

6. **Save the publication**

Spacing around inline graphics

By simply pressing [Spacebar], you can add space between the text and an inline graphic. You can also use indents and tabs to set space between one or more inline graphics. Using indents and tabs is especially helpful when creating a table with inserted inline graphics. Whenever you place an inline graphic, PageMaker assigns it autoleading format independent of the paragraph's leading. This might create odd line spacing in a particular paragraph of text. You can resize your inline graphic and increase the paragraph's leading to accommodate the inline graphic.

FIGURE H-10: Inline graphic

Inline graphic selected

Baseline shift

Inline graphic dimensions and percentages

FIGURE H-11: Inline graphic at 80% of its original size

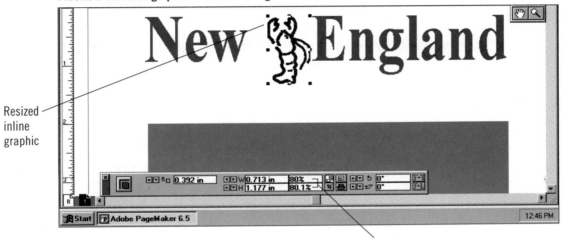

Resized inline graphic

New percentages

FIGURE H-12: Adjusting the graphic's baseline position

Pointer changes, allowing you to move the graphic up or down

Current value for baseline shift

PageMaker 6.5

Skewing an Object

PageMaker lets you **skew**, or distort, an object's dimensions horizontally only. Skewing stretches the selected object at an angle, giving it a distorted appearance. Using the Control palette in object view, you can skew a graphic horizontally only by plus or minus 85 degrees at .01 degree increments. Joe wants to create a skewed box to add a unique visual effect to his poster.

Steps

1. **Click View on the menu bar, point to Zoom To, then click 50% Size**
   Joe can now view the top half of the poster in greater detail. Before Joe draws his box, he sets up vertical ruler guides and turns on the Snap to Guides option. This will make it easier to draw the box to the exact measurements. Joe uses the Control palette once again for the precise placement of the ruler guides.

2. **Drag a vertical ruler guide to the .75" mark on the horizontal ruler**
   Joe wants his box to be 6" long, so he will need a second vertical ruler guide at the 6.75" mark on the horizontal ruler.

3. **Drag a second vertical ruler guide to the 6.75" mark on the horizontal ruler**
   Now Joe needs to activate the Snap to Guides option.

4. **Click View on the menu bar, then click Snap to Guides**
   This option gives the ruler guides a "magnetic" effect, making it easy to align items to the guides. It allows you to measure and size graphics precisely. Joe is now ready to draw his box.

5. **Click the Rectangle tool in the toolbox, using the ruler guides and the Control palette as a reference point for the exact measurements, move ✛ to display .75 in in the Position X text box on the Control palette and .75 in in the Position Y text box**

6. **Drag ✛ down and to the right until the Width sizing text box on the Control palette displays 6 in and the Height sizing text box displays .5 in, then release the mouse button**
   See Figure H-13. Notice the box's size dimensions in the Control palette. Joe now wants to add a gray shade fill and to eliminate the line border on the box.

7. **Click Element on the menu bar, then click Fill and Stroke**
   The Fill and Stroke dialog box opens. See Figure H-14. Joe wants to create a gray filled box.

8. **Click the Fill list arrow, click Solid, and make sure Black is selected in the Color list box, click the Tint list arrow and click 20, click the Stroke list arrow, click None, then click OK**
   Joe will use the Control palette to skew the box and create a unique shadow effect for the headline.

9. **Double-click the Skew text box on the Control palette, type 55, then click the Apply button**
   See Figure H-15. The box now is skewed horizontally. In the next lesson, Joe will use the skewed box he created to complete his headline design.

10. **Save your publication**

DesignTip

Skewing can create a unique effect with headlines as long as you do not overuse it on a page.

FIGURE H-13: The box's dimensions on the Control palette

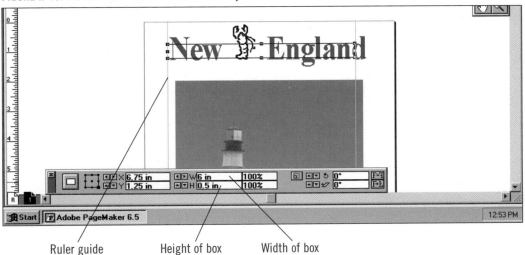

Ruler guide   Height of box   Width of box

FIGURE H-14: Fill and Stroke dialog box

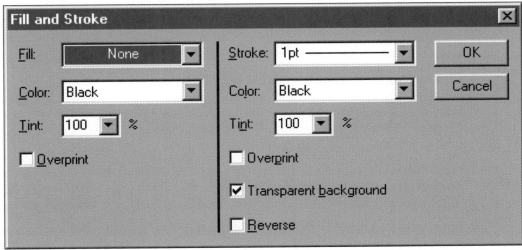

FIGURE H-15: The box skewed horizontally

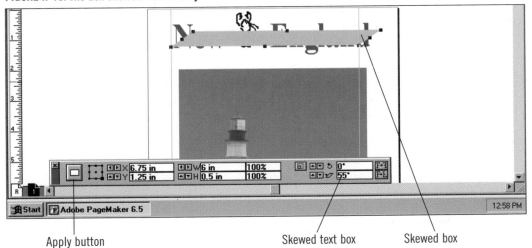

Apply button   Skewed text box   Skewed box

Reflecting an Object

PageMaker lets you **reflect** an object to its mirror image, either vertically or horizontally. Joe wants to create a visual link between the top and bottom headlines in the poster. Joe would like to duplicate the skewed box behind the New England logo. Then he will reflect the skewed box and place it behind the bottom phone number headline.

Steps

1. Click the **Pointer tool** in the toolbox, then click the **gray box** to select it.

2. Click **Element** on the menu bar, point to **Arrange**, then click **Send to Back**
   The gray box moves behind the New England text and inline graphic. Before deselecting the box, Joe wants to copy the skewed box and paste a reflected copy behind the bottom headline.

This replaces Step 3.
3. Click Edit on the menu bar, click Copy, then press [⌘][V] to paste a copy of the gray box

3. Click **Edit** on the menu bar, click **Copy**, then press **[Ctrl][V]** to paste a copy of the gray box
   PageMaker pastes a copy on top of the headline. Before Joe moves the new skewed box, he wants to create a vertical reflection.

4. Click the **Vertical reflecting button** on the Control palette
   The box instantly reflects vertically, as shown in Figure H-16. Joe wants to change the publication view so he can easily move the graphic to the point of response at the bottom of the page. To remove skewing or reflecting from an object, select the object, click Element on the menu bar, then click Remove Transformation.

This replaces Step 5.
5. Press [⌘] (zero) in the publication window

5. Press **[Ctrl]** and right-click twice in the publication window
   The view returns to Fit in window. Joe notices that the Control palette covers the bottom of the page, so he decides to move it to the middle of the page before he moves the box.

6. Position the pointer on the vertical title bar on the Control palette, press and hold the **left mouse button**, then drag the Control palette to the middle of the page
   See Figure H-17. Now Joe can see the bottom of the page, and he is ready to move the box.

7. Drag the **reflected box** to the bottom of the page on top of the New World Airlines phone number, even with the left margin
   See Figure H-18. Joe needs to send the reflected box behind the text.

This replaces Step 8.
8. Press [shift][⌘][[]

8. Press **[Shift][Ctrl][[]**
   This shortcut is the same as selecting Element, Arrange, and then Send to Back. The box moves behind the text, and Joe is satisfied with the placement of the skewed box. He decides to move the Control palette back to the bottom of the publication window.

9. Drag the **Control palette** back to the bottom of the publication window above the horizontal scroll bar
   Joe no longer needs the ruler guides, so he drags them off the pasteboard to remove them.

10. Click the **vertical ruler guide** at the .75" mark, drag it to the left of the pasteboard over the vertical ruler, drag the second ruler guide off the pasteboard to remove it, then save your publication
    There is now a visual link between the New England headline at the top of the poster and the New World Airlines phone number at the bottom of the poster.

FIGURE H-16: **The reflected skewed box**

Reflected box—

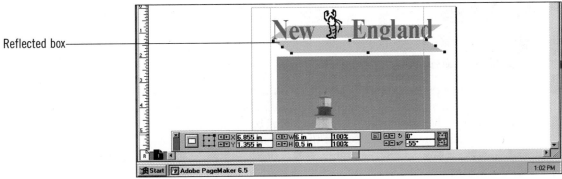

FIGURE H-17: **Control palette moved to the middle of the publication window**

Vertical title bar
used to move
Control palette

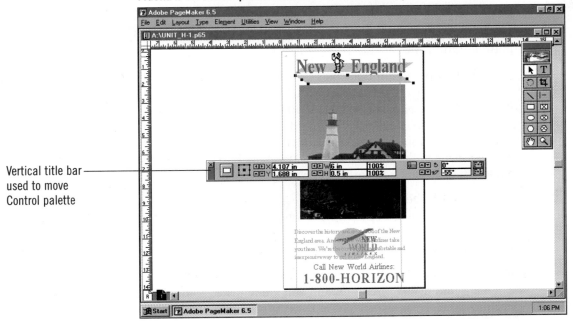

FIGURE H-18: **The reflected skewed box placed on top of the phone number**

Box positioned over
phone number

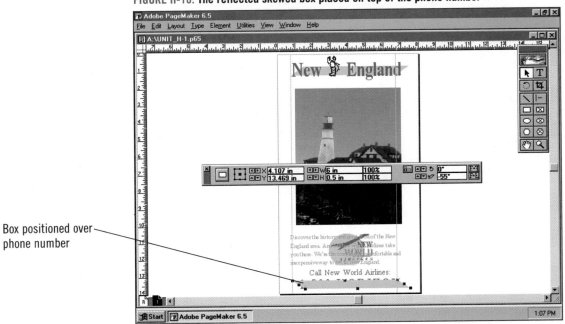

PageMaker 6.5

Changing an Object's Links

Using the Links dialog box in PageMaker, you can monitor and control object linking in your publication. When you place graphics in your publication, PageMaker automatically creates a link to the graphic's source file. The Links dialog box lists the source files of every graphic placed in your publication. Because the text on top of the New World Airlines logo is hard to read, Joe decides to lighten the graphic. Only black and white graphics can be lightened, so Joe will change the link to a black-and-white version of the New World Airlines logo.

1. Click **View** on the menu bar, point to **Zoom To**, click **50% Size**, then scroll to view the bottom half of the poster

2. Click **File** on the menu bar, then click **Links Manager**
   The Links Manager dialog box opens, as shown in Figure H-19. The Info command displays the filename of a selected linked object, the file type, and the page on which the linked object appears. If the placed graphic's source file has been changed, a plus sign (+) appears in front of the filename. You must click the Update button to update the placed graphic with the new changes made to the source file. Joe will use the Links Info dialog box to establish a different link file for the New World Airlines logo.

3. Click **Logo.tif**, then click **Info**
   The Link info dialog box opens, in which you can unlink a file or establish a link with another file. Joe wants to select the black-and-white version of the logo, which is called Logo_bw.tif.

4. In the filename list box, click **Logo_bw**, then click **Open**
   The Link info dialog box closes and you are returned to the Links dialog box. Notice the document name has changed from LOGO.TIF to LOGO_BW.TIF.

5. Click **OK**
   Now the New World Airlines logo in your publication is the black-and-white version, as shown in Figure H-20. Joe still has to lighten its appearance to make the text more readable.

6. Save the publication

MacintoshUser

This replaces Steps 4 and 5.
4. In the filename list box, click **Logo_bw**, then click Open
PageMaker displays a dialog box asking you to confirm the change of link target.
5. Click Yes
Resume at Step 5.

FIGURE H-19: Links dialog box

Color version of ———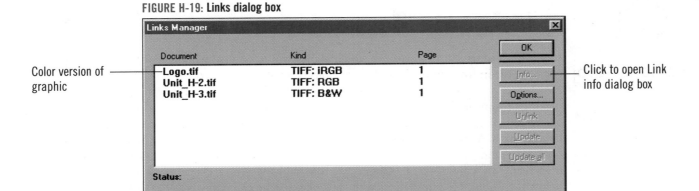
graphic

Click to open Link
info dialog box

FIGURE H-20: The newly linked logo

Newly linked
black-and-white
version

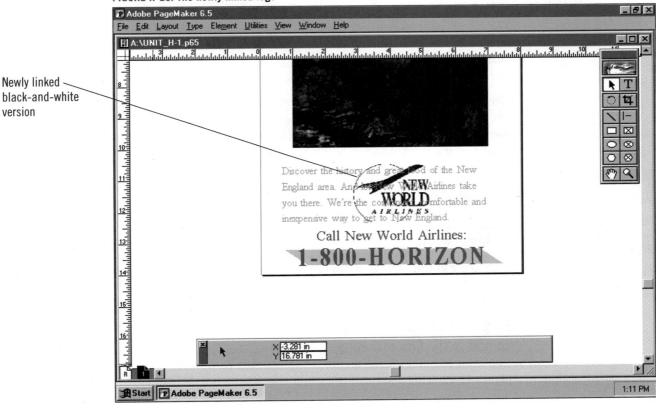

Importing files using Publish and Subscribe

PageMaker's Publish and Subscribe feature allows you to share information between application programs. PageMaker allows you to import text or graphics created in a different application program. Using this system, the application program used to create a file, called the **publishing** application program, creates a separate file called an **edition**, which can be imported, or **subscribed to**, by other application programs, including PageMaker. The subscribed editions are automatically updated when changes occur in the original publishing edition. You can also edit an edition placed in your publication by double-clicking it. The original publishing program opens, allowing you to make changes.

PageMaker 6.5

PageMaker 6.5

Using Layers

In addition to its stacking feature, which allows you to control whether individual objects on a page appear in front of or behind other objects nearby, PageMaker also lets you arrange multiple objects on a page into stacked sets, called **layers**. Using the layers feature is comparable to placing groups of objects onto sheets of transparency film, and then stacking the sheets to create a single page. All publications are created with a single layer; PageMaker 6.5 also allows you to add layers. A layer can be temporarily hidden to allow you to make fine adjustments to other objects in your publication. You can also use layers to add production notes that can be viewed on screen, but will not print.  Joe would like to create a separate layer for the text block below the photo. He can then hide the layer so that he can easily edit the logo underneath. Joe is now sure he wants to include the text in the final output of his publication. Using the layer, he can also show his boss the page layout with or without text.

MacintoshUser

This replaces Step 1.
1. Press [⌘][0] (zero), click Window on the menu bar, then click Show Layers

QuickTip

All placed text and graphics will be placed on the selected layer.

1. Press **[Ctrl]**, click the **right mouse button** twice, click **Window** on the menu bar, then click **Show Layers**

The Layers palette opens. This palette allows you to create, edit, lock, and delete layers. In addition, you can show and hide selected layers. The most frontward layer appears at the top of the palette. All publications have a single default layer. Joe would now like to create a new layer for the text block below the photo.

2. Click the **right arrow** ▶ on the Layers palette, then click **New Layer**

The New Layer dialog box appears. Joe will give a descriptive name for the new layer. Joe will also accept the assigned selection color. The objects placed on the layer will display the selection handles in the selected color. This gives you the opportunity to determine an object's layer. The total number of the layers is limited only by the amount of RAM (memory) on your computer.

3. Type **City text**, then click **OK**

Next, Joe will add the text block to the City text layer. You can use the Layers palette to move objects between layers. Notice this new layer is listed first on the palette and it now becomes the **target layer**.

4. Click the **Pointer tool** ▶ in the toolbox, click the red colored text block below the photo

A small box appears to the right of the default layer name on the Layers palette as shown in Figure H-21.

5. Drag the **small box** at the far right end of the [Default] entry on the Layers palette up next to the **City text** entry

The color handles on the text block turn to the color of the City text layer, as shown in Figure H-22. This text box is on a separate layer from the rest of the objects in the publication. Now Joe can temporarily hide the City text layer so he can resize the Sunset Tours Graphic.

6. Click the **Show/Hide button** 🔲 for the City text entry on the Layers palette

See Figure H-23. The text is now hidden from the layout. Now Joe can easily increase the size of the graphic.

7. Click the **New World Airlines logo**, click the **top right proxy reference point**, then use the Width sizing percentage box on the Control palette to increase the size of the logo to **100%**

Joe is satisfied with the new size of the logo, and now he needs to show the text block again.

8. Click 🔲

The text now reappears.

9. Save the publication

FIGURE H-21: Layers palette with the new City text layer

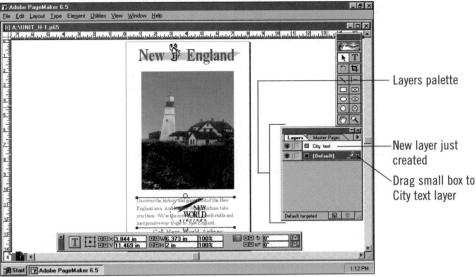

Layers palette

New layer just created

Drag small box to City text layer

FIGURE H-22: Text block moved to City text layer

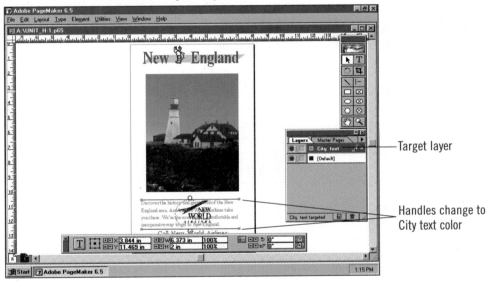

Target layer

Handles change to City text color

FIGURE H-23: City text layer hidden

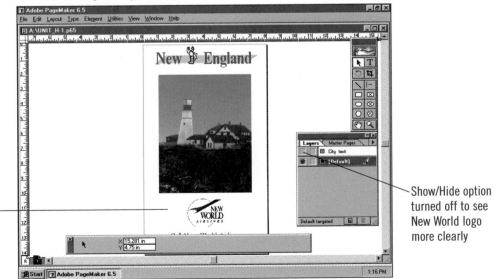

Text layer is hidden

Show/Hide option turned off to see New World logo more clearly

Using Image Control

PageMaker lets you alter or enhance the appearance of grayscale and line art TIFF and PICT images using the Image control dialog box. However, you cannot change color TIFF images. Using **image control** is like having access to a photographic darkroom in which you can lighten and adjust the contrast of black-and-white photographs and images. Image control helps you to improve the appearance of images you place in your publication. You can lighten images so they can be printed behind text or graphics. Or you can adjust the image's contrast to increase or decrease the gray levels of the image. See Table H-2 for a description of options and commands.

The text on top of the New World Airlines logo is still hard to read, so Joe will adjust the lightness of the logo to appear faded. To do this, Joe wants to lighten the logo so he can keep it behind the text.

Steps

DesignTip

Graphics placed behind text should be light enough that the text can be read easily.

MacintoshUser

Note that your Image Control dialog box differs from Figure H-24.

This replaces Step 4.

4. Click the Lightness up arrow until about 80% of the large rectangle is filled with white

QuickTip

If you click Cancel in the Image Control dialog box, the image reverts to a solid black-and-white image.

1. Click the text block on top of the New World Airlines logo
   The text is selected.

2. Click the eye icon 👁 for the City text entry on the Layers palette, then click the logo to select it

3. Click Element on the menu bar, point to Image, then click Image Control
   The Image Control dialog box opens, as shown in Figure H-24.

4. Change the Lightness to 80% using the scroll box and scroll arrows to the right of the text box
   Notice that the Apply button in the Image Control dialog box becomes active. Joe can click Apply to preview his changes before he clicks OK to accept his changes.

5. Click Apply
   PageMaker redraws the graphic in the publication window as shown in Figure H-25. Joe is satisfied with the appearance of the logo.

6. Click OK, then click the leftmost box next to the City text entry on the Layers palette to redisplay this layer
   The graphic is now a light gray shade, and Joe can clearly see the text on top of the logo.

7. Save and print your publication, then exit PageMaker

FIGURE H-24: Image Control dialog box

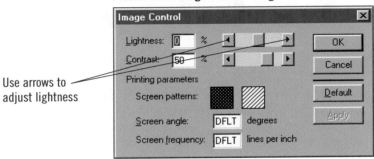

Use arrows to adjust lightness

FIGURE H-25: Image Control dialog box moved in the publication window

Dialog box in new position

Lightened logo makes text more readable

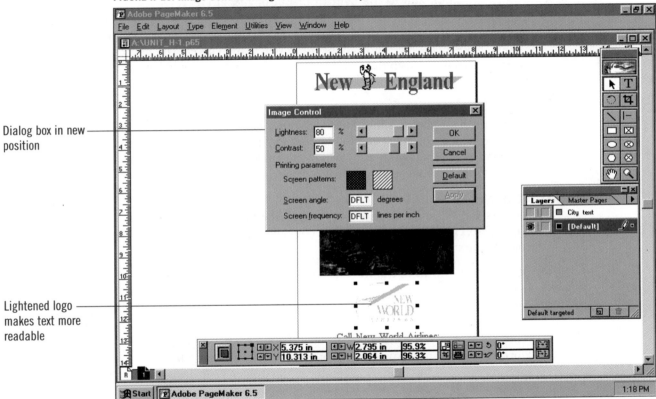

TABLE H-2: Image Control dialog box options and commands

option/command	description
Lightness	Lightens or darkens an image; the more white in the box, the lighter the image
Contrast	Changes the balance between the dark and light parts of the image; greater contrast will "blacken" the image, lower contrast will add more gray parts to the image
Cancel	Undoes any changes and closes the dialog box
Default	Reverts the dialog box to the default settings
Apply	Lets you see the changes you make to an image's lightness and contrast without closing the dialog box

PageMaker 6.5

Design Workshop: Posters

Joe's series of posters highlighting the New World Airlines destinations requires large graphics that make the viewer want to plan a trip to one of those destinations. Each poster needs to make a positive statement and to attract attention. Joe reviews his work to see if his design meets his original plan.

Details

Do the graphics add to the overall effect of the poster?

Joe used a picture of a lighthouse to showcase the scenery in New England. Covering about 75% of the surface area with text and graphics enhances the quality of the poster. The lobster inline graphic helps make the top headline jump out at the viewer. The inline graphic is sized and evenly spaced in between the two words, New England. Joe could have added color to enhance the inline graphic.

Is the message clear?

A poster can handle any amount of text; however, people need to be able to read information from a distance. You must choose the font and point size carefully. When Joe reproduces this poster at full size, the body copy will be nearly 30 points, which is almost a half inch. That is perfect for Joe's needs.

Does the headline's shadow effect enhance the poster?

Joe uses skewed and reflected boxes to link the top and bottom headlines in his poster. The skewed box creates a unique effect. Joe could have improved their overall appearance by adding color to the shaded, skewed box.

Does the poster lend itself to additional posters in a series?

Joe hopes to use this same basic layout for posters advertising other New World Airlines destinations. The large photo and top headline can easily be changed to accommodate other cities. For the top headline inline graphic, Joe will need to identify a well-known icon that will represent each city as well as be easily identifiable by potential travelers. For example, for Miami, Florida, he could use a sunshine logo; for St. Louis, Missouri, he could use an arch graphic; or for San Francisco, he could use a graphic of the Golden Gate Bridge. For the photo, he will select a representative picture from each place.

Practice

► Concepts Review

Label each of the publication window elements shown in Figure H-27.

FIGURE H-27

Match each of the terms with the statement that describes its function:

7. **Image control**
8. **Reflect**
9. **Skew**
10. **Inline graphic**
11. **Proxy**

a. Distorting a graphic to its mirror image
b. Display of a selected graphic on the Control palette
c. Distorting a graphic's dimensions
d. Graphic as part of a text block
e. Allows you change the lightness and contrast of an image

12. **Image control works with all the following graphic types, except:**
    a. Line art or monochrome TIFF
    b. Grayscale TIFF
    c. Color TIFF
    d. PICT

13. **The term skewing means to:**
    a. Change a graphic's size
    b. Change a graphic's dimensions
    c. Distort a graphic
    d. Both b and c

14. **Which of the following transformations can be made to multiple selected objects?**
    a. Skewing
    b. Scaling
    c. Rotating
    d. All of the above

15. **All the following transformations can be made to an inline graphic, except:**
    a. Resize
    b. Adjust its baseline position
    c. Rotate
    d. All of the above can be made to an inline graphic

16. **To edit an inline graphic:**
    a. Select the graphic with I, then make the changes on the Control palette
    b. Select the graphic with ▶, then make the changes on the Control palette
    c. Replace the graphic using the Place document dialog box
    d. PageMaker doesn't allow edits to an inline graphic

17. **To lighten a black-and-white line art TIFF image in PageMaker, you would use:**
    a. Image control
    b. Fill and Line
    c. Either a or b
    d. TIFF images cannot be lightened in PageMaker

18. **Each time you place a graphic, PageMaker:**
    a. Stores a copy of the placed file's information in the PageMaker publication
    b. Creates a link to the source file
    c. Neither a nor b
    d. Both a and b

▶ Skills Review

1. **Minimize a PageMaker file size.**
   a. Start PageMaker and open the file UNIT_H-4 from your Student Disk.
   b. Click Element on the menu bar, then click Link Options.
   c. In the Graphics section, click the Store copy in publication check box to deselect this option.
   d. Click OK.
   e. If necessary, click Window on the menu bar, then select Show Control Palette.
   f. Click File on the menu bar, click Place, select the graphic file UNIT_H-5 from your Student Disk, then click Open *(Macintosh users: click OK)*.
   g. Move the pointer to display 1" in the Position X text box and 1" in the Position Y text box.
   h. Click the left mouse button.

2. Scale a graphic.

a. Make sure the Control palette displays the Proportional Scaling off indicator; if not, click the button to turn it off.

b. Double-click the value in the Width sizing text box, then type "7".

c. Double-click in the value in the Height sizing text box, then type "10".

d. Click the Apply button.

e. If necessary, use the Pointer tool to center the graphic.

f. Save the publication.

3. Place an inline graphic.

a. If necessary, scroll the publication window so the bottom of the page is visible.

b. Click the Text tool in the toolbox.

c. Position the insertion point in the bottom headline right before the words "World" and "You."

d. Click File on the menu bar, then click Place.

e. Select the graphic file UNIT_H-6 from your Student Disk, then make sure the As inline graphic option button is selected.

f. Click Open *(Macintosh users: click OK)*.

4. Modify an inline graphic.

a. Click the Pointer tool in the toolbox.

b. Click the inline graphic to select it.

c. Make sure the Proportional scaling on indicator on the Control palette is displayed.

d. Double-click the Width sizing text box, then type "1.5".

e. Click the Apply button.

f. Position the pointer over the inline graphic, then press and hold the left mouse button.

g. Drag the pointer until the baseline shift reads approximately .125".

h. Move the pointer over the text block with the inline graphic, then click once to select the headline.

i. Select the bottom left proxy reference point on the Control palette.

j. Double-click the value in the Position Y text box, then type "14".

k. Click the Apply button.

5. Skew and reflect an object.

a. Select the inline graphic.

b. Click the Horizontal reflecting button on the Control palette.

c. Place a vertical ruler guide at the .5" mark on the horizontal ruler.

d. Place another vertical ruler guide at the 8.5" mark on the horizontal ruler.

e. Click View on the menu bar, then click Snap to Guides.

f. Click the Rectangle tool in the toolbox. Using the ruler guides, draw a box to be placed behind the bottom headline. The dimensions should be approximately 8" wide and .5" high.

g. Click Element on the menu bar, then click Fill and Stroke.

h. Click the Fill list arrow, then click Solid.

i. Make sure Black is selected in the Color list box, then select a tint of 30%.

j. Select None in the Stroke list box.

k. Click OK.

l. Make sure the center proxy reference point on the Control palette is selected, double-click the Skew text box, type "35", then click the Apply button.

m. Click Element on the menu bar, point to Arrange, then click Send to Back.

n. If necessary, use the Pointer tool to center the skewed box behind the headline.

6. Change an object's link.

   a. Click the Pointer tool in the toolbox, then click to select the text block below the photo. Press [Ctrl] and click the left mouse button on the logo behind the text block to select it *(Macintosh users: click the Pointer tool in the toolbox, then click to select the text block below the photo. Press ⌘ and click the mouse button on the logo behind the text block to select it).*

   b. Open the Links Manager dialog box.

   c. Select the file ST_LOGO.TIF from your Student Disk.

   d. Click Info.

   e. In the filename list box, select the file ST_B&W from your Student Disk.

   f. Click Open, then click OK *(Macintosh users: click Link, click Yes, then click OK).*

7. Using layers.

   a. If necessary, click Window on the menu bar, then click Show Layers.

   b. Click the right arrow on the Layer palette, then click New Layer.

   c. Type "Sunset text", then click OK.

   d. Make sure the Pointer tool in the toolbox is selected, then click the text block beneath the photo.

   e. Drag the box from the [Default] layer next to Sunset text on the Layers palette.

   f. Click the Eye icon next to Sunset text in the Layers palette.

   g. Click the Sunset Tours logo, click the top center proxy reference point, and then using the Control palette decrease the logo size to 100%.

   h. Click the gray box next to Sunset text where the Eye icon was previously located.

8. Use Image control.

   a. Make sure the Sunset Tours logo is selected.

   b. Click Element on the menu bar, point to Image, then click Image Control.

   c. Adjust the Lightness to lighten the image.

   d. If necessary, move the dialog box so you can see the Sunset Tours logo and the dialog box in your publication window.

   e. Click Apply.

   f. Continue to adjust the lightness, then click Apply until the graphic image is lightened to your satisfaction.

   g. Click OK.

   h. Save and print the publication, then exit PageMaker.

▶ Independent Challenges

1. You volunteered to help your theater department promote its fall play. Your job is to design material to help promote the production. This includes posters that students will hang around campus in various locations. Your budget is small, but you discover you can inexpensively produce tabloid-size (11" × 17") posters at your local printer's. You can work only in black and white, but color paper stock is available. You need to create three different posters for variety.

To complete this independent challenge:

1. Create a three-page document with tabloid-sized pages.
2. Use any type and graphics you choose to create headlines and complementary graphics. Use graphics from various units in this book to help your design.
3. Determine the play's name, running dates, location, and times of each performance.
4. Use reflected, rotated, or skewed graphics or text in each of the three posters, but do not overuse these effects.
5. Add a layer to the default layer, then hide the layer so that you can make an adjustment to another part of your publication.
6. Use Image control on appropriate graphics to create unique effects with the Lightness and Contrast controls.
7. Do not use text smaller than 72 points in the publication. Headlines should be at least 150 points.
8. Save your publication as Theater poster to your Student Disk and print it, then submit your posters.

2. Posters surround your world. Even billboards are sometimes considered posters. Posters can hang inside frames or on walls with staples or tape. But what makes a poster attractive?

To complete this independent challenge:

Make a list of the next 10 posters you see and critique them using what you learned in this unit.

1. Answer the following questions:
   - What is the quality of the photography?
   - Are graphics used at all?
   - How large is the text, and does the size help the design of the poster?
   - Is the poster selling or promoting something? Is it successful in its sales or promotional pitch?
   - Why?
2. Submit your findings and evaluation.

3. Occasionally, you do some design work for New World Airlines. You have been asked to create a poster advertising New World Airlines nonstop flights from Omaha to St. Louis. You will rearrange the layout of an already existing New World Airlines publication to design the poster.

To complete this independent challenge:

1. Open the file UNIT_F-1 on your Student Disk, and save it as IC_H-3.
2. Delete the Toronto Needle, the New World Airlines logo, the airplane, and the arrows.
3. Make the page size to 8" × 14". Change the Orientation to Wide.
4. Create new headlines that are at least 150 points in size.
5. Use the Control palette in object view to transform objects in your poster by sizing, skewing, reflecting, cropping, or rotating them.
6. Place the file UNIT_H-6 located on your Student Disk as an inline graphic in a headline.
7. Add a new layer to the default layer, then hide the layer so that you can more easily make changes to another part of your publication.

8. Place the file ST_B&W located on your Student Disk into your poster, then lighten the graphic so that it can be placed behind text.

9. Save the publication as OMA-STL poster on your Student Disk, then print it.

4. Your senior class trip was approved by the school board. As the senior class secretary, you have been nominated to create a poster advertising the trip to your classmates.
To complete this independent challenge:

1. Search the World Wide Web for information on the destination of your choice.

2. Sketch the design of your poster using the guidelines that you learned in this unit.

3. Create an 8" × 14" proof version of the poster in PageMaker using your sketch as a guide. Be sure to minimize the size of your PageMaker publication file. You can place graphic files from your Student Disk as dummy graphics and inline graphics, but add your own text to the poster.

4. Use the Control palette in object view to create unique effects with graphic images and to transform objects in your poster by sizing, rotating, skewing, reflecting, or cropping them.

5. Modify an inline graphic that you have placed in a text block to enhance your design.

6. Add a new layer to the default layer so that you can hide the layer if necessary, making it easier for you to change another part of the poster.

7. Place the file LOGO.tif located on your Student Disk somewhere in your poster. Modify the link for the New World Airlines logo to the LOGO_BW file. Use Image control to lighten the logo.

8. Critique the final design of your poster. Save the publication as Class trip poster to your Student Disk and print it. Hand in your sketch, all printouts, and your critique.

▶ Visual Workshop

Joe needs your assistance creating the second poster for advertising a second New World Airlines destination. Create the poster shown in Figure H-28 advertising flights to St. Louis, using the file UNIT_H-7 from your Student Disk. Add the triangular shapes by creating and skewing a 3-sided polygon, and then make a reflected copy.

FIGURE H-28

Adding
Color to Publications

Objectives

► **Plan a brochure**
► **Apply color to text and graphics**
► **Plan color use in PageMaker**
► **Use a color library**
► **Create a new color**
► **Apply spot colors**
► **Edit a color**
► **Create a tint**
► **Trap colors**
► **Create color separations**
► **Design Workshop: Brochures**

Color adds impact to your publications. In this unit you will learn how to create colors and apply those colors to graphical elements and text. You will learn to use PageMaker's color libraries to give you an expanded variety of colors that can be applied to your publications. Then you will learn how to edit colors and produce tints. Finally you will create color separations from your publication that could be used by a commercial printer to print your publication.   Joe Martin needs to create a color brochure to be mailed to frequent flyer members with their next mileage summary. This brochure describes travel through Rome, Italy, which is one of the New World Airlines and Sunset Tours joint vacation destinations.

Planning a Brochure

Brochures come in all sizes and styles depending on the type of information and the audience for which they are designed. Some brochures include most if not all of the details of a product or service, such as a 10-page color brochure that you would receive at a car dealership. This brochure has large, colorful pictures of cars and a detailed explanation of the car's features. A "teaser" brochure, in contrast, wants you to respond to receive more information (usually in the form of another brochure) about a product or service. **Teaser brochures** do not have a lot of text—they depend on graphics and color to make the viewer want to find out more. ✐ Joe wants to create a teaser brochure announcing new guided tours through Rome, sponsored by New World Airlines and Sunset Tours travel agency, to New World Airlines frequent flyers. To design the color brochure, Joe considers the following guidelines:

Details

Determine the purpose of your brochure

If your brochure is going to be a teaser brochure, you don't want to include too much information. You will rely more on pictures and other graphics. If your brochure is going to be an informational brochure, you want to consider unique ways of presenting the information, including page size, paper quality, photo quality, and the layout of graphics and supporting amount of text. Joe decides that this will be a teaser brochure for two reasons. First, respondents will give him a database of people who are interested enough in New World Airlines to fill out a card and mail it back. Second, Joe's follow-up brochure is large and expensive to produce. If he knows exactly who should receive the follow-up brochure, his audience is already a targeted, interested group.

Be creative with the brochure's size

Most designers experiment with paper size and the way the paper folds when they begin the design process. One of the most popular brochure sizes is a vertical three-panel, two-fold brochure based on a letter-size (8½" × 11") page. You can be creative and try horizontal folds, varied paper sizes, or even a folder-type brochure with one-page handouts. Joe decides to make a four-panel, three-fold brochure based on a legal page size of 8½" × 14".

Be consistent with other marketing materials

Brochures describing a single product or service should maintain consistency with other corporate brochures. The New World Airlines logo placed in the brochure will help provide a consistent corporate identity. Joe develops a layout for his brochure that could be replicated easily for future brochures highlighting any of New World Airlines tours.

Include point of response

It is important to give the reader a point of response. Include a phone number where those people who are interested can call. Some brochures include a reply card that can be mailed for more information. Because Joe is creating a teaser brochure, he includes a perforated cutoff self-mailer, a portion of the brochure for people to fill out and mail back for more information.

Figures I-1 and I-2 show Joe's sketches of the teaser brochure.

FIGURE I-1: Joe's sketch of the outside panels (page 2)

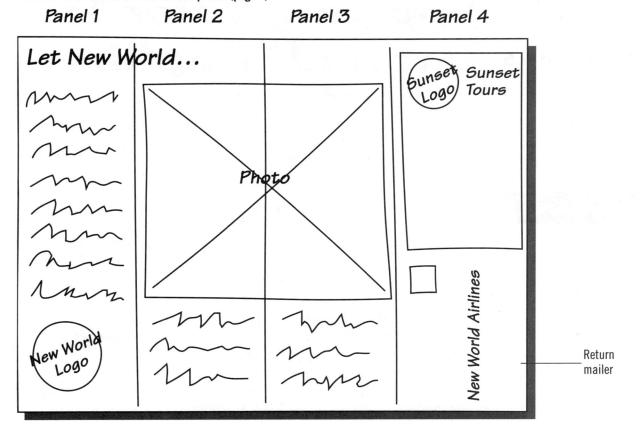

Panel 1   Panel 2   Panel 3   Panel 4

Let New World...

Photo

Sunset Logo   Sunset Tours

New World Logo

New World Airlines

Return mailer

FIGURE I-2: Joe's sketch of the inside panels (page 3)

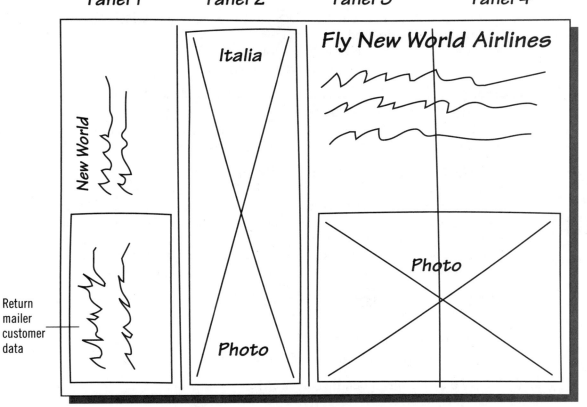

Panel 1   Panel 2   Panel 3   Panel 4

Italia

Fly New World Airlines

New World

Photo

Photo

Return mailer customer data

Applying Color to Text and Graphics

You can apply color to graphical elements such as boxes and lines. In addition, you can apply colors to headlines, body type, or other types of text. You apply colors to text using the Character Specifications dialog box or the Colors palette. Joe wants to add red color to the headline on page 2 to be consistent with the color of the headlines on page 3. Then he wants to add blue color to the box around the self-mailer included in the brochure to make it stand out.

Steps

1. **Start PageMaker and open the file UNIT_I-1 from your Student Disk**
   Notice that this publication has three pages, but contains information only on pages 2 and 3. This is so you can see both pages that you are working with at the same time, by treating them as facing pages.

2. **Click the headline at the top of page 2 with ▶ to select it, click View on the menu bar, point to Zoom To, then click 50% Size; click the Text tool T in the toolbox, then drag I over the headline to highlight it**
   Joe changed the view to see the headline better. He must highlight the desired text in order to apply color to it. Joe will use the Character Specifications dialog box to apply red color to the headline.

3. **Click Type on the menu bar, then click Character, click the Color list arrow, then click Red**
   The color black is the default. You can replace it with red, blue, or green.

4. **Click OK, then click the Pointer tool ▶ in the toolbox to deselect the text**
   The headline text is now red, as shown in Figure I-3. Next Joe needs to change the color of the box around the self-mailer to help set it off from the rest of the brochure, drawing the reader's attention to the publication's point of response.

5. **Use the scroll bars to move down and to the right so you can see the self-mailer box, then click the dashed line box around the self-mailer information**
   Joe wants to apply the blue color only to the dashes that make the box. He will leave the color inside the box white.

6. **Click Window on the menu bar, then click Show Colors**
   The Colors palette appears in the publication window, as shown in Figure I-4. If necessary, drag it to the right edge of the window and resize it to match the one in Figure I-4. For a description of all the options on the Colors palette, see Table I-1. The Line, Fill, and Both buttons appear across the top of the Colors palette. You need to select one of these options to apply a color to an object. Since Joe wants to apply the color only to the dashed line box, he chooses the Line button.

7. **Click the Line button ▨ on the Colors palette**
   See Figure I-5. Now Joe selects his color.

8. **Click Blue on the Colors palette**
   The dashes change to blue. Joe is satisfied with the color.

9. **Click File on the menu bar, then click Save**

Trouble?
To see the complete names of the colors on the Colors palette, you can resize the palette by dragging the sizing box in the lower-right corner.

FIGURE I-3: Applying color to text

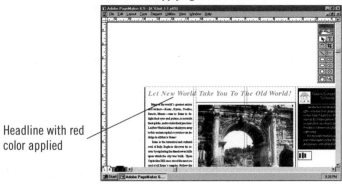

Headline with red color applied

FIGURE I-4: Colors palette in publication window

Selected box

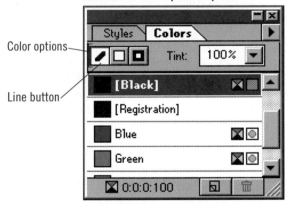

Colors palette

FIGURE I-5: Colors palette options

Color options

Line button

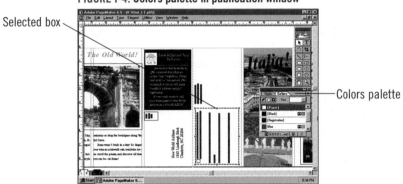

TABLE I-1: Colors palette options

option	description
[Paper]	Indicates the color of the paper on which you are currently printing
[Black]	Indicates one of the process colors (black prints over all other colors)
[Registration]	Indicates the percentage of each of the colors in your publication
Blue	Indicates choice of Blue, Green, or Red
100% ▼	Indicates if the color is a tint by showing the percentage of color
▣	Apply selected color as both fill and lines
▣	Apply selected color as fill only
▱	Apply selected color to lines only

Planning Color Use In PageMaker

When you create a PageMaker publication that will eventually be sent to a commercial printing press, you need to consider the two types of color that you can use in the publication: spot colors and process colors. **Spot color** is one specific ink used to create a color. For example, to create green using spot colors, you use one of PageMaker's online color libraries to specify the green that suits your publication. **Color libraries** are "industry standards" for creating specific colors. **Process colors** are made from four basic colors combined in percentages to create other colors. The four basic colors are cyan (C) (a shade of blue), magenta (M) (a shade of red), yellow (Y), and black (K). This process is commonly referred to as **CMYK**. Most color publications you see, including this book, are printed using process colors. To create green using process colors, you mix 100% of cyan and 100% of yellow for a one to one ratio. Joe needs to create color separations that will be given to a commercial printer to create the brochure as shown in Figure I-6. Joe uses the following guidelines when deciding to use spot or process colors or both methods:

 ### Use spot colors to keep production costs low

Each time you use a different color, you add to the overall cost of producing your publication. If you are on a limited budget for producing a publication, adding one spot color will add the extra impact needed to make your publication stand out without adding excessive costs. A publication with three or fewer colors should be produced using spot colors. Spot colors are sometimes needed to match an exact color. Joe's budget will allow him to use process color for this brochure; however, he will still need to use a spot color to match exactly the yellow color in the New World Airlines logo.

 ### Use process colors to produce a greater variety of colors and reproduce photographs

When using process colors, you pay for four inks, CMYK, but you can create a wide variety of colors. Process colors must be used to produce color photographs. Process colors should also be used if you need to create a publication with four or more spot colors. The process colors can be used to create the specified spot color; however, it is important to note, most commercial printers don't guarantee that process colors will create an exact match to an "industry standard" predefined library color. Joe needs to use process colors in his brochure because he will be using color photographs.

Use both spot and process colors to give you the most flexibility

QuickTip

If you wish to print a color photograph in your publication, you must use CMYK process colors to create the wide variety of colors in the photograph. If you use process colors in your publication, you can also use process colors to create your own specific spot colors.

Using spot and process colors together in a publication is the most expensive method for printing a publication. However, using both color methods will give you the most flexibility in producing a publication with colors you want. You can print color photographs and also specify an exact spot library color for a graphical element such as a company logo. In order to create the most attractive and stunning brochure possible, Joe will use both spot and process colors in his publication.

FIGURE I-6: Color separations of a publication page

Cyan

Magenta

Yellow

Black

Using commercial printers

Because printing a color publication is costly, make sure you discuss with a printing representative the colors you plan to use and whether the printing company has the appropriate equipment and time to handle the job. After you give your PageMaker publications to the printing company, the printing company creates a film copy for each spot color used in your publication, known as **separations**. Each film separation is then used to make printing plates. The plates are placed directly onto the printing press to make impressions on the paper in the publication. In color printing, each color ink has its own set of plates and the paper passes through each plate once. For four-color process printing, four plates are created and each paper receives four passes of color. Each ink is an additional cost: therefore, four-color printing is more complex and more costly than one- or two-color printing. However, the commercial printer can create a wide variety of different colors using a four-color process.

PageMaker 6.5

Using a Color Library

One of the greatest challenges in printing is matching colors in your PageMaker publication with the color of the final output from a commercial printer. Color representation can vary between monitors and even vary on different days using the same monitor. Several companies have developed color matching systems that are used by designers and printing companies as standards to print consistent colors. PageMaker supports several color matching systems which are stored as color libraries in the Define Colors dialog box. See Table I-2 for a list of PageMaker color libraries. Joe recreated the New World Airlines logo in PageMaker so he could have more control over the colors in the logo. The circle behind the New World Airlines text is a specific color in the Pantone Matching System (PMS). It is a color known as Pantone color 123. Joe wants to add this color to the Colors palette. When this publication is sent to the commercial printer, it will require a separate ink to print the Pantone color 123.

Steps

QuickTip

Before selecting a library color, make sure your commercial printer can print your publication using the specified matching system color.

1. **Click Utilities on the menu bar, then click Define Colors**
   The Define Colors dialog box opens.

2. **Click New, then click the Libraries list arrow**
   A list of PageMaker's color libraries appears.

3. **Click PANTONE® Coated**
   The Color Picker dialog box opens for the PANTONE® Coated library, as shown in Figure I-7. To choose a Pantone color, you can scroll through the list or type a specific Pantone number in the text box. The designer who originally created the New World Airlines logo used the spot color Pantone color 123 for the golden sun behind the text and airplane. Joe wants to use the exact color for his logo in this brochure.

4. **Drag ▶ over the text in the PANTONE CVC text box, then type 123**
   A golden color is highlighted in the color window. The color on your monitor might not match the color shown in the figures in this book.

5. **Click OK**
   See Figure I-8. Notice PANTONE 123 CVC automatically appears in the text box. Joe closes the dialog box so he can apply the color to the logo.

6. **Click OK twice**

7. **Use the scroll bars to move to the far left to display the New World Airlines logo on page 2, click the border of the circle in the logo with ▶, then click the Both button ▣ on the Colors palette**
   Joe wants to add Pantone color 123 to both the line and fill of the circle. It is important that the logo match the exact color specifications for the company logo.

8. **Click PANTONE 123 CVC (yellow box) on the Colors palette**
   PageMaker changes the circle's color from white to the spot color Pantone 123, as shown in Figure I-9.

9. **Save the publication**

FIGURE I-7: Color Picker dialog box for the PANTONE® Coated library

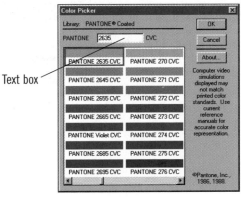

Text box

FIGURE I-8: The new color

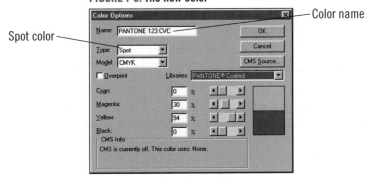

Spot color

Color name

FIGURE I-9: Logo with new color applied

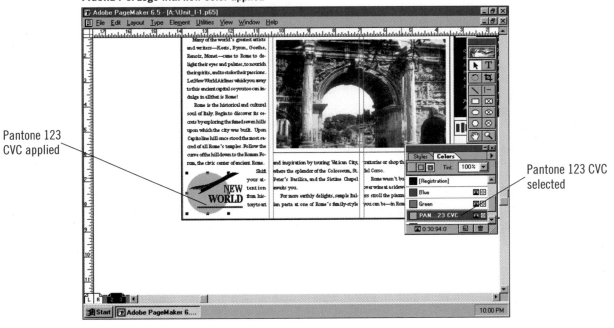

Pantone 123 CVC applied

Pantone 123 CVC selected

TABLE I-2: A sample of PageMaker's color matching libraries

library name	type	number of colors	library name	type	number of colors
Dainippon	Spot	1280	**TOYO**	Spot	1050
PANTONE	Process	3006	**PANTONE**	Spot	736
Focoltone	Process	763	**Trumatch**	Process	2093

PageMaker 6.5

Creating a New Color

When using process colors, you can mix the four CMYK colors to create any color you want. To create a new color, use the Define Colors dialog box. ◀━━ In addition to the spot color Joe used for the circle, he needs to use process colors so the commercial printer can print color photographs in his publication. He wants to create an additional spot color to use for the text and airplane graphic in the company logo in his publication. This time Joe will use process colors to create the new spot color.

Steps

1. **Click Utilities on the menu bar, then click Define Colors**
   The Define Colors dialog box opens. Joe needs to click Paper to clear the previously selected color settings in order to create a new color.

2. **Click [Paper] in the Colors list box, then click New**
   The Color Options dialog box opens. Joe wants to create a blue color to apply to the text in the logo and to the boxes around the photos. Joe will give the color a name. You can customize the name to your preference, using any number of characters. However, the new color name must be unique—do not use an existing name.

3. **Type Royal Blue in the Name text box**
   This is the name that will identify the new color that Joe is creating by using process colors.

4. **Click the Type list arrow, click Process, then make sure CMYK is selected in the Model text box**
   With CMYK selected, PageMaker bases your new color on the four components of process colors: cyan, magenta, yellow, and black.

MacintoshUser

This replaces Step 5.
5. Double-click the Cyan text box, type 100, then press [Tab]

5. **Double-click the Cyan text box, type 100, then press [Tab] twice**
   See Figure I-10. PageMaker displays an example of the color you are creating. The Magenta text box is highlighted. Joe decides to add magenta to darken the cyan color.

6. **Type 75 in the Magenta text box, then press [Tab] once**
   See Figure I-11. The color changes from cyan to a darker blue.

DesignTip

Publications stand out when color is used selectively and not excessively.

7. **Click OK**
   The Color Options dialog box closes and the Define Colors dialog box reopens. Notice that the color you just created is in the Colors list box.

8. **Click OK**
   The Define Colors dialog box closes. Royal Blue is added to the Colors palette.

FIGURE I-10: **Cyan added to the new color**

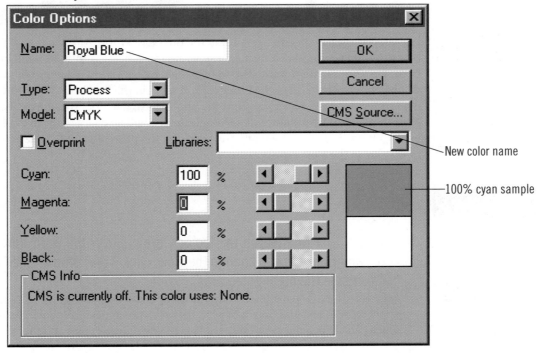

New color name

100% cyan sample

FIGURE I-11: **Cyan and magenta combined to create the new color**

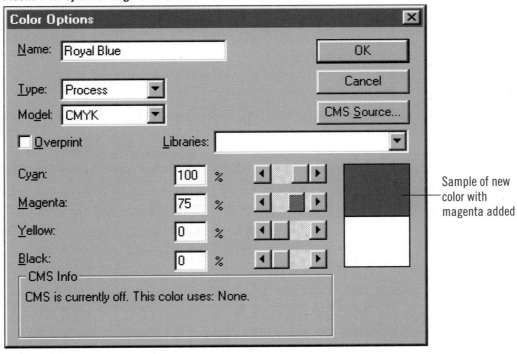

Sample of new color with magenta added

Using process colors to create Pantone colors

You can mix process colors to create Pantone colors. If you have a Pantone swatch book, you can determine the percentage of the process colors needed to create a Pantone color. The only disadvantage is that some commercial printers won't guarantee that mixing process colors will exactly match the Pantone color.

Applying Spot Colors

Earlier you used a specific spot color for the New World Airlines logo. When the brochure is printed by the commercial printer, a separate ink called Pantone 123 will be used to print color in the brochure in addition to the four process colors (cyan, magenta, yellow, and black), which will be used to create all of the other color images in the brochure. The printer will also apply the new spot color to the boxes around the photos. ![scribble] Joe would now like to apply the colors to both the text and graphics in his brochure. Joe will be charged for five colors; however, he will not be charged for the spot color created using the process colors. First he would like to add the new color to the New World Airlines logo.

Steps 1234

MacintoshUser

This replaces Step 1.

1. Click the Text tool **T** in the toolbox, drag I over the word New in the logo, press [⌘][1]to change the view, click Royal Blue on the Colors palette, then click out-side the highlighted area

---

1. **Click the Text tool **T** in the toolbox, drag I over the word New in the logo, press [Ctrl] and right-click to change the view, click Royal Blue on the Colors palette, then click outside the highlighted area**
   See Figure I-12. The word is now in the newly created Royal Blue color. Note that when you first apply color to text and drawn objects, they may not appear fully colored, or may appear cut off. Once you change the view, however, PageMaker redraws them and they display correctly.

2. **Drag I over the word Airlines, click Royal Blue on the Colors palette, then click out-side the highlighted area**
   The word "Airlines" is now Royal Blue. Next, Joe wants to apply PageMaker's default Red color to the word "World" in the logo.

3. **Highlight the word World, click Red on the Colors palette, then click outside the highlighted area**
   Joe is satisfied with the color of text. Now Joe wants to add the Royal Blue color to the air-plane graphic.

4. **Click the Pointer tool **▶** in the toolbox, click the airplane graphic, then click Royal Blue on the Colors palette**
   Joe's PageMaker version of the logo is now complete and the colors match his ongoing iden-tity plan for the logo's use. Next Joe wants to apply the new Royal Blue color to the boxes that surround the photos.

MacintoshUser

This replaces Step 5.

5. Press [⌘][0] (zero), click to select the box around the photo on page 2, click the Line button **✏** on the Colors palette, then click Royal Blue

---

5. **Press [Ctrl] and right-click, click the box around the photo on page 2 to select it, click the Line button **✏** on the Colors palette, then click Royal Blue**
   Notice that just the line has the Royal Blue color. Joe then decides a solid color fill will help make the photos stand out.

6. **Click the Fill button **■** on the Colors palette, then click Royal Blue**
   See Figure I-13. Now both the line and fill change to Royal Blue.

7. **Click the box around the photo of the church in the bottom right corner of page 3, click the Both button **■** on the Colors palette, then click Royal Blue**
   Once again the box behind the photo turns to the new color Royal Blue. Joe would like to finish applying Red to the brochure's headlines on page 3.

8. **Click **T**, drag I over the rotated headline Italia! on page 3, click Red on the Colors palette, highlight the headline on page 3 beginning with the words "Fly New World...," then click Red on the Colors palette**

9. **Click **▶** to deselect the text, then save the publication**

FIGURE I-12: Royal Blue added to text

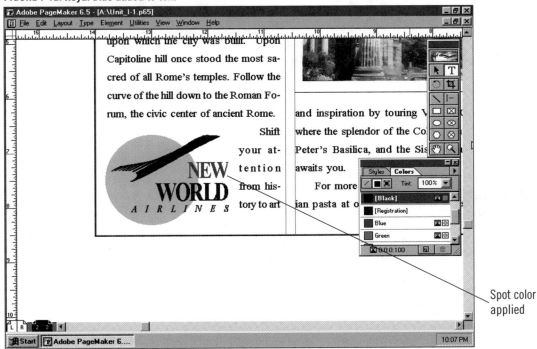

Spot color applied

FIGURE I-13: Box with Royal Blue applied

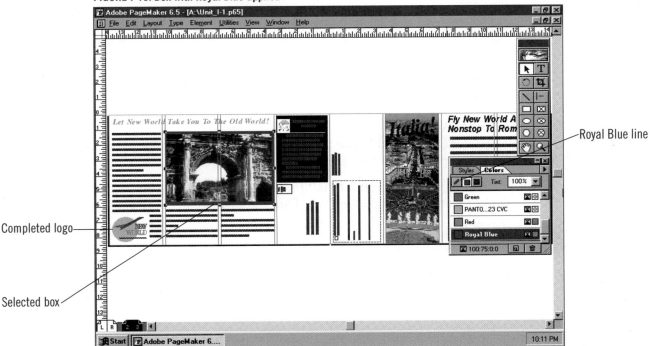

Royal Blue line

Completed logo

Selected box

Applying colors to imported graphics

You can apply a color to imported grayscale TIFF, EPS, or PIC file formats. Color TIFF files imported in a PageMaker publication will print in their original colors, even if you apply a color to the image. To apply a color to an imported graphic, select the image and then choose the color from the Colors palette. If you decide to return the graphic image to its original colors, click [Registration] on the Colors palette.

PageMaker 6.5

Editing a Color

You can edit any color before or after you use it in a publication. Use the Define Colors dialog box to edit a color. After the color is edited, PageMaker automatically changes the color wherever you applied it in the publication. When you import an EPS image in your publication, PageMaker automatically adds the image spot colors to PageMaker's Colors palette. ✎━━ Joe doesn't think the shade of blue is the color he wants, so he plans to deepen the Royal Blue color by increasing the amount of magenta.

MacintoshUser

This replaces Step 1.
1. Click the box around the photo on page 2 to select it, then press [⌘][1]

1. **Click the box around the photo on page 2 to select it, then press [Ctrl] and right-click**
   Joe would like to darken the color around this box. He needs to open the Define Colors dialog box to edit his color.

2. **Click Utilities on the menu bar, then click Define Colors**
   The Define Colors dialog box opens.

3. **Click Royal Blue, then click Edit**
   The Color Options dialog box opens.

4. **Use the scroll bar to increase the Magenta percentage to 100**
   See Figure I-14. Joe notices the color in the top half of the preview box has changed. The bottom half of the preview box remains the original color. Joe is still not satisfied with the appearance of the color. He refers to a color chart that gives formulas for mixing colors to create new colors. He determines that he needs to add yellow to make the color a "royal" blue.

QuickTip

To remove a fill color from an object, select the object, click Element on the menu bar, point to Fill, then click None.

5. **Double-click the Yellow text box, type 25, then press [Tab] once**
   Joe likes the new color.

6. **Click OK twice**
   The Color Options and Define Color dialog boxes close. See Figure I-15. PageMaker automatically updates the color boxes behind the photos.

MacintoshUser

This replaces Step 7.
7. Press [⌘][0] (zero) to return the view to Fit in Window)

7. **Press [Ctrl] and right-click to return the view to Fit in Window**
   Notice that the color in the New World Airlines logo and the page 3 photo border is updated as well.

8. **Save the publication**

FIGURE I-14: Color Options dialog box

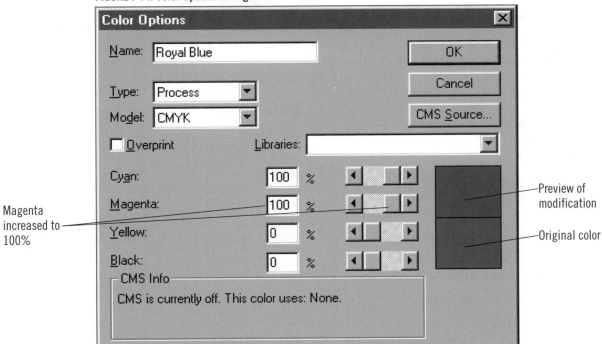

Magenta increased to 100%

Preview of modification

Original color

FIGURE I-15: Edited color applied in the publication

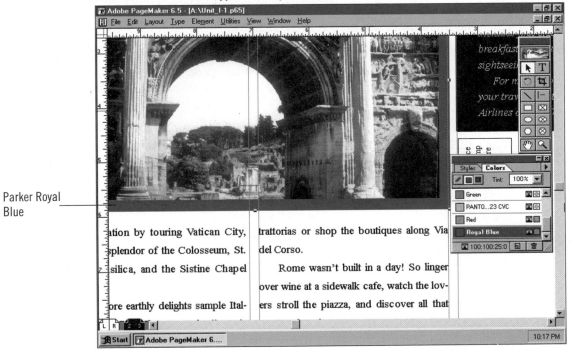

Parker Royal Blue

Editing color in an EPS image

When you place a color EPS file in a publication, PageMaker imports all colors stored in the image onto the Colors palette. The colors appear on the Colors palette with an EPS graphic place icon **PS** symbol placed in front of the newly imported color. Imported colors can be converted from spot colors to process colors, or you can modify a spot color. Process colors that are part of an EPS file cannot be edited in PageMaker.

Creating a Tint

A **tint** is a new color based on a percentage of a color you created or based on one of PageMaker's default colors. When you use only spot colors in your publication, tints can save money because the commercial printer uses only one ink to create original color as well as the tint. Tints appear on the Colors palette with a percent sign (%) in front of the CMYK color square. Joe wants to lighten the box behind the text in the fourth panel on page 2. He decides to create a new red tint.

Steps

1. Click **Utilities** on the menu bar, click **Define Colors**, click **[Paper]** in the Color list box, then click **New**
   The Color Options dialog box opens.

2. Type **75% RED** in the Name text box
   It is best to begin the name of your tint color with the percentage of the original color.

3. Click the **Type list arrow**, then click **Tint**
   See Figure I-16. The bottom half of the dialog box changes to display only the color selected in Base Color list box. Joe wants to create a tint of the red, so he will select red as his base color.

4. Click the **Base Color list arrow**, then click **Red**

5. Double-click the **Tint text box**, type **75**, press **[Tab]**, then click **OK** twice
   The Color Options and Define Colors dialog boxes close, and "75% RED" appears on the Colors palette. A % appears on the right edge of the color's entry on the Colors palette to indicate that this is a tint. Joe wants to use the new tint color in the reversed text box on page 2 in the fourth panel.

6. Make sure the **Both button** 🔳 on the Colors palette is selected, click the **black box** surrounding the text box in the fourth panel on page 2, then click **75% RED** on the Colors palette
   The box fills with the tint and the line changes from black to 75% RED, as shown in Figure I-17. Joe is pleased with the new color. The 75% RED provides a clear background for the text, and the tint unites the red headlines in the brochure.

7. Save the publication

CLUES TO USE

Applying tints using the Colors palette

A second type of color tint, created using the Colors palette, is an **object-level tint**. To create an object-level tint, select the desired object to be applied with the color tint, click the desired color on the Colors palette, and click the Tint percentage list arrow on the Colors palette, as shown in Figure I-18. Click the desired percentage tint in this list. This is a quick method for applying tint color. If you will be using a specific tint color numerous times in your publication, you might want to choose to create a new color tint so that the defined tint color will always appear on the Colors palette.

FIGURE I-16: Creating a tint using the Color Options dialog box

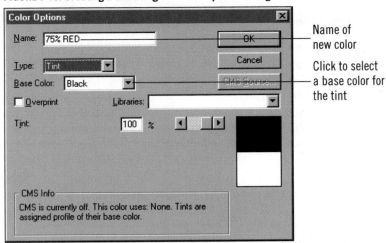

Name of new color

Click to select a base color for the tint

FIGURE I-17: 75% RED tint applied

Tint applied to box

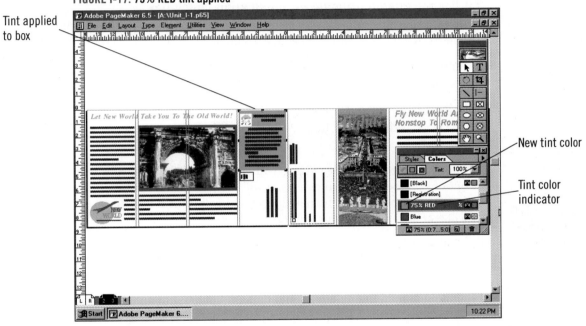

New tint color

Tint color indicator

FIGURE I-18: Creating a tint using the Colors palette

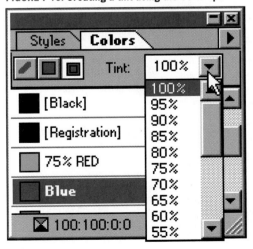

PageMaker 6.5

PageMaker 6.5

Trapping Colors

Trapping is a technique for compensating for gaps between colors when creating color separations. The gap between colors is called **misregistration**. Misregistration occurs when one or more of the colors in a multiple-color process (like CMYK) is not printed in exact alignment with the other colors. Figure I-19 shows an example when colors are printed out of registration. The Trapping Options dialog box allows you to enable PageMaker to apply trapping automatically on the different objects in your publication. Trapping is only used on color separations, and you will not see any results of trapping on the screen. However, the effects will appear on color separations. Trapping affects text and graphic objects drawn using PageMaker. Imported graphics and photographs are not affected by the trapping options. Joe wants to make sure he enables trapping to ensure that the New World Logo will print in registration.

1. **Click File on the menu bar, point to Preferences, then click Trapping**
   The Trapping Preferences dialog box opens. See Figure I-20.

2. **Click the Enable trapping for publication check box**
   By selecting this option, you instruct PageMaker to automatically apply trapping to all objects in your publication. Now Joe would like to fine-tune the trapping options.

3. **Double-click the Trap width Default text box, type .005 then press [Tab]**
   The default trap measurement is used for all colors except black.

4. **In the Black width text box, type .01**
   The black width is set at 1.5 to 2 times the default trap.

Trouble?

PageMaker does not trap imported graphics. An imported graphic should be trapped within the program that created the image.

5. **Click OK**
   The dialog box closes. See Figure I-21. You cannot see the effects of enabling the trapping options on the screen. However, you will see the effects when creating color separations at a commercial printer. In the next lesson you will learn how to create color separations that will take advantage of your trapping settings.

6. **Save your publication**

FIGURE I-19: **Examples of colors printed out of registration and printed in registration**

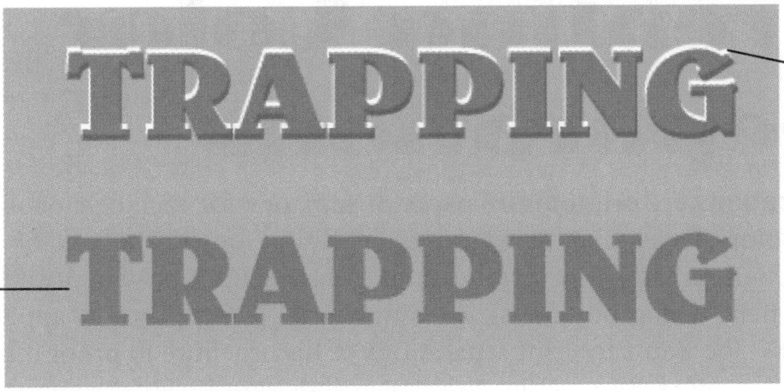

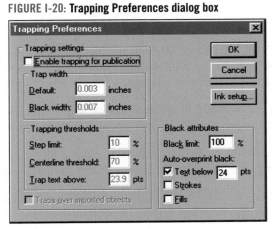

Colors not aligned correctly, resulting in undesirable white gaps

PageMaker compensates for possible misregistration, eliminating gaps

FIGURE I-20: **Trapping Preferences dialog box**

FIGURE I-21: **The final publication layout with trapping applied**

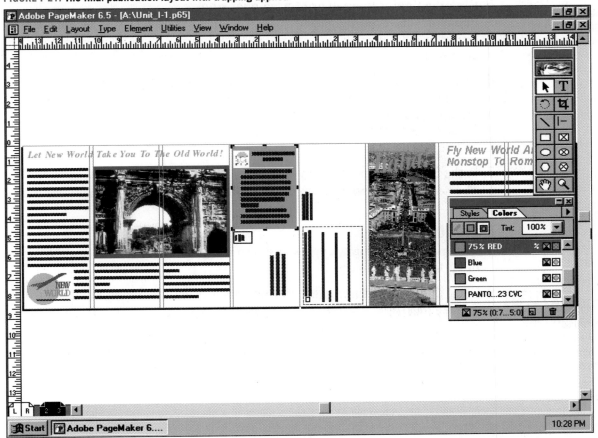

Creating Color Separations

Separations are printouts on paper or film, one for each of the four process colors. If you used spot colors, PageMaker prints out a separation for each spot color applied to your publication. When you create color publications, PageMaker lets you print separations from the Print Document dialog box that your commercial printer uses to apply color to your publication. Joe wants to print separations of his brochure to proof it before sending it to the commercial printer. By printing the separations, Joe can make sure the graphic objects and text blocks have been assigned the correct spot or process colors.

Steps

1. **Click File on the menu bar, then click Print**
   The Print Document dialog box opens. First Joe needs to change the orientation of his publication from portrait to landscape.

2. **Click the Landscape orientation icon [icon] at the bottom of the dialog box**
   Joe needs to open the Print Paper dialog box to switch to legal size paper.

3. **If you are using a PostScript printer, click Paper**
   The Print Paper dialog box opens, as shown in Figure I-22.

4. **If you have a printer capable of printing on legal-size paper, make sure Legal appears in the Size list box in the Paper section; if you can print only on letter-size paper, make sure Letter appears in the Size list box**

5. **Click the Center page in print area check box**
   This centers the information on the page. This option is helpful if you can print only on letter-size paper and your publication is based on legal-size pages. PageMaker can reduce the legal-size pages to fit on smaller paper and will center the information on the page you print.

6. **Click the Printer's marks and Page information check boxes**
   Printer's marks are the cropping and registration marks used by commercial printers to line up separations on the printing press and then trim the print job to the final size after it's printed. **Page information** adds the filename, date, and separation name to the bottom of each separation page.

7. **In the Scale section, click the Reduce to fit option button**
   The Reduce to fit option reduces the brochure to fit on whatever paper size you chose in Step 4.

8. **Click Color**
   The Print Color dialog box opens, as shown in Figure I-23. Notice the small "X" next to each of the four process colors.

9. **Click the Separations option button, scroll down the Separations color list box to display PANTONE 123 CVC, click PANTONE 123 CVC, click the Print this ink check box, click Print, save the publication, then exit PageMaker**
   PageMaker sends the file to the specified printer one separation at a time, starting with the cyan plate and ending with the Pantone 123 plate. A total of five separations print for page 2, and four separations print for page 3 (because you applied no PANTONE 123 CVC to page 3).

Trouble?
If you are using a non-postscript printer, click Setup, select Legal in the Paper Size list box if your printer accepts legal size paper or select Letter if your printer holds only letter-size paper, then click OK and continue with Step 6.

Trouble?
If PageMaker displays the message "All links may not print as expected," click Print Pub to continue.

FIGURE I-22: **Print Paper dialog box**

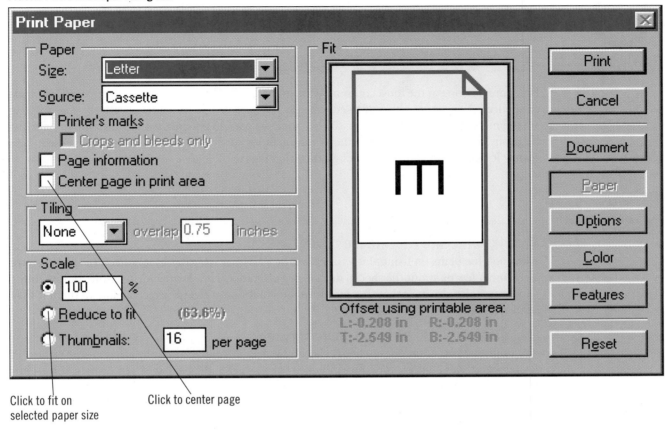

Click to fit on selected paper size

Click to center page

FIGURE I-23: **Print Color dialog box**

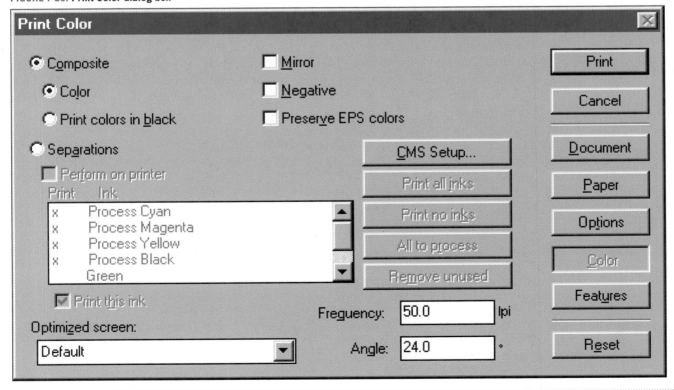

PageMaker 6.5

PageMaker 6.5

Design Workshop: Brochures

Brochures are one of the most common ways for people to learn more about a company's products or services. A brochure is meant to educate. By using color in a brochure effectively, you can help get the message across to the reader. Color should be used to enhance the information or help distinguish the differences or unite the commonalities of the information being presented. Let's review Joe's completed brochure design shown in Figure I-24.

Does the brochure educate the reader?

Although Joe plans on using this as a teaser, the brochure educates as it entices. In the brochure a customer learns about the special deals being offered by New World Airlines and Sunset Tours. Customers also discover that there is more information on the subject available to them if they send away for it.

How does color add to the brochure's design?

Although Joe could have designed the brochure using just black ink, the effect of the photos of Rome would not be the same. If members of Joe's target audience have been to Italy, color photos will spur their memories of past vacations better than black and white photos. Besides the photos, Joe used color conservatively, not splashing it onto every text block or every part of white space.

Does the paper size and folding technique help or hinder the design?

Joe's design using standard legal-size paper is relatively common in the printing industry. He will have no problems finding an economical way to print the brochure. The brochure's folds are also simple, folding the longest measurement in half, then in half again.

Does the brochure make it easy for potential customers to respond?

Potential response is where Joe's design really pays off. By using just one flap for both addressing the piece to customers and a reply card on the reverse side, Joe saves money and makes responding easier for customers. How? Joe can have the printing company add a perforation along the fold line to separate the card easily from the rest of the brochure. The bulk of the brochure stays intact for the customer, and the response card is mailed back to New World Airlines.

FIGURE I-24: Joe's completed brochure

Let New World Take You To The Old World!

Many of the world's greatest artists and writers—Keats, Byron, Goethe, Renoir, Monet—came to Rome to delight their eyes and palates, to nourish their spirits, and to stoke their passions. Let New World Airlines whisk you away to this ancient capital so you too can indulge in all that is Rome!

Rome is the historical and cultural soul of Italy. Begin to discover its secrets by exploring the famed seven hills upon which the city was built. Upon Capitoline Hill once stood the most sacred of all Rome's temples. Follow the curve of the hill down to the Roman Forum, the civic center of ancient Rome.

Shift your attention from history to art

NEW WORLD A I R L I N E S

Place Stamp Here

and inspiration by touring Vatican City, where the splendor of the Colosseum, St. Peter's Basilica, and the Sistine Chapel awaits you.

For more earthly delights, sample Italian pasta at one of Rome's family-style trattorias or shop the boutiques along Via del Corso.

Rome wasn't built in a day! So linger over wine at a sidewalk cafe, watch the lovers stroll the piazza, and discover all that you can be— in Rome!

New World Airlines
1845 Lindbergh Blvd.
Charlotte, NC 28204

New World Airlines
1845 Lindbergh Blvd.
Charlotte, NC 28204

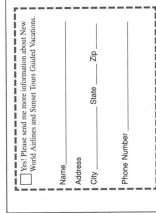

Yes! Please send me more information about New World Airlines and Sunset Tours Guided Vacations.

Name
Address
City   State   Zip
Phone Number

Fly New World Airlines Nonstop To Rome

New World Airlines has convenient non-stop flights from Chicago, Miami, Atlanta, New York, and Boston to Leonardo da Vinci International Airport in Rome. Leave your cares at the gate as you begin your Italian adventure in the comfort and security of a New World Airlines and Sunset Tours.

Practice

► Concepts Review

Label each of the publication window elements shown in Figure I-25.

FIGURE I-25

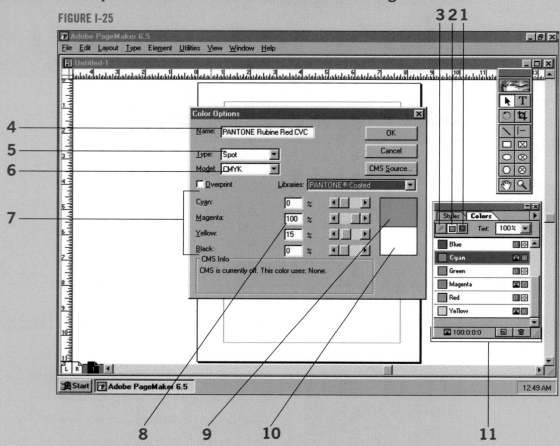

Match each of the terms with the statement that describes its function.

12. **Process colors**
13. **Spot color**
14. **Tint**
15. **Color library**
16. **Separations**

a. Based on a specific color ink
b. Printouts on paper or film of each color used for commercial printing of publications
c. PageMaker's storage for color matching systems
d. The four main colors used in combinations to create many other colors
e. A new color based on a percentage of another color

17. Which of the following is true about brochures?
   a. Brochures can be used as teasers to entice the reader to find out more information.
   b. Brochures should be distinctive in design from other corporate brochures.
   c. Brochures come in all different sizes.
   d. Both a and c are true.
   e. All of the above are true.

18. The four process colors are:
   a. Cyan, magenta, yellow, red
   b. Cyan, magenta, green, yellow
   c. Cyan, magenta, yellow, black
   d. Red, yellow, blue, black

19. Spot colors are not:
   a. Percentages of another color
   b. Created using a color matching system
   c. Based on a specific color ink used in printing
   d. All of the above

20. Colors can be applied to:
   a. Text
   b. Graphical elements
   c. Lines
   d. All of the above

21. Tints are based on:
   a. Color matching systems
   b. Process colors
   c. Black
   d. All of the above

22. The purpose of a color matching system is to create:
   a. Colors that display vibrantly on a color monitor
   b. Color separations
   c. Process colors
   d. Consistent color representation between monitors and print output

23. Color separations are:
   a. Previews of final color composite output
   b. Printouts on paper or film of process colors
   c. Printouts on paper or film of spot colors
   d. Both b and c

▶ Skills Review

1. Create a new color.
  a. Start PageMaker and open the publication UNIT_I-2 from your Student Disk.
  b. Click Utilities on the menu bar, then click Define Colors.
  c. Click [Paper] in the Colors list box, then click New.
  d. In the Color Options dialog box, make sure CMYK is selected.
  e. Double-click the Cyan text box, type "100", then press [Tab] twice *(Macintosh users: press [Tab] once)*.
  f. Type "50" in the Magenta text box, then press [Tab] twice *(Macintosh users: press [Tab] once)*.
  g. Type "100" in the Yellow text box, then press [Tab].
  h. In the Name text box, type "Forest Green," then click OK twice.

2. Apply color to a graphic and remove a color.
  a. If necessary, click Window on the menu bar, then click Show Colors to display the Colors palette in the publication window.
  b. Click the horizontal box around the word "Speaker" in the upper-left corner on page 2 to select it.
  c. Click the Both button on the Colors palette, then click Forest Green.
  d. Click the vertical box intersecting the box on the far right side of page 2.
  e. Apply the Forest Green color to both the fill and line of the selected box, then click outside the box to deselect it.
  f. Select the vertical box to which you just applied the color.
  g. Click [Registration] on the Colors palette to return the object to its original color.
  h. Apply the Forest Green color to both the fill and line of all horizontal boxes on page 2 and in the left two columns on page 3.

3. Edit a color.
  a. Click Utilities on the menu bar, then click Define Colors.
  b. Click Forest Green in the Color list box, then click Edit.
  c. Use the scroll bar to increase the Magenta percentage to 75%.
  d. Click OK twice to close the Color Options and Define Colors dialog boxes.
  e. Make sure your new color is automatically applied to all objects set to that color.

4. Use a color library.
  a. Click Utilities on the menu bar, then click Define Colors.
  b. Click [Paper] in the Color list box, then click New.
  c. Click the Libraries list arrow, then click PANTONE Coated.
  d. Scroll to the right, then select the color named Rubine Red.
  e. Click OK twice.
  f. Click New to create a second color.
  g. Click the Libraries list arrow, click PANTONE Coated.
  h. Select the text in the PANTONE CVC text box, then type "3955" to create a second Pantone color.
  i. Click OK three times to close the Define Colors dialog box.
  j. Scroll down the Colors palette to see the new Pantone colors that you created.

5. Apply color to text.
   a. Click the Text tool in the toolbox, then highlight the headline text inside the Forest Green box in the upper-left corner on page 2.
   b. Click Rubine Red on the Colors palette to apply the color to the text.
   c. Repeat Steps a and b above to apply the Rubine Red color to all headline text inside Forest Green boxes.

6. Create a tint.
   a. Click Utilities on the menu bar, then click Define Colors.
   b. Click New.
   c. Click the Type list arrow, then click the Tint.
   d. Click Forest Green in the Base Color list box.
   e. Use the scroll bar to select 50% in the Tint text box.
   f. Click in the Name text box then type "50% Forest Green."
   g. Click OK twice.
   h. Apply the new 50% Forest Green color to all vertical boxes in the brochure.

7. Trap colors.
   a. Click File on the menu bar, point to Preferences, then click Trapping.
   b. Click the Enable trapping for publication check box.
   c. Type ".005" in the Trap width Default text box, then press [Tab].
   d. Type ".011" in the Black width text box.
   e. Click OK.

8. Create color separations.
   a. Click File on the menu bar, then click Print.
   b. If you are using a PostScript printer, click Paper. If you are using a non-PostScript printer, go to Step e.
   c. Click the Center page in print area check box.
   d. Click the Reduce to fit option button.
   e. Click Color.
   f. Click the Separations option button.
   g. Click PANTONE Rubine Red 2X CVC, then click the Print this ink check box.
   h. Repeat Step g for PANTONE 3955 CVC.
   i. Click Print.
   j. Save your publication, then exit PageMaker.

PageMaker 6.5

► Independent Challenges

1. You work for Sunset Tours in the Young Audience Tours division. You have decided to create a brochure that can be sent to all New World Airlines customers who are between the ages of 18 and 24, announcing new spring break trips to the Caribbean Islands. This brochure will serve as a teaser with the purpose of encouraging the reader to send back an attached mailer for more information. This brochure will be printed using four-color process inks. Include photos and color elements to enhance the overall message of the brochure.

To complete this independent challenge:

1. Plan and sketch the brochure design.
2. Open a new publication and determine the size, shape, and possible ways to incorporate a reply card. Use a size other than letter or legal, and a format other than three- or four-panel.
3. Place the Caribbean-related photos called PHOTO1 and PHOTO2, located on your Student Disk, in the brochure.
4. Add headlines and copy for the brochure, then apply color to the sections you think are appropriate. If necessary, you can use the Word document, PROPOSAL, located on your Student Disk, for text describing the Caribbean.
5. Create a spot color using the process colors. Apply the color to the headlines.
6. Create an additional spot color using one of PageMaker's color libraries. Apply the color to appropriate graphical elements included in your brochure.
7. Create color separations for each of the process colors. Be sure to include a separation for each additional spot color.
8. Save the brochure as Caribbean brochure to your Student Disk.
9. Submit your sketch and final brochure.

2. Visit a local bank or financial planner and find brochures about investment opportunities. Try to find brochures that include full color. Review the examples, then redesign one of the brochures to improve its appeal. Answer the following questions as you plan your design:

1. What is the purpose of the brochure? Is it meant to be informational or serve as a teaser to encourage the reader to inquire for more information?
2. Do the different brochures from a single company present a single corporate identity?
3. Does the brochure give the reader the opportunity to inquire for more information?
4. Does the size of the brochure seem appropriate? Does the information presented seem to fit the dimensions proportionately?

To complete this independent challenge:

1. Sketch your version of the brochure.
2. Open a new publication and save it as Financial brochure to your Student Disk.
3. Create columns in your publication if necessary.
4. Place the Word document TEXTHLD and the graphic file PLACEHLD to serve as dummy text and graphics.
5. Add boxes and lines to enhance the overall design of the brochure.
6. Create new colors that can be applied to headline and other appropriate text blocks.
7. Create a new color from a PANTONE® Coated library. Use this color and apply it to graphical elements in your publication.
8. Create a new tint color and apply it to either text or graphics.
9. Include a point of response. This could be a mailer or simply be an address and phone number depending on your brochure.
10. Create color separations for each of the process colors. Be sure to include a separation for each additional spot color.
11. Save the publication, then print it.
12. Submit your sketch and final brochure.

3. You work for a small but promising software company called Digital Art Media Ltd. You have been asked by the president, Harry O'Grady, to create a brochure for his new CD ROM titles: Golf For The Vertically Challenged, Health Care Clip Art, and CHUNKY the fuzzy Bear. This brochure will serve as a teaser with a mailer included that the reader can send back for more information.

To complete this independent challenge:

1. Create a vertical four-panel, three-fold brochure.
2. Place the Word document TEXTHLD.DOC and the graphic file PLACEHLD.TIF into your publication as necessary to serve as dummy text and graphics.
3. Create colors that can be applied to text and drawn graphic designs. Use one color from the Pantone® Coated library.
4. Create a tint and apply it in your design.
5. Create color separations for each of the process and spot colors.
6. Save the publication as CD-ROM brochure to your Student Disk, and print a composite of the brochure.

4. You work for a travel agency that is offering package trips to several locations in Florida and the Bahamas in conjunction with a major airline. You have been given the job of creating a teaser brochure which describes the vacation destinations.

To complete this independent challenge:

1. Search the World Wide Web for information on vacation packages in Florida and the Bahamas.
2. Using the information that you find, create a sketch of both the inside and outside panels of your brochure following the guidelines that you learned in this unit. Be sure to include a logo for the agency and a return mailer or point of response.
3. Create a brochure in PageMaker from your sketch. You can use the dummy graphic file PLACEHLD on your Student Disk in place of graphics or photos, but add your own headlines and text from the information that you have found on the World Wide Web.
4. Use color to add to the brochure's design. Create a new spot color from the four process colors and also from a predefined library color. Apply these colors to different elements in your brochure.
5. Edit the spot color that you created from the four process colors.
6. Create a tint from one of PageMaker's default colors and use it as the background color for a text block in the publication.
7. Create color separations for your brochure, being sure to turn the Trapping option on first.
8. Critique your final brochure to make sure that it achieves its purpose. Save the brochure as Bahamas brochure to your Student Disk, then print it. Hand in your sketch, critique, and all printouts.

▶ Visual Workshop

Create a new tri-fold brochure from this file highlighting New World Airlines and Sunset Tours' European vacations to London, Paris, and Rome. Figure I-26 serves as a guide for what your completed publication should look like. Use the file TEXTHLD, located on your Student Disk, to take the place of each text block. Save the publication as European brochure to your Student Disk and print it. Then turn on the Trapping feature, and print color separations for your brochure. Save the publication.

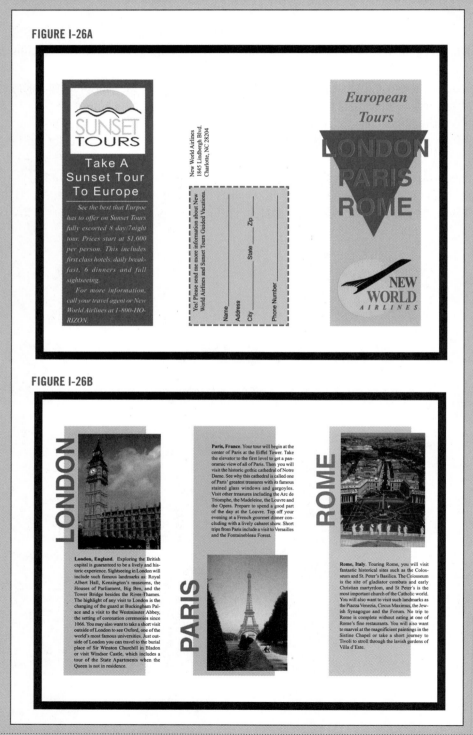

PageMaker 6.5

Working
with Long Publications

Pagemaker provides the tools that you can use to easily add an index and a table of contents to your publication. In this unit you will learn how to mark text in your stories that you want to be included in an index, how to use shortcuts for identifying text to be used in the index, how to edit index entries, how to create cross-references, and how to generate an index. In addition, you will learn how to create a table of contents and how to use the Drop Cap PageMaker Plug-in. New World Airlines is promoting its flights from Southwest cities to Boston. In conjunction with this promotion, Joe Martin needs to create a visitor's guide for potential visitors. He has already created a layout and placed stories, but now he wants to make the guide more user-friendly by adding an index and a table of contents.

Designing an Index

When planning a publication with many pages, you should consider adding an index to help your readers find specific information in your document. You can create a comprehensive index, or you can create an index based on major topics, or **key words**. When sketching his design, shown in Figure J-1, Joe used the following guidelines to help him create an effective index:

Details

 Determine your reader's need for an index

Some publications need comprehensive indexes, others only need an index with key words. Use comprehensive indexes for technical or detailed publications. Use a more general key word index for publicity or marketing publications. Joe will index his publication using key words.

 Provide alternative methods for finding key/words in an index

When designing an index, you need to take into consideration the different ways readers might use the index to find a specific topic. For example, adding cross-reference index entries gives readers a greater chance to find the information they need. You can also add secondary index information—or information about the discussion of one topic in relation to another—to primary index references. Joe will add both cross-references and secondary index references where appropriate.

 **Add graphics to index pages**

DesignTip

Index pages should be broken up using two or more columns per page but never more than four columns on a standard 8½" × 11" size page.

Many publications end with numerous pages of "heavy" textual pages. You can break up the monotony of these pages and draw readers' attention to these pages by adding graphic designs or photographs. While looking at a graphic design or photograph, readers might see an index topic that causes them to refer back to the publication. Joe will add photos of Boston that he didn't use in the previous page layouts.

PageMaker 6.5

Adding Index Entries

To include a word or group of words in an index, you use the Index Entry command. This command adds an index marker, which is visible only in story editor. The **index marker** signals text to be included in the index. Later, when you generate an index, you use the Index Entry dialog box to determine if each index entry has a page reference or is a cross-reference to another entry. Joe begins creating the index by marking key words in the first story on page 4.

Steps

1. **Start PageMaker and open the file UNIT_J-1 from your Student Disk**
   The visitor guide for Boston, which Joe has been working on, appears in the publication window. Joe uses story editor to mark key/words to be added to the index.

2. **Click the body text block on page 4, click Edit on the menu bar, then click Edit Story**
   The text block opens in story editor. Now Joe is ready to mark his first index entry.

3. **Select the text Freedom Trail in the second paragraph, click Utilities on the menu bar, then click Index Entry**
   The Add Index Entry dialog box opens, as shown in Figure J-2. You must first determine if the topic Freedom Trail is a page reference or cross-reference index entry.

4. **Make sure the Page reference option button is selected**
   In the Topic section of the dialog box, you identify topics to be indexed. You can also choose to add subcategories to create a more detailed index. See Figure J-3 for an example of secondary and tertiary topics. Secondary topics are indented under the primary topic and tertiary topics are indented under the secondary topic. Joe decides this index entry Freedom Trail is a primary topic. Next Joe needs to determine the beginning and ending page range of the topic's discussion.

5. **Make sure the Current page option button in the Page range section is selected**
   The final option in this dialog box allows you to format the page number. Joe decides not to use this option.

Trouble?

When exporting stories from PageMaker, you will lose index information associated with index topics.

6. **Click OK**
   The dialog box closes and PageMaker inserts an index marker in front of the word "Freedom", as shown in Figure J-4.

Sorting index topics

Using the Index Entry dialog box, you can sort topics alphabetically by the spelling entered in the Sort text boxes. However, the topic will appear in the index as it is spelled in the Topic text box. Figure J-5 shows an example where St. Louis is entered in the Topic text box and Saint Louis is typed in the Sort text box. When the index is generated, the index entry will be printed as St. Louis in the index, but it will be sorted as Saint Louis because of the sort specification entered in the Sort text box.

FIGURE J-2: Add Index Entry dialog box

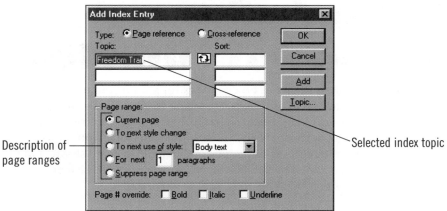

Description of
page ranges

Selected index topic

FIGURE J-3: Example of secondary and tertiary topic index

Primary index topics

Secondary topics

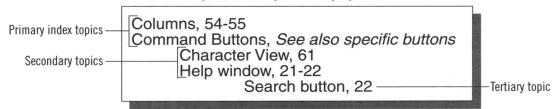

Columns, 54-55
Command Buttons, *See also specific buttons*
    Character View, 61
    Help window, 21-22
            Search button, 22

Tertiary topic

FIGURE J-4: Index marker in front of Freedom Trail

Index topic

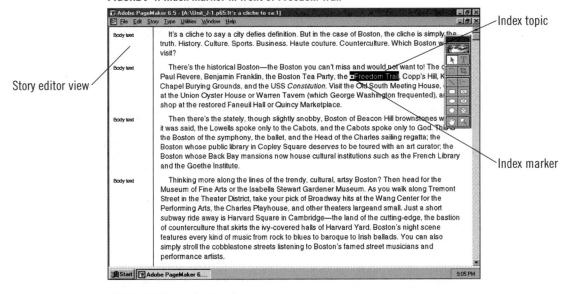

Story editor view

Index marker

FIGURE J-5: Example of topic sort

Index entry
appears as "St."

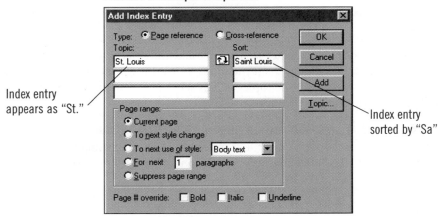

Index entry
sorted by "Sa"

Using Index Keyboard Shortcuts

Once you have an understanding of how to index topics, you can use shortcuts that allow you to quickly add index items. One shortcut suggestion is to use keyboard shortcuts in the publication window. When you use keyboard shortcuts to mark index entries, you won't see the index marker. However, using keyboard shortcuts will save you time from entering story editor. In addition to marking index entries, you can use a different keyboard shortcut to index a person's proper name so that it is sorted by last name first. Joe will use index shortcuts to quickly index important topics that he wants to include in the index.

1. Click **Story** on the menu bar, then click **Close Story**
   The story editor window closes, and you return to the publication window.

2. Move ▶ over the second paragraph on page 4, then press [Ctrl] and right click
   The view changes to Actual Size. Joe wants to add the topic Copp's Hill to the index.

3. Click the **Text tool** 🔲 in the toolbox, select the text **Copp's Hill**, then press [Ctrl][Y]
   The Add Index Entry dialog box opens, as shown in Figure J-6. Joe accepts the specifications in the Add Index Entry dialog box.

4. Click **OK**
   Joe wants to return to story editor to make sure an index marker is displayed in front of the topic Copp's Hill.

5. Click the **Pointer tool** 🔲 in the toolbox, move ▶ over the text on page 4, then triple-click
   The story appears in the story editor window. There is an index marker in front of the word "Copp's". Joe wants to continue selecting index topics using the keyboard shortcut.

6. Click **Story** on the menu bar, click **Close Story**, click 🔲, select the text **King's Chapel Burying Grounds**, then press [Ctrl][Shift][Y]
   Although you can't see it, an index marker is automatically inserted in front of the word "King's". Indexing terms using this shortcut bypasses the Add Index Entry dialog box. The topic is also automatically added as a primary index topic. Joe continues indexing topics using keyboard shortcuts in the publication window.

7. Repeat Step 6 to index the following entries: **USS *Constitution*, Old South Meeting House, Union Oyster House, Warren Tavern, Faneuil Hall,** and **Quincy Marketplace**
   The next item Joe needs to index is the proper name George Washington. Joe wants the name to be indexed by the last name.

8. Select the text **George Washington**, then press [Ctrl][Alt][Y]
   Once again, even though you can't see it, PageMaker has placed an index marker in front of George, and the entry will appear in the index as Washington, George, referencing page 4. Next, Joe wants to be sure all the topics he has selected for the index have been marked, so he uses story editor to view the index markers.

9. Click 🔲, move ▶ over the text on page 4, then triple-click
   The story appears in the story editor. The index topics selected using the keyboard shortcuts have been marked with index markers, as shown in Figure J-7.

MacintoshUser

This replaces Step 2 and 3.
2. Move ▶ over the second paragraph on page 4, then press [⌘][option][1] and click the mouse button
3. Click the Text tool 🔲 in the toolbox, select the text "Copp's Hill", then press [⌘][Y]
Resume at Step 4.

MacintoshUser

This replaces Step 6.
6. Click Story on the menu bar, click Close Story, click 🔲, select the text "King's Chapel Burying Grounds", then press [⌘][shift][Y]

MacintoshUser

This replaces Step 8.
8. Select the text "George Washington", then press [⌘][option][Y]

FIGURE J-6: Add Index Entry dialog box in layout view

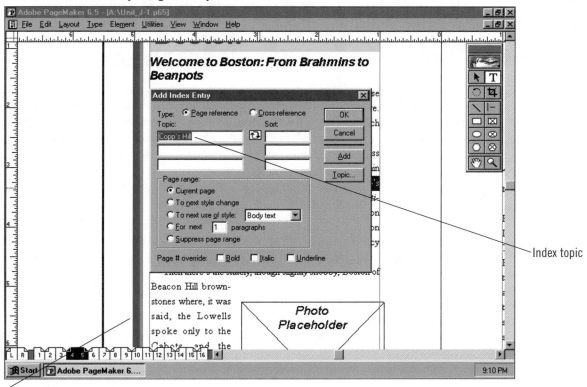

Index topic

Layout view

FIGURE J-7: Index markers in story editor

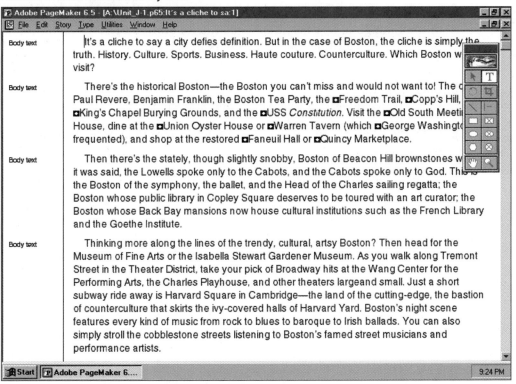

Using the Index Shortcut Menu

In addition to keyboard shortcuts, there is a shortcut menu command—the Change command—you can use in story editor. This command allows you to index all occurrences of words or phrases with one command. Joe wants to create a secondary-level reference for Faneuil Hall underneath the primary index reference Downtown Boston. He will begin by using a keyboard shortcut to open the Add Index Entry dialog box. Then he will use the Change command to index all occurrences of the word "Boston."

Steps

MacintoshUser

This replaces Step 1.
1. Select the text "Faneuil Hall", press [⌘][Y], click the Promote/Demote button ⬍

QuickTip

To index a complete name such as Thomas Martin Brooks, insert a nonbreaking space between Thomas and Martin by pressing [Ctrl][Shift][H] (Macintosh users: press [option] [spacebar]), then index the name using [Ctrl][Shift][Z] (Macintosh users: [⌘] [option][Y]). PageMaker indexes the name as Brooks, Thomas Martin.

1. **Select the text Faneuil Hall, press [Ctrl][Y], click the Promote/Demote button ⬍**
   Notice that the phrase Faneuil Hall is now displayed in the second Topic text box. The insertion point is flashing inside the first Topic text box prompting you to type. Joe types the primary index reference.

2. **Type Downtown Boston, then click OK**
   Notice two index entry markers appear in front of Faneuil. See Figure J-8. This tells you that the entry is indexed in two different places: as Faneuil Hall and under Downtown Boston. Now Joe wants to index all occurrences of Boston.

3. **Click Ɪ at the beginning of the story, click Utilities on the menu bar, then click Change**
   The Change dialog box opens. Joe types the word "Boston" in the Find what text box.

4. **Type Boston in the Find what text box, press [Tab], then type ^; (caret and semicolon) in the Change to text box, then click the All stories option button**
   Joe has entered the information necessary to index all occurrences of the word Boston. See Figure J-9.

5. **Click Change all**
   PageMaker adds every instance of Boston to the index.

6. **Click the Close button in the Change dialog box, then close each story editor window that is open**

7. **Save and close your publication**

FIGURE J-8: Two index entry markers in front of Faneuil

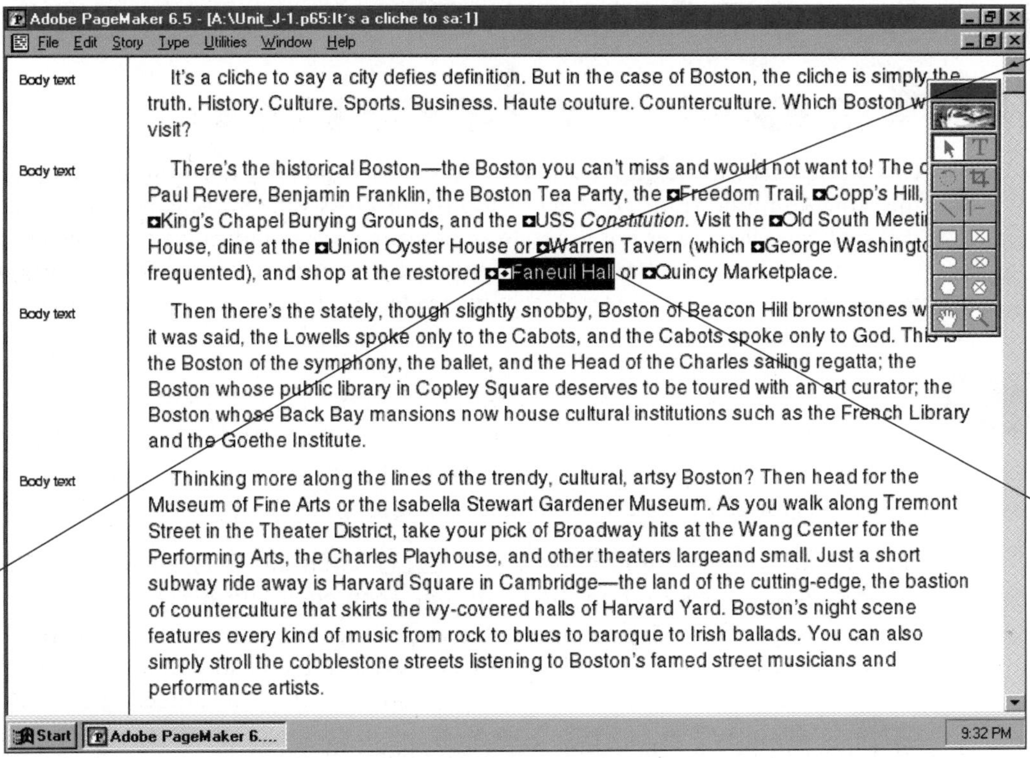

Secondary index marker

Index topic

Primary index marker

Adobe PageMaker 6.5 - [A:\Unit_J-1.p65:It's a cliche to sa:1]

File Edit Story Type Utilities Window Help

Body text

It's a cliche to say a city defies definition. But in the case of Boston, the cliche is simply the truth. History. Culture. Sports. Business. Haute couture. Counterculture. Which Boston w visit?

Body text

There's the historical Boston—the Boston you can't miss and would not want to! The Paul Revere, Benjamin Franklin, the Boston Tea Party, the ◻Freedom Trail, ◻Copp's Hill, ◻King's Chapel Burying Grounds, and the ◻USS *Constitution*. Visit the ◻Old South Meeti House, dine at the ◻Union Oyster House or ◻Warren Tavern (which ◻George Washingt frequented), and shop at the restored ◻◻Faneuil Hall or ◻Quincy Marketplace.

Body text

Then there's the stately, though slightly snobby, Boston of Beacon Hill brownstones w it was said, the Lowells spoke only to the Cabots, and the Cabots spoke only to God. This the Boston of the symphony, the ballet, and the Head of the Charles sailing regatta; the Boston whose public library in Copley Square deserves to be toured with an art curator; the Boston whose Back Bay mansions now house cultural institutions such as the French Library and the Goethe Institute.

Body text

Thinking more along the lines of the trendy, cultural, artsy Boston? Then head for the Museum of Fine Arts or the Isabella Stewart Gardener Museum. As you walk along Tremont Street in the Theater District, take your pick of Broadway hits at the Wang Center for the Performing Arts, the Charles Playhouse, and other theaters largeand small. Just a short subway ride away is Harvard Square in Cambridge—the land of the cutting-edge, the bastion of counterculture that skirts the ivy-covered halls of Harvard Yard. Boston's night scene features every kind of music from rock to blues to baroque to Irish ballads. You can also simply stroll the cobblestone streets listening to Boston's famed street musicians and performance artists.

Start   Adobe PageMaker 6....   9:32 PM

FIGURE J-9: Change dialog box

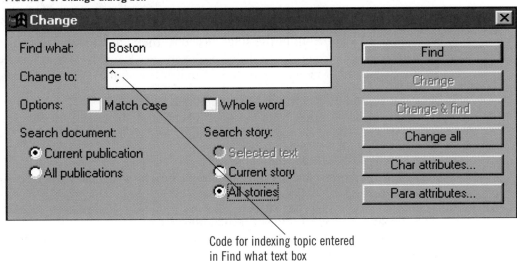

Change

Find what: Boston

Change to: ^;

Options: ☐ Match case   ☐ Whole word

Search document: Search story:
  ⦿ Current publication   ○ Selected text
  ○ All publications   ○ Current story
                                 ⦿ All stories

Find
Change
Change & find
Change all
Char attributes...
Para attributes...

Code for indexing topic entered
in Find what text box

PageMaker 6.5

PageMaker 6.5

Creating a Cross-reference

Cross-references are helpful to readers who want to find related or additional topics. You will use the same Add Index Entry dialog box to identify cross-references. However, unlike primary references, PageMaker does not generate an index marker to indicate a cross-reference. The placement of your cursor in the story is irrelevant when creating a cross-reference. ✎ Joe wants to add several cross-references to help his readers find pertinent information.

Steps 1 2 3 4

1. **Open the file UNIT_J-2 from your Student Disk**
   The visitor guide is nearly complete with most of the index selections selected.

2. **Click the pages 6 and 7 page icon [6][7], click the story under "Boston Highlights" to select it, click Edit on the menu bar, then click Edit Story**
   The story editor window opens. Joe decides to add a cross-reference for the Children's Museum. He wants to remind his readers that there is additional information about the Children's Museum in the Family Attractions section of the guide.

3. **Click Utilities on the menu bar, then click Index Entry**
   The Add Index Entry dialog box opens. Remember, because a cross-reference does not generate an index marker, it is not necessary to place the insertion point before the phrase Children's Museum in this story. First, Joe changes the type of index entry from a page reference to cross-reference.

4. **Click the Cross-reference option button**
   Notice that the bottom half of the dialog box changed. See Figure J-10. Joe needs to type in the Topic text box the topic he wishes to cross-reference.

5. **Type Children's Museum in the Topic text box, then click X-ref**
   The Select Cross-Reference Topic dialog box opens. See Figure J-11. Next Joe needs to cross-reference Children's Museum to the topic Family Attractions.

6. **Click the Topic section list arrow, then click F**
   The index entries beginning with the letter "F" appear in the Level 1 list box. See Figure J-12. Joe sees that he created an index entry for Family Attractions, so he selects it.

7. **Click Family Attractions, then click OK**
   The dialog box closes. Next Joe must determine how he wants the cross-reference to appear in the index.

QuickTip

Make sure you select the See also option and not the See [also] option.

8. **Click the See also option button, then click OK**
   Notice that no new index marker is displayed in story editor to indicate that Children's Museum is a cross-reference.

9. **Close story editor, then save the publication**

FIGURE J-10: **Cross-reference option button selected**

Option button selected

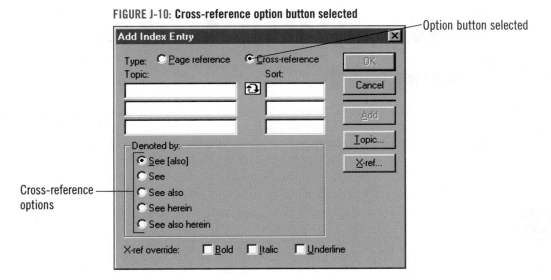

Cross-reference options

FIGURE J-11: **Select Cross-Reference Topic dialog box**

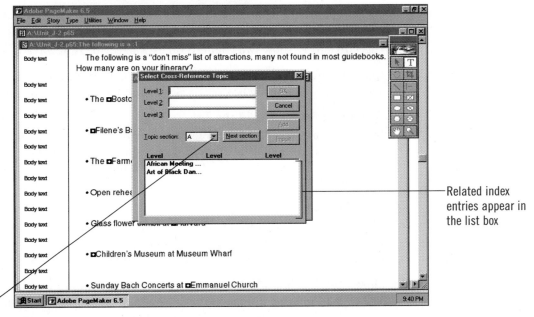

Related index entries appear in the list box

Topic section list arrow

FIGURE: J-12: **Index list box for the letter F**

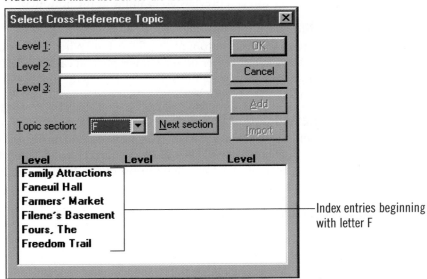

Index entries beginning with letter F

PageMaker 6.5

Setting the Index Format

After you have identified all the topics to be indexed, you use the Create Index command to format the index information. You can specify how index entries will be arranged in the index, and you can also change the paragraph style applied. Joe is ready to format the index.

Steps

1. **Click the pages 16 and 17 page icon** ⌷16⌷17⌷
   First Joe wants to create a two-column layout.

2. **Click Layout on the menu bar, click Column Guides, type 2 in the Number of columns text box, then click OK**
   Pages 16 and 17 show two columns on each page. Joe is now ready to create the index.

3. **Click Utilities on the menu bar, then click Create Index**
   The Create Index dialog box opens. See Figure J-13. Joe types the index title.

4. **Type Index To Boston in the Title text box**
   Index titles can be up to 30 characters in length. Notice that the Remove unreferenced topics option is selected at this time. This option removes any unreferenced topics for which entries were deleted or for which a topic was removed if an index marker was deleted. Joe leaves this option turned on. Next Joe chooses the Format option.

5. **Click Format**
   The Index Format dialog box opens, as shown in Figure J-14. The first choice Joe needs to make is whether to include index section headings. He also can choose to include empty index sections, such as the section Q if there are no entries for Q.

6. **Make sure the Include index section headings check box is selected**
   The next formatting option choice is Nested or Run-in. These options determine whether subentries are separate paragraphs or included in one paragraph. When you select either Nested or Run-in, you can preview an example at the bottom of the dialog box.

7. **Click the Run-in option button**
   Notice the example at the bottom of the dialog box. When Run-in is selected, the subentries for an index entry run together in one paragraph, and each subentry is separated by a semicolon. After examining the options for displaying the index, Joe decides he prefers the Nested format.

8. **Click the Nested option button**
   The remaining text boxes are used to enter other index format specifications. These specifications determine how PageMaker will enter characters and spaces to separate parts of your index entries. See Table J-1 for a description of the Index Format options. Joe decides to keep the default settings.

9. **Click OK to close the Index Format dialog box**

FIGURE J-13: Create Index dialog box

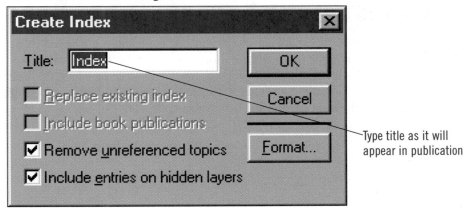

Type title as it will
appear in publication

FIGURE J-14: Index Format dialog box

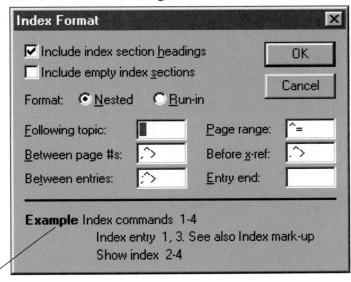

Shows selected
format style

TABLE J-1: Index Format options

option	description
Following topic	Space used to separate the topic and the page number. The default is two spaces.
Between page #s	Space used to separate multiple page references. The default is an en space (a space equal to the width of the "n" character).
Between entries	Character used to separate level entries in a run-in format or character used to separate cross-references. The default is a semicolon and en space.
Page range	Character used to separate first and last page references in a series. The default is a dash.
Before x-ref	Character that appears before a cross-reference. The default is a period and en space.
Entry end	Character that appears at the end of every entry in a nested format or following the last cross-reference in the topic. The default is no character.

PageMaker 6.5

Generating an Index

After setting the format for an index, you can generate it and insert it into your publication. PageMaker creates the index information as a new story that you can place in your publication as you would any other story. If you continue to add or to edit index entries, then you must regenerate the index for the changes to appear in the placed index story. Joe will place the index on the last two pages of his publication.

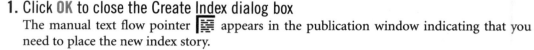

1. Click **OK** to close the Create Index dialog box
   The manual text flow pointer appears in the publication window indicating that you need to place the new index story.

2. Move to the margin intersection in the top left corner of page 16, press **[Shift]** and click, but do not release **[Shift]**

3. Continue to hold **[Shift]** and click in the second column on page 16 and in the first and second columns on page 17 to finish placing the story

4. Move to page 16, then press **[Ctrl]** and right-click
   See Figure J-15. The newly generated index is displayed in the publication.

5. Save the publication

Trouble?

You might need to adjust the text kerning if an index topic's page references run together.

MacintoshUser

This replaces Step 4.
4. Move to page 16, then press [⌘][0] (zero)

CLUES TO USE

Special index paragraph styles

PageMaker automatically creates special index paragraph styles and applies them to the index story when you generate an index. See Figure J-16. These styles can be edited using the same method you use to change normal styles. The names of index styles should not be changed because PageMaker looks for the original index style names each time you regenerate an index.

FIGURE J-15: Index generated using Create Index command

Title

Section

Primary
entry

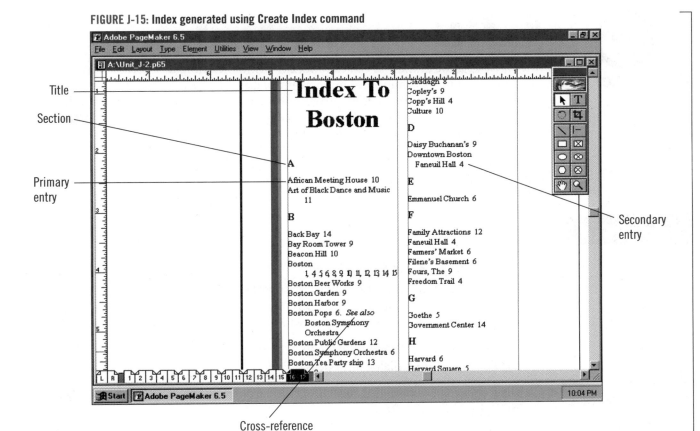

Secondary
entry

Cross-reference

FIGURE J-16: Styles palette with the index styles

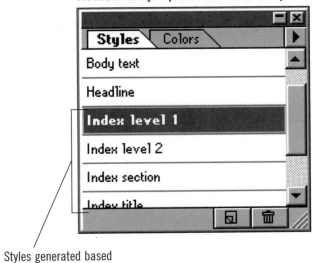

Styles generated based
on formatting options

PageMaker 6.5

Editing an Index

After reviewing the index, you can edit index entries by selecting the specific index entry or by using the Show Index command. The Show Index dialog box allows you to use edit commands on all index entries from all stories in your publication. See Table J-2 for a detailed description of the special codes used when PageMaker cannot locate a publication page. ✐⬤▬ After reviewing the index he just created, Joe wants to edit several index references.

MacintoshUser

The pointer appears as ▶ in this window.

QuickTip

You can delete index entries using the Show Index dialog box by selecting the index item you want to delete and then clicking Remove.

1. Click the **pages 4 and 5 page icon** ⎡4|5⎤, triple-click the story on page 4, then select the **index marker** in front of the word "Goethe" at the end of the third paragraph
   The index entry only includes the word "Goethe" and not the word "Institute," so Joe will add the word "Institute" using the Index Entry dialog box.

2. Click **Utilities** on the menu bar, then click **Index Entry**
   The Edit Index Entry dialog box opens.

3. Click I in the Topic text box after the word "Goethe," press [Spacebar], type **Institute**, then click **OK**
   The dialog box closes. When Joe regenerates the index, this index entry will be corrected to read Goethe Institute. Joe does not want to go to each index entry that he wants to correct. Joe will use Show Index command to correct other index entries.

4. Click **Utilities** on the menu bar, then click **Show Index**
   The Show Index dialog box opens. See Figure J-17. This dialog box allows you to edit any index entry in the publication. Joe needs to display the Omni index entry.

5. Click the **Index section list arrow**, click **O**, click **Omni** in the Index section list box, then click **Edit**
   The Edit Index Entry dialog box opens, as shown in Figure J-18. Joe needs to add the word "Theater" after the indexed word "Omni."

6. Click I in the Topic text box after the word "Omni," press [Spacebar], type **Theater**, then click **OK** twice

7. Click **Story** on the menu bar, then click **Close Story**
   Now that Joe has finished editing the index entries, he needs to regenerate the index.

8. Click the **pages 16 and 17 page icon** ⎡16|17⎤, click **Utilities** on the menu bar, then click **Create Index**
   The Create Index dialog box opens. Notice that new options are now available.

9. Make sure the **Replace existing index check box** is selected, click **OK**, then save the publication
   PageMaker automatically replaces the index with the new index.

FIGURE J-17: Show Index dialog box

Click to select index section

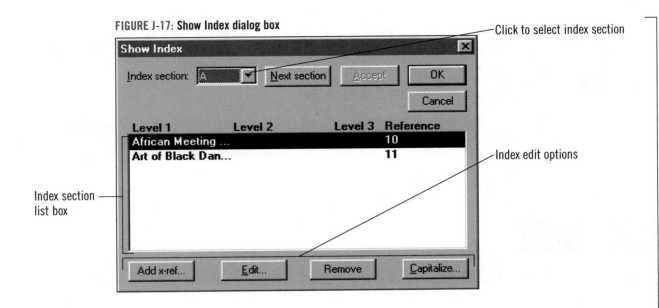

Index section list box

Index edit options

FIGURE J-18: Edit Index Entry dialog box

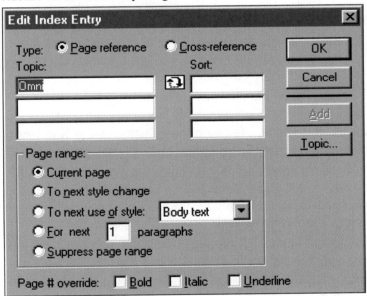

TABLE J-2: Index special characters

character	description
LM	Left master page
RM	Right master page
PB	Pasteboard
UN	Unplaced story in story editor
OV	Text outside of text blocks in layout view
?	Text included in a page range that has changed

Creating a Table of Contents

PageMaker 6.5

PageMaker can automatically generate a table of contents (TOC) for your publication. Designing a TOC is as important as designing the index; however, it is generally less work since you have already created the main headings by the time you generate the TOC. You select styles or individual paragraphs for the TOC and use the Create TOC command on the Utilities menu. PageMaker then searches for the paragraphs you selected for the TOC and creates a new story, the TOC, to be placed in your publication. ✒️ Joe uses the Create TOC command to generate a table of contents.

Steps

1. Click the **pages 2 and 3 page icon** ⌐2|3⌐, click **Type** on the menu bar, then click **Define Styles**
   The Define Styles dialog box opens.

2. Click **Headline+** in the Style list box, then click **Edit**
   The Style Options dialog box opens. Joe needs to select the styles to be included in the table of contents. He decides to include Headline style. That way every story with a headline will appear in the TOC.

3. Click **Para**, click the **Include in table of contents check box**, then click **OK** three times
   Choosing Paragraph tells PageMaker to identify what page the story appears on in the publication. Joe is ready to generate the TOC.

4. Click **Utilities** on the menu bar, then click **Create TOC**
   The Create Table of Contents dialog box opens. See Figure J-19.

5. Type **In This Guide...** (include the ellipses) in the Title text box, make sure that the **Page number after entry option button** is selected and that the ^t code appears in the Between entry and page number text box, then click **OK**
   The code ^t tells PageMaker to insert a tab between the text and page number. The dialog box closes and PageMaker generates the table of contents. The manual text flow pointer ▦ appears. Now Joe needs to place the TOC on page 3.

6. Click ▦ at the top left margin intersection on page 3, click **Window** on the menu bar, then click **Show Styles**
   The new text is a table of contents with "In This Guide..." as the title. See Figure J-20. PageMaker has created three new styles for the TOC based on the Headline style. Next, Joe edits the styles.

MacintoshUser

This replaces Step 7 and 8.

7. Press [⌘] and click TOC Headline on the Styles palette, click Char, click in the Size text box and type 16, then click OK twice

8. Press [⌘] and click TOC Index title on the Styles palette, click Char, click in the Size text box and type 16, then click OK twice

Resume at Step 9.

7. Press **[Ctrl]** and click **TOC Headline** on the Styles palette, click **Char**, click in the **Size text box** and type **16**, then click **OK** twice

8. Press **[Ctrl]** and click **TOC Index title** on the Styles palette, click **Char**, click in the **Size text box** and type **16**, then click **OK** twice

9. Click the **Close button** on the Styles palette, then save the publication

Type title as it will appear
in publication

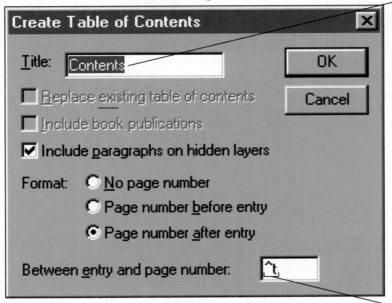

Code indicates tab

FIGURE J-20: **TOC placed on page 3**

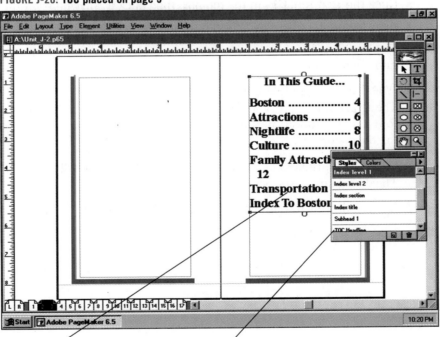

TOC Headline style is based on
style of headline text

New headline style produced
the Create TOC command

CLUES TO USE

Marking individual paragraphs to be included in a TOC

You can add more stories or select individual paragraphs to include more items within a table of contents. To add an individual paragraph to the table of contents, click the Text tool pointer ⊥ within the paragraph you want included, click Type on the menu bar, then click Paragraph. The Paragraph Specifications dialog box opens. Click the Include in table of contents check box, then click OK. Click the Create TOC command on the Utilities menu, then click OK in the Create Table of Contents dialog box to regenerate the TOC with the new paragraph.

PageMaker 6.5

Adding a Drop Cap

Many publications use a design feature called a drop cap. A **drop cap** is the first letter in a story that is enlarged and lowered so the top of the letter is even with the first line of text and the base of the letter drops next to the rest of the paragraph. You determine the size of the drop cap based on how many lines you want it to descend into the paragraph. The Drop Cap command is a PageMaker Plug-in. Joe wants to add a drop cap to the first paragraph of the page 4 story to help the story stand out on the page.

Steps

MacintoshUser

This replaces Step 1.
1. Click the pages 4 and 5 page icon [4|5], then press [⌘][1] to change the view to Actual Size

1. Click the **pages 4 and 5 page icon** [4|5], then press **[Ctrl]** and right-click to change the view to Actual Size

2. Scroll to the center of the first paragraph of the story on page 4 in the publication window

3. Click the **Text tool** [T] in the toolbox, then click ℐ anywhere within the first paragraph

4. Click **Utilities** on the menu bar, point to **Plug-ins**, then click **Drop Cap**
   The Drop cap dialog box opens. See Figure J-21. Joe wants the drop cap to descend four lines into the paragraph.

5. Type **4** in the Size text box, then click **Apply**
   The Apply button previews the drop cap action before you close the dialog box. A drop cap four lines tall appears next to the first paragraph. Joe decides to accept this addition by closing the dialog box.

6. Click **Close**, then click anywhere in the story to deselect the drop cap
   The dialog box closes. See Figure J-22.

7. Save and print the publication, then exit PageMaker

Creating pull quotes

A **pull quote** is a small amount of text enlarged within a story to catch the reader's attention. To create a pull quote, click the Text tool pointer in the text that you want to use for the pull quote, copy the text you want to use for the pull quote, paste the text where you want the pull quote to appear in the publication, click Type on the menu bar, click Paragraph, then click Rules. The Rules dialog box opens allowing you to add a fine line above and below a specified paragraph of text. The rule lines will set off the text from the rest of the story. All you need to do then is to increase the size of text in the paragraph. See Figure J-23. Using lines attached to a paragraph of text is beneficial because the lines stay attached to the paragraph and flow with that paragraph if the text is modified.

FIGURE J-21: Drop cap dialog box

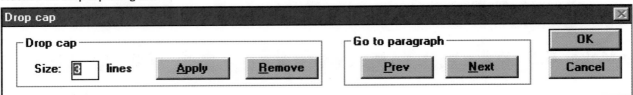

FIGURE J-22: Drop cap placed in first paragraph

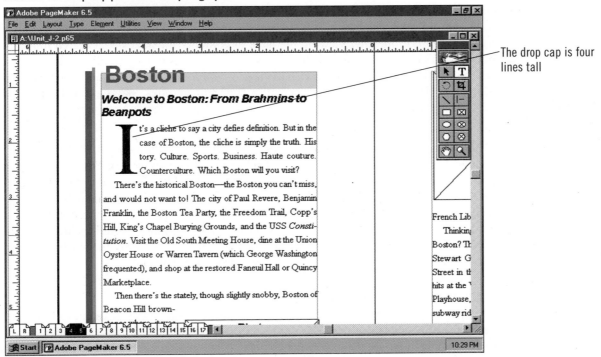

The drop cap is four lines tall

FIGURE J-23: Pull quote feature

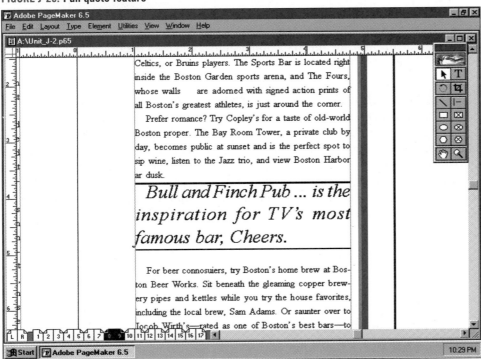

Design Workshop: Books with TOCs and Indexes

A book's table of contents (TOC) is usually the first place a reader looks after viewing the book's cover. It is important to include a TOC so that the reader can quickly glance at the overall contents of the publication. After viewing the table of contents, a reader's next search might be in the publication's index. It is also important to include an index in your publication so that readers can quickly find a topic that they wish to view. As you found out in this unit, PageMaker provides the tools that allow you to quickly create a TOC and an index. The Boston Visitor Guide TOC and index pages are shown in Figure J-24. Let's review Joe's design.

Does the visitor guide table of contents and index give enough information?

The publication's TOC and index are the reader's road map for your book. You must know your target audience in order to determine how information should be included in the TOC and the index. Readers prefer a more detailed TOC and index for most technical manuals; however, for marketing books, the TOC and index must quickly capture the reader's attention. For these books, the TOC should include only the main topics and the index should include key words. Since Joe's Boston Visitor Guide is a marketing piece, he included only the stories with headlines in his table of contents, and he used key words to create his index.

Does the text format make the index easy to read?

There can be a tendency to reduce the type size of a publication's index in an effort to reduce the total number of pages. However, this is not recommended since the size of text in an index must be large enough to be read by everyone in your target audience. PageMaker gives you many different index formats to improve the readability of the index. You can include index section entries, which help break up the consecutive index entries. By selecting a nested format, you can separate each subentry in a new paragraph. In addition, you can enter a space or special characters following each topic, between page numbers, between page ranges, before cross-references, and/or at the end of an entry. Joe added section headings and used the nested format to improve the readability of the index.

Does the overall layout of the index encourage the reader to view the index?

Many indexes, especially multiple-page indexes, encourage readers to quickly bypass the pages. However, if you add photos, graphics, or small boxed stories, you can capture your reader's attention, causing the reader to read these objects. You could also add related material in a colored or gray-shaded, boxed, sidebar story. An example would be adding a list of all the phone numbers listed in the book, or a listing of all the important figures included in the publication. Joe initially has not added any additional objects to his index; however, he will add a photo of Boston to fill the blank spot on the page.

FIGURE J-24: Boston Visitor guide TOC and index

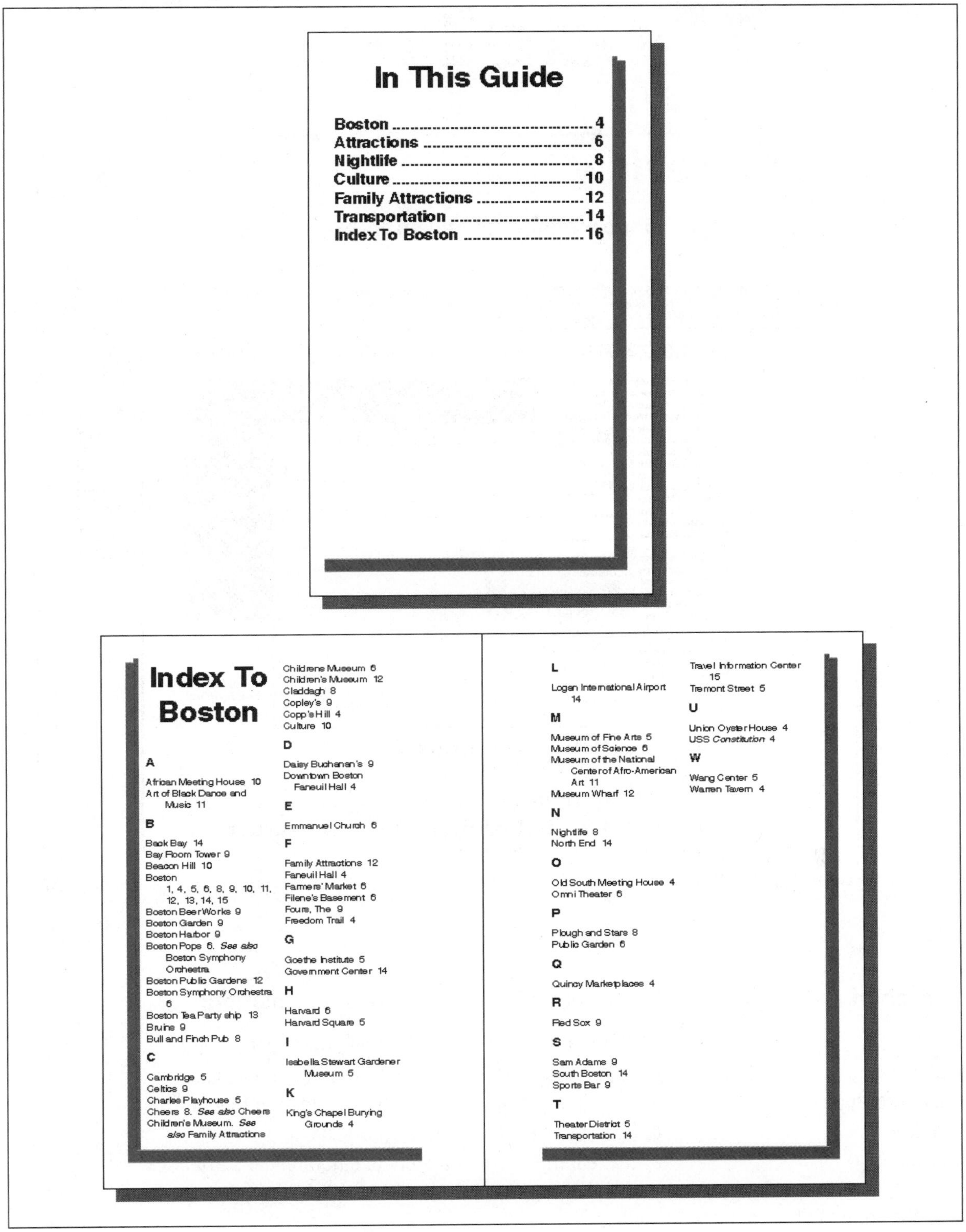

In This Guide

Index To Boston

PageMaker 6.5

Practice

► Concepts Review

Label each of the publication window elements shown in Figure J-25.

FIGURE J-25

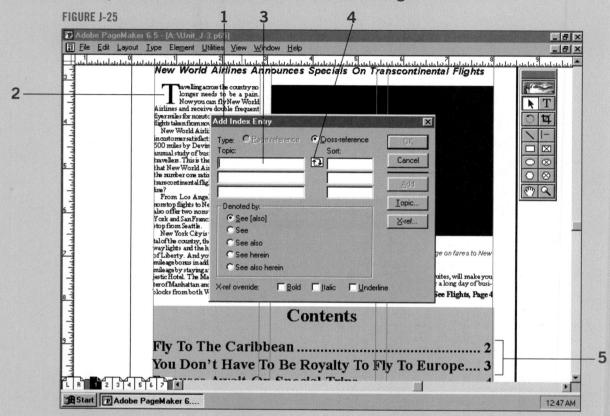

Match each of the terms with the statement that describes its function:

6. **Pull quote**
7. **Index entry**
8. **Cross-reference**
9. **Drop cap**
10. **Show index**

a. Information used to find related or additional topics
b. Allows you to edit commands on all index entries
c. A word or group of words to be included in the index
d. First letter in story that is enlarged
e. Text enlarged within a story to catch reader's attention

11. **Using the Index Entry command, you can:**
    a. Add headlines to the table of contents
    b. Set cross-references
    c. Remove unneeded index entries
    d. All of the above

12. **Which of the following is true about a cross-reference?**
    a. A cross-reference can be created in the layout view.
    b. A cross-reference is added to an index using the Index Entry command.
    c. Both a and b are true.
    d. None of the above are true.

13. **To generate an index:**
    a. Click Edit on the menu bar, select element, then click Generate Index.
    b. Click Utilities on the menu bar, then click Create Index.
    c. Click the Promote/Demote button in the Cross-reference dialog box.
    d. Both b and c

14. **Which of the following is an option in the Index Format dialog box?**
    a. Edit the type, style, and size of the index
    b. Format space separating multiple page references
    c. Add an index title
    d. All of the above

15. **The Show Index command allows you to:**
    a. Generate the index
    b. Use edit commands on all index entries
    c. Display all of the indexed topics
    d. Both b and c

16. **All of the following about drop caps are true, except:**
    a. Drop cap is a PageMaker Plug-in.
    b. Drop caps can be used only in the first paragraph of a story.
    c. A drop cap can drop six lines into the paragraph.
    d. All of the above are true.

17. **To add lines above and below a pull quote, which dialog box will you use?**
    a. Rules
    b. Pull Quote
    c. Line and Fill
    d. Either a or c

▶ Skills Review

1. **Add index entries.**
   a. Start PageMaker and open the file UNITJ-3 from your Student Disk.
   b. Click the body text block in the first column on _page 2, click Edit on the menu bar, then click Edit Story.
   c. Select the text "New World Airlines."
   d. Click Utilities on the menu bar, then click Index Entry.
   e. Click the Page reference option button, if necessary, to select this option.
   f. Click the Current page option button in the Page range section.
   g. Click OK.

2. Use index keyboard shortcuts.

   a. Select the word "Caribbean" using the Text tool pointer, then press [Ctrl][Y] *(Macintosh users: press [⌘][Y]).*

   b. Click OK to accept specifications in the Add Index Entry dialog box.

   c. Using the Text tool pointer, select the text "San Juan," then press [Ctrl][Shift][Y] *(Macintosh users: press [⌘] [shift][Y]).*

   d. Repeat the previous step to index the following entries: Puerto Rico, St. Thomas, Virgin Islands, frequent flyer miles, Charlotte Amalie, Sunset Tours.

   e. Close story editor.

   f. Move the pointer below the headline "Fly to the Caribbean," then press [Shift] and right-click *(Macintosh users: press [⌘][option]).*

   g. Using the Text tool pointer, select the text "Michelle Snow," then press [Ctrl][Alt][Y] *(Macintosh users: press [⌘][option][Y] and click).*

3. Use the index shortcut menu.

   a. Press and hold [Shift] and right-click *(Macintosh users: press [⌘][0]),* click the Pointer tool in the toolbox, move the pointer over the story on page 3, then triple-click.

   b. Click the insertion point at the top of the story, click Utilities on the menu bar, then click Change.

   c. Type "New World Airlines" in the Find what text box, press [Tab], then type "^;" (caret and semicolon only) in the Change to text box, click the All stories option button, click Change all, then click the Close button in the Change dialog box.

   d. In the third paragraph, select the text "Eagle Club restaurants," press [Ctrl][Y] *(Macintosh users: press [⌘][Y]).*

   e. Click the Promote/Demote button, type "Eagle Flight Program" inside the first Topic text box, then click OK.

   f. Click Story on the menu bar, then click Close Story. Repeat closing for other stories that might have been opened when you used the Change command.

4. Create a cross-reference.

   a. Click the pages 4 and 5 page icon, click the story under the heading "SkyCar Rentals Earn 300 Miles," click Edit on the menu bar, then click Edit Story.

   b. Click Utilities on the menu bar, then click Index Entry.

   c. Click the Cross-reference option button.

   d. Type "SkyCar" in the Topic text box.

   e. Click X-ref.

   f. Click the Topic section list arrow, then click E.

   g. Click Eagle Flight Program.

   h. Click OK.

   i. Click See also option button.

   j. Click OK.

   k. Close story editor, then save the publication.

5. Generate an index.

   a. Click the pages 6 and 7 page icon.

   b. Click Utilities on the menu bar, then click Create Index.

   c. Type "Wings Index" in the Title text box.

   d. Click Format.

   e. Make sure the Include index section headings check box is selected.

   f. Click the Nested option button if it is not already selected.

   g. Click OK to close the Index Format dialog box, then click OK again to close the Create Index dialog box.

   h. Press [Shift], position the semi-Autoflow text flow pointer under the heading "Wings" at the top of the first column on page 6, click and continue placing the text on the pages.

6. Edit an index.

  a. Click the pages 4 and 5 page icon, triple-click the top story on page 4 under the headline "Bonuses Await On Special Trips," then select the index marker in front of the word "South" in the first paragraph.

  b. Click Utilities on the menu bar, then click Index Entry.

  c. Position the insertion point in the Topic text box after the word "South," press [Spacebar], type "Korea," then click OK.

  d. Click Utilities on the menu bar, then click Show Index.

  e. Click the Index section list arrow, click S, click Sunset in the Index entry list box, then click Remove.

  f. Click OK to close the Show Index dialog box, then close story editor.

  g. Click the pages 6 and 7 page icon, click Utilities on the menu bar, click Create Index, then click OK to generate the index.

7. Create a table of contents.

  a. Click the page 1 page icon.

  b. Click Type on the menu bar, then click Define Styles.

  c. Click Reg. Headline in the Style list box, then click Edit.

  d. Click Para, click the Include in table of contents check box, then click OK three times.

  e. Click Utilities on the menu bar, then click Create TOC.

  f. Type "In This Issue..." in the Title text box.

  g. Click the Page number after entry option button in the Format section if it is not already selected.

  h. Make sure "^t" appears in the Between entry and page number text box.

  i. Click OK to close the dialog box.

  j. Drag-place the TOC across the three columns in the shaded box at the bottom of the page.

  k. Click Window on the menu bar, then click Show Styles.

  l. Press [Ctrl] *(Macintosh users: press [⌘])* and click the TOC Reg. Headline on the Styles palette, click Char, type "16" in the size text box, then click OK twice.

  m. Repeat Step 1 for the TOC index style.

  n. Widen the TOC, if necessary, so that each story title and page number fits on one line.

  o. Click the Close button on the Styles palette.

8. Add a drop cap.

  a. Click View on the menu bar, then click Actual Size.

  b. Scroll to center the first paragraph of the story on page 1 in the publication window.

  c. Click the Text tool in the toolbox, then click the Text tool pointer anywhere within the first paragraph.

  d. Click Utilities on the menu bar, point to Plug-ins, then click Drop Cap.

  e. Type "4" in the Size text box if necessary, then click Apply.

  f. Click Close, then click anywhere in the story to deselect the drop cap.

  g. Save and print the publication, then exit PageMaker.

 Independent Challenges

1. As the investment manager for Omaha Investor Group Inc., you are required to create a report for your investors that describes the performance of all investments. You decide that a booklet publication will best convey your report. To make the booklet more user-friendly, you have decided to add an index and a table of contents (TOC). In addition, you will enhance the appearance by adding a drop cap at the beginning of each of the main sections.

To complete this independent challenge:

1. Open the file UNIT_J-4 from your Student Disk. On page 1, triple-click inside the abstract and index the following two topics: Omaha Investors Group Plan Summary and group funds. Close story editor.
2. Move to pages 4 and 5, triple-click inside the story below the headline on page 4. Use the Change command to index all occurrences of Omaha Investors Group in the publication.
3. Using keyboard shortcuts, index the following topics in points #1 and #2 on page 4 of the publication: Fixed Income Fund, Guaranteed Investment contracts, Bank Investment contracts, FDIC, money market fund, Windlow Stock Fund.
4. Create cross-references for Guaranteed Investment contracts to Fixed Income Fund, and Bank Investment contracts to Fixed Income Fund.
5. Create an index on page 10. Name the index "Plan Summary Index."
6. Edit your index using the Show Index command, select S, then delete the index entry for Standard. Close the Show Index dialog box.
7. Move to pages 2 and 3 to create a TOC. Use the Headline style for creating the items in the TOC. Name the TOC "Plan Summary Contents..." Improve the appearance of the TOC by editing the TOC styles.
8. Add a drop cap in the first paragraph under the "Investment Fund Report" headline on page 4 and also in the first paragraph under the "Fund Performance" headline on page 9.
9. Save the publication, then print it.

2. As you have already learned, creating an index in PageMaker is a fairly simple task and can be of great assistance to readers when they are trying to find certain topics in your publication.

To complete this independent challenge, open a multi-page publication that you have previously created and to which you would like to add an index, and then complete the following:

1. Use the story editor to index all the important topics.
2. Use keyboard shortcuts and the Change command to index multiple usage of the same topic.
3. Use the Index Entry command to create cross-references.
4. Generate the index and give it a descriptive name. Review the index to determine if there are any mistakes.
5. Use the Show Index command to edit any unnecessary topics or mistakes.
6. Add drop caps to improve the appearance of the publication.
7. Save the publication as Indexed publication to your Student Disk, then print it.

3. Remember, designing a table of contents (TOC) is just as important as designing an index for your publication. However, it is easier, since by the time you are ready to create the TOC, you have already created the main headings for your publication.

To complete this independent challenge, open one of the previous publications to which you would like to add an index, and then complete the following:

1. Use the story editor to index all the important topics including all proper names. Use keyboard shortcuts and the Change command to index multiple usage of the same topic.
2. Use the Index Entry command to create cross-references.
3. Generate the index. Give the index a descriptive name. Review the index to determine if there are any mistakes.
4. Use the Show Index command to edit any unnecessary topics or mistakes.
5. Create a TOC. Edit the TOC styles to improve the appearance of it.
6. Add drop caps to improve the overall appearance of the publication.
7. Save the publication, then print it.

4. As the marketing manager for a major airline, you have been asked to create a visitor's guide for potential visitors to New York City, one of the airline's most popular destinations. In order to complete this independent challenge, you need to design the layout for the guide and place the stories, and then add an index and table of contents (TOC).

1. Search the World Wide Web for information on New York City's major tourist attractions.
2. Create a guide by placing text from the file TEXTHLD and graphics with the file PLACEHLD, both located on your Student Disk. Replace at least the first page of your guide's text with information that you find on the World Wide Web about attractions in New York.
3. Make a sketch of your index, using the guidelines that you learned in this unit. Index all of the important subjects and names in your guide using story editor and using shortcuts in the publication window.
4. Create at least two cross-references for your index.
5. Generate your index and review it for any mistakes or changes that you would like to make, then edit your index to make these changes.
6. Create a TOC for your guide and then edit the TOC's styles.
7. Add drop caps to your publication. Create a pull quote that will catch the reader's attention.
8. Review the design of your TOC and index.
9. Save the publication as NYC guide to your Student Disk, and then print it. Hand in your sketch, all printouts, and the critique of your TOC and index.

▶ Visual Workshop

Open the file UNIT_J-5 from your Student Disk. Create an index and table of contents (TOC) as shown in Figure J-26. Save the publication as HealthLine, then print it.

FIGURE J-26

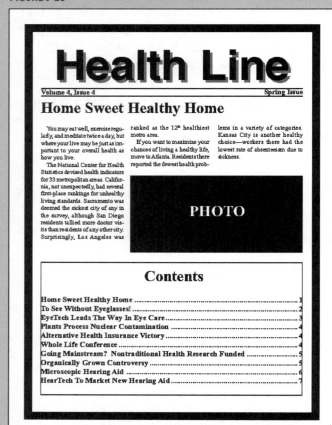
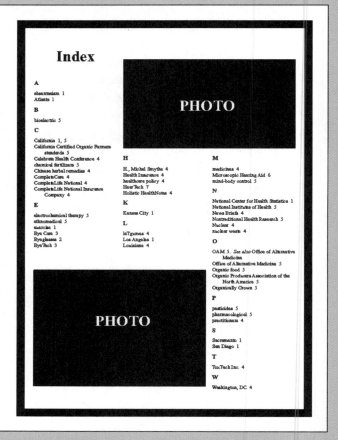

Publishing

Electronically

Objectives

▶ **Review file formats used for electronic viewing**

▶ **Plan a home page**

▶ **Name PageMaker pages as HTML pages**

▶ **Assign PageMaker pages as HTML pages**

▶ **Associate PageMaker styles with HTML styles**

▶ **Create hypertext links**

▶ **Export HTML files**

▶ **Identify PDF specifications**

▶ **Create PDF index bookmarks**

▶ **Create a PDF file**

▶ **Use Acrobat™ Reader to view a PDF file**

▶ **Design Workshop: Web pages**

In previous units you learned how to create different kinds of publications that eventually ended up in a final paper format for distribution to your intended audience. In this unit you will learn how to produce a publication that can be distributed to and viewed electronically by your intended audience on the World Wide Web. You will also learn how to use Adobe Acrobat Distiller to create a publication that can be distributed and viewed by anyone using a Macintosh, Windows, or Unix-based computer, or that can be downloaded from the World Wide Web. First Joe Martin will finish creating a New World Airlines home page which can be used on the World Wide Web. Then he will convert the Boston Visitor Guide into an Adobe Acrobat file, which can be viewed by customers using a personal computer.

Reviewing File Formats Used for Electronic Viewing

PageMaker started the desktop publishing revolution in the early 1980's when it was first introduced as a means for creating and outputting high-quality, camera-ready publications. PageMaker recently pioneered new options for creating publications. These two new tools allow creation of publications that can be distributed electronically for viewing on the Internet. The first option is to create an HTML (Hyper Text Markup Language) file, which can be used on the World Wide Web. You can use PageMaker's Export HTML function to create the HTML file from an existing PageMaker publication. The second option is to use the Adobe Acrobat program to convert a PageMaker publication into a file that can be shared by users regardless of their computer platform. Acrobat Distiller creates a file called a portable document format file, or PDF file. This lesson discusses both options in more detail.

HTML Author

The **World Wide Web**, also known as the "**Web**" or "WWW", is a network setup that allows the use of a graphical interface on the Internet. **HTML** is a programming language used to create publications, known as **web pages**, that can be read on the World Wide Web using special software called a **web browser**. HTML Author allows you to use PageMaker to create graphical page layouts. **HTML Author** automatically translates your publication's layout into a separate file using HTML programming code. This allows you to create your web pages using PageMaker instead of writing HTML programming code from scratch. These web pages can be viewed by anyone on the Internet using a web browser such as Netscape Navigator. A **home page** is the first screen viewed on a web site. An example of a home page that could be found on the World Wide Web is shown in Figure K-1.

The disadvantage of HTML and the World Wide Web is that you are limited in your page layout design because you must conform to the standards defined by HTML. For example, you are limited to certain fonts, type sizes, leading, type formats, and paragraph alignments as well as indent and tab positions. The advantage to using HTML is that your file can be distributed to a large audience on the World Wide Web.

PDF

The **Adobe Acrobat Distiller** program allows you to convert any PageMaker publication into a PDF file. **PDF files** retain all page designs and layouts created in PageMaker. See Figure K-2. If page layout and design are critical to your publication, then you might want to consider producing a PDF file. The PDF file can be included in your home page and downloaded from the Internet. PDF files can be distributed and viewed or printed by anyone using Adobe Acrobat Reader. Acrobat Reader can be downloaded free from the Adobe home page on the World Wide Web. To convert a PageMaker publication, you must install and use Acrobat Distiller, which is included in PageMaker 6.5. The Acrobat Distiller program produces the PDF files that can be read by Acrobat Reader.

FIGURE K-1: An example of a home page on the Internet

FIGURE K-2: Screen shot of a PDF file

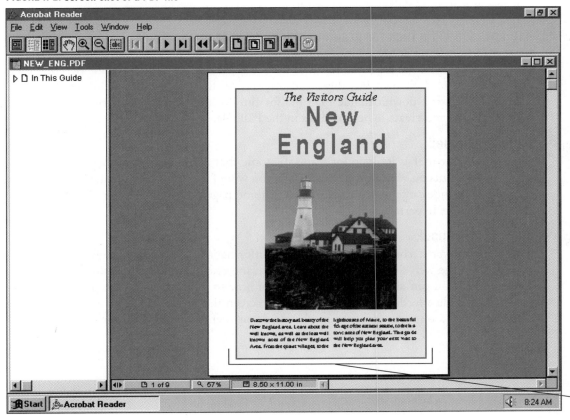

Publication retained page design and layout

Planning a Home Page

When designing a home page for the World Wide Web, it is very important to consider your target audience. Some people who use the Internet like to "surf the Net," which means they jump from home page to home page using hypertext links. **Hypertext links** are specially formatted blocks of text that open other web pages or change the view to other parts of the current document when they are clicked. Thus it is important to design a home page that instantly captures your viewers' attention and conveys useful information. When planning a home page, you must carefully consider what information to include and what information should be available through hypertext links. Joe is designing a home page for New World Airlines. He will also create a home page for Sunset Tours that will be linked by a hypertext link from the New World Airlines home page. See Figure K-3. He will use the following guidelines to design effective home pages:

Use graphic images discretely

Using color graphics at the top of your home page seems like the most likely method for catching your viewer's attention. However, large complex graphics can slow the time it takes to access your home page which might cause some viewers to cancel the link and link to another home page instead. Joe's home page uses only a color graphic of the company logo on the main home page.

Give concise listing of home page content

When your viewers first access your home page, they do not want to be overwhelmed with a screen full of text. List the contents of your web site on the home page with a short description. The hypertext link pages can include greater amounts of text if necessary. Joe's home page will include several bulleted points that will be hypertext linked to other pages on the web site. Joe will also include one or two sentences describing each hypertext page link.

Use downloadable files for graphic images or long publications

Most readers will not spend a lot of time reading on a PC screen, especially if they are using a web service that charges for the amount of time they are using the web. Include files that users can download to their own PC, then read or print on their own time. Joe's home page will include a link for a downloadable PDF file for the Boston Visitor Guide. He will be able to include photos and create hypertext links in the PDF file.

Include an index

Sometimes your user is looking for a specific topic that might not be easily described in the main bullet points on your home page. Just as you would in a long document, you might want to include an index of the key topics in your home page and web site. Joe's home page will include an index hypertext link.

Allow for feedback

Give your viewer a chance to request more information concerning products or services described on the web site. This is a very effective and easy method for meeting potential customer needs. You can also solicit suggestions on how to improve the home page. Joe's home page will include a feedback hypertext link to a screen that will allow users to request further information or a response from the marketing department at New World Airlines.

FIGURE: K-3: Joe's sketch of his home pages

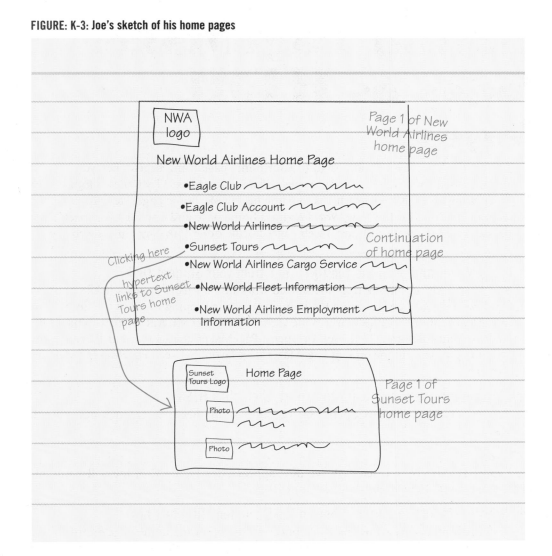

Naming PageMaker Pages as HTML Pages

After you create the basic layout and design of your home page using PageMaker, you can use HTML Author to identify which PageMaker pages will be exported as HTML files. Joe's first step in creating an HTML export file is to name his HTML home page. He will create two different export files: one for the New World Airlines home page and one for his Sunset Tours home page. Later he can create additional web pages for the other link pages in his web site.

1. Start PageMaker and open the file UNIT_K-1 from your Student Disk

The New World Airlines home page Joe started working on earlier appears in the publication window. Joe continues to create the home page while keeping in mind the limitations of creating publications for the World Wide Web. Joe uses HTML Author first to name his HTML documents. Before HTML Author opens, PageMaker checks to see if there are any compatibility problems in the present PageMaker page layout between PageMaker styles and HTML styles.

2. Click File on the menu bar, point to Export, then click HTML

The Export HTML dialog box opens. See Figure K-4. Joe needs to create a new HTML document.

3. Click New

The Export HTML: New Document window appears. See Figure K-5. Joe will name his HTML document "New World Airlines Home Page."

4. Type New World Airlines Home Page in the Document Title text box

This document title is the name that will appear at the top of the home page on the World Wide Web. This name should not be confused with the filename that Joe will create later for the HTML file that he exports. Next Joe will assign the PageMaker pages to the New World Airlines home page.

Trouble?

Your browser icon in the Export HTML dialog box may be different. You can change browsers by clicking on the icon and selecting a different browser.

QuickTip

If you wish to change the document name, open the HTML Export dialog box, click the Contents tab, select the document you want to change, click Edit, type the new name in the Edit Document Title text box, then click Done twice.

FIGURE K-4: Export HTML dialog box

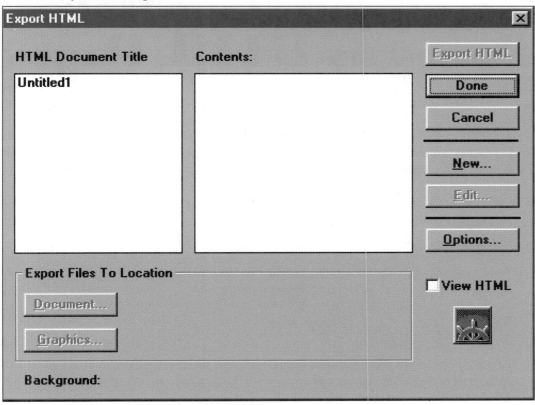

FIGURE K-5: Export HTML: New Document dialog box

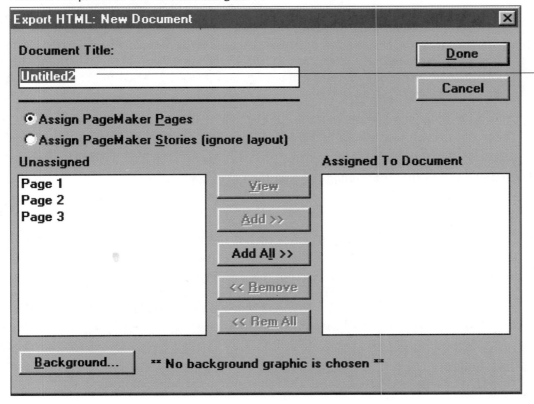

Type title as it will
appear at the top
of the home page

PageMaker 6.5

Assigning PageMaker Pages as HTML Pages

You can assign more than one PageMaker page to each HTML file. PageMaker gives you the option to define either pages or stories that will be exported as HTML files. You can export up to 50 different HTML files from just one PageMaker publication. This allows you to create your entire web site in one PageMaker publication. By creating separate HTML files, each file has its own HTML address on the Web, and each file can be accessed by others without accessing your main home page. Joe will now assign pages to his New World Airlines home page.

Steps

1. Click **Page 1** in the Unassigned list box, then click **Add>>**
This marks page 1 of the current PageMaker file to be included in the new HTML file. Notice page 1 has now moved to the Assigned To Document list box. See Figure K-6. Joe will now add page 2 since it contains additional information that should be part of the New World Airlines home page. Page 3 will be assigned to a different home page.

2. Click **Page 2** in the Unassigned list box, then click **Add>>**
Now Joe needs to assign a filename for the HTML file to be exported. The filename should be only eight characters long and should not contain any special characters or spaces between letters. The filename must end with .HTML, a special ending that is called a **file extension**. The World Wide Web reads this file extension and recognizes the file as HTML. The .HTML file extension is not part of the eight character restriction.

3. Click **Done**, click **Document** in the Export Files to Location section, type **NWAHMPG.HTML** in the File Name For HTML Document text box, then click **OK**
The name and location of the HTML files to be created are displayed in the Export Files To Location section. Later, when you click the Export HTML button, the document will be saved to that location. Joe wants to make more changes to the file before he exports it. Next, he wants to create a second HTML export file from the same PageMaker publication. This export file will be the Sunset Tours home page and it will be joined to the New World Airlines home page by a hypertext link.

4. Click **New**, then type **Sunset Tours** in the Document Title text box
This will be the web page title for the HTML file to be linked to the New World Airlines home page. The New World Airlines home page will recognize this document name as the link.

5. Click **Page 3** in the Unassigned list box, then click **Add>>**
Page 3 of the current publication is assigned to the second HTML document. Next, Joe needs to assign a filename to his second HTML page.

6. Click **Done**, click **Document**, type **SUNSET.HTML** in the File Name for HTML Document text box, then click **OK**
Joe has assigned names to both of his export files. See Figure K-7. The document names for his HTML files are listed in the HTML Document Title list box. By clicking on a document title he can verify which PageMaker pages are assigned to that HTML file. In later lessons, Joe will create the actual HTML documents for these pages, and create the link between the New World Airlines HTML file and the Sunset Tours HTML file.

7. Click **Done**
The HTML Author dialog box closes, and you return to the publication window.

FIGURE K-6: Assigning pages in Export HTML: New Document dialog box

HTML document name ─────

PageMaker publication page numbers ─────

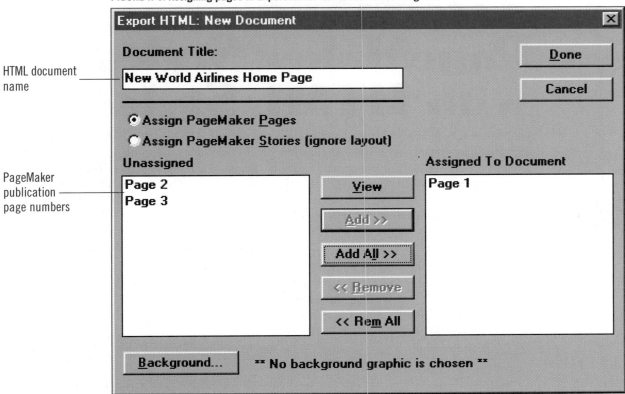

FIGURE K-7: HTML documents containing PageMaker pages

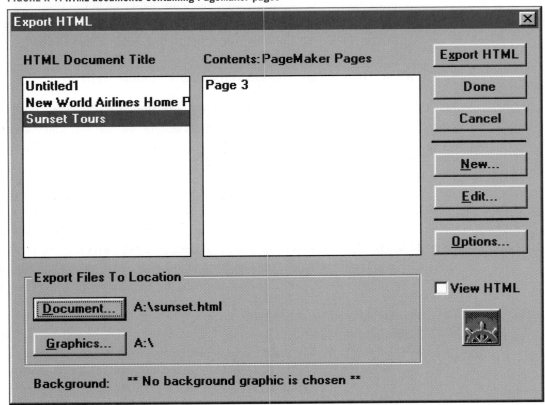

PageMaker 6.5

Associating PageMaker Styles with HTML Styles

The easiest way to apply text formats is to use the default HTML styles. However, you can also use other PageMaker styles by changing the PageMaker styles mapping to match the HTML styles in the HTML Author Preferences window.  Each of PageMaker's default styles will be automatically converted to an HTML style when Joe exports his document as an HTML file. However, Joe has created a custom style that he would like to map to the HTML Body Text style as well; he will have to map this style manually.

1. **Click Window on the menu bar, click Show Styles, click the right arrow ▶ on the Styles palette, then click Add HTML Styles**
   PageMaker automatically generates style names that appear on the Styles palette that correspond to HTML markup tags or styles. See Figure K-8. Remember, you can adjust the size of the Styles palette by dragging the bottom border. Next, Joe increases the view of the publication page.

2. **Position the pointer over the text "New World Airlines Home Page", then press [Ctrl] and right-click**
   Now Joe can apply an HTML headline style to the New World Airlines home page main headline.

   > **MacintoshUser**
   >
   > This replaces Step 2.
   > 2. Position the pointer over the text "New World Airlines Home Page", then press [⌘] [option], then click the mouse button

3. **Click the Text tool T in the toolbox, click any place in the text New World Airlines Home Page, then click HTML H1 on the Styles palette**
   PageMaker applies the HTML H1 style to the main headline in the home page. See Figure K-9.

4. **Click Ⓘ in the line of text "What You'll Find Here," click HTML H2 on the Styles palette, click Ⓘ in the line of text beginning with "Please select…", then click HTML H3 on the Styles palette**
   Notice how the text changes as the HTML headline styles are applied. Next Joe selects the Body text style.

5. **Click Ⓘ in the paragraph beginning with the words "Eagle Club"**
   Notice Body text is selected on the Styles palette. Joe does not want to apply the HTML Body Text style to each paragraph in the body of his publication; rather he wants to associate the PageMaker Body text style with an HTML body style.

6. **Click File on the menu bar, point to Export, click HTML, then click Options**
   PageMaker displays the Options dialog box. Joe notices that the PageMaker Body text style is already associated with the HTML Body Text style. Joe has also created a separate style called "text," which he would like to associate with an HTML body style.

7. **Scroll down the HTML Style list box, click Heading, which is the HTML style corresponding to the PageMaker text style, then click Body Text on the pop up menu**
   See Figure K-10. Notice the selection in the PageMaker Style text box changes to HTML Body Text. The HTML Body Text style is now applied to all text in the PageMaker publication that used Joe's text style.

8. **Click Done**
   The HTML Author dialog box closes. Notice Body text is selected on the Styles palette, showing the style of the text where the insertion point is located. Because you set the HTML preferences to accept the PageMaker Body text style as the HTML Body Text style, HTML Author translates the PageMaker style to HTML style.

9. **Save the publication**

FIGURE K-8: **HTML styles listed on Styles palette**

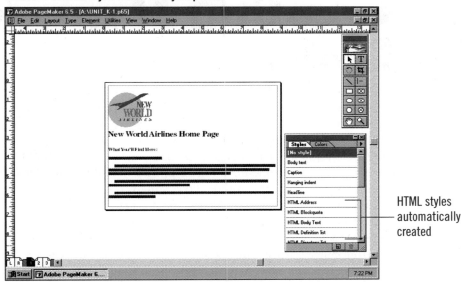

HTML styles
automatically
created

FIGURE K-9: **HTML style applied to home page headline**

HTML H1 style
applied

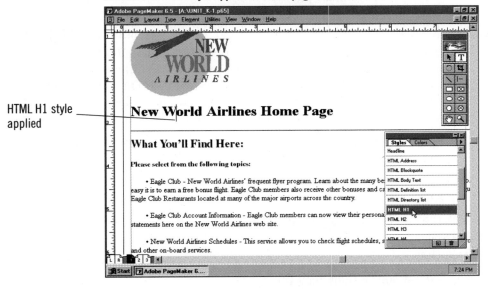

FIGURE K-10: **Options dialog box displaying PageMaker and HTML styles**

New associated
HTML style with the
PageMaker style

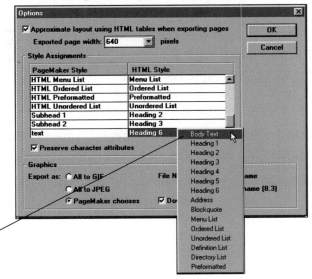

Creating Hypertext Links

One of the main benefits to browsing the World Wide Web is the ability to use hypertext links to move from page to page in the same document or to move from a page in a document to a page in another document. You can create hypertext links using any text in your publication. The hypertext links appear highlighted on your home page. When you click the highlighted text, you link or jump to the new page or destination: you use an **anchor** to link to a new page within the same HTML document; you use a **uniform resource locator (URL)** to link to a different HTML document. HTML Author allows you to create up to 500 anchors and/or URLs anywhere in a PageMaker publication. Joe has included a lot of information in his New World Airlines PageMaker publication. He has assigned specific PageMaker pages to different HTML home pages to broaden his Internet viewing audience. Now Joe wants to create a hypertext link from the Sunset Tours bullet point in the New World Airlines home page to information describing tours to Europe in the Sunset Tours home page. Joe will use a URL to create the link since the tour information will be in a separate HTML file when Joe exports the HTML files he has created using his PageMaker publication.

MacintoshUser

This replaces Step 1.
1. Click the pages 2 and 3 page icon, click the pointer tool, position the pointer at the top left corner of page 3, then press [⌘] [option], then click the mouse button

QuickTip

If you want your reader to be able to link to specific sections in a long document, you can create hypertext anchor links in a table of contents for a document.

1. **Click the pages 2 and 3 page icon, click the pointer tool, position the pointer at the top left corner of page 3, then press [Ctrl] and right-click**
   Joe wants Internet viewers who are reading his New World Airlines home page to be able to read about the tour packages described in his SUNSET.HTML file. He needs to create a hypertext link that will link from the New World Airlines home page to the Sunset Tours home page here on page 3. Joe wants to use the Sunset Tours logo as his hypertext anchor.

2. **Click the Sunset Tours logo to select it, click Window on the menu bar, then click Show Hyperlinks**
   The Hyperlinks palette opens. Joe will create an anchor to the Sunset Tours home page using the logo.

3. **Click the right arrow on the Hyperlinks palette, then click New Anchor**
   The New Anchor dialog box opens as shown in Figure K-11. Joe needs to type the name of the anchor.

4. **Type Sunset Tours, then click OK**
   The anchor is now set up. Now Joe will set up the link on the New World Airlines home page that will take viewers to the Sunset Tours home page.

5. **Scroll over to the top left corner of page 2, click the Text tool in the toolbox, highlight the text Sunset Tours, click Window on the menu bar, click Show Colors, click the color Blue, then close the Colors palette**
   Blue is a standard color used in home page to indicated hypertext links. Joe will add bold formatting and an underline to help make the link stand out on the page.

6. **Make sure the text Sunset Tours is still highlighted, click Type on the menu bar, point to Type Style, then click Bold**

7. **Make sure the text Sunset Tours is still highlighted, click Type on the menu bar, point to Type Style, then click Underline, then click anywhere in the window to deselect the text**
   See Figure K-12. When reading the New World Airlines home page, a viewer can click this highlighted text to open the HTML file containing the information about Sunset Tours to Europe.

FIGURE K-11: New Anchor dialog box

Type the name of the anchor

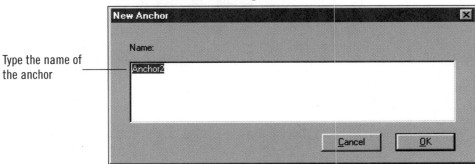

FIGURE K-12: Hypertext link

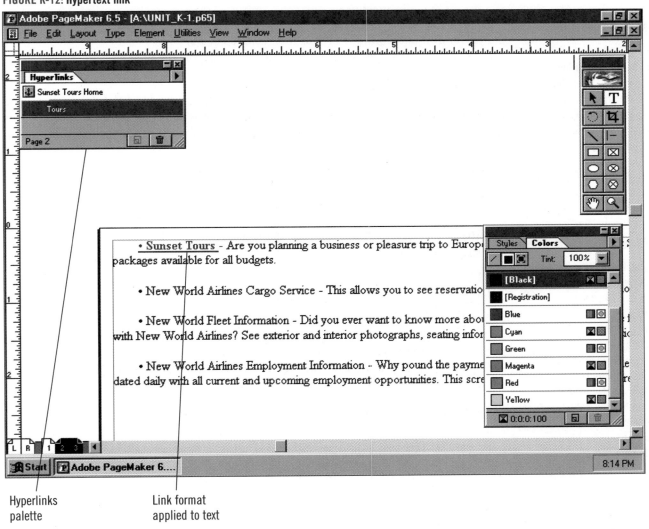

Hyperlinks palette

Link format applied to text

PageMaker 6.5

Exporting HTML Files

Once you have finished assigning PageMaker pages to HTML pages, assigning HTML styles, and creating HTML anchors and/or hypertext links, you can export the final HTML document. The HTML export file is a special file that translates the PageMaker format commands into HTML style tags. This HTML file can be used to create a page or pages on the World Wide Web. 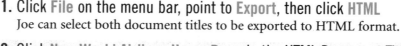 Joe uses HTML Author to export his final HTML documents. Two separate HTML files are created for the World Wide Web. Then he exits PageMaker and opens the HTML file in Notepad to view the HTML file.

Steps

1. Click File on the menu bar, point to Export, then click HTML
Joe can select both document titles to be exported to HTML format.

This replaces Step 2.
2. Click New World Airlines Home Page in the HTML Document Title list box, press and hold [⌘] and click Sunset Tours, then release [⌘]

2. Click New World Airlines Home Page in the HTML Document Title list box, press and hold [Ctrl] and click Sunset Tours, then release [Ctrl]
Both files are selected. See Figure K-13. Now Joe can export the files.

3. Click Export HTML
PageMaker generates the HTML files, checks for errors, and then completes the export. The exported HTML files are created in the same directory as the original PageMaker publication. Joe wants to view the file that PageMaker created for the New World Airlines home page. First he needs to exit PageMaker.

4. Close the Hyperlinks palette, click File on the menu bar, click Exit, then click Yes when prompted to save the publication
The original publication is saved as a PageMaker file.

MacintoshUser

This replaces Steps 5 through 7.
5. Click the Apple icon on the menu bar, then select SimpleText
If SimpleText is not listed on the Apple menu, select Find File from this menu, type SimpleText, click Find to search for the application, then double-click the filename to start the application once it is located.
6. Click File on the menu bar, click Open, then open the file NWAHMPG.HTML
7. Click File on the menu bar, then click Quit

5. Click the Start button on the taskbar, point to Programs, point to Accessories, then click Notepad
The Windows Notepad application opens.

6. Click File on the menu bar, click Open, click All Files in the Files of type list box, then open the file NWAHMPG.HTML from your Student Disk
The file opens in Notepad, as shown in Figure K-14. Notice the codes of text that will be interpreted by the software that administers the World Wide Web. When Joe puts the home pages on the World Wide Web, he must remember to include both HTML files and all of the graphics files, saved in GIF format.

7. Click File on the menu bar, then click Exit

FIGURE K-13: Selecting HTML files to export

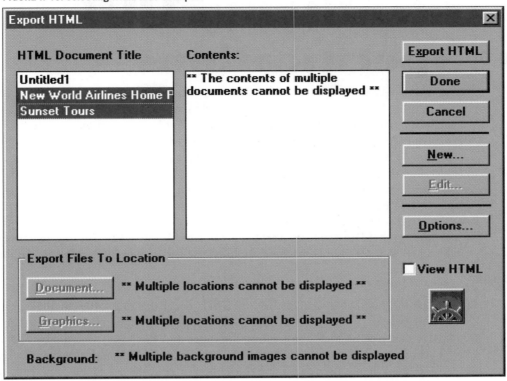

FIGURE K-14: The NWAHMPG.HTML file in Notepad

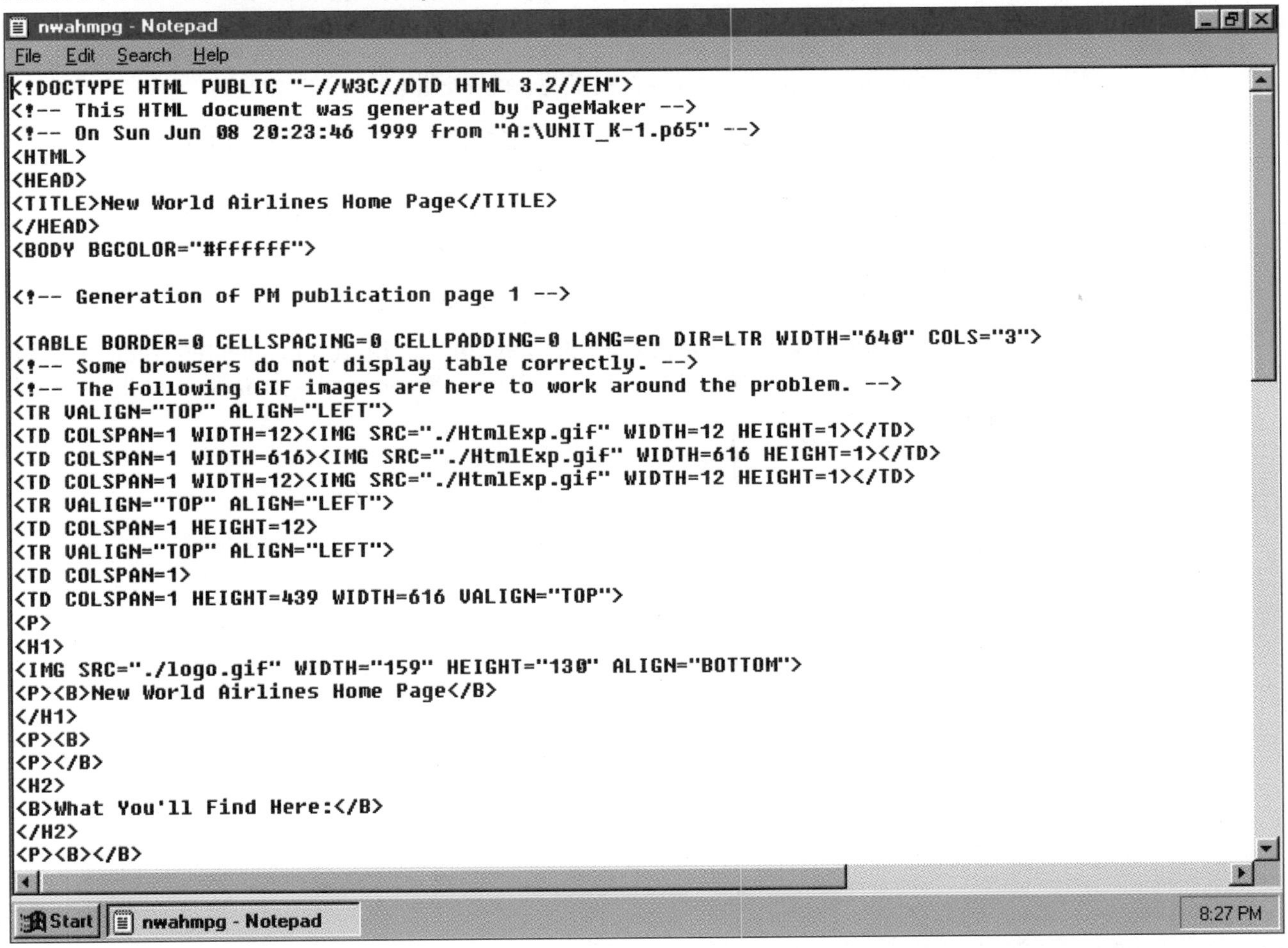

```
nwahmpg - Notepad
File  Edit  Search  Help
<!DOCTYPE HTML PUBLIC "-//W3C//DTD HTML 3.2//EN">
<!-- This HTML document was generated by PageMaker -->
<!-- On Sun Jun 08 20:23:46 1999 from "A:\UNIT_K-1.p65" -->
<HTML>
<HEAD>
<TITLE>New World Airlines Home Page</TITLE>
</HEAD>
<BODY BGCOLOR="#ffffff">

<!-- Generation of PM publication page 1 -->

<TABLE BORDER=0 CELLSPACING=0 CELLPADDING=0 LANG=en DIR=LTR WIDTH="640" COLS="3">
<!-- Some browsers do not display table correctly. -->
<!-- The following GIF images are here to work around the problem. -->
<TR VALIGN="TOP" ALIGN="LEFT">
<TD COLSPAN=1 WIDTH=12><IMG SRC="./HtmlExp.gif" WIDTH=12 HEIGHT=1></TD>
<TD COLSPAN=1 WIDTH=616><IMG SRC="./HtmlExp.gif" WIDTH=616 HEIGHT=1></TD>
<TD COLSPAN=1 WIDTH=12><IMG SRC="./HtmlExp.gif" WIDTH=12 HEIGHT=1></TD>
<TR VALIGN="TOP" ALIGN="LEFT">
<TD COLSPAN=1 HEIGHT=12>
<TR VALIGN="TOP" ALIGN="LEFT">
<TD COLSPAN=1>
<TD COLSPAN=1 HEIGHT=439 WIDTH=616 VALIGN="TOP">
<P>
<H1>
<IMG SRC="./logo.gif" WIDTH="159" HEIGHT="130" ALIGN="BOTTOM">
<P><B>New World Airlines Home Page</B>
</H1>
<P><B>
<P></B>
<H2>
<B>What You'll Find Here:</B>
</H2>
<P><B></B>
```

Start | nwahmpg - Notepad   8:27 PM

PageMaker 6.5

Identifying PDF Specifications

In addition to creating and using HTML files for electronic transmission, you can also create PDF files. In order to create a PDF file from a PageMaker file, you need to open your publication in PageMaker. Then, you will use the Create Adobe PDF command on the File menu to create a PostScript file of your PageMaker publication. This PostScript file is used by Acrobat Distiller to create the PDF file. You have the option to create the PDF file immediately while still running the PageMaker program, or at a later time after exiting PageMaker. If you choose the option to create the PDF immediately, PageMaker executes Acrobat Distiller directly, and your computer must have at least 24 MB of RAM in order to open the program. If you choose the create separately option, PageMaker creates a PostScript file of the publication, and then you must quit PageMaker and start Acrobat Distiller to convert the PostScript file into a PDF file. ◄▬▬▬ Because Joe only has 16 MB of RAM on his machine, he must use the Prepare PostScript file for distilling separately option.

1. **Start PageMaker and open the file UNIT_K-2 from your Student Disk**

   A newsletter Joe created in PageMaker appears in the publication window. Joe used PageMaker commands for creating the index and the table of contents. This is important because Joe can mark the index and TOC to become bookmarks for hyperlinked text in the PDF file. When a user clicks one of the bookmarks, the screen automatically jumps to the selected topic reference in the publication.

2. **Click File on the menu bar, point to Export, then click Adobe PDF**

   The Export Adobe PDF dialog box opens, as shown in Figure K-15. Joe needs to choose the workflow. Because Joe's system does not have enough memory to run PageMaker and create a PDF file at the same time, Joe must create a PostScript file to distill later.

3. **Click the Prepare PostScript for distilling separately option button if it is not already selected**

   Next, Joe wants to make sure the PDF file is optimized for screen display.

4. **Click Control**

   The Control dialog box opens, as shown in Figure K-16.

5. **Make sure the RGB (best for screen display) option button is selected, then click OK**

   In the next lesson, Joe will make sure his PDF file will contain bookmarks, and then he will export the PDF file.

FIGURE K-15: Export Adobe PDF dialog box

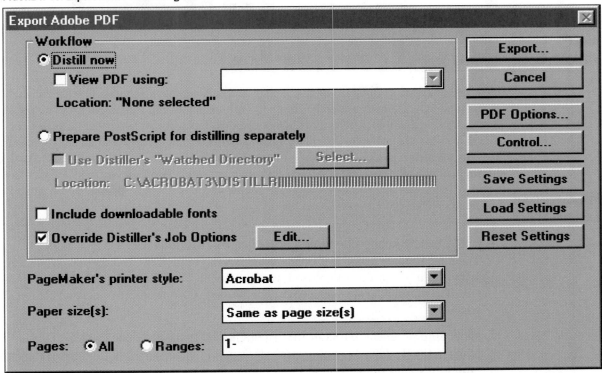

FIGURE K-16: Control dialog box

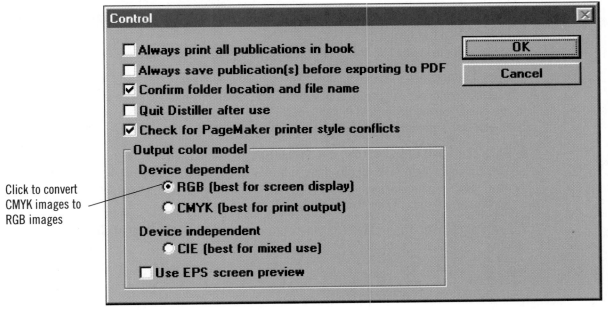

Click to convert
CMYK images to
RGB images

Creating PDF Index Bookmarks

Joe wants to create thumbnails of all the pages in his PageMaker publication so he can view them in the new PDF file he is creating. The PDF Options allow you to control how the publication is converted into a PDF file. You can select options that will add hypertext links to your publication. You can create hypertext links for the table of contents (TOC) and for the topics included in your index. You can also create bookmarks based on the TOC and the index. **Bookmarks** are another method for creating hypertext links in your publication. Bookmarks are displayed in a narrow window when you open the PDF file in Acrobat Reader. ◢▬▬ Joe wants to create bookmarks in the PDF file.

Steps

1. In the Export Adobe PDF dialog box, click **PDF Options**

   The PDF Options dialog box opens, as shown in Figure K-17. It might take your computer several minutes to open this window. See Table K-1 for a description of the options contained in this dialog box. Joe needs to select bookmark options he wants that are not already selected.

2. Make sure all check boxes in the Hyperlinks section are selected, make sure all check boxes in the Bookmarks section are selected, and make sure **Add Document Information check box** near the bottom of the page is selected

3. Click **OK**

   The PDF Options dialog box closes and the Export Adobe PDF dialog box is displayed. Joe is ready to identify the PageMaker pages to be included in the PDF file.

4. Click to the right of the dash in the Ranges text box in the Pages section, then type **5** to complete the range

   Joe is ready to create the PostScript file to be used in Acrobat Distiller.

5. Click **Export**

   PageMaker checks for conflicts between the options you have selected and the PageMaker file. Next, you are prompted to confirm the filename of the new PostScript file to be created. PageMaker automatically places a .ps file extension on the end of the filename.

6. Click the **Save in list arrow**, click **Desktop**, then click **Save**

   This process might take two to three minutes to complete depending on your computer's processor and processing speed. To distill the PostScript file into a PDF file in Adobe Acrobat, Joe needs to exit PageMaker.

7. Exit PageMaker, then click **Yes** when prompted to save the PageMaker publication

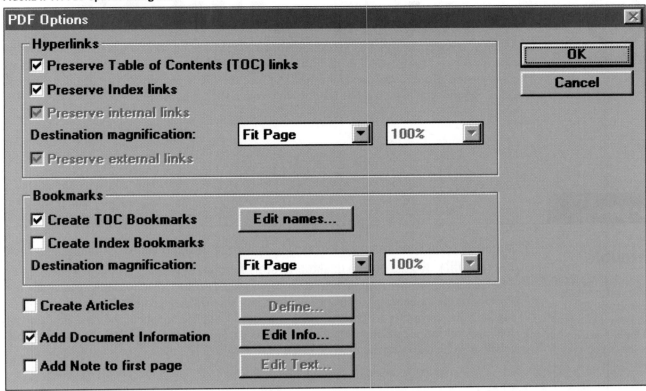

TABLE K-1: **PDF options**

option	description
Link TOC entries	Adds hypertext link between text in the TOC and the page referred to in the TOC. This option converts all TOC items.
Create Bookmarks (TOC section)	Adds bookmarks links for each TOC item in the bookmarks section in Adobe Acrobat.
Destination magnification	Displays magnification shown when the page is accessed by a hypertext link.
Link Index entries	Adds hypertext link between text in the index and the page referred to in the index. This option converts all index items.
Create Bookmarks (Index section)	Adds bookmarks links for each index item in the bookmarks section in Adobe Acrobat.
Create Articles	Converts threaded PageMaker stories into threaded Acrobat stories.
Add Document Information	Allows you to add text appearing in the File, Document Info, General dialog box in Acrobat Distiller.
Add Note to first page	Allows you to create notes that appear in the first page of your PDF file.

Creating a PDF File

PageMaker 6.5

Now that you have created a PostScript file from a PageMaker publication, you can use Acrobat Distiller to convert the PostScript file into a PDF file, which is stored in the Watched Directory. The conversion process takes several minutes. Once the file is converted, you can exit Acrobat Distiller. ✎ Joe uses Acrobat Distiller to create a PDF file.

Steps

1. Minimize open windows as necessary to make the desktop visible, then double-click the file **UNIT_K-2.ps** on the desktop to start Acrobat Distiller

The Acrobat Distiller dialog box opens. Acrobat Distiller automatically processes the PostScript file and converts it to a PDF file. This process takes a couple of minutes depending on your computer hardware. When Acrobat Distiller is finished, the message "End of Job" appears in the bottom of the Messages list box. See Figure K-18. Next, Joe quits Acrobat Distiller so he can view the newly created PDF file.

2. Click **File** on the menu bar, then click **Exit**

Acrobat Distiller closes, and UNIT_K-2.pdf is visible on the desktop, as shown in Figure K-19. Distiller always places the resulting PDF file in the same directory in which the original PostScript file was located.

3. Click the file **UNIT_K-2.ps** on the desktop to select it, press **[Delete]**, then click **Yes** to delete this file

Be sure to delete the file with the extension .ps, not .pdf.

FIGURE K-18: Acrobat Distiller dialog box

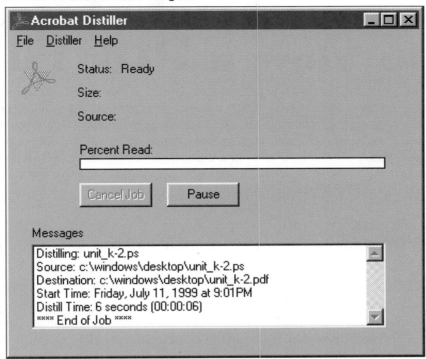

FIGURE K-19: Newly created PDF file visible on the desktop

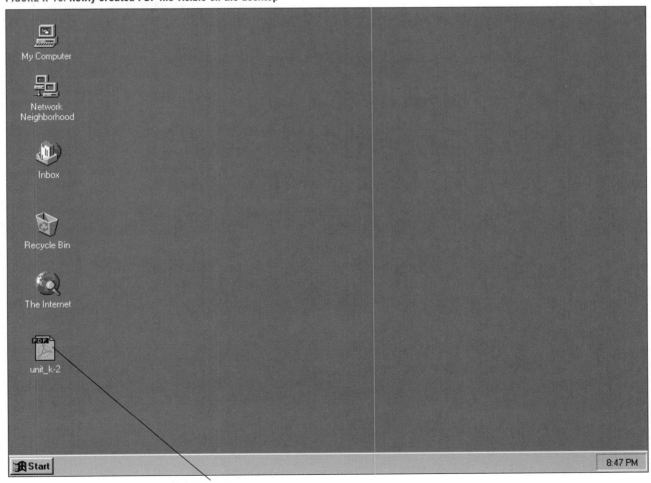

Delete this file

Using Acrobat Reader to View a PDF File

Using Acrobat Reader, you can view and print PDF files. A PDF file can be viewed or printed on any computer platform as long as you have that platform's version of Acrobat Reader. When you open the PDF file, you will notice that all page formats, layouts, colors, and graphics are retained from the original file. The viewer, however, cannot alter any of the pages in the PDF file. ✒️ Joe wants to verify that the options he selected before creating the PDF file, such as creating bookmarks, work as he expects them to work. Joe opens and views the newly created UNIT_K-2.PDF file using Acrobat Reader.

Steps

1. **On the desktop, double-click the unit_k-2.pdf icon**
   The newly created PDF file opens in Acrobat Reader. See Figure K-20.

2. **Click the Fit Page button 🔲 on the button bar to scale the page to fit within the publication window**
   Notice the entire first page of the newsletter appears in the publication window. Joe wants to view the page bookmarks that he created using the PDF Options in PageMaker.

3. **Click the Bookmarks and Page button 📃 on the button bar**
   The bookmarks section is displayed in the left side of the publication window. Notice the right arrows to the left of the topics that are listed in the bookmarks section.

4. **Click the right arrow ▷ before the In This Issue bookmark**
   All the stories that were marked in the original PageMaker publication's TOC also appear as TOC topics for this PDF file. See Figure K-21. As Joe drags the pointer over the TOC topics listed in the bookmark section, he notices that the pointer changes to ☝. This pointer indicates to the user that the item is a hypertext link.

5. **Position the pointer over the TOC topics listed under the heading "In This Issue", move ☝ over the topic "Fly To The Caribbean...", then click once**
   The hypertext link automatically changes the view to the story about the Caribbean on page 2. Next, Joe wants to check out the links he created in the index.

6. **Click the Wings Index at the bottom of the bookmarks section of the publication window, click the Actual Size button 📄 on the button bar, then position the pointer over the page number next to the index entry SkyCar Rental**
   The pointer changes to ☝ when it is placed on top of a topic's page number, as shown in Figure K-22. After clicking the index page number, Joe's publication window will move from page 6 to the hypertext link on page 4.

7. **Click the mouse button**
   The hypertext link automatically jumps to page 4.

8. **Click File on the menu bar, then click Exit**

9. **Delete the file UNIT_K-2.pdf from the desktop**

MacintoshUser

This replaces Step 8.
8. Click File on the menu bar, then select Quit

FIGURE K-20: PDF file created using Acrobat Distiller

Button bar

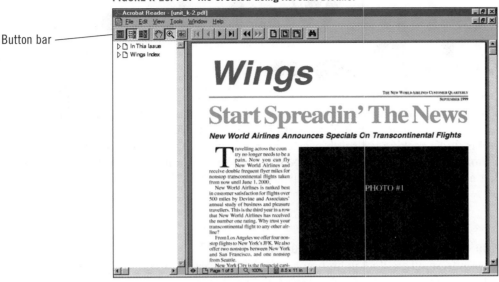

FIGURE K-21: Contents of the In This Issue TOC

Bookmark section with TOC topics

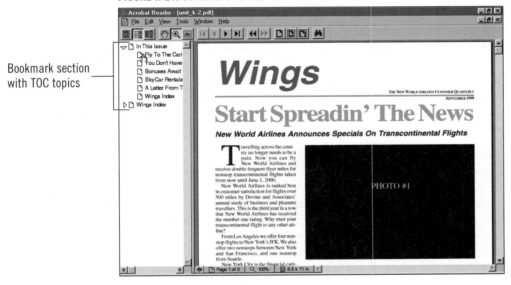

FIGURE K-22: Index hypertext link

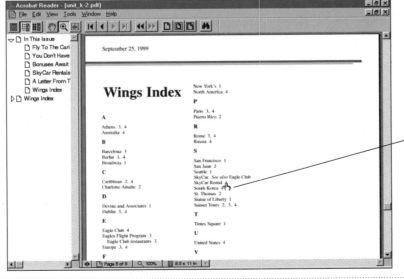

Pointer indicates hyperlink to story

Design Workshop: Web Pages

PageMaker 6.5

The World Wide Web is one of the most exciting technologies to emerge in recent years. The potential benefit for individuals and businesses is almost unlimited. The challenge for web page designers is to create unique web pages that capture the attention of web browsers. Part of the challenge includes making your web page easy to use while at the same time presenting useful information to the browser. The New World Airlines home page with hypertext links is Joe's first experience with designing web pages. See Figure K-23. Let's review Joe's home page design.

Details

Does the home page capture the reader's attention?

Joe uses simple, small graphics in his home page. He believes that larger, more complex graphics would slow the access time to the New World Airlines home page. However, Joe decides that he can use additional graphics to enhance the design without dramatically slowing down the access speed.

Is the home page easy to use?

Besides capturing the reader's attention, the home page has to be easy to use. Just as Joe made Sunset Tours a hypertext link, he will add hypertext links in each of the main paragraphs in the home page. After viewing other home pages on the Web, he decides that the addition of buttons within his home page document at the top will help experienced browsers access the needed information more quickly. The use of buttons means browsers would not have to read through the text to find the links. Buttons also add an element of fun to the web page.

Does the information benefit the reader?

You can have the best looking home page, but if you do not give readers the information they need, they will click to the next web site. Joe believes he has included useful information on the home page. Readers can find out about the great benefits of joining the frequent flyer club, or members of the frequent flyer club can pull up their account to find out their accumulated miles. Passengers can find out about flight schedules as well as special discount flight rates. In the future, Joe hopes to allow passengers and their awaiting parties the ability to access the latest up-to-date flight information. Joe has an even more ambitious project in mind—he hopes that in the very near future passengers will be able to make reservations using the New World Airlines home page.

New World Airlines Home Page

What You'll Find Here:

Please select from the following topics:

• Eagle Club - New World Airlines' frequent flyer program. Learn about the many benefits to joining the Eagle Club. Learn how easy it is to earn a free bonus flight. Eagle Club members also receive other bonuses and can treat themselves and their guests in the Eagle Club Restaurants located at many of the major airports across the country.

• Eagle Club Account Information - Eagle Club members can now view their personal mileage information and recent summary statements here on the New World Airlines web site.

• New World Airlines Schedules - This service allows you to check flight schedules, special discount flight rates, aircrafts, menus, and other on-board services.

• <u>Sunset Tours</u> - Are you planning a business or pleasure trip to Europe? If so, you must learn about Sunset Tours' extensive packages available for all budgets.

• New World Airlines Cargo Service - This allows you to see reservation information, cargo information, and a list of cities served.

• New World Fleet Information - Did you ever want to know more about the airplane that you will be flying in on your next flight with New World Airlines? See exterior and interior photographs, seating information, maintenance information, and other fleet statistics.

• New World Airlines Employment Information - Why pound the pavement when you can pound the Internet? This job service is updated daily with all current and upcoming employment opportunities. This screen will also link you to other related employment listings.

Practice

► Concepts Review

Label each of the publication window elements shown in Figure K-24.

FIGURE K-24

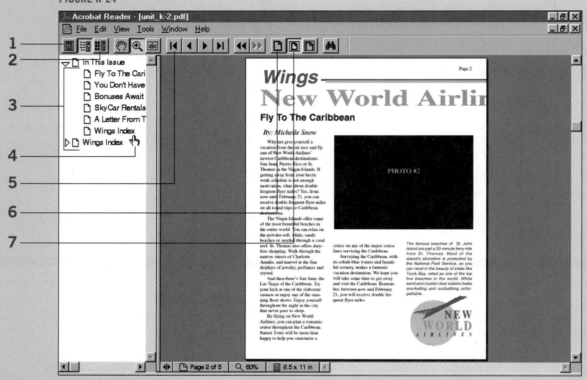

Match each of the terms with the statement that describes its function.

8. **HTML**
9. **World Wide Web**
10. **PDF**
11. **Thumbnails**
12. **Web browser**

a. A file format that can be viewed and printed from a Windows, Macintosh, or Unix-based platform
b. A network setup that allows use of a graphical interface on the Internet
c. Language used to create publications on the World Wide Web
d. A program for finding and viewing web pages
e. Page preview icons

13. **HTML Author is a:**
   a. PageMaker File Export option
   b. PageMaker Plug-in
   c. Program that can only be accessed if you are attached to a web browser
   d. Both b and c

14. **Which of the following can be used to create files that can be downloaded from the World Wide Web?**
    a. HTML Author
    b. Adobe Acrobat™ Reader
    c. Adobe Acrobat Distiller
    d. Both a and c

15. **HTML is an acronym that stands for:**
    a. Hyper Text Marking and Linking
    b. Hyper Text Markup Language
    c. Higher Text Marking Language
    d. None of the above

16. **When planning web pages, you should limit your use of graphic images because:**
    a. HTML limits web pages to a maximum of five graphic images
    b. Complex graphics can slow the time it takes for your home page to be accessed
    c. Web viewers are most interested in the textual information available on your web pages
    d. All of the above

17. **PDF is an acronym that stands for:**
    a. Portable Document File
    b. Portable Distribution Format
    c. Passive Document Flexibility
    d. None of the above

18. **Hypertext links can be used to connect to:**
    a. Text or graphics within the web page
    b. Text or graphics on other web sites
    c. Open graphic files on the web
    d. Both a and b

19. **Uniform resource locator (URL) is a:**
    a. Programming language for creating web pages
    b. Method of linking web pages on the Internet
    c. PDF viewer
    d. None of the above

► Skills Review

1. **Name and Assign PageMaker pages as HTML pages.**
    a. Start PageMaker and open the file UNIT_K-3 from your Student Disk.
    b. Click File on the menu bar, point to Export, then click HTML.
    c. Click New, then type "Boston Home Page" in the Document Title text box.
    d. Click Page 1 in the Unassigned list box, click Add>>.
    e. Click Page 2 in the Unassigned list box, click Add>>, click Done, then click Document.
    f. Type "BOS_HP.HTML" in the File Name for HTML Document text box, then click OK.
    g. Click New, type "Boston Nightlife" in the Document Title text box.
    h. Click Page 3 in the Unassigned list box, click Add>>, click Done, then click Document.
    i. Type "BOS_NITE.HTML" in the File Name for HTML Document text box, then click OK.
    j. Click Done to close the HTML dialog box.

2. **Associate PageMaker styles with HTML styles.**
    a. Click Window on the menu bar, click Show Styles, click the right arrow, then click ADD HTML Styles.
    b. Position the pointer below the Boston logo, then press [Ctrl] and right-click *(Macintosh users: press ⌘ [option]) then click the mouse button.*

   c. Click the Text tool in the toolbox, click in the line of text below the logo, then click HTML H1 on the Styles palette.

   d. Click in the next line of text, then click HTML H2 on the Styles palette.

   e. Click in the paragraph beginning with "This home page...".

   f. Click File on the menu bar, point to Export, click HTML, then click Options.

   g. Scroll down the HTML Style list box, click Heading5, then click Body Text on the pop-up menu.

   h. Click Done.

   i. Save the publication.

3. Create hypertext links.

   a. Click the pages 2 and 3 page icon, position the pointer at the top left corner of page 2, then press [Ctrl] and right-click *(Macintosh users: press ⌘ [option], then click the mouse button)*.

   b. Make sure the Text tool in the toolbox is selected, select the text "The Nightlife," click Windows on the menu bar, then click Show Hyperlinks.

   c. Click the right arrow on the Hyperlinks palette, then click New Anchor.

   d. Type "BOS_NITE.HTML", then click OK.

   e. Make sure the text "The Nightlife" is still selected, click Window on the menu bar, click Show Colors, click the color Blue, then close the Colors palette and deselect the text.

4. Export HTML files.

   a. Click File on the menu bar, point to Export, then click HTML.

   b. Click Boston Home Page in the HTML Document Title list box, press and hold [Ctrl], click the second file Boston Nightlife, then release [Ctrl].

   c. Click Export HTML.

   d. Click File on the menu bar, click Close, then click Yes when prompted to save the publication.

5. Identify PDF specifications.

   a. Open the file UNIT_K-4 from your Student Disk.

   b. Click File on the menu bar, point to Export, then click Adobe PDF.

   c. Click the Prepare PostScript file for distilling separately option button if it is not already selected.

   d. Click Control, then make sure the RGB (best for screen display) option button is selected.

6. Creating PDF Index bookmarks.

   a. In the Export Adobe PDF dialog box, click PDF options.

   b. Make sure all check boxes in the Hyperlinks section are selected, make sure all check boxes in the Bookmarks section are selected, and make sure Add Document Information checkbox near the bottom of the page is selected.

   c. Click OK to close the PDF Options dialog box.

   d. Click to the right of the dash in the Ranges text box in the Pages section, then type "10" to complete the range.

   e. Click Export

   f. Click the Save in list arrow, click Desktop, then click Save.

   g. Click Save.

   h. Click File on the menu bar, click Exit to exit PageMaker *(Macintosh users: click Quit)*, then click Yes when prompted to save the PageMaker publication.

7. Create a PDF file.

a. On the desktop, double-click the file UNIT_K-4.ps to open it in Distiller and convert it to a PDF file.

b. Click File on the menu bar, then click Exit to exit Acrobat™ Distiller (*Macintosh users: click Quit*).

c. On the desktop, click the file UNIT_K-4.ps to select it, press [Delete] (*Macintosh users: drag the file to the trash*), then click Yes.

8. Use Acrobat™ Reader to view a PDF file.

a. On the desktop, double-click the unit_k-4.pdf icon.

b. Click the Fit Page button on the button bar to scale the page to fit within the publication window.

c. Navigate through the file and test the links you've created.

d. Exit Acrobat™ Reader.

e. If you need to turn in a copy of your PDF file, save a copy of unit_k-4.pdf to a separate disk.

f. Delete unit_k-4.pdf from the desktop.

▶ Independent Challenges

1. You work for a newly created and prosperous company known as WorldLink, which specializes in helping businesses establish web sites on the World Wide Web. A local record store named Rocket Music Connection wants you to create a web site for their stores. The Rocket Music Connection wants a home page that gives their viewers a brief overview of the web site. Viewers would then be able to use hypertext links to connect with web pages specific to their desired music preferences. These web pages would have information about the latest releases as well as weekly updates on specials at the Rocket Music Connection.

To complete this independent challenge:

1. Plan and sketch the home page and hypertext links to other web pages.

2. Open a new publication, choose a page size of 8½" × 11", landscape orientation, 6 pages. Open story editor and create the text for the home page. Start by typing an introductory paragraph. Then type six short paragraphs describing pages that the readers can link to using hypertext links. A linked page could describe the latest music release, store location, concert schedule, and so on. You can include your own graphics or use GIF files on your Student Disk as graphic placeholders. These graphics must be placed as inline graphics. Remember the World Wide Web requires that you only use graphic files with the GIF extension.

3. Create at least one hypertext link page in your publication.

4. After you create the basic layout, use the HTML Author to assign PageMaker pages to HTML pages. Assign the home page(s) as ROCK_HP.HTML and the hypertext link page as LINK_P1.HTML.

5. Apply and associate PageMaker styles with HTML styles.

6. Create a hypertext link from your home page to your hypertext link page.

7. Export the home page and hyptertext link home page using the HTML Export command in HTML Author.

8. Save then print your publication.

2. As you have already learned, creating a PDF file is an alternative to traditional publication creation and distribution. Use one of your favorite PageMaker publications that you have already completed to create a PDF file using PageMaker and Adobe Acrobat.

1. Open your publication in PageMaker, open the Create Adobe PDF dialog box, then modify the PDF workflow options to prepare a PostScript file for distilling separately. Using the Auto-list command in the Select option dialog box, select your destination watched directory. Finally, use the Edit command to select the range of pages to be included (all) in the PDF file and to make sure that RGB is selected if necessary.

2. Use the PDF Options dialog box to create bookmarks for the TOC and the index if applicable in your publication. Export the PDF file, and then exit PageMaker.
3. Convert the PostScript file you just created, using Acrobat Distiller. After it has been distilled, exit Distiller.
4. Double-click your new PDF file to open it using Acrobat™ Reader. View your PDF file, and test all of the functions using the button bar.

3. Create a PDF file for the Holistic Health Notes newsletter.
   To complete this independent challenge:

1. Open the publication UNIT_K-5 on your student disk.
2. Modify the Headline style to be included in the table of contents.
3. Use the Create TOC command to create a table of contents for the publication. Place the table of contents in the box at the bottom of page 1.
4. Save the publication.
5. Use the Auto-list command in the Select option dialog box to select a watched directory.
6. Use the Edit command and complete the range of pages in the Ranges text box in the Pages section.
7. Use the PDF options dialog box to create bookmarks for the TOC.
8. Export the PDF file and then exit PageMaker.
9. Start Acrobat Distiller, then open the PDF file using Acrobat™ Reader.

4. Because so many people today are "surfing the Net", it is important to have a home page that pro-vides viewers with useful information and which captures their attention before they jump to another home page. You have been asked by your employer to critique a few of your competitor's home pages to determine whether or not your company's home page needs to be redesigned in order to be more attractive and informative to your customers.

To complete this independent challenge:

1. Search the World Wide Web for at least three home pages belonging to companies in the industry of your choice. Bookmark these pages so that you can easily jump from page to page. Explore some of the links that you find on the home pages.
2. Critique each home page using the guidelines that you learned in this unit:
   Are graphic images used discretely?
   Is there a concise listing of the home page's content?
   Does it include downloadable files for graphical images or long publications?
   Does it include an index?
   Does it allow for feedback?
   How would you improve each home page?
3. Sketch a home page for your company that includes the best qualities from each of the home pages that you have explored. Make sure to show where you have included hypertext links.
4. Hand in your sketch and all critiques.

▶ Visual Workshop

As the marketing director for a local retail center called SouthPointe, it is your job to create a web site for the center. Create a home page that describes the businesses, gives the location of the center, provides an additional means of advertising for the different retailers at the center, and allows for feedback from customers. Create the home page and hypertext link home page, as shown in Figure K-25. Export the home page and hyptertext link home page using the Export HTML command in HTML Author. Save your publication as SouthPointe, and then print your publication.

FIGURE K-25A

Welcome to SouthPointe! Denver's Retail and Business Center.

You've found Denver's premier shopping and business center. Learn about SouthPointe's featured business of the month, or visit the web site of one of our other retail stores. You can also ask our information booth for more information about SouthPointe.

Our Featured Business of the Month: **Johnson Printing**

Johnson Printing brings you cutting-edge technology to help you in all of your printing needs. Johnson Printing offers the most competitive prices in the area, along with the fastest and friendliest service. You can even make your own copies on professional copy machines, guaranteeing the finest quality black and white or color reproductions.

 **ChuckXPress**

Whether you need your letter or package delivered across town or across the state of Colorado, ChuckXPress is there to deliver it for you. ChuckXPress also has a wide selection of boxes available in all sizes and shapes to protect your valuable contents.

 Sunset Tours

Tired of the cold Denver winters? Then let Sunset Tours plan your next vacation to the sunny Caribbean! Sunset Tours also prides itself on the finest tour packages in all of Europe. The best thing about Sunset Tours is the affordable prices that fit almost any budget. So go ahead and give yourself a break!

Click Here for SouthPointe's Information Booth

FIGURE K-25B

SouthPointe's Featured Business of the Month:

Johnson Printing brings you cutting-edge technology to help you in all of your printing needs. Johnson Printing offers the most competitive prices in the area, along with the fastest and friendliest service. You can even make your own copies on professional copy machines, guaranteeing the finest quality black and white or color reproductions.

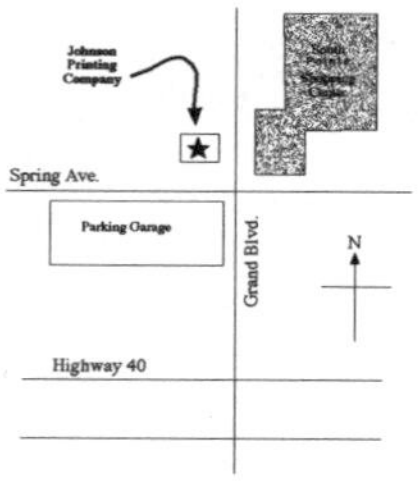

Additional
Projects

Objectives

- ► **Create a letterhead**
- ► **Create a fax cover page**
- ► **Create an advertisement**
- ► **Create a flyer**
- ► **Create a brochure**
- ► **Create a newsletter**
- ► **Create a PDF file**

This unit provides seven additional projects for you to practice the skills you learned in the lessons of this book. Begin each project by organizing how you want the information to flow on the page, using the planning techniques you learned in earlier units. The layout and design of your publications should be simple and easy to understand, yet creative enough to involve the reader totally in each publication's message. ▬ Sunset Tours, an independent travel agency, provides quality self-guided and packaged tours in the United States and around the world. Matt Candela of Sunset Tours needs to finish some projects he has been working on over the last couple of weeks.

PageMaker 6.5

Creating a Letterhead

Matt's first project is to create a new Sunset Tours letterhead using a different business address and a newly designed logo. The information on Sunset Tours' previous company letterhead was poorly organized and difficult to read. Corporate letterhead should contain a slogan statement, name, address, phone number, and fax number. In addition to containing this valuable information, it should be well-designed and should effectively project the company's image. To help complete this project, open a new PageMaker document, set page dimensions, then create and import the information needed to design a professional-looking letterhead. Use the sample letterhead Matt sketched, shown in Figure L-1, to create the new letterhead.

1. **Start PageMaker and open a new publication, then set page specifications for the letterhead in the Document Setup dialog box**
   This publication should be single-sided because it is a one-page publication. Set the left and bottom margins with the same setting and top and right margins with the same setting. All of the margins should be less than 1".

2. **Save the letterhead with a meaningful name to your Student Disk**
   Give the letterhead a name that you can easily recognize.

3. **Place the logo SUNLOGO, located on your Student Disk, in the publication, then resize it to the dimensions necessary for your layout**
   The Sunset Tours logo appears, as shown in Figure L-2. Matt waits to experiment with the placement of the logo until he creates the letterhead text.

4. **Use the Text tool** **T** **to enter the company address, phone number, fax number, and a company slogan**
   Matt creates two text objects independent of each other, so he can move each object around the page. Matt formats the text before he experiments with its position on the page.

QuickTip

See Unit B for help designing a letterhead and other office stationery.

5. **Use the Font, Size, and Type Style commands on the Type menu to format the letterhead text**
   Before deciding on the best look for your letterhead text, try a number of different font types, sizes, and styles.

6. **Add the shaded bar, and move the logo and the text objects into their final positions**
   Use the design guidelines you learned in this book to place the logo and text. As you experiment with different logo and text positions, print the letterhead designs you favor to see how they look on paper. Printing the letterhead at different stages of development provides good clues on how the document needs to change. Remember, your letterhead needs to be simple and visually pleasing.

7. **Finish the project by checking for spelling errors, then save and print your publication**

8. **Be prepared to explain the design of your letterhead**

FIGURE L-1: Sketch of Sunset Tours' letterhead

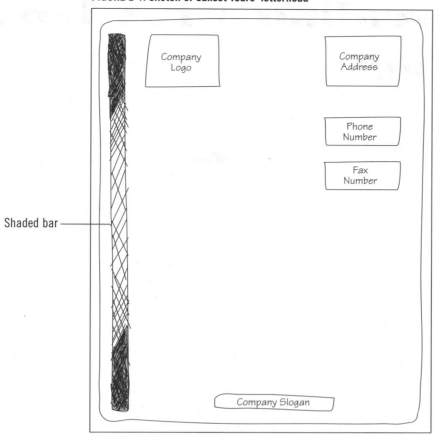

Shaded bar ————

Company Logo

Company Address

Phone Number

Fax Number

Company Slogan

FIGURE L-2: Sunset Tours logo

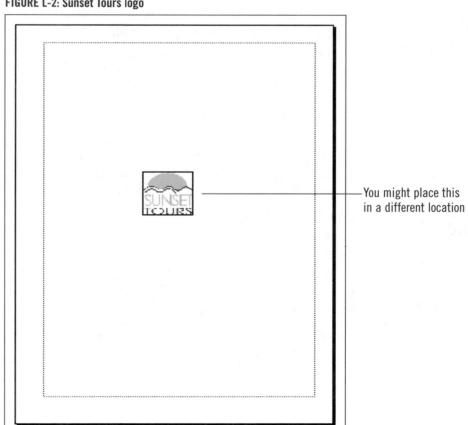

You might place this
in a different location

Creating a Fax Cover Page

Use your drawing skills to help Matt finish the fax cover page he started earlier today. Sunset Tours' old fax cover page was not designed well and could not easily accommodate new information. The fax cover page needs to be concise and professional looking. A fax cover page that is too detailed or that includes intricate designs or photographs does not print well on the majority of facsimile printers and slows the transmission of the fax. As with corporate letterhead, a fax cover page needs to include some basic information such as the date, sender and recipient names, phone and fax numbers, number of pages, and a subject area. It should also contain the company logo and address and instantly identify the intended party and the pages that follow. Use the sample fax cover page Matt sketched, shown in Figure L-3, to help you design your fax cover page.

1. Open the file UNIT_L-1 from your Student Disk
The fax cover page appears. So far, Matt has entered the text and placed the Sunset Tours logo on the fax cover page. Take this information and organize it into a simple but effective fax cover page.

2. Use the Rectangle tool ▢ to draw an unfilled box (use a line larger than 1 point) over the margin guides of the document
Use the box resize handles to move the box lines over the margin guides, if necessary. Placing the box over the margin guides gives your fax cover sheet boundaries to follow when you place text or other elements on the page. Next, create some unfilled boxes to place around the fax cover text. Putting boundaries around the text provides defined areas to write the necessary sending and receiving information.

QuickTip

See Unit B for help designing business stationery.

3. Choose a position on the vertical ruler, then draw a box ¼" high from the left vertical margin guide to the right vertical margin guide
You might need to turn on the Snap to Guides option. The sides of the box should snap to the vertical margin guides. Drag the box resize handles to stretch the box to fit between the vertical margin guides, if necessary. While the box is selected, experiment with different line widths and styles. Keep in mind, as you experiment with line widths and styles, that the purpose of this box is to surround text.

4. Duplicate the box four times, then drag the boxes into logical positions
Each box will contain one of the five lines of text from "Sender Name"/ "Recipient Name" to "Subject:". Use a horizontal ruler guide to help position the boxes relative to each other, if necessary. Once you place the boxes on the page, move the fax cover page text inside the boxes.

Trouble?

The boxes shown around text in Figure L-3 represent areas of the page, not drawn boxes. Create and place boxes as described in Steps 2 through 4.

5. Drag the text objects inside the boxes
Before you drag the objects inside the boxes, plan how you want the text organized. You have the width of the page to work with, so make use of all the space.

6. Use the Constrained Line tool ▭ to draw a vertical line to separate the text objects
Be sure to print the fax cover page at different stages of development, so you can see exactly how all the elements fit together.

7. Finish the project by checking for spelling errors, then save and print your publication

8. Be prepared to explain the design of your fax cover page

FIGURE L-3: Sketch of Sunset Tours' fax cover page

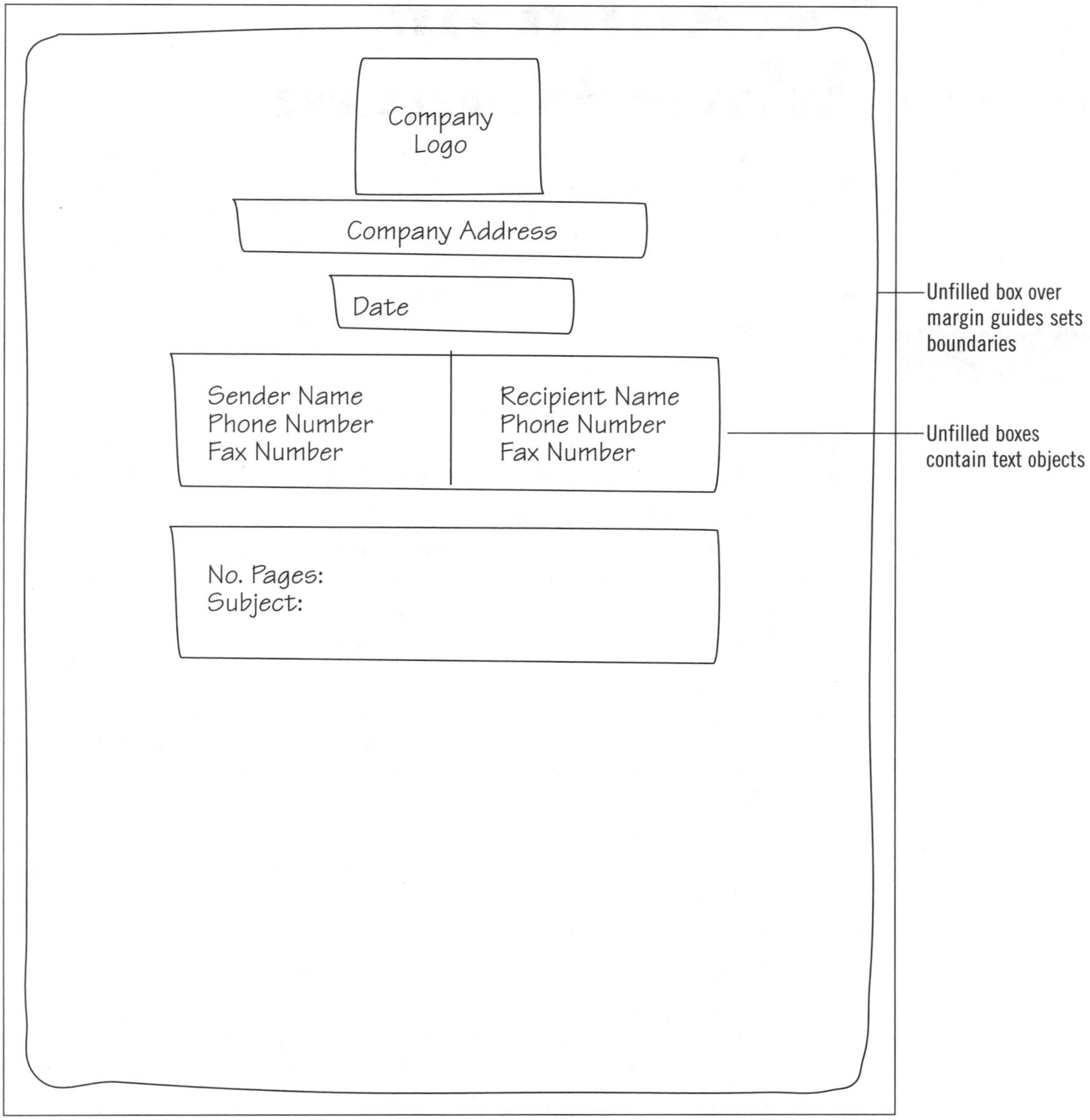

Company
Logo

Company Address

Date

Sender Name
Phone Number
Fax Number

Recipient Name
Phone Number
Fax Number

Unfilled box over
margin guides sets
boundaries

Unfilled boxes
contain text objects

No. Pages:
Subject:

Creating an Advertisement

One of Matt's jobs at Sunset Tours is to create print advertisements for trade magazines and newspapers. Ads must be simple yet eye-catching. They should pique the readers' interest and make them want to learn more. You do this by incorporating graphics and text in a meaningful way. Matt began developing an advertisement on tours to Europe last week but has not had time to complete it. He needs to finish this one-color advertisement, which will run in a national travel magazine on European tours. The magazine publisher will only accept ads that are one color and submitted on 8½"×11" paper. 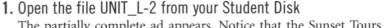 Use the sample ad Matt sketched, shown in Figure L-4, to help complete the ad.

QuickTip

See Unit F for help designing a print advertisement.

1. **Open the file UNIT_L-2 from your Student Disk**
   The partially complete ad appears. Notice that the Sunset Tours logo is imported but not positioned on the page. You need to begin by placing the text and the logo in better positions.

2. **Place the Sunset Tours logo and the title text on the page, then place the ad text**
   Remember that the ad and logo need to stand out on the page. When you think you have a good layout design, print and review the page. After you are satisfied with the design, you need to format the text.

3. **Use the Control palette to change the font type, font size, and text tracking to achieve the desired look**
   Be careful not to rush through the text formatting portion of your ad. You want to ensure that the main points of the ad are clear and easily absorbed. You might need to adjust the text position again because of the formatting you choose. Remember to be simple and clear in your layout design and to include plenty of white space.

4. **Add bullets to the text list**
   The bullets should draw attention to the features being highlighted in the list but not away from the rest of the ad. Adjust the spacing between the bullets and the text to achieve a professional look.

5. **Use the alignment commands to adjust the alignment of text or use the alignment buttons on the Control palette**
   The default alignment of text is left, which is appropriate for most text objects; however, some text lines look better with a different alignment. Experiment with text alignment in the ad.

6. **Finish the project by checking for spelling errors, then save and print your publication**

7. **Be prepared to explain the design of your advertisement**

FIGURE L-4: Sketch of Sunset Tours' advertisement

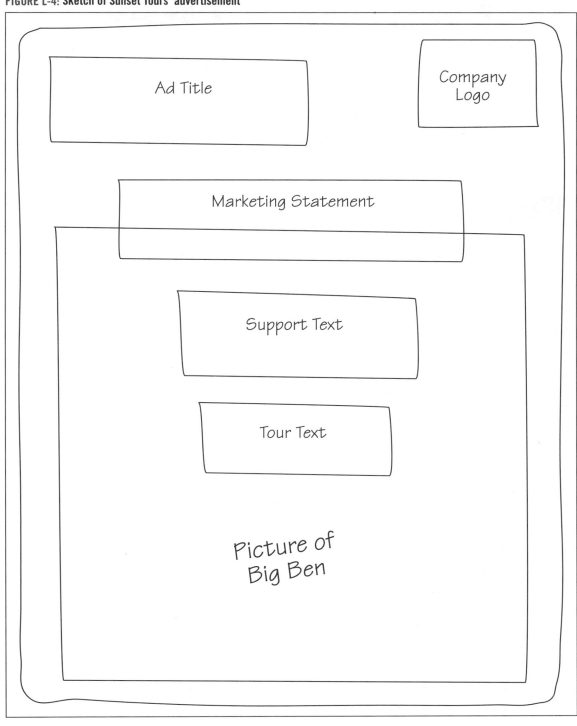

PageMaker 6.5

Creating a Flyer

Every month Sunset Tours produces a flyer that highlights special package tours to its "country of the month." Sunset Tours decided to highlight four full-package tours to Russia for next month. As with an advertisement, a flyer needs to have a simple, eye-catching design. The flyer must direct the reader to the important information on the page by using color, shading, or different text style attributes, such as bold or italic. Flyers might not provide readers with all the information they need, so be sure to provide a way for readers to contact the company for more information. Matt can finish the flyer by resizing a graphic, rotating and recoloring text, and adjusting text tracking and leading. Use the sample flyer Matt sketched, shown in Figure L-5, to help finish designing the flyer.

QuickTip

See Unit H for help designing a flyer.

1. Open the file UNIT_L-3 from your Student Disk

The partially completed flyer appears. Notice that the graphic of Russia does not fill the page. You will need to resize the graphic to fit the width of the page (within the vertical margin guides).

2. Use the Control palette to resize the Russia graphic proportionally to the width of the page, then rotate the word "Russia!" inside the graphic

Be careful how much you rotate the text; it needs to be readable. Print the page to check the size of the object and the rotation position of the text in the object. Now change the color of the text in the graphic so it stands out.

3. Use the Character Specifications dialog box to change the text color of the word "Russia!" to contrast with the Russia graphic color

4. Use the Character Specifications dialog box to format the font, font style, leading, and tracking of the two lists on the page

The tabs Matt set between the cities and the day and prices in the lower list need to be reformatted using the Tab command. Matt just set a normal tab, by pressing [Tab], between the cities and the days and prices. Because each text line is a different length, using the Tab key does not align the text properly.

5. Set and adjust a tab in the lower list to line up all the days and prices in two clearly separate columns

The position of a tab is dependent on the size of the text object and the formatting of the text. You might need to experiment with the tab or the size of the text object to achieve just the right look. If possible, make sure that you are finished formatting the text before you set the tabs, because later text formatting can change a tab's position.

6. Finish the project by checking for spelling errors, then save and print your publication

7. Be prepared to explain the design of your flyer

FIGURE L-5: Sketch of Sunset Tours' flyer

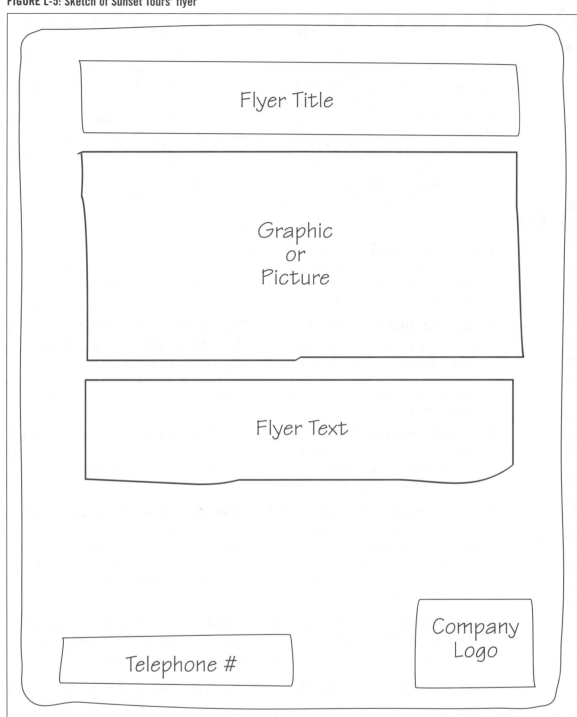

Flyer Title

Graphic
or
Picture

Flyer Text

Telephone #

Company
Logo

PageMaker 6.5

Creating a Brochure

In order to attract a larger customer base, Sunset Tours has decided to create full-color 8½"×11" brochures on its most popular and profitable tours. One of the most popular tours that Sunset Tours offers is a seven-day cruise to Mexico on an American Cruise Lines ship. Matt's two-page brochure introduces the Mexican ports of interest that the traveler will see during the cruise. In this project you will place text into the brochure from a Microsoft Word document, add a color from a color library to the Colors palette, then create a tint color. To complete this project, use the design ideas from Unit I to plan your brochure. Make sure the brochure provides enough information for the reader to act on. Well-placed color and graphics add to the overall appeal of the brochure and can dramatically affect how the reader responds to the information. Use the sample brochure Matt sketched, shown in Figure L-6, to help you finish designing the brochure.

Steps

QuickTip

See Unit I for help designing a brochure.

1. **Open the file UNIT_L-4 from your Student Disk**
   The first thing you need to do is place the text in the document so you can arrange the layout for both pages. The text for the brochure is in a Word document, which you import using the Place command.

2. **Place the Word document file, BROCHURE, located on your Student Disk, on page 2 of the brochure, resize the text object, then use ☟ to move text to page 3**
   Be sure to leave white space around the picture in the center of the two pages. You can use the ruler guides to help place the text object. Before you continue, you might want to resize the text objects on both pages so they match each other horizontally, then print the pages to check your work.

3. **In the text object on the left page, wrap the text around the Sunset Tours logo**
   Experiment with the logo's position to determine the best place for it in the text object. Once you finish adjusting the logo, add a new color to the menu that you will use in the box at the bottom of pages 2 and 3.

4. **Add the Orange Yellow color from the Crayon color library to the Colors palette, then add the new color to the box at the bottom of pages 2 and 3**
   Make sure the Orange Yellow color is a process CMYK color. Matt uses the Orange Yellow color because it matches the color used in the Sunset Tours logo. Now, Matt moves to the last page of the brochure and creates a tint from the Orange Yellow color to apply to the turquoise-colored box.

5. **Move to page 4 of the publication, create a tint from the Orange Yellow color, name the new color "Tint #1," then apply the color to the turquoise colored box**
   Remember to use Orange Yellow as your base color when you create the tint.

6. **Finish the project by checking for spelling errors, then save and print your brochure**

7. **Be prepared to explain the design of your brochure**

FIGURE L-6: Sketch of Sunset Tours' brochure

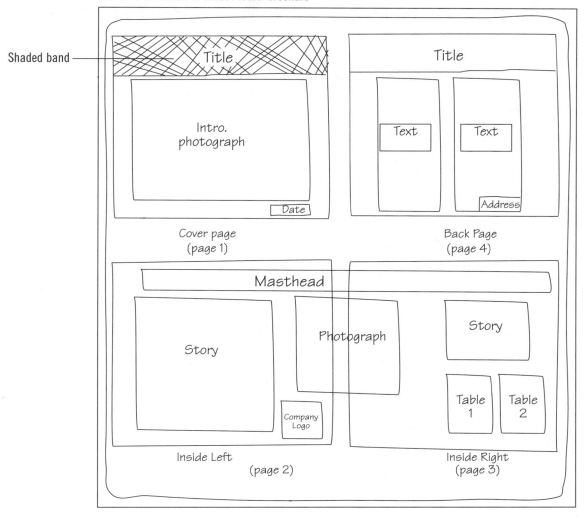

PageMaker 6.5

Creating a Newsletter

Upon arriving at his office today, Matt is told by his boss that he misplaced the disk that contained the company newsletter he had been working on. The only thing Matt has left to work from is a hard copy of the newsletter he printed the day before and a text document that contains the text for the publication. Re-create Matt's work by referring to his hard copy of the newsletter. Set the page specifications for the publication first, and then place the text and graphics. Make your publication look like the page examples in Figures L-7, L-8, L-9, and L-10.

1. Open a new PageMaker publication, set the page specifications and save the file with an appropriate name, then place the text from the document NEWSLTTR, located on your Student Disk

   Don't spend too much time designing the page at this stage, just get the information in place. Now check the Link Options: Default dialog box to make sure that placed graphics are not stored in the newsletter.

2. Deselect the text you just placed, open the Links Manager dialog box, then make sure there are no graphics stored in the publication

   Storing graphic files in the newsletter would dramatically increase its file size.

QuickTip

See Unit E for help designing a newsletter.

3. Create the masthead for the newsletter, place the graphic file PICTURE1 on page 1, then format the information as shown in Figure L-7

   Use the ruler guides to help you place the information on the page.

4. Create text styles for the body text, the caption text, and the header text, then apply the styles to the text

5. Place the graphic files PICTURE2, PICTURE3, and PICTURE4, located on your Student Disk, on the publication pages, then format the information as shown in Figures L-8, L-9, and L-10

6. Finish the project by checking for spelling errors, then save and print your newsletter

7. Be prepared to explain the design of your newsletter

FIGURE L-7: Newsletter page 1

The Sunset

SUNSET TOURS

CUSTOMER QUARTERLY JOURNAL
JANUARY 1995

Inside the Bostonian World

From Brahmins to Beanpots

by Joan Wilcox

It's a cliche to say a city defies definition. But in the case of Boston, the cliche is simply truth. History. Culture. Sports capital. Business center. Haute couture and counterculture. Which Boston will you visit?

There's the historical Boston—the Boston you can't miss, and wouldn't want to! The city of Paul Revere, Benjamin Franklin, the Boston Tea Party, the Freedom Trail, Copp's Hill and King's Chapel Burying Grounds, and the USS Constitution. Visit the Old South Meeting House, dine at the Union Oyster House or Warren Tavern (which George Washington frequented), and shop at the restored Faneuil Hall or Quincy Marketplaces.

A Winter evening in the Boston Public Garden

Then there's the stately, though slightly snobby Boston of Beacon Hill brown-stones where, it was said, the Lowells spoke only to the Cabots, and the Cabots spoke only to God. This is the Boston of the symphony, the ballet, and the Head of the Charles sailing regatta; the Boston whose public library in Copley Square deserves to be toured with an art curator. The Boston whose Back Bay mansions now house cultura institutions such as the French Library and the Goethel Institute.

Thinking more along the lines of the trendy, cultural, artsy Boston? Then head for the Museum of Fine Arts or the Isabella Stewart Gardener Museum. As you walk Tremont Street in the Theater District take your pick of Broadway hits at the Wang Center for the Performing Arts, the Charles Playhouse, and other theaters big and small. Just a short subway ride away is Harvard Square in Cambridge—the land of the cutting-edge, the bastion of counterculture that skirts the ivy-covered halls of Harvard Yard.

Boston's night scene features every kind of music from rock to blues to baroque to Irish ballads. Or simply stroll the cobblestone streets listening to Boston's famed street musicians and performance artists.

Boston isn't a city as much as it's an experience. And one thing is for sure—there's a Boston that's perfect for you!

Inside. . . .

A Publication of Sunset Tours

FIGURE L-8: Newsletter page 2

The Streets of Boston

by Matt Candela

Logan International Airport is the gateway to Boston for most visitors, although since the renovation of the spectacular South Station, more and more travelers are arriving by train. Getting to Boston is not the problem. However, getting around once you're here may be.

Actually Boston is a "small" big city—a walker's paradise. You can walk from one end of town to the other in little more than half an hour. Most historical and cultural sites are grouped in "neighorboohs" such as the North End, South Boston, Government Center, Back Bay, so you can map out comfortable walking tours each day. But should you want to venture farther afield take a native's advice—don't drive!

Historic Faneuli Hall, built in 1742, in the foreground and the Custom House tower in the background

There's a not-so-funny joke in Boston that the only people foolish enough to drive in Boston are the tourists—because ignorance is bliss! Tourists soon find out what the natives mean—Boston is perhaps the most frustrating driving experience in America. The hub of the city is clustered around a crazy-quilt of narrow streets that out-of-towners would call alleys. Many are one-way, so if you get lost you can't simply go around the block to get back to where you started. Street signs are often missing or confusing. A local newspaper, acting on tourist frustration and complaints, once sent a team of local reporters out to follow the traffic signs from the center of Boston to Logan International Airport: They couldn't do it!

> "There's a not-so-funny joke in Boston that the only people foolish enough to drive in Boston are the tourists—"

Besides the hopelessly intricate streets, there's the fear factor. Anyone who has had the unfotunate experience of driving in Boston knows that Bostonians are notoriously agressive drivers. If you do decide to rent a car, be ready for an experience that is a cross between bumper cars and the Indy 500.

And forget about parking on the streets. The locals will have every available space—most of which are resident sticker only—and those that are public are ruthlessly monitored by meter readers. There's no second chance if they catch your parking meter expired. Expect an expensive ticket, and expect to pay up immediately! If you stick to public parking garages, expect to pay big bucks.

So how should you get around town? Thankfully, Boston has an excellent public transit system. There are subways and trolleys that can take you around town and out to many suburbs. There are trains, taxis, and buses galore. For schedules, maps, and directions, call Sunset Tours at 1-800-555-TRVL.

Boston Highlights

When visiting Boston make sure you see the *real Boston*. The following list is a "don't miss" list of attractions, many of which are not found in the guidebooks. How many are on your itinerary?

- The Boston Pops, especially the July 4th concert at the Hatch Shell
- Filene's Basement for shopping bargains
- The Farmers' Market at Haymarket every Friday and Saturday
- Open rehearsal of the Boston Symphony Orchestra on Wednesday evening or Thursday morning
- Glass flower exhibit at Harvard
- Mapparium (inside-out glass globe of the world) at the Christian Science Center
- Sunday Bach Concerts at Emmanuel Church
- The Omni Theater at the Museum of Science
- Watching street performers in the Public Garden

2 *The Sunset*

FIGURE L-9: Newsletter page 3

Cape Cod and the Islands

by Matt Candela

A visit to Massachusetts isn't complete until you've ventured outside of Boston to the second most visited area—Cape Cod. Curving 75 miles out into the Atlantic, like a arm crooked at the elbow, Cape Cod is quintessential New England. Known for its storybook New England towns and miles of glorious beaches, Cape Cod is also tourist heaven in summer. There is no better place for shopping, seafood restaurants galore, and more art galleries than you'll have time to browse. Traffic can be a nightmare, so if you want to get off the beaten path, check out the miles of bike trails that wind through Cape Cod beach, marsh, and woodland.

While you're on the Cape, plan to venture off it to one of Massachusetts' famous islands: Nantucket or Martha's Vineyard.

The "Vineyard," as locals call it, is the historical getaway for the rich and famous. It's also home for more than 80,000 tourists during peak season. The draw is its spectacular beaches and "quaint" atmosphere. After the bustle of Boston, Martha's Vineyard is the perfect place to rejunevate.

Nantucket is known for its cranberry bogs, clapboard cottages, and ornate mansions. In the 19th century, Nantucket was the busiest whaling port in the world, and it boasts one of the best whaling museums in the world. Today, it's a summer retreat for artists and writers—and tourists.

You can reach both islands by ferry in less than 2 hours, but you have to book ahead, especially if you want to ferry your car During summer, you will have to book hotel rooms very far in advance. The best hotel bargains are found off-season, in spring or late fall.

Since 1679 the lighthouse on Little Brewster island (the oldest in the United States) has welcomed sea-travelers from all over the world.

July 1999 3

FIGURE L-10: Newsletter page 4

Boston For Kids

First stop for kids is the Boston Public Gardens, where the famous swan boats are on everyone's list of things to do. While there kids can marvel at the famed bronze ducklings, lifesize statues created by an area artist of the literary *Make Way for Ducklings entourage*.

Next stop is the award-winning Children's Museum, located on Museum Wharf. You can't miss the Museum—at its entrance is a 40-foot tall milk bottle that can hold 50,000 gallons of milk! This hands-on museum has innovative, interactive displays from computers to giant soap bubbles to Grandmother's Attic, where everyone can dress up in vintage clothing. Admission is $7 for adults, $6 for kids 2-15, and $2 for kids younger than 2. The Museum can get quite crowded, so plan to arrive early.

Next door to the Children's Museum is a replica of the Boston Tea Party ship, the famous vessel from which angry colonists disguised as Mohawk Indians dumped tea to protest British taxation.

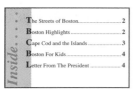

The U.S.S. Constitution, built in Boston in 1797, is one of the oldest U.S. Navy ships still afloat. The Constitution was undefeated in 40 battles during her commision. Today the Constitution, shown here at a 4th of July celebration, is an active U.S. Naval museum.

And don't forget those most New England of ships—whalers. What is a trip to Boston without a whale-watching cruise? Because of safety consideration, kids have to be 36" or taller to board a whale cruise ship, but once aboard there's excitement for everyone as you head out to sea in search of great humpbacks and finbacks. Cruises run from April to October; each can take up to six hours roundtrip, so it's not suitable for very young children. Costs average $25/person. Reservations are required.

While you and the kids are at the harbor, stop by and see the *U.S.S. Constitution*, known as "Old Ironsides." This mighty ship got her nickname when cannon balls bounced off her oak decking during battle. If you happen to be in Boston during the 4th of July, you can see the *Constitution* as she is towed in the harbor with flags flying and cannons booming.

Letter From The President

On behalf of the 260 Sunset Tours employees nation wide, I would like to thank you for choosing our agency for your travel needs. Because of your confidence in our package tours throughout the world, we have expanded our services to Africa and South America.

We would like to reward all those who travel with us with an automatic 15% discount on the purchase price of any international package tour. Plan your trip between now and January 1, 1999 and recieve an automatic discount on the purchase price of your trip. Call your local Sunset Tours agent for complete terms and details.

I would also like to take this opportunity to introduce our World Class program. The Sunset Tours World Class program offers many great services and discounts with our partner corporations around the world. We have worked hard so you can receive hotel discounts, car rentals upgrades, special restaurant services as well as discounts to major cultural attractions.

The flying partner for our World Class program is New World Airlines. And if you want to earn free travel fast, the New World Airlines Frequent Flyer program is your best choice. Members earn a free international roundtrip ticket on New World Airlines starting at just 30,000 miles. New World Airlines flies to every major city in the United States, as well as some of the most important cities in the world including London, Paris, Rome, Frankfurt, Moscow, Seoul and Toyko.

Thank you for allowing us to be your travel host and we look forward to serving you in the near future.

- J.C. Reynolds-

The Sunset
TOURS

Staff:	Editor-in-Chief:	David Beskeen
	Managing Editor:	Steve Johnson
	Production Manager:	Cheryl Martin
	Production Artist:	Mark Keener
	Publications Manager:	Holly Todd
	Circulation Manager:	Karen Craig
	Copublishers:	Matt Candela
		Joan Wilcox

Address: The Editor, *The Sunset*
1847 Jefferson Blvd.
Charlotte, North Carolina 22001
1-800-555-5504

4 *The Sunset*

PageMaker 6.5

Creating a PDF File

Matt wants to get some more practice converting PageMaker publications to PDF files. He created a sample publication, using pages from other publications, plus placeholder text and graphic frames, to use for a practice conversion. Matt's final PDF file displays as shown in Figure L-11.

Steps

QuickTip

See Unit K for help creating a PDF file.

1. Open the file UNIT_L-5.p65 from your Student Disk

2. Using PageMaker's Export Adobe PDF function, modify the PDF workflow options to prepare a PostScript file for distilling separately and to select all the pages in the publication for export

3. Use the Control command to select RGB color

4. Use the PDF Options dialog box to create bookmarks, then create the PDF file, saving any intermediate files to the desktop

5. Open the PDF file to view your new publication using Acrobat Reader

FIGURE L-11: Sample newsletter PDF file

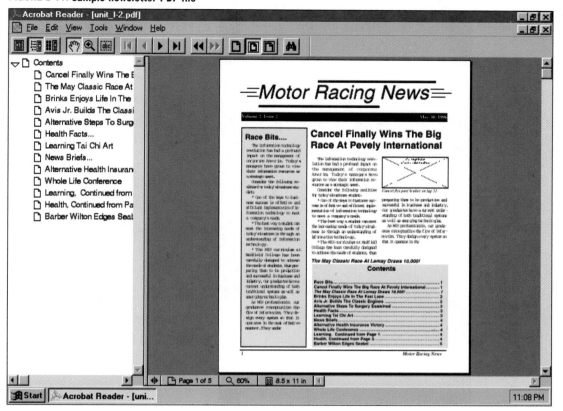

Glossary

Abstract A summary at the beginning of a report.

Active application The application or program that is running. *See also* Task List.

Adobe Acrobat A software family that allows you to create and view portable document formats that can be read on multiple computer platforms such as IBM-compatible, Macintosh, or Unix-based machines.

Adobe Acrobat Distiller An application program that converts a Postscript export file into a portable document format publication.

Adobe Acrobat Reader An application program that allows you to view and print portable document format publications.

Alignment The position of text within a page or column: left, right, centered, or justified.

Anchor A hypertext link that goes to another page within the same HTML document.

Application A task-oriented software program that you use for a particular kind of work, such as word processing or database management.

Autoflow Automatically places text flowing from one column to the next, filling up as many columns and pages as necessary.

Balance columns Aligns the top or bottom of text blocks threaded in a story on a single page or facing pages.

Base line An imaginary line that text rests on.

Base line leading Measures the leading from the base line of the line to the text.

Bitmapped Windows Paint File An image created by dot resolution.

Bookmark A method for creating hypertext links in a PDF publication.

Bullet A small graphic, usually a round or square dot, used before items in a list.

Camera-ready A paper publication that can be sent directly to a printing company to be printed.

Character view The view on the Control palette used to change character-related commands such as font, type style, leading, baseline shift, and other settings.

Clip art Graphic images or photographs stored as electronic files.

Clipboard A temporary storage area for cut or copied text or graphics.

CMYK The four process colors: cyan (C), magenta (M), yellow (Y), and black (K).

Color libraries Industry standards for creating specific colors.

Color Matching System A method used by commercial printers to make sure the color used in a publication matches the color of the final output.

Color palette A moveable panel that applies color to both text and graphics to a graphic element's outside border line, inside fill, or both the line and fill.

Column guides Vertical, dotted, nonprinting lines that mark the right and left side of defined columns in a publication page.

Constrained-line tool Draws a straight line at a 45-degree angle.

Crop To cut down a graphic to improve the image by eliminating unnecessary portions.

Cross reference An index entry that describes related or additional topics.

Cursor Indicates the place where new text will be inserted when typed. *See* Insertion point.

Cut A command that removes selected text or a graphic from a document and places it on the Clipboard.

Cutlines Text that describes photos or graphics in a newsletter.

Cyan One of the four basic process colors; a shade of blue. *See* CMYK.

Default settings Predefined settings such as page margins, page size, and number of pages.

Definition points Adjustable points that define the shape of a text wrap.

Desktop An electronic version of a desk that provides a workspace for different computing tasks on a computer screen.

Desktop publishing The ability to integrate text, graphics, spreadsheets, and charts created in different programs into one document on a computer.

Dialog box A window that appears temporarily to request information. Many dialog boxes have options you must choose before Windows can carry out a command.

Directory Part of a structure for organizing files on a disk. A directory can contain files and other directories (called subdirectories).

Dots per inch (dpi) A measure of the dots in a line that create an image. The higher the DPI number, the better the quality of the printout.

Drag Placing Defining the size of a text block at the same time the text is imported.

Draw Microsoft software that allows you to create geometric drawings.

Drop cap The first letter in a story that is enlarged and lowered so the top of the letter is even with the first line of text and the base of the letter drops next to the rest of the paragraph.

Element Individual or grouped items in the publication window. *See also* Object.

Ellipse Tool A tool used to draw circles or ovals in PageMaker.

Encapsulated PostScript file A file created using PostScript code to create an image.

Export To create a new text file using PageMaker's story editor.

Fact sheet An informational publication.

Fill The area within a drawn graphic element.

Fit in window command Adjusts page(s) to fill publication window so you see all of the page(s) and some of the surrounding pasteboard.

Flag The graphical element that serves as your identification and gives a purpose to your newsletter. Also known as masthead or nameplate.

Floating palette A moveable window within the publication window.

Font The specific design of the characters.

Format The appearance of text or paragraph settings.

Frames Placeholders that allow you to design your page layout before placing final versions of text and graphics.

Grabber hand An icon that acts like a hand on a piece of paper with which the page can be moved in any direction in the publication window.

Graphic A picture, chart, or drawing object in a document.

Graphic elements An umbrella term that describes anything on a page other than the text.

Graphical user interface (GUI) A software program that works hand-in-hand with the MS-DOS operating system to control the basic operation of a computer and the programs that run on it.

Greeked text Text on page that cannot be read but represents text on the screen.

Guides Nonprinting lines such as ruler, column, and margin, which are used to align text on the page.

Gutter Space between columns.

Handles Square marks that appear on text and graphics when selected.

Home page The first screen viewed on a Web site.

HTML (Hypertext Markup Language) A programming language used to create Web pages.

HTML Author A PageMaker Plug-in that creates an HTML file that can be viewed on the Internet.

Hypertext link Enables the user to open related Web pages by clicking on the link.

Hyphenate Inserting hyphens into words in order to separate the word between the end of one line and the beginning of the next line.

I-Beam The shape of the pointer when the text tool is selected from the toolbox.

Icon picture or symbol used to represent a command.

Image control A dialog box used to lighten and adjust the contrast of black and white photographs and images.

Indent The distance between the text boundaries and page or column guides.

Index entry A word or group of words included in an index.

Inline graphic An object placed within a text block that moves with the text block or when text in the text block moves.

Insertion point Indicates the place where new text will be inserted when typed. *See also* Cursor.

Internet A collection of networks that connects computers all over the world using phone lines and cables.

Jump The continuation of a story from a previous page.

Justification Adjusting the space between characters so that the text is aligned with a particular margin.

Kerning Adjusting the space between characters in the selected text.

Lamination A permanent plastic coating which preserves documents.

Landscape A term used to refer to horizontal page orientation; the opposite of portrait, or vertical orientation.

Layers A PageMaker publication that allows you to create multiple versions within a single publication, and which allows you to write notes that can only be viewed on-screen.

Leaders Repeated pattern between tabbed items. Examples of leaders include repeated dots or dashes.

Leading Vertical space between lines of text. Leading is the total height of a line from the top of the tallest character in the line to the top of the tallest characters in the line below.

Line style A line's design, such as a single, double, dashed, or reverse line.

Line tool Draws a straight line at any angle.

Line weight The thickness of a line.

Linked file An independent text or graphic file that is used as part of a PageMaker publication.

Magenta One of the four process colors; a shade of red. *See* CMYK.

Margin guides A magenta-colored box inside the page border indicating the page's margins.

Master Page A nonprinting page used for placing text and/or graphics that will appear on all pages of the publication.

Menu A list of available commands in an application window.

Menu bar A horizontal bar containing the names of the application's menus. It appears below the title bar.

Misregistration The gap between colors that occurs when one or more of the colors in a multiple-color process is not printed in alignment with the other colors.

Mouse A hand-held input device that you roll on your desk to position the mouse pointer on the Windows desktop. *See also* Mouse pointer.

Mouse pointer The arrow-shaped cursor on the screen that follows the movement of the mouse; used to select items, choose commands, start applications, and select words in applications.

Notepad A simple text editor that lets you create memos, record notes, or edit text files.

Nudge buttons Small arrow buttons on the Control palette that make changes by using preset measurements.

Object An imported or a drawn graphic that you can select and transform. *See also* Element.

Object view The view on the Control palette used to transform a graphic by changing size, position, rotation, or reflection.

Orientation A page position either portrait (vertical) or landscape (horizontal).

Orphan A short line that ends a paragraph at the top of a column or page.

Page icons Miniature icons that represent pages in the publication. To move to a different page, click the desired page icon at the lower-left corner of the screen. In a single-page document, only one page icon appears.

PageMaker Plug-ins Customized features to automate repetitive or complex publishing tasks.

Paragraph rule A line that can appear above or below a paragraph of text.

Paragraph view The view on the Control palette used to change Paragraph-related commands such as indents, alignment, styles.

Pasteboard The white area surrounding and including the publication page. You can use the pasteboard as a work area to hold text or graphics until you place them in your publication. Any area beyond the pasteboard is represented by yellow or a color other than white.

PDF (Portable Document Format) An independent file that retains all page design and layouts of the file in which it was originally created and can be copied and viewed by anyone using Acrobat Reader.

Picas A character measurement system used by many commercial printers. Six picas equal one inch.

Place To import text or graphics into a PageMaker file.

Point ½ of an inch, used to measure characters.

Point of response The phone number or the address where the reader can respond to information in the publication.

Pointer guides Dotted lines in the horizontal and vertical rulers which indicate the position of the pointer tool.

Pointer tool Selects, moves and resizes objects.

Portrait A term used to refer to vertical page orientation; the opposite of landscape or horizontal orientation.

Power points Areas that are read first in a document because of their potential impact on the reader.

Process color Colors made from four basic colors (cyan, magenta, yellow, and black) combined in percentages to create many colors. *See also* CMYK.

Promote/Demote Index option used to create secondary or tertiary topics.

Proof A smaller-scaled version of the final publication used for editing.

Proportional leading The default setting that allows for proportional amounts of space above the tallest character and the lowest character in a line.

Publication page The solid-lined, boxed area used to create and modify text and graphics to build a publication. The maximum size allowed in PageMaker is 42" × 42".

Publication window The area that includes the page where the publication will be created.

Publications Brochures, newsletters, reports, advertisements, flyers, letterhead, forms, simple one-page letters, magazines, and even books that can be created using a desktop publishing program such as PageMaker.

Pull quote Text enlarged within a story to catch the reader's attention.

RAM (Random Access Memory) The memory that can be used by applications to perform necessary tasks while the computer is on.

Reflecting Flipping an object either from top to bottom or from right to left.

Resize To change the size of a graphic by dragging its handles.

Resolution Print quality, measured in dots per inch.

Reverse text White or lightly-shaded text or lines on a black or dark background.

RGB A color system composed of red (R), green (G), and blue (B). These colors are predefined in each new PageMaker publication.

Rotate To move a graphic or text block at any angle.

Rulers Used to size and align text and graphics accurately.

Sans Serif font A font without small strokes at the ends of the characters.

Scale To increase or decrease an object's dimensions either proportionally or unproportionally.

Scanner A device that converts printed text or graphics to digital files.

Scroll bar A bar that appears at the bottom and/or right edge of a window whose contents are not entirely visible. Each scroll bar contains a scroll box and two scroll arrows. You click the arrows or drag the box in the direction you want the window to move.

Secondary index topic An index entry that appears subordinate to the main or primary index entry.

Select To highlight an item so that a subsequent action can be carried out on the item.

Selection handles The small black squares at the corners and sides of the graphic that indicate that the graphic is selected.

Selection marquee A rectangular frame created by dragging the pointer; you can select several objects at once in PageMaker by drawing a selection marquee around the group of objects you want to move or edit.

Semi-Automatic flow The ability to place text which flows to the bottom of a column or page and then waits for you to place text in the next column or page.

Separations Printouts on paper or film, one for each of the four process colors.

Serif font A font with small strokes at the ends of the characters.

Size The dimensions of characters, usually measured in points.

Skewing Stretches the object at an angle, giving it a distorted appearance.

Snap to guides A feature that causes graphic elements to "magnetically" align to a PageMaker guide.

Spot color A specific ink used to create a color.

Stack Overlapping objects on a page.

Story editor A word processing program within PageMaker.

Style The appearance of type; for example, italics or bold.

Surf To navigate the Internet by jumping from home page to home page using hypertext links.

Tabs Nonprinting characters used to position text at specific locations within a text block.

Tagged Image File Format (TIFF) A file format used for storing graphics or photographs that can be used in PageMaker or other software programs.

Task List A window that displays the active applications and programs. You can use the Task List to switch between active applications and programs.

Teaser A publication designed to motivate the reader to request more information about the product or service.

Template Predesigned page layouts which have dummy text and graphics and can be replaced with your own text and graphic objects.

Tertiary index topic An index entry that appears subordinate to a secondary index topic entry.

Text block Text selected with the pointer tool from the toolbox.

Text file A document file containing words, letters, or numbers, but no special computer instructions, such as formatting.

Text tool Tool used for entered or deleted text.

Text wrap Flowing text around a graphic object at a specified distance.

Threaded text A text block that is connected to or linked to another text block flowing from a column or page to another column or page.

Thumbnail A small sketch that shows only the large elements of the page.

Tint A new color based on a percentage of a color you created or based on one of PageMaker's default colors.

Title bar Displays the open publication's filename.

Toolbox Contains fourteen tool icons for creating and modifying text and graphics. The toolbox is a floating palette, which is a moveable window within the publication window.

Tracking Spacing between characters.

Transform Change an object's appearance by sizing, rotating, skewing, reflecting, or cropping.

Trapping A technique for compensating for gaps between colors when creating color separations.

Typographer A person who designs or sets type in the commercial printing industry.

URL (Uniform resource locator) The unique address assigned to each page on the World Wide Web, identifying its server location and filename.

Watched directory A folder used to store files during the PDF creation process.

Web browser A program such as Netscape used to read Web pages on the Internet.

Web pages Publication files that can be read on the Internet.

Widow A line of text that begins a paragraph at the bottom of a column or page.

Windowshade handles Bars that mark the beginning and end of a selected text block.

Word wrap A feature that makes text flow to the next line.

WWW (World Wide Web) A network setup that allows the use of a graphical interface on the Internet.

Zero point The point at which the zero marks on the rulers intersect.

Zero point marker The tool at the intersection of the horizontal and vertical rulers.

Index

Index

Index